Civil Juries
and the Politics of Reform

Civil Juries and the Politics of Reform

Stephen Daniels and Joanne Martin

Northwestern University Press

The American Bar Foundation

Northwestern University Press
625 Colfax
Evanston, Illinois 60208-4210

Printed in the United States of America

ISBN 0-8101-1121-7

The paper used in this publication meets the minimum requirements of the American National Standard for Information Sciences—Permanence of Paper for Printed Library Materials, ANSI Z39.48–1984.

To our parents

Ann Marrone Daniels (1923–80)
Barbara Whitehead Martin
Charles Clifton Daniels
William Allen Martin

Contents

Preface ix

1 Juries and the Politics of Reform 1
A System Run Amok, in Crisis, Out of Balance 4
A Threat to the American Way of Life: Consequences 12
The Problem of Veracity: Critics of the Reform Rhetoric 15
Conclusion: Reform and the Politics of Ideas 26

2 The Public Policy Process and the Importance of Agenda Setting: The Case of Civil Justice Reform 29
Agendas and Solutions Seeking Problems 30
Kingdon's Model of Agenda Setting 32
Defining Public Policy Problems: Stone's Concept of Strategic Representation 37
Conclusion: Analyzing the Rhetoric of Reform 58

3 Civil Juries: An Empirical Mapping 60
Juries and the Disputing Process 62
The Jury Verdict Data 66
General Patterns in Jury Verdicts 69
Conclusion 90
Appendix 3.1: Jury Verdict Reporters 91

4 Medical Malpractice 92
"More a Lottery than a Rational System": Rhetoric and Context 94
The Disputing Pyramid 114
Jury Verdict Patterns 126
Conclusion: The "Vagaries" of Justice 148
Appendix 4.1: Nine-Point Injury Scale 150

5 Products Liability 152
"Let's Restore Balance": Rhetoric and Context 153
The Disputing Pyramid 161
Jury Verdicts: 1988–90 168
Verdict Patterns within Injury Settings 175
Verdict Patterns over Time: 1970–90 183
Conclusion: Don't Kill the Messenger till You Read the Message 194

6 Punitive Damages 199
"A Monstrous Heresy . . . [A]n Unsightly and Unhealthy Excrescence": Rhetoric and Context 200
Patterns and Changes in Punitive Damage Verdicts 213
Conclusion and General Summary 238

7 Juries and Civil Justice Reform: Politics, Policy, and Knowledge 244
Politics 244
Policy 248
Knowledge 252

Notes 259

Index 306

Preface

Civil justice reform reached a symbolic pinnacle as a result of the 1994 congressional elections. It made the victorious Republican party's top ten list with its inclusion in the "Contract with America" signed by over 300 Republican candidates. "The Common Sense Legal Reform Act" is number nine on that list. Attaining this rather dubious status shows the salience of civil justice reform in the public mind, as well as its prominence on the policy agenda for the 104th Congress and many state legislatures. Underlying this promise for legal reform are the familiar refrains of a litigation explosion, a lawsuit crisis, a liability crisis, an insurance crisis, skyrocketing jury awards, unscrupulous attorneys, and on, and on. This legal system run amok is blamed for everything from the unavailability of essential health care and medicines, the loss of business competitiveness in the world economy and the concomitant effects on economic well-being and jobs, to the closing of public parks and the demise of high school football. These costs and others are presented as a justification for immediate, fundamental reform in the civil justice system. Or as the Republicans' top ten list says, what we need is some common sense reform—and who can be against "common sense"?

This book is about juries and civil justice reform, and it challenges "common sense." We are skeptical of the efficacy of many proposed and enacted reforms, and we are concerned about the consequences of those measures. Beyond the self-interest of those groups lobbying for reform, we can see little reason for endorsing this reform agenda. We come to this position after spending a number of years collecting and analyzing data on civil jury verdicts from different parts of the country. We—and others—do not find empirical evidence of a system run amok with skyrocketing awards, and so on. Or, we find little or no empirical information available regarding many of the claims made by the reformers about juries and the civil justice system.

The difference between the picture of juries and the civil justice system portrayed by the reform movement on the one hand and the picture emerging from our research and other systematic studies on the other has been an issue of increasing concern for us. It is the reason we decided to write this book. The book presents a critical analysis of the images of juries and civil justice that animate reform in light of the available empirical evidence. This analysis relies heavily upon our own research on jury verdicts, but does so in the context of other empirical studies. This, we believe, will be a useful contribution to the ongoing discussion of reform. Policy mistakes can be costly, and the appropriateness and efficacy of proposed and enacted policy solutions will depend, to a large degree, on their connection to the reality of demonstrable problems. There is, however, more to our concern than just the gap between the picture portrayed by the reform movement and the best available evidence. The book also analyzes those images in a more theoretical context and explores their nature, their use (often successful), and the possible reasons why the marked difference between the reform rhetoric's picture and the best available evidence has made so little difference in terms of policy. To do this we have turned to a theoretical literature in political science on the public policy process itself, one that emphasizes agenda-setting, the defining of policy problems, and what is called the "politics of ideas."

The book is divided into seven chapters. The first chapter serves as a general introduction with an emphasis on the "politics of ideas." The second chapter critically analyzes the reform rhetoric and its images of juries and civil justice from the perspective of agenda-setting and problem definition in the public policy process. Chapters 3 through 6 build on this critical analysis by comparing those images to the findings of our own research on jury verdicts and the findings in the extant literature. Chapter 3 introduces our research on verdicts and provides the conceptual framework used to organize the discussion in the following chapters, each focusing on one of the most visible issue areas in the reform rhetoric: chapter 4—medical malpractice; chapter 5—products liability; and chapter 6—punitive damages. Each of these three chapters includes an analysis of the images found in the reform rhetoric, a review of relevant findings in the extant literature, and a detailed discussion of our findings on jury verdicts.

While some readers may find the detailed discussion of quantitative data in some of the chapters a less than exhilarating prospect, we ask that you bear with us. These data are important in their own right for what they can tell us about civil juries, and the story they tell is a key part of our challenge to the reformers' notion of "common sense." These data present a picture fundamentally different than the one animating reform, and that picture only emerges from the details. Accordingly, in presenting and discussing our jury verdict data we have chosen not to rely on sophisticated statistical techniques, but on a straightforward description of the data at progressively lower levels of aggregation. With a minimal amount of ordering on our part, we want the data themselves to tell their own story.

The final chapter serves as the book's conclusion by leaving the detailed discussion of empirical findings and returning to the general themes regarding agenda-setting, the defining of policy problems, and the politics of ideas with which we began. Among the issues this chapter addresses is the influence of the partisan political battle over reform on the academic literature—in both law and social science. Those interests with a stake in the policy debate (on both sides) have been lobbying the academic literature and trying to shape research agendas in order to create an intellectual and even "scientific" justification for their various partisan goals. We find this troubling. Left unchallenged, such partisan efforts can thoroughly undermine the integrity of the scientific enterprise. We hope that one of the things this book does is to offer such a challenge.

The views we express in this book are ours alone. The American Bar Foundation, an independent research institute, has supported our work on jury verdicts and civil justice reform. Support for some of the research (on medical malpractice verdicts) also came from the National Science Foundation's Law and Social Sciences Program (grant no. SES87-09794) and the M. D. Anderson Foundation. No monetary support came from the American Bar Association, from any other professional organization, or from any entity with a direct or indirect stake in the outcome of the reform debate. We have been able to follow our findings in whatever direction they led us. The advantages of being affiliated with an institution that vigorously honors and defends independence in research are incalculable. For these advantages we are indebted to the Foundation's Board of Directors. We would also like to thank John P. Heinz, who was the ABF's director when our research began, and the present director, Bryant G. Garth. Two former members of the ABF's Board also warrant special mention: Justice William Erickson of the Colorado Supreme Court, at whose suggestion our research on jury verdicts began; and Charles M. Thompson, Esq., of South Dakota, who provided a practitioner's perspective and helped bring our work to the attention of the bar.

There are many others we must also acknowledge. Rick Bernet, Chris Browning, Leah Feldman, Ami Jaeger, Mark Nielsen, Mitchell Pravatiner, Ruth Sosniak, and Greg Stuart served as research assistants on our jury verdict projects. Most of the coding was done by the Center for Legal Studies (CLS) at Sangamon State University in Springfield, Ill. Professor Nancy Ford, first as the Center's director and later as the director of Sangamon State's Institute for Public Affairs, provided an excellent institutional setting for meeting our data coding needs. Very special acknowledgement must go to Rebecca Wilkin, now assistant to the Vice-President for Academic Affairs at Sangamon State. As CLS's assistant director she managed the coding for our jury verdict data. She helped design the coding instruments, trained the coders, supervised the coding and data entry, and ensured the accuracy and integrity of the data. She is simply the best.

Tom Davies and Bob Hayden started with us on the jury verdict projects, but moved on to other places (the University of Tennessee and the University of Pittsburgh, respectively); they nonetheless continued to provide ideas, comments, and support. John E. Collins, a lawyer practicing in Dallas, helped us in locating jury verdict data and provided invaluable insight into the political dynamics of civil justice reform. Professor Neil Vidmar read drafts of some of the chapters of this book and offered many useful criticisms and suggestions, most of which we wisely accepted. He has followed our jury verdict research for some time and provided very helpful comments on some of our earlier work as well. Professor Joseph Sanders has also been a helpful critic of our earlier work. Last, but certainly not the least, is Johanna Womack, who typed, retyped, and often retyped again the many drafts of the manuscript. Occasionally seen rotating our edited pages in unusual directions in the attempt to decipher the scribbling with which we left her, she did a magnificent job.

CHAPTER ONE

Juries and the Politics of Reform

Juries lie at the heart of the ongoing public policy debate over reform in the American civil justice system. They are credited with detonating an "explosion" of litigation that triggered a "skyrocketing" growth in the size of verdicts, causing nothing short of a "crisis." Cast not only as a problem in and of themselves, juries—and jury verdicts—are seen as symbolic or representative of a variety of fundamental problems in the civil justice system—a system alleged to have run amok, to be arbitrary, unpredictable, irrational, unfair, and dangerously out of balance. As a consequence, as one pair of commentators put it, "today, jury trials are the hot focus of much law reform debate, as reformers suspicious of juries repeatedly urge policymakers to modify the right to a jury trial."[1]

Complaints about juries, however, are not a recent phenomenon. Writing over 60 years ago, Jerome Frank expressed a sentiment that seems all too current: "proclaiming that we have a government of laws, we have, in jury cases, created a government of often ignorant and prejudiced men."[2] Frank perceived juries as capricious and prejudiced. They ignore legal rules and doctrines, allow nonlegal and often irrelevant factors, such as the status of parties and witnesses, to sway their judgment. Indeed, he claimed "that the defendant is a wealthy corporation and the plaintiff is a poor boy . . . often determine who will win or lose."[3]

Today's reform debate is crowded with horror stories of juries awarding "astronomical figures that boggle the mind"[4] in cases often involving hapless and innocent (typically "deep pocket") defendants. Juries are said to be incompetent—or perhaps less unkindly, ill-equipped—to decide issues in complex trials in areas such as antitrust, products liability, medical malpractice, or accountancy, because these cases often involve complicated technical and scientific evidence. It is asserted that juries are likely to be misled or confused in such cases by a "battle of experts" waged over the technical or scientific evidence, thereby eliminating any chance for a fair, rational decision. Even worse, juries may be asked to decide complex issues about indirect effects and statistical probabilities. From this perspective, the gullibility of juries coupled with the contingency fee system in which plaintiffs' lawyers take their fees as a percentage of the winnings provide a powerful incentive for greedy lawyers to initiate frivolous lawsuits.[5]

Reformers, note Clermont and Eisenberg, "catalog problems with juries,"[6] placing them at the symbolic center of the debate over reform. For this reason, our discussion in this book centers on juries. Examining and critically analyzing the claims made about juries provides a wide window through which to look at the broader rhetoric of reform. The reformers' characterization of the civil justice system as being in crisis and in immediate need of reform has not only influenced policymakers, but also has become a part of popular culture. Our purpose in this book is twofold. The first is to critically analyze the rhetoric of reform. We will argue that rhetoric has been more important than reality in the debate over civil justice reform. Analyzing the rhetoric is important not only for understanding the politics of reform, but also theoretically in terms of our understanding of the civil justice system and the public policy process.

The second purpose, complementing the first, is to present an alternative picture of juries and the civil justice system using the findings of our own empirical research and those in the extant literature. Some scholars who study the civil justice system have persistently criticized the rhetoric of reform. These critics argue that there is a wide gap between the reformers' characterization and what is empirically known or, more important, not known about the system. A principal concern for us is the nature of the gap between rhetoric and empirical knowledge, and an exploration of that gap helps us better understand the current political debate over juries and civil justice reform. It is important to know if the reformers' characterization of the civil justice system has any basis in reality or is best seen as the artifact of an intense, high-stakes political battle. The rhetoric presents its image as authoritative and the only reasonable portrayal of juries and the civil justice system. At stake, ultimately, are long-standing rights in the legal system now called into question because of allegations by reformers regarding the negative effects or costs of their use. Underlying this argument is a normative standard that evaluates those rights on the basis of their alleged deleterious effects rather than as ends in themselves serving political and social goals that do not lend themselves to easy quantification and cost benefit analysis. Also at stake is the very way in which the civil justice system itself is seen and understood—not simply by academics and researchers but by policymakers, key elites, and the public. The system's legitimacy is in question.

Most simply, the rhetoric of the reform movement is a weapon in a battle for the public mind, more a skirmish over ideas and perceptions than over the veracity of factual assertions. It offers a prime illustration of political scientist Deborah Stone's assertion that, when stripped to its essentials, policymaking is a "struggle over ideas[,] . . . a constant struggle over the criteria for classification, the boundaries of categories, and the definition of ideals that guide the way people behave."[7] This is "part of a struggle to control which images of the world govern policy."[8] At the core of this process is the identification of "problems," and as Stone observes, problems "are not given, out there in the world waiting for smart analysts to come along and define them correctly. They are created in the minds of citizens by other citizens, leaders, organizations, and government agencies, as an essential part of political maneuvering."[9]

David Ricci sees this struggle to control which images govern policy as a part of what he calls the "politics of ideas."[10] In an era in which expertise has come to play an important role in the political process, in which there is uncertainty about traditional values, and in which older party structures and patterns of voting behavior have eroded, ideas and images have become a central part of the policy process. Ideas and images, Ricci notes, are aggressively marketed, and he describes this as a "pervasive reality" controlling the format of ideas conveyed in the mass communications media in America.[11] Ideas and images in the political realm are marketed just like products in the commercial realm; citizens, like consumers, are treated as a passive audience receiving messages about issues as the marketers define them.[12] The rhetoric of civil justice reform can be understood as one manifestation of the politics of ideas.[13]

The remainder of this chapter is divided into three parts. The first section explores some of the major points of the reformers' criticisms of the civil justice system, with special emphasis on juries. The second looks at the reformers' claims about the consequences of the system's failures. These two sections serve as a general introduction to the rhetoric of reform. Our focus is on those seeking reform for one important reason. Those who desire fundamental policy changes first and foremost must set the terms of political debate by arguing for their version of a particular issue. Our interest is in the ideas and images used in this effort as political phenomena. To demonstrate the gap between what academic researchers have learned and the political rhetoric, the third section presents some critiques of the reformers' claims by empirical scholars of juries and civil justice. This section also addresses the rhetoric of reform as a political phenomenon rather than an "objective" or disinterested description of reality. Chapter 2 will offer a theoretical context for examining the substance of the reform rhetoric's image. Chapters 3 through 6 explore the gap between political rhetoric and empirical knowledge.

A System Run Amok, in Crisis, Out of Balance

As the earlier reference to Jerome Frank illustrates, criticisms of juries and the civil justice system are not new. Since the mid-1980s, however, the civil justice system and juries in particular have been under strenuous assault. The critics assert that juries are capricious, biased toward plaintiffs, unpredictable, and overgenerous in their verdicts. They find juries often incompetent to pass judgment on issues brought before them, particularly in complex cases such as medical malpractice and products liability. Further, the critics claim that jury trials add to the already crippling delays and backlogs plaguing American courts, thereby increasing the "costs" of justice.

This next section discusses four basic allegations found in the recent critical attack on juries.[14] While these criticisms are about juries, we also note the reformers' more general concerns about the substantive rules and procedures structuring the civil justice system.

Juries and the "Litigation Explosion"

Based upon a complex series of assumptions, juries are blamed for a large part of the alleged "litigation explosion"—particularly in tort litigation. Key components of this notion are plaintiffs' lawyers and the contingency fee system. Jury verdicts and the contingency fee system are seen as working synergistically to bring increasing numbers of claims to the courthouse door and even to trial. According to this logic, juries are strongly biased in favor of plaintiffs and exhibit this bias by making large damage awards. Expectations of easy victory and handsome awards encourage contingency fee lawyers and their clients to file more lawsuits, many of them frivolous. This fuels the explosion of civil litigation. These expectations also set the going rate for the even larger number of matters that settle short of trial.[15]

Examples used to support this criticism abound and range from the shallow and ridiculous to the sublime and sophisticated. Among the former are the many "real life" stories used to illustrate the symptoms of failure in the civil justice system. Such stories have been widely used in the debate over the civil justice system, and we will make reference to them throughout the book. As they are always evocative and frequently outrageous, the reader must keep in mind that the stories are distorted versions of real events or simply complete fabrications. By way of example, in a broadly disseminated 1986 speech, insurance executive William McCormick presented several vivid vignettes highlighting the vagaries of jury verdicts. One involved a Little League baseball player hit on the head by a ball he was unable to catch. His parents sued the coaches for negligence for playing their son in the outfield. The jury decided in their favor. Another told of a burglar who fell through a painted-over skylight on a public school roof and then successfully sued the school district winning a high six-figure award.[16]

A widely distributed 1985 speech by Robert Malott, CEO and chairman of FMC Corporation and chair of the Business Roundtable, also criticized juries for making "absurdly generous liability awards."[17] His evocative anecdotes included the tale of a fat man who suffered a heart attack trying to start a Sears lawnmower. He sued Sears and won an award of over one million dollars. Another told of the psychic who sued her doctor and the hospital, claiming that a CAT scan had destroyed her psychic powers. She also received a $1 million dollar damage award. Verdicts such as these in frivolous cases, said Malott, "strain credulity."[18] These examples have been recycled many times. They appeared in a 1986 solicitation letter from the American Tort Reform Association (ATRA). The tale of the CAT-scan case also appeared in the report of Vice President Quayle's Council on Competitiveness,[19] in a *Chicago Tribune* editorial in 1993,[20] as well as in books written by Peter Huber[21] and Walter Olson.[22]

In addition to these anecdotes of horrific verdicts, the reform literature also makes frequent reference to summary figures on jury awards. Typically these are nationwide mean or average amounts for jury verdicts in medical malpractice or products liability cases, with occasional reference to the frequency and size of punitive damage awards or the number of million dollar awards. Numbers purporting to describe the size of awards in a variety of arenas appeared regularly in various forums from the mid-1980s into the 1990s. These summary figures are used to support the notion that the high awards reported in the reformers' anecdotes are all too typical. For example, a 1985 *Forbes* article reported that in 1984 the average products liability award was $1.07 million and the average medical malpractice award was $990,000. These figures were subsequently cited in other reform assessments of jury activity.[23] The highly influential Reagan administration *Report of the Tort Policy Working Group on the Causes, Extent and Policy Implications of the Current Crisis in Insurance Availability and Affordability* reported an average award in 1985 of $1,017,716 for medical malpractice cases and $1,850,452 for products liability cases. During 1985 and 1986—the height of the "insurance crisis"—the many national publications carrying stories on the crisis all included summary figures on the large size of the "typical" jury verdict.[24]

Sometimes figures on the size of awards are taken from a particular locale with the implication that these figures are representative of the country as a whole. More often than not, these figures come from a study of Cook County, Illinois (Chicago), conducted by the RAND Corporation's Institute for Civil Justice (ICJ). The Reagan administration's *Report* used these ICJ figures to talk about the size of punitive damage awards. According to the *Report,* the average punitive damage award in Cook County for 1980–84 was $489,000. In personal injury cases the average punitive damage award was even higher—$1,152,000.[25] Interestingly, the *Report's Update,* written to counter criticism of the *Report,* relied on the ICJ Cook County data to claim that the average punitive damage award in personal injury cases for 1980–84 was $1,934,000. This higher figure was also cited by Richard Mahoney and Stephen Littlejohn (Chair/CEO and Public Relations Director, respectively, of the Monsanto Corporation) in an article published in *Science.*[26] The same figure appeared in a press kit prepared by the ATRA and circulated to the media before oral arguments in the Supreme Court in the 1989 case, *Browning-Ferris Industries, Inc. v. Kelco Disposal, Inc.,* an Eighth Amendment challenge to punitive damages.[27]

Congressional and state legislative hearings and state tort reform commissions in the mid- to late 1980s also tended to incorporate summary figures on jury awards. So, too, did briefs in the increasing amount of appellate litigation challenging the constitutionality of large jury awards. For instance, the petitioner's Supreme Court brief in *Pacific Mutual Life Ins. Co. v. Haslip,*[28] a due process challenge to the constitutionality of punitive damages, included numerous references to the size of punitive damage awards in Alabama, the state in which the case originated. The brief was accompanied by an extensive appendix listing punitive awards over a two-year period. The *amicus* brief for the American Tort Reform Association and a number of other tort reform groups asserted: "(p)unitive damages are today awarded with a frequency and in amounts that are startling. . . . And these awards may be enormous: punitive verdicts exceeding $1 million, while not the norm, have become almost commonplace."[29]

The Increasing Size of Awards and Frequency of Victory

Underlying the allegations set out above is the assumption that in recent years the size of awards has increased substantially, as has the frequency with which plaintiffs win generally or are awarded punitive damages. The idea presented is one of change, change for the worse—a straight-line view that looks back to some golden age when plaintiffs rarely won and, when they were successful, were awarded modest amounts. The rate at which this change has occurred, say the critics, has been dramatic. While purportedly taking place across the board, the greatest focus has been on increases in the high-visibility, big ticket areas of medical malpractice, products liability, and punitive damages.

As early as 1984, the president of an insurance industry information and lobbying group wrote in an industry trade journal about the need for civil justice reform. Relying on jury verdict data from the ICJ study of Cook County, he characterized the changes in award sizes as "skyrocketing," with the average award nearly tripling during a seven-year period in the 1970s.[30] In this account, medical malpractice awards "skyrocketed 700%"; worker injury cases increased "more than 250%"; and awards "jumped 830% for slip and fall injuries, road construction injuries, and other street and sidewalk hazard cases."[31]

Similar claims appeared throughout the middle to late 1980s in reports on the insurance crisis. A 1986 cover story in *Time,* "Sorry, Your Policy Is Canceled," presents on its first page a graph depicting a sharp upward trend in the number of $1 million verdicts nationwide.[32] A 1985 story in *Business Week,* "Stopping the Bloodbath in Medical Malpractice," presented a similar graph, showing a dramatically increasing number of $1 million verdicts in malpractice cases.[33]

The Reagan administration's *Report* included a section titled "The Explosive Growth in Damage Awards,"[34] which opened with the following sentence: "Another area of great concern is the explosive growth in tort damages over the last decade."[35] Figures were given on the growth of the average medical malpractice award nationwide, showing that such verdicts "increased from $220,018 in 1975 to $1,107,716 in

1985, a 363% increase. Average products liability jury verdicts during this same period increased from $393,580 to $1,850,452, a 370% increase."[36] The *Report* also noted the increases in the numbers of million dollar verdicts in malpractice and products liability cases. "In 1975 there were three million dollar medical malpractice verdicts and nine million dollar product liability verdicts. . . . In 1984, the numbers had grown to 71 million dollar medical malpractice verdicts and 86 million dollar product liability verdicts, an increase of over 1200% in the number of such verdicts."[37] Using ICJ figures from Cook County, the *Report* also took note of increases in the size of the average punitive damage award stating that, "the average punitive damage award in Cook County, Illinois increased from $63,000 in 1970–74 to $489,000 in 1980–84. Of particular interest is that the average Cook County punitive damage award in personal injury cases increased from $40,000 in 1970–74 to $1,152,174 in 1980–84."[38]

Vice President Quayle's Council on Competitiveness cited even more dramatic figures on punitive damage awards: "A 1987 study by the Institute for Civil Justice, which examined 24,000 jury trials in Cook County, Illinois, found that the average punitive damage award increased, in inflation adjusted dollars, from $43,000 in 1965–69 to $729,000 in 1980–84—a jump of 1,500%. In personal injury cases, the rise has been even more dramatic."[39]

The first chapter of Peter Huber's influential book, *Liability: The Legal Revolution and Its Consequences,* is full of facts and figures used to show how the civil justice system has changed for the worse in recent years. For instance, he claims that "the plaintiff's probability of winning has also risen steadily. The likelihood of success rose from 20 to 30 percent in a product case in the 1960s to more than 50 percent in the 1980s, with similar increases in other classes of lawsuits."[40] Equally important are the changes in the size of jury awards. Since the early 1960s, said Huber, the average judgment in tort cases increased fivefold in constant dollars. Verdicts against cities "rose almost tenfold."[41] He also noted an increase in high-end awards: "The first jury verdict exceeding $1 million came in 1962; in 1975 there were fewer than twenty; today there are over 400 a year."[42] More recently, Justice Sandra Day O'Connor asserted in her dissent in *TXO Production Corporation v. Alliance Resources Corporation,*[43] a constitutional challenge to punitive damages, that "as little as 30 years ago, punitive damage awards were rarely assessed and usually small in amount. Recently, however, the frequency and size of such awards have been skyrocketing."[44]

In addition to the changes in jury verdicts and success rates, critics of the civil justice system have also commented on the negative effects of changes in the procedures and substantive law structuring the system. Changes in the law have been the special concern of the reform movement's "high theorists." These are the writers whose task is to give the reform movement an intellectual and theoretical justification—a justification beyond pure political self-interest. Peter Huber and Professor George Priest are perhaps the most widely known of these "high theorists." They have written extensively about changes in the law, particularly with regard to the issue of liability. Writing in 1985, Priest argued: "[s]ince 1960, our modern civil liability regime has experienced a conceptual revolution that is among the most dramatic ever witnessed in the Anglo-American legal system. Legal rules that had been entrenched for decades, and the attitudes and presuppositions that supported them, were suddenly repudiated and replaced by rules and presuppositions radically different."[45] In a 1987 article, he found a cause for the "insurance crisis" of the mid-1980s in the changes that made it easier for people to sue for recovery in personal injury cases, to win, and to win increasingly large jury awards.[46]

This perception about the role of change in substantive and procedural law is also a basic theme of Walter Olson's book, *The Litigation Explosion*,[47] an extended argument about the consequences of replacing the old ways and old rules with naive new ideas. Insurance executive McCormick's 1986 speech had a similar theme. He told his audience that the old legal system we knew (and presumably loved) no longer existed. The system no longer provided a clear definition of law. As a result, the legal system "encourages plaintiffs to sue, hampers defense, makes incredible awards, and has stretched the line that defines responsibility from 'true negligence' to what almost amounts to 'innocent bystander.' "[48]

The Limited Competence of Lay Juries

The remaining allegations about juries address more fundamental issues that go to the very idea of using lay juries. Critics assert that juries are not competent to decide issues and award damages in complex, lengthy trials because juror attention span decreases in long trials, especially in antitrust, products liability, or medical malpractice cases involving complicated technical matters. In addition, juries are likely to be misled or confused by the inevitable "battle of experts" over the technical evidence, thereby eliminating any chance for a fair, rational decision. As Jeffrey O'Connell and Brian Kelley phrased it in their book *The Blame Game: Injury, Insurance and Injustice,* "You have to wonder, if you or a loved one were critically injured and permanently disabled, whether you'd want your financial future to turn on a battle of warring experts—with a thoroughly confused jury caught in between."[49] Even worse, juries may be asked to decide on complex issues for which there is no hard technical evidence, but rather only claims about indirect effects and statistical probabilities. Uninformed, gullible lay jurors may accept expert testimony uncritically, ignore it, or just not understand it at all.

Peter Huber devoted an entire book to what he called "junk science," the legal rules allowing its use, and its effectiveness when used before lay juries. "Junk science is impelled through our courts by a mix of opportunity and incentive. 'Let-it-all-in' legal theory creates the opportunity. The incentive is money: the prospect that the Midas-like touch of a credulous jury will now and again transform scientific dust into gold."[50] Junk science and gullible juries, in Huber's view, encourage lawsuits that are in fact frivolous and make it easy to win, and to win big. To illustrate his argument, Huber retold the story of the psychic and the CAT scan. He characterized it as the "most fantastic verdict recorded so far" and a story "worthy of a tabloid" one might find at the grocery store checkout counter.[51] "[W]ith the backing of expert testimony from a doctor and several police department officials, a sooth-sayer who decided she had lost her psychic powers following a CAT scan persuaded a Philadelphia jury to award her $1 million in damages."[52] And this case, said Huber, is not unique. He stated that similar scientific frauds "are attempted almost daily in our courts, and many succeed. . . . Many culminate in large awards. . . . Junk science verdicts, once rare, are now common."[53] This issue was also addressed in the report of Vice President Quayle's Council on Competitiveness, which quoted from Huber's book and included the CAT-scan story.[54]

Capriciousness and Bias

Another major criticism of juries, today as in the past, is that they are capricious. As a result, the jury system is a bizarre lottery, lacking predictability and consistency as to who wins and how much winners are awarded. This allegation has special relevance in areas like medical malpractice and products liability where damage awards can be very high. William McCormick complained that "certainty and predictability have been two casualties of the developments of the past 25 years.

Without certainty and predictability, plaintiffs sue, defendants don't know how to protect themselves and we in the insurance industry can't price, and in some cases can't accept risks."[55] Dr. Otis Bowen, Secretary of Health and Human Services in the Reagan administration, criticized the jury in the medical malpractice system: "it has become more a lottery than a rational system for compensation for the injured."[56] Huber, in *Liability*, complains of the "mounting randomness and incoherence of jury outcomes" in products liability cases.[57] In his conclusion, he characterized the situation as "today's wide-open legal casino."[58] Jeffrey O'Connell titled a 1979 book on the civil justice system *The Lawsuit Lottery* to describe the "capricious nature of our legal system as it applies to personal injury cases."[59]

A related complaint, which appears to contradict the idea of capriciousness, is that juries are biased. Rather than being a random lottery, jury decision making is characterized as consistently and inappropriately favoring some interests to the detriment of others. An old and widely asserted claim is that juries are biased against businesses, professionals, governmental bodies, and other deep pocket defendants. One need only turn back to Jerome Frank's criticisms from the early 1930s to get a sense of the long history of this claim. The problem in Frank's estimation, and in that of many contemporary critics, is that juries generally decide in favor of individual plaintiffs suing deep pocket defendants and consistently award these plaintiffs large amounts of money.

Professor Dorsey Ellis, writing about punitive damages, commented on jury bias in favor of injured plaintiffs and against defendants, especially when the defendants are profit-making entities. Such entities, he said:

> do not rank high in the public's esteem, even when a cross-section of the community is systematically surveyed. And, regardless of our aspirations, juries do not reflect a cross section of the community. Noticeably absent from most panels are those who are most likely to understand the functions of profits in an enterprise economy—managers and professionals. Hence, the antagonism toward large, profit-making institutions is likely to be greater in a cross-section of jurors than in a cross-section of the community. There is good reason to believe, moreover, that this bias will manifest itself in the jury's decision on the defendant's liability for punitive damages.[60]

Richard Mahoney of Monsanto asserted that there is a "statistically proven relationship between the punitive damage award and the relative wealth and unpopularity of the defendant."[61]

There is, in fact, a statistical study of reported jury verdicts in personal injury cases which allegedly found "that juries sometimes respond emotionally, awarding some objectively similar cases higher damages than others."[62] Bovbjerg and his colleagues argued that "some cross-cutting factor like sympathy must be influencing some awards. Sympathy can have a large influence because the law gives so much leeway to juries to go beyond 'legitimate' (and observable) factors in their decisionmaking."[63] They suggest that plaintiffs' lawyers choose cases "according to their expert judgment on how juries will respond to various idiosyncrasies of a case, including relative ability to generate sympathy . . . [and] . . . high-sympathy cases are more predominant in high stakes litigation."[64]

While the notion of bias is, at one level, in apparent contradiction with that of capriciousness, the two are similar in one respect. The underlying logic is that juries are incompetent to decide cases fairly and rationally. The difference between the two allegations lies in the presumed result of jury incompetence. The concept of capriciousness expects a result of chaos, while that of bias predicts a kind of consistency and order, albeit based upon inappropriate criteria.

A Threat to the American Way of Life: Consequences

Great effort has gone into "demonstrating" the cumulative and wide-ranging effects of the failings of juries and the civil justice system on American society and the economy. The litany of the "costs" is extensive, ranging from the unavailability of essential health care and medicines, the loss of business competitiveness in the world economy and the concomitant effects on economic well-being and jobs, to the closing of public parks and the end of high school sports. Such consequences are presented as a part of a causal argument used to justify immediate, fundamental reform. Without major reform, the reformers argue, such problems will quickly worsen, but with reform, essential health services, economic prosperity, and even high school sports will be maintained.

During the "insurance crisis" of the mid-1980s, many discussions of the failings of the civil justice system concentrated as much on the consequences of those failings as on the failings themselves. It was these consequences that elevated the issue to a crisis level in the public mind. No aspect of American life escaped; no group was spared. Said FMC Corporation's Robert Malott, "even ministers are being sued for malpractice. . . . some 40,000 ministers have bought malpractice insurance—while others have become reluctant to counsel members of their congregation and are sending them to psychiatrists instead. Where will this end? Is no group sacrosanct in our litigation-prone society?"[65]

A very evocative theme evolved from this generation of commentary; that theme was "who pays for the system's failure?" Reinforcing the notion that it is not just businesses or doctors or manufacturers who suffer the burdens, Robert Malott commented, "Who ends up paying for our current mania for litigation? It's obvious that we all do. The growing tide of liability litigation is imposing enormous costs on consumers, on business, and on society as a whole."[66] Similarly, William McCormick noted that "runaway tort litigation means we all pay higher prices for everything, whether it's in product prices, insurance rates or in municipal, state or federal taxes."[67]

In 1986, this theme—who pays—animated a public relations campaign mounted by the Insurance Information Institute (III). This effort was introduced in the article "We All Pay the Price."[68] Built around the concept of the "lawsuit crisis" and with the intent of "informing" the public, it employed a series of eye-catching, dramatic print advertisements intended to drive home to the general public the idea that "we all pay the price" for the products of jury decision making.[69] Advertisement titles included "The Lawsuit Crisis Is Bad for Babies," "The Lawsuit Crisis Is Penalizing School Sports," and "Even the Clergy Can't Escape the Lawsuit Crisis."[70]

Many of the journalistic accounts of the insurance crisis during the mid-1980s also portrayed the effects of this "crisis" in terms of its effects on everyday life. *Time* magazine's cover story for March 24, 1986, entitled "Sorry, Your Policy Is Canceled," spoke in vivid, almost frightening terms about the consequences of the insurance crisis and what was happening in the civil justice system.[71] The cover story for the January 27, 1986, issue of *U.S. News & World Report,* "Sky-High Damages: The Impact on Consumers and Professionals,"[72] was similar in substance and tone as was a story in the March 10, 1986, issue of *Business Week* entitled "The Insurance Crisis: Now Everyone Is In a Risky Business."[73] This theme was not limited to the national media. For instance, an editorial in the *Dallas Morning News* said: "You've been seeing a lot of media attention given lately to something called the 'liability crisis.' Is it only hype? No, it's real. . . . What we have here is a true, classic crisis, because if you've bought many goods and services—from fish to baby delivery—in the past year or so, you have paid a bundle for it."[74]

The idea that we all pay the price for the failings of juries and civil justice took another direction in the work of Peter Huber. He quantified the idea of consequences by devising a measure he called the "tort tax."[75] He said: "The tax directly costs American individuals, businesses, municipalities, and other government bodies at least $80 billion a year, a figure that equals the total profits of the country's top 200 corporations. But many of the tax's costs are indirect and unmeasurable, reflected only in the tremendous effort, inconvenience, and sacrifice Americans now go through to avoid its collection. . . . the tax's hidden impact on the way we live and do business may amount to a $300 billion dollar annual levy on the American economy."[76] Huber later increased the estimate of direct costs to $117 billion a year[77] and said that "would be about $1,000 per household."[78] Huber's $300 billion estimate has been widely cited as authoritative, and perhaps its most symbolically important use was in the report of Vice President Quayle's Council on Competitiveness.[79]

While the $300 billion estimate provided a summary measure of consequences, Huber personalized its effects by applying his "tort tax" to everyday situations. He said that it "accounts for 30 percent of the price of a stepladder and over 95 percent of the price of childhood vaccines. It is responsible for one-quarter of the price of a ride on a Long Island tour bus and one-third of the price of a small airplane."[80] More dire and threatening than estimates of costs are claims about the unavailability of critical goods and services and the decline of economic prosperity and the concomitant loss of jobs.

Robert Malott told of drugs no longer available, like Bendectin, or barely available, like the DPT vaccine.[81] William McCormick commented on the limited availability of the DPT vaccine and added that "day care centers across the county are closing their doors. . . . Nonprofit organizations and local government boards are now having trouble finding anyone willing to serve. . . . And some manufacturers of life-saving products have quit because the threat of products liability suits is so overwhelming."[82] Specifically, McCormick noted that only two companies remained in the business of making anesthesia machines. Another company withdrew a drug designed to prevent sudden infant death syndrome because of the liability problem.[83] Richard Mahoney of Monsanto supplemented the litany of dire effects of the crisis by noting that one company had "halted the development of a suitcase-sized kidney dialysis machine because of the threat of punitive damages" and suggested that manufacturers may not "pursue the derivation or distribution of a vaccine to prevent AIDS."[84] He also said that his own company had halted the development of an asbestos substitute because of the threat of punitive damages. Mahoney quoted the Monsanto employee directing the ill-fated project as saying that "seven-figure jury awards on claims without merit are enough to send shivers down anyone's spine."[85] Mahoney also told of the threat to competitiveness and economic well-being. Jury verdicts, especially those involving punitive damages, are "known only too well by major American companies, costing everybody in lost jobs, new and improved products, and international competitiveness."[86]

In the 1990s this particular view of consequences—competitiveness, innovation, economic well-being, and jobs—came to dominate as the focus shifted from the insurance crisis of the middle 1980s. The most visible and symbolically important use of the competitiveness idea was by Vice President Quayle and his Council on Competitiveness.[87] In a speech at the 1991 Annual Meeting of the American Bar Association, Quayle stated that "[O]ur system of civil justice is, at times, a self-inflicted competitive disadvantage" in the global marketplace.[88] This idea animated much of the Bush administration's activity on tort reform, especially with regard to products liability legislation. For instance, in testimony before the Senate Subcommittee on the Consumer, Secretary of Commerce Robert Mosbacher outlined the Bush administration's position in precisely such terms, saying that the existing products liability system is "a very serious barrier."[89] He said that it "imposes excessive costs and creates unwarranted uncertainty for American companies. It denies job opportunities to American workers by contributing to plant closings and deterring business expansion. It harms American consumers by raising prices, diminishing the quality of goods, and denying access to socially beneficial products that manufacturers will refuse to produce."[90]

This picture of the drastic effects of a system gone awry, with its failings touching critically upon everyone's life, has obviously not gone unchallenged. The plaintiffs' bar and various consumer groups have responded to these characterizations of the civil justice system and the effects of its failures. Additionally, the academic community has begun to question some of the underlying assumptions of this portrait of crisis. The next section focuses on some of these efforts.

The Problem of Veracity: Critics of the Reform Rhetoric

Despite the often impassioned recounting of the failures of the civil justice system, juries, and the consequences of their ruinous behavior;

despite the apparent commonsensical character and inherent believability of the allegations; and despite the authority and status of those making the claims (from academics to business leaders and high-level governmental officials), deep-seated skepticism has been expressed regarding the veracity of the allegations made and the need for, or even the wisdom of, the reforms proposed. Some of this skepticism, of course, comes from those political interests opposed to reform. For instance, an amicus brief filed by the Trial Lawyers for Public Justice in support of the respondent in *Pacific Mutual Life Ins. Co. v. Haslip*[91] attacked the claims and empirical evidence used in the petitioner's briefs to document punitive damages as a problem area requiring a constitutional ban. That brief argued: "Despite the rhetoric of the attack on punitive damages, the empirical evidence simply does not support assertions that such awards are 'routine' or 'astronomical' or 'mindboggling' or 'skyrocketing.'"[92] The goal of this brief is clear in its concluding sentence: "This Court should not alter a longstanding tradition of state common law in response to a 'crisis' which simply does not exist."[93]

Such criticisms from those interests opposed to the reformers' efforts are to be expected in what has become a heated political and even ideological debate. What is perhaps more important is that concerns about the veracity of the reformers' claims about juries and the civil justice system are also coming from those not directly involved in the political fray. Serious criticisms have emerged from some scholars who study—empirically—juries, litigation, and the civil justice system. Increasingly, these researchers are finding either a wide gap between the reformers' claims and the best available evidence or assertions being made about issues for which there is little or no systematic evidence at all. Some legal journalists are also beginning to seriously question the veracity of the claims that lie at the heart of the reformers' characterization of juries and the civil justice system.

Our intent here is not to review all or even most of the recent commentaries on the claims of the tort reform movement. Rather, we will draw from several of the more recent and thorough efforts to outline the difference between rhetoric and what the best available evidence has to say. This discussion will be in two parts. First, we turn to the conclusions of three reviews examining some of the most basic claims that lie at the heart of the reform movement. While there are other analyses of such claims, what distinguishes these efforts is their concern with the entire litigation process—not just juries and jury verdicts—and with the importance of empirical information in the process of making public policy in this arena. Second, we look at commentaries focusing in whole or in part on the work of Peter Huber of the Manhattan Institute—one of the most visible critics of the civil justice system and one of the chief advocates for reform. He has become the ubiquitous voice of reform, and accordingly, he has attracted a fair number of critics. In a way, as the jury has come to symbolize much that is wrong with the civil justice system, Huber has become a symbol of what is wrong with the reform rhetoric.[94]

Reform Rhetoric v. Empirical Findings

Among the most thorough reviews of the reformers' claims about juries and the civil justice system are those by Michael Saks[95] and by Joseph Sanders and Craig Joyce.[96] Although they approach these issues from different perspectives—Saks in a more general sense and Sanders and Joyce specifically in terms of the reform effort in their state of Texas—these academic writers are ultimately concerned with a policy process in which the substantive claims being made and the policies being proposed are at odds with the best available empirical evidence. Or even worse, that situations arise when those claims and policies involve matters about which there is no reliable evidence. Important to Saks and to Sanders and Joyce are three related matters: what the problem(s) is (are), according to the reform movement; how that problem is identified and defined; and what solutions are offered or already enacted to deal with the problem. Each of the reviews comes to the same basic conclusion and questions, fundamentally, the veracity of the reformers' empirical claims about the civil justice system—claims which are then used to define a set of serious policy problems for which the reformers had ready-made solutions.

Writing in 1992, in an exhaustive and detailed review, Michael Saks bluntly concludes that the reformers' negative characterization of juries and the civil justice system used in the reform effort is "built of little more than imagination."[97] In light of the best available empirical evidence, "much of what we think we know about the behavior of the tort litigation system is untrue, unknown, or unknowable. . . . [O]ur current understanding of the tort litigation system is constructed of inference built upon evidence that is surprisingly incomplete and inadequate."[98] In his estimation, "a comprehensive picture, based on the best available evidence, suggests a system that behaves quite differently from what is widely assumed."[99]

It is worth quoting Saks's summary of this picture because he touches on each of the basic allegations about juries we have outlined.

> A tiny faction of accidental deaths and injuries become claims for compensation; even actionable injuries rarely become lawsuits. In both federal and state courts, torts has not been the largest or the fastest growing area of civil litigation. The great majority of all kinds of civil suits result in negotiated settlements. On average, these settlements undercompensate the plaintiff's losses. Modest losses are fully or overcompensated, but the larger the loss suffered, the more pronounced the undercompensation. The great majority of jury verdicts reach the same result that judges would make in the same cases. The degree of judge-jury agreement is all the more striking when we recognize that the clearest cases are removed from the system before trial. In the aggregate, jury awards are remarkably predictable. Over half the variation can be accounted for merely by knowing the severity of the plaintiff's injuries. Paralleling settlements, however, jury awards overcompensate small losses, undercompensate larger losses, and on average undercompensate plaintiffs. Judicial review at and after trial tends to reduce rather than increase awards, most dramatically for punitive damages.[100]

In short, for Saks, the key claims used to demonstrate that the civil justice system is *the* problem (the cause of phenomena like the insurance crisis of the mid-1980s or the loss of economic competitiveness in the early 1990s) and to identify the problem's particular manifestations (like runaway or biased juries and an explosions of tort litigation) simply do not measure up.

In a 1993 review essay devoted exclusively to medical malpractice, Saks came to the same conclusion:

> More and better research is replacing assumptions, anecdotes, and fragmentary or poorly analyzed data. The picture that is evolving of the malpractice litigation system is remarkably different from the one that had been created earlier out of anecdotes and casual assertions. . . . Ironically, while these findings could support a variety of conclusions and, in turn, a variety of reforms, they provide hardly any basis for the reforms that are most commonly promoted.[101]

It is important to note that Saks's two critical reviews do not lead him to conclude that the civil justice system is working just fine with no identifiable problems. Rather, his concern is that the evidence suggests that the "problems" identified by the reformers are not the ones an outside observer would see. His review raises the possibility not of a system run amok with excess, but of a system not doing enough.[102] The "solutions" proposed to remedy these "problems"—while perhaps serving some narrow self-interests for the reformers—would do nothing to deal with the problems about which an outside observer might be concerned. In fact, Saks fears that the proposed "solutions"—including some already enacted—might actually make matters worse. In short, Saks is as concerned with the process as he is with the substantive issues.

Sanders and Joyce,[103] with their more specific focus on reform in Texas, come to much the same conclusion with regard to the veracity of the empirical claims that defined the civil justice system as the problem the reformers seek to remedy. They also arrive at a similar assessment about solutions. Sanders and Joyce found that most reform proposals discussed in Texas and other state legislatures in the late 1980s were directed primarily at juries. This reflected the perception that the civil justice system is the cause of the "insurance crisis." Rather than dealing with the substantive rules of tort law, most reforms focused on "the remedial aspect of the law, that is, on damage awards. They are designed to influence insurance rates by slowing the growth in filings and the size of awards."[104]

After reviewing this reform logic in light of the available empirical information on the litigation process as a whole (from the occurrence of injury, to the decision to make a claim for compensation, to the decision to file a lawsuit, to disposition of that suit through trial or otherwise, to possible appeal), Sanders and Joyce are far from sanguine in their commentary. They find crucial parts of the factual argument at the heart of the reform movement and the problem it seeks to remedy—particularly with regard to the growth in the frequency of litigation and the size of tort recoveries—to be highly problematic.[105] The claims about the various manifestations of the problem—such as the frequency of claims, lawsuits filed, trials held, jury verdicts, and jury behavior—are highly questionable in their opinion.[106] As a result, they conclude that the types of reforms being enacted in Texas and other states are unlikely to succeed. "These most recent reforms are incomplete and arguably ill-focused (depending upon whose interests most concern the observer)."[107] Like Saks, Sanders and Joyce do not believe that the civil justice system is without problems worthy of attention, only that the "problems" being attacked have little or nothing to do with what the best available evidence tells us about the system.

Sanders and Joyce, like Saks, are not just concerned with the gap between the assertions comprising the reform view of the civil justice system and the best available empirical information. Their concern goes much deeper, to how little is actually known in any systematic way about the behavior of the system. Having the appropriate empirical information is essential, in their view, for identifying problems and crafting appropriate solutions. In Saks's words, the "asserted harmful discontinuance in the behavior of the tort litigation system can be evaluated and dealt with effectively only if the necessary evidence and analysis are developed."[108] That evidence, however, is not yet available according to these reviewers.

Yet, the shortcomings of our collective knowledge about the civil justice system "has barely slowed policymakers, scholars, and other commentators. Their discussions about the behavior of the tort liability system often have proceeded without even assembling the fragments that do exist, much less pausing to figure out how they fit together."[109] In their discussions of the shortcomings of the Texas reform effort—the 1987 Omnibus Tort Reform Act—Sanders and Joyce provide an example of precisely what worries Saks about the policy process. Sanders and Joyce focused on "the process by which tort reform came to Texas in 1987."[110]

The 1987 Texas legislation emerged from the Texas House/Senate Joint Committee on Liability and Tort Reform, created by the legislature in 1986.[111] Other states also set up similar committees or commissions about this time to deal with the "insurance crisis."[112] The committee's charge "was to study the availability and cost of commercial, professional, and governmental liability insurance and the impact of the tort recovery process on the insurance industry."[113] Rather than setting out to actually study the situation (as at least some committees or commissions in other states did) the Texas committee assumed that the liability crisis was a documented fact.[114] The committee "adopted as its principal sourcebook for resolving the tort law aspects of that crisis"[115] the Reagan administration's *Report of the Tort Policy Working Group*.[116] Because of that report's wide and often uncritical use and its symbolic importance in the reform debate as the Reagan administration's statement that the civil justice system is *the* problem, Sanders and Joyce spent the better part of their review systematically criticizing the veracity of this report's picture of the civil justice system.[117]

The lack of concern about the existence, quality, and integrity of pertinent empirical evidence in the Texas policy process can be traced, in part, say Sanders and Joyce, to the makeup of the committee itself. Its membership consisted entirely of Texas state legislators, none of whom "brought to the task relevant subject matter expertise of an academic sort."[118] Additionally, the makeup of the committee's staff only aggravated this problem: "its staff included no academicians or objective outside experts of any description to assist the Committee either in sifting through the testimony of eighty-six highly interested witnesses, or in preparing the Committee's final report."[119] Sanders and

Joyce's evaluation of this committee and the reform process in Texas is clear. The reform package "transparently represents the product of a political process essentially uninformed by a distinterested, professional examination of the underlying problem, the result almost certainly will be misbegotten."[120]

Saks's and Sanders and Joyce's reviews raise serious questions about both the substance of the claims made in this policy debate and the policy process itself with regard to civil justice issues. As to substance, the issue is the wholly negative characterization of juries and the civil justice system and the concomitant notion of crisis animating the reform effort—ideas presumed as true rather than systematically and empirically described. For the policy process, the issue is the frustrating and troubling realization that the reform movement has moved forward with some degree of success (nearly every state legislature passed some type of reform in the late 1980s) with little or no rationality in its approach, there being limited or no empirical analysis or attention to developing appropriate and workable solutions.

Ultimately, the message contained in these reviews is one of concern for the efficacy of the solutions offered or, worse, already put into place. As Saks noted in his 1993 article on medical malpractice, "If problems are not understood or even described accurately, hasty law reforms may not accomplish the reformers' aims or improve the civil justice system."[121] This sentiment echoes that of Malcolm Feeley in his commentary on the the failure of the criminal justice reforms of an earlier decade. He concluded that one can find the roots of failure in the mistaken notion of a crisis in the courts, in "the exaggerated assertions about the problems faced by the courts, the historical perspective that informs (or, more properly, fails to inform) so much analysis, and the easy—and often wrong—answers implied in so many crisis-generated discussions."[122]

The Politics of Ideas

Another concern about the rhetoric of reform goes directly to the politics of the rhetoric and its role in what is ultimately a political process. It questions whether the rhetoric is nothing more than sophistry or simply propaganda, making the accuracy of the claims contained in its logic irrelevant so long as those claims further certain political goals.[123] This concern is perhaps most evident in discussions reflecting upon the work of Peter Huber of the Manhattan Institute. A review of some of the issues raised in these discussions offers a means of exploring the rhetoric of reform as a part of what is basically a political process. Huber has written widely on issues surrounding civil justice reform for a variety of audiences.[124] He also writes a regular column for *Forbes* magazine, appears on radio and television news interview programs, speaks often before business and trade groups, and regularly testifies before congressional committees in favor of civil justice reform.[125]

In short, Huber is a policy entrepreneur—a full-time advocate for a particular worldview and resulting set of proposals that are generated by that construct.[126] The defining characteristic of policy entrepreneurs, like that of business entrepreneurs, says political scientist John Kingdon, "is their willingness to invest their resources—time, energy, reputation, and sometimes money—in the hope of future return. That return might come to them in the form of policies of which they approve, satisfaction from participation, or even personal aggrandizement in the form of security or career promotion."[127] These entrepreneurs seek visibility for themselves and their ideas. Among other things, they "try to highlight the indicators that so importantly dramatize their problems. They push for one kind of problem definition rather than another."[128] Kingdon observes that "entrepreneurs are central to the softening-up process" needed to get an issue on the policy agenda.[129]

In playing such a role, Huber has become the ubiquitous voice of reform. Either he or his ideas appear whenever reform is discussed or debated. As a consequence, he has attracted a substantial amount of attention and criticism, and to at least some of his critics he also personifies the problems in the reform movement's rhetoric. This perception is epitomized in an *American Bar Association Journal* article by legal journalist Kenneth Jost.[130] Jost's article was a head-on attack on the reform movement, and Huber became a primary focus because of his role in that effort. The title of the article itself reflects the reason for Jost's assault: "Tampering with Evidence: The Liability and Competitiveness Myth."

The reason for Jost's title and the theme of his article are laid out in his opening paragraphs which are worth quoting because they summarize his entire argument:

> Americans anxious about the United States' precarious position in the world economy were given a new but familiar target to blame last summer: the legal system. From the nation's second highest office, Americans were told that "unrestrained litigation" was exacting a "terrible toll" on the U.S. economy: costing U.S. consumers up to $300 billion, deterring U.S.

manufacturers from product innovation, and hampering their ability to compete with foreign companies.

"A self-inflicted competitive disadvantage" was how Vice President Quayle described it. The message struck a responsive chord in people naturally distrustful of lawyers and accustomed to hearing of daffy lawsuits and extravagant jury awards and settlements.

It also provided new impetus for a bill being pushed in Congress by a business and insurance industry coalition to change the rules for trying damage suits involving product-related injuries.

That message is fundamentally false—the product of dubious anecdotes, questionable research, concocted statistics, factual and legal misstatements, and willful disregard of contradictory evidence. (emphasis added)[131]

Jost outlines here the darker side of the reform movement and its rhetoric—something not revealed in academic critiques like those of Saks and Sanders and Joyce. Jost's criticism of the rhetoric of reform is not simply about empirical accuracy, good science or rational policymaking. It is about political gain and the use of symbols and ideas in the interest of political gain—it is about the politics of ideas. Jost believes that Huber's work should be evaluated in this context.

Jost suggests that many claims found in the rhetoric of reform, including Huber's, are manipulated to present the desired picture at the cost of accuracy. Jost finds Huber's approach to the issues consciously one-sided rather than a balanced or objective analysis. For instance, he essentially accuses Huber and coeditor Litan of stacking the deck in choosing contributors to their book *The Liability Maze*[132] to emphasize the negative effects of the tort system on innovation and competitiveness. "The most damning evidence on innovation came from papers on automobiles, pharmaceuticals and general aviation aircraft, each written by someone with long-standing financial ties to the industry he examined."[133] Jost notes that nowhere in the book are these ties or their one-sidedness explained.[134] Huber and Litan did not deny that their intent was to show just one side of the issue. They made "no bones about what the experts on innovation were asked to do. Huber says he contacted business groups and asked them to suggest authors who could 'give us your best on how this is killing innovation.' Says Litan, 'We were fairly confident that the innovation people would find that there was an effect on innovation.' "[135]

Jost finds Huber's approach to the issues to be cavalier.[136] To illustrate this, he highlights the way Huber calculated the "liability tax" of $300 billion and characterizes the estimate as being "about as genuine as a $3 bill."[137] Jost explains that the estimate was derived by taking a widely cited figure of $80 billion as the direct cost of all insurance in the U.S. and multiplying by $3.50—the indirect cost. The $3.50 came from a 1987 American Medical Association study of doctors' costs for avoiding liability—$3.50 for $1 in direct costs. In response to criticisms of this estimate, reports Jost, "Huber says that the AMA study was 'biased, no doubt,' and then adopts an agnostic stance toward his own calculation. 'Nobody knows what the indirect cost is,' he says. 'What I said was that if the same multipliers operate in other areas, it's $300 billion. If they don't, it's not.' "[138]

Jost is not the only writer to look skeptically at Huber the policy entrepreneur. Kenneth Chesebro wrote perhaps the most scathing commentary on a Huber work—Huber's 1991 book *Galileo's Revenge: Junk Science in the Courtroom.*[139] In a lengthy and heavily footnoted law review essay, Chesebro criticized both Huber's factual description of the junk science "problem" and his legal analysis of the rules surrounding the use of scientific materials—in particular the so-called "*Fyre* Rule."[140] Said Chesebro: "The analysis of Huber's treatment of facts . . . reveals a work that relies almost exclusively on anecdotal information and inflated rhetoric, misrepresents numerous aspects of its subject matter, and presents no considered, objective or empirically based measure of the extent of the 'junk science' problem."[141] Bluntly, he called Huber's factual description biased.[142] He characterized Huber's legal analysis as dubious and his history of the "*Fyre* Rule" fictitious.[143] There is very little truth, Chesebro claimed, in "Huber's description of the *Fyre* rule, of how its elimination prompted the rise of junk science, and thus how its rebirth would help destroy junk science."[144] A telling weakness of Huber's legal analysis—telling for Chesebro for what it says about Huber's approach to scholarship—"is that throughout his extensive discussion of *Fyre*, Huber provides no citations to support his version of the birth, growth, death, and possible new rise of the *Fyre* rule. Close examination reveals that, in fact, virtually nothing that Huber says about *Fyre* is true."[145]

Chesebro went beyond criticizing Huber's book and addressed what he calls "the selling of Peter Huber" by the Manhattan Institute "public relations juggernaut."[146] Relying on Manhattan Institute materials he described the Institute's vigorous public relations activities in disseminating Huber's work and ideas. The Institute's political objective was to change the minds of the public and "to sell ideas, shape public perceptions of a 'legal system in crisis,' and manufacture a supposedly spontaneous public outcry about the need to reform the legal system."[147] Its political objectives were financed, Chesebro said in a lengthy footnote that drew directly from Manhattan Institute materials, largely by corporations and actively conservative foundations. For instance, Chesebro noted that "[b]y 1989, total contributions had grown to $2,113,000, 41% of which came from conservative and/or corporate foundations such as the John M. Olin Foundation, Sarah Scaife Foundation, Lynde and Harry Bradley Foundation, J. M. Foundation, Smith Richardson Foundation, and Starr Foundation. . . . Thirty-three percent came from Fortune 500 corporations, chiefly insurance companies and pharmaceutical and chemical manufacturers, including $50,000-plus each from Aetna, State Farm Insurance, Citicorp, and Chase Manhattan Bank."[148]

Huber's influential book *Liability: The Legal Revolution and Its Consequences*[149]—a book consciously aimed at a general, rather than an exclusively academic or professional audience—has also been fiercely criticized in some law journals. Like Jost and Chesebro, these reviewers look at Huber's work in the context of a political process in which a particular set of interests are trying to alter the rules regarding civil litigation to be more in their favor. Professor Joseph Page, reviewing the book in the *Georgetown Law Journal*,[150] wrote "within the context of the current debates over tort reform, *Liability* serves the immediate political interests of those who favor pro-defendant changes in the law of torts."[151] Professor Robert Hayden characterized the book as a combination of "dubious scholarship with a polemical ideological argument. The scholarship is dubious because it ignores or misstates contrary evidence and overstates its own case. The argument is polemical and ideological because it fails to take into account possible alternative explanations for the phenomena it examines and sees conspiracy among those who oppose its tenets."[152]

A review in the *Stanford Law Review* by Professor Mark Hager was no kinder than those of Page and Hayden. A close scrutiny of Huber's work, says Hager, "reveals a book riddled with flaws and errors—factual, historical, logical, philosophical, and moral—so serious as to make its defined status as 'authoritative' a disturbing prospect."[153] Hager sees the book as troubling for another reason, and that has to do with the connection between intellectual and scholarly work on the one hand, and particular political agendas on the other. From Hager's perspective, the positive, even enthusiastic, reaction to Huber's book in the *Wall Street Journal, Forbes,* and "dust jacket plaudits from a number of business spokesmen and right-wing law professors"[154] is "a paradigmatic case study of intellectual corruption in the corporate state."[155] Hager ties work like Huber's to the rise of what he calls a "reactionary intelligentsia" during the 1980s:

This reactionary intelligentsia, through a network of well-funded think tanks, university and business connections, and intimate linkages to policy-making bureaucracies, has established precisely the sort of stable, institutionalized economic and intellectual power base that left-liberal intellectuals have been criticized for having, but have never actually had. One index to this development lies in the litany of right-wing think tanks whose names—Heritage Foundation, Hoover Institute, American Enterprise Institute, Cato Institute, Manhattan Institute—have become almost household words to the reading public.[156]

Even those more sympathetic to reform expressed some apprehension about Huber's work and the role played by the Manhattan Institute. The *Wall Street Journal* carried a front-page profile of Huber that not only raised questions about the accuracy of Huber's claims about the legal system, but also described the Manhattan Institute's support and marketing of Huber's work.[157] It noted that Huber had been brought onboard to produce "a book on the liability system aimed at [a] popular 'cross-over' audience of influential leaders."[158]

Conclusion: Reform and the Politics of Ideas

How can we begin to analyze and make sense of the reform debate, its rhetoric, and the characterization of juries and the civil justice system upon which it depends? As the work of Saks and of Sanders and Joyce reveals, there is a substantial gap between the substantive claims of the reform rhetoric and what the best available empirical information can tell us. The criticisms of the work of Peter Huber and the efforts of the Manhattan Institute suggest that there is more to understanding that gap and its political significance than looking at it as the result of a lack of rationality and a lack of reliance on the work of detached analysts in the policy process.

One of the important issues that Jost raises, at least in terms of the products liability arena, is that pointing out the existence of the gap between rhetoric and academic knowledge, as Saks and Sanders and Joyce did, seems to have made little difference. He says, "Despite the demonstrated flaws in its evidence, the product liability reform lobby's major points have gained wide acceptance—to the frustration of its opponents."[159] Image, it appears, is everything in what is a hotly contested political fight and not a rational decision-making process.

What the efforts of policy entrepreneurs like Huber and the Manhattan Institute tell us is that ideas and images are extremely important in the debate over civil justice reform, especially ideas and images that are used to characterize juries and the civil justice system, identify and define problems, and describe solutions. In short, as we suggested at the beginning of this chapter, the public policy process is essentially a struggle over ideas and which images of the world will govern policy.[160]

As if to echo Deborah Stone's argument about the battle over ideas, the mission statement of the Manhattan Institute's Judicial Studies Program says: "An essential element of successful policy advocacy is taking the initiative; the side proposing change most often ends up setting the agenda, while the side opposing change finds itself in the unenviable position of defending the status quo."[161] More specifically, this statement says:

> the rhetoric of liability reform must incorporate transcending concepts, like consumer choice, fairness, and equity, while simultaneously pointing out the opposition's indifference or opposition to these values. Across a wide cultural horizon today powerful new ideas like choice, empowerment, and voluntarism are capturing the public imagination; they can and should be brought into the debate about legal reform. At the same time, it is vital that defenders of the current system—the plaintiff's bar, in particular—not be allowed to divert attention from these issues, or skirt the question of costs. The present system is not only coercive, capricious, and regressive, it encourages fraud and deception on a massive scale, and seriously hinders the engines of industrial renewal and economic growth; the ultimate cost of expanded liability is a loss of competitiveness and lower standards of living, a point that must continuously be driven home. . . .
>
> If, sometime during the present decade, a consensus emerges in favor of serious judicial reform, it will be because millions of minds have been changed.[162]

This is the politics of ideas.

The politics of ideas and the struggle to control which images of the world govern policy, ultimately, are about what issues and problems government will pay attention to in the policy process. At both the state and federal levels, government has paid attention to the issue of civil justice reform. Ricci argues that we must pay attention "to the question of which ideas will be received successfully. . . . Ideas are easier to produce than votes, money, and bureaucratic positions, and there are, as a result, always plenty of them available. . . . What is crucially important . . . is the process by which some ideas come to the fore and then inspire government policies, while others do neither."[163] The next chapter outlines a general framework, drawn from the political science literature on the policy process, that will provide a theoretical context for examining the substance of the reform rhetoric's ideas and images with Ricci's concern in mind. This framework deals with agenda setting.

CHAPTER TWO

The Public Policy Process and the Importance of Agenda Setting: The Case of Civil Justice Reform

The successful placement of an issue on the policy agenda, said political scientist John Kingdon, requires changing the way people think about that issue.[1] The rhetoric of civil justice reform is part of a political effort to do just that, an effort that has been successful to a large degree despite the critics' contention that the reformers' portrayal of juries and the civil justice system is inaccurate. To understand this, we must move beyond simply analyzing the reformers' substantive claims, to an examination of the reform rhetoric as a part of a political effort to gain a place on the policy agenda. Chapter 2 provides a framework for doing this.

Specifically, this chapter analyzes the rhetoric of reform from the perspective of agenda setting within the public policy process and critically examines the major symbolic devices used in marketing the rhetoric's ideas and images. These devices—the rhetoric's form—are important because they help explain the reformers' success in gaining a place on the policy agenda. This chapter is divided into three main parts. The first discusses the major premise underlying our approach to the politics of agenda setting—that policy problems are not self-evident, but rather are socially constructed in the political arena. This is the politics of ideas. The second part then examines the rhetoric of reform in terms of John Kingdon's model of agenda setting, one in which the politics of ideas is an integral part.[2]

The last and largest part concentrates on the ways in which policy problems are defined. If indeed policy problems are not self-evident but rather are socially constructed, then *how* they are constructed or defined is the key part of this political process. If gaining a place on the policy agenda requires changing the way people think about an issue, then the devices and strategies used to accomplish this merit examination. This third part of the chapter critically analyzes the reform rhetoric using Deborah Stone's conceptual arguments about the symbolic devices and types of language used to characterize or strategically represent some situation as a policy problem.[3]

Agendas and Solutions Seeking Problems

For those who study the public policy process, the "agenda" refers to those issues which receive serious and active attention from key political actors or the public—issues about which it is believed that governmental action is appropriate and worthwhile.[4] John Kingdon subdivides the agenda into the "governmental agenda" and the "decision agenda." The former covers "the list of subjects that are getting attention."[5] The latter is somewhat narrower and includes "the list of subjects within the governmental agenda that are up for an active decision."[6]

Richard Cobb and Charles Elder,[7] also political scientists interested in agenda setting, describe matters in a similar fashion. For them, there are two important agendas: the public or systemic agenda and the policy or institutional agenda. The first is roughly akin to Kingdon's governmental agenda, but broader. It "consists of all issues that are commonly perceived by members of the political community as meriting public attention and as involving matters within the legitimate jurisdiction of existing governmental authority."[8] The second is much like Kingdon's decision agenda and consists of "that set of items explicitly up for the active and serious consideration of authoritative decisionmakers."[9] For Cobb and Elder, the public agenda is the more important and more interesting of the two as few issues emerge on the policy agenda without first appearing on the public agenda.[10]

Policy entrepreneurs like Peter Huber and advocacy organizations like the Manhattan Institute have attempted to position the issue of civil justice reform squarely on the governmental or public agenda, and to place their proposed solutions on the decision or institutional agenda. As the opening paragraph of the Manhattan Institute mission statement says: "It may not be an overstatement, in fact, to say that debate and sentiment have reached a new plateau; in contrast to just one or two years ago, when liability reform hovered on the fringes of mainstream discussion, liability reform now vies with more traditional issues such as welfare, education and environmental policy in the debate about the nation's future."[11] In short, the reform movement has been successful in placing the issue of civil justice reform on the public agenda and in getting their proposed solutions on the policy agenda. By the late 1980s, nearly every state's legislature addressed one or more of the reform movement's proposals as had Congress and the Supreme Court.

Among the most important findings regarding agenda setting is that policy problems are not obvious or self-evident. Says Kingdon, "at any time, important people in and around government could attend to a long list of problems. . . . Obviously, they pay attention to some potential problems and ignore others. . . . problems are not entirely self-evident."[12] Consequently, those wanting to get their issues and ideas on the public agenda, and ultimately the policy agenda, invest great effort and resources in getting the attention of important people in and around government and sometimes in influencing the public at large. They must identify and define their issues as problems worthy of concern and demanding of immediate attention, and also be able to offer up acceptable solutions for these problems.

What this means is that policy problems are not discovered, but rather they are socially constructed. "They arise not so much from events and circumstances as from the meanings that people attribute to those events and circumstances."[13] How "conditions" become defined or labeled as "problems" is a key part of the process of gaining agenda status. Consistency with the best empirical evidence is not a necessity in this process which is governed as much or more by passion and partisanship than reason. Deborah Stone summarizes the political character of problem definition nicely:

> [P]roblem definition is never simply a matter of defining goals and measuring our distance from them. It is rather the *strategic representation* of situations. Problem definition is a matter of representation because there is no objective description of a situation, there can only be portrayals of people's experiences and interpretations. Problem definition is strategic because groups, individuals, and government agencies deliberately and consciously design portrayals so as to promote their favored course of action. Dissatisfactions are not registered as degrees of change on some thermometer, but as claims in a political process. Representations of a problem are therefore constructed to win the most people to one's side and the most leverage over one's opponents.[14]

Viewed from this perspective, the efforts of policy entrepreneurs like Huber and the organizations that sponsor and support them make sense as strategic representation.

Some critics of the reform rhetoric would hope to see more rationality and systematic investigation in the policy process so that actual problems in the civil justice system can be identified and appropriate solutions devised.[15] However, the strategic representation of situations begins with a set of preexisting, favored "solutions"—what some particular political interests ultimately wish to achieve. These solutions are then attached to conveniently devised "problems." In short, problems are not systematically identified so that appropriate solutions may then be crafted. Instead, the process is inverted; solutions are devised and then problems that justify those solutions are defined. As Kingdon found in his analysis, "people generate and debate solutions because they have some self-interest in doing so . . . not because the solutions are generated in response to a problem."[16] The gap between reform rhetoric and reliable empirical information that so bothers critics like Michael Saks and Joseph Sanders and Craig Joyce looks quite different from this perspective. What they characterize as a problem—a potentially dangerous diversion from rationality, detached analysis, and the best available evidence—is in effect a set of tactics in a political process used to win allies in an effort to gain a place on the agenda. Candid debate and dispassionate empirical analysis will not necessarily be in the best political interest of the reformers, and there is no reason to expect them to adopt such an approach.

The characterization of juries and the civil justice system that forms the foundation of the reform rhetoric and animates both the debate and the concrete solutions presented is understandable only as a part of the tactics of gaining a place on the agenda for a preferred set of policy changes. Drawing on the work of John Kingdon, the next section presents a scheme for understanding the politics of agenda setting within the policy process. It pays particular attention to what is involved in changing the agenda to include some new idea or problem.

Kingdon's Model of Agenda Setting

John Kingdon's work provides a rough model of the agenda-setting process in which Stone's idea of *strategic representation* can be placed and used. Although he devised this model as a description of the process with regard to the Congress, its basic logic and structure can be applied more generally. Kingdon sees the process of agenda setting as involving three separate areas or streams of activity—problems, policies, and politics—that may come together at certain critical times and allow new ideas on the public and even the decision agenda. "Solutions (policy proposals) become joined to problems, and both of them are joined to favorable political forces. This coupling is most likely when a policy window—an opportunity to push pet proposals or one's conception of problems—is open. . . . Policy windows are opened either by the appearance of compelling problems or by happenings in the political stream."[17] Kingdon's model does not guarantee that certain ideas—like civil justice reform—will gain agenda status nor predict what will happen. It is a model based on contingency for which those who would take advantage of it must be prepared.

Perhaps the most important factor in this model of the policy process is the window of opportunity, created either by a compelling problem or by happenings in the political stream. The chances of an idea gaining agenda status are best when these windows coincide—the perception of a compelling problem in a political environment receptive to that perception—*and* the presence of an available set of solutions (activity in the policy stream). Ultimately, opening a political window of opportunity requires receptivity to an idea by those in key positions in and around government. Participants in the political arena, says Kingdon, are likely to perceive and be influenced by three things: "swings in the national mood, elections bringing new administrations to power and new partisan or ideological distributions to Congress (or other legislative bodies), and interest groups of various description who press (or fail to press) their demands on government."[18]

The Political Stream

The combination of national mood and elections is most important in bringing new items to the agenda.[19] Engendering or even creating broad public and elite concern about an issue helps develop a receptivity among key political actors for particular solutions and/or problem definitions. Policy entrepreneurs and advocates for a particular idea may work industriously over many years fertilizing and cultivating the ground, waiting for the opportunity to arise that will allow their seed to germinate. This notion is illustrated quite well by the Manhattan Institute's mission statement which says in part: "If, sometime during the present decade, a consensus emerges in favor of serious judicial reform, it will be because millions of minds have been changed."[20]

Kingdon calls this the "softening up" process. "Many good proposals have fallen on deaf ears because they arrived before the general public, the specialized publics, or the policy communities were ready to listen."[21] Many of the claims about juries and the consequences of the civil justice system's behavior along with the activities of policy entrepreneurs outlined in chapter 1 are a part of this "softening up" process—the attempt to shape the national mood so the right climate for the reformers' agenda could be created. Some specific examples illustrate the ways in which the reformers sought to shape the national mood in the effort to get civil justice reform on the agenda. A number of insurance companies and trade groups have invested heavily in public relations and lobbying campaigns to bring their view of juries and the civil justice system to the general public, elites, and opinion leaders.[22] In 1982 one such effort called "Project Justice" began in Illinois.[23] The product of combined insurance, business, professional, and service provider interests, "Project Justice Illinois . . . [was] considered a prototype tort reform coalition."[24] It was formed to disseminate information to the public, to opinion leaders, and to policymakers, and to coordinate lobbying efforts, all in the interest of civil justice reform.[25] As the "insurance crisis" of the middle 1980s began making its way onto the public agenda, similar organizations with symbolically charged names began appearing across the country.[26]

While the insurance trade associations encouraged the creation of these public relations/lobbying organizations, they were themselves vigorously engaged in the "softening up" process. In 1986 the Insurance Information Institute (III) announced its own public relations campaign in an article entitled "We All Pay the Price: An Industry Effort to Reform Civil Justice." Its purpose was to "extend the advertising effort to the broad general public. We must gain the widest possible awareness and support before we can expect political leaders to improve the system."[27] The article estimated that the campaign would reach 90% of the adults in the country through "a broad-based advertising campaign using network television, major newspapers and national news magazines."[28] Built around the concept of the "Lawsuit Crisis," the campaign employed a series of eye-catching dramatic print advertisements intended to drive home to the general public the idea that "we all pay the price" for the products of jury decision making.[29] Advertisement titles included: "The Lawsuit Crisis Is Bad for Babies," "The Lawsuit Crisis Is Penalizing School Sports," and "Even the Clergy Can't Escape the Lawsuit Crisis."[30] Each was clearly intended to instill fear and anxiety as a way of defining in the public mind a problem which could only eliminated through civil justice reform. These advertisements appeared in the Sunday magazine sections of major newspapers across the country,[31] as well as in *Readers Digest*, *Time*, and *Newsweek*.[32] The "Civil Justice Campaign" also included press and speakers kits, and "insurance agents and company personnel [were] being asked to participate in the campaign by placing additional advertisements in their local media to generate community interest."[33]

While perhaps the best-funded and most vigorous campaign aimed at changing the national mood, III's effort was by no means the only visible public relations activity. From late 1985 through 1986, the insurance brokerage firm of Johnson and Higgins launched an advertising campaign pointing out the system's role in creating the "insurance crisis" of the middle 1980s. It too relied on dramatic illustrations in print advertisements to convey its message.[34] Individual insurance companies also sponsored their own public relations campaigns. Aetna Insurance, for example, ran a major campaign during 1987, called "Speaking out for Civil Justice Reform." It involved an eight-part series of advertisements targeted to appear in a number of widely circulated publications along with a direct mail campaign to various opinion leaders. Each advertisement had a theme which described a particular aspect of the civil justice "problem"—cost, delay, overlitigiousness, or runaway jury verdicts—and the kinds of solutions Aetna wished to present as necessary. The mailing included a personally addressed letter signed by William O. Bailey, vice chairman of Aetna, reprints of the eight advertisements making up the series, and summary of a 1987 Louis Harris poll conducted for Aetna on the civil justice system and reform.

Shaping the national mood may place an idea on the broad public agenda; but according to Kingdon's model, it is another matter to get it on the decision agenda. Here elections become very important. They can bring a new administration or legislative majority to Washington or a state capital, often with a "mandate" for change. A new administration may signal greater receptivity for certain ideas—a potential window of opportunity for those seeking a place on the agenda. The Reagan and Bush administrations provided just this opportunity for the civil justice reform movement whose goals fit nicely into the antiregulation views that dominated both administrations. In fact, both administrations wholeheartedly embraced the reformers' cause, giving it high-level attention and visibility as evidenced in the widely circulated and highly influential Reagan Justice Department's *Tort Policy Working Group Report* and the Bush administration's Council on Competitiveness headed by Vice President Quayle. A new legislative majority may also signal a greater receptivity for certain ideas. The Republican victory in the 1994 election giving the party control of both houses of Congress promises to provide such an opportunity. Federal tort reform legislation ("The Common Sense Legal Reform Act") is one of the ten items in the Republican candidates' "Contract with America."

The symbolic importance of a change in administration and support at the presidential level cannot be overestimated, especially when the President is as highly popular as Reagan. An idea seeking a place on the agenda can draw on that popularity and authority, making it more acceptable and giving it a kind of moral force. An administration's statements on the issue are likely to be viewed with a less critical eye, especially by those within the President's party. For instance, one of the things that Sanders and Joyce complained about was the uncritical acceptance of the claims found in the *Tort Policy Working Group Report* by reformers in Texas, particularly Republicans.

The Problem Stream

Windows of opportunity may open in the problem stream as well as in the political stream. Government is largely reactive and needs some concrete reason for acting on one concern rather than another. A window of opportunity may open in the problem stream as a result of the existence of a compelling problem—one that *seems* to demand immediate and substantial governmental action. Some things, like a natural disaster, may be seen rather obviously as compelling problems, but "problems" that deal with social or economic matters are often not self-evident. This raises two important questions: how something is defined as a problem, and then how it is identified when it occurs.

In trying to shape the national mood, a key part of the reformers' effort has been to bring attention to a "problem" in the civil justice system that will require their favored "solutions" (e.g., limitations on damages and contingency fees, changes in causes of action, and changes in procedures), and then to make a convincing argument that the problem is so compelling due to its consequences that immediate action is needed. It is in this stream of activity that ideas and rhetoric are especially important because it is here that the battle over which image of reality will govern policy is fought. Ultimately, the turf being fought over is the public mind. As Kingdon notes, "there are great political stakes in problem definition."[35]

Defining and identifying problems are evaluative and hence interpretative tasks requiring judgments based on certain standards or measures. Most of the rhetoric of civil justice reform involves statements or claims about the standards used in defining the problem, the identification of the problem using those standards, and the evaluations of the consequences that make that problem compelling. Each of these issues has been hotly contested in the political debate surrounding the reform effort. These are the issues and claims that concern Saks, Sanders and Joyce, and Jost, among others. It bears repeating that it is important to look not only at how consistent the image is with the best available empirical evidence, but also at how that image is constructed. The policy process is not well described by a rational decision-making model that defines problems and evaluates them as compelling on the basis of objective standards and methods. Instead, it is better depicted as a model of reasoning by metaphor and analogy. "It is trying to get others to see a situation *as* one thing rather than another."[36] As Deborah Stone said, it is a matter of strategic representation.

In the next section we will explore in detail some of the major devices used by the reformers to construct their image of the civil justice system and the consequences of its behavior. This is especially important in light of Jost's observation noted in chapter 1 that the reformer's claims have gained wide acceptance despite their demonstrated flaws.

Defining Public Policy Problems: Stone's Concept of Strategic Representation

Three aspects of strategic representation used in defining and identifying policy problems are particularly important in Stone's view: the use of symbols and symbolic devices, the use of numbers, and ideas of cause and effect. We will look at each of these in turn as they relate to the rhetoric of reform.

Symbols and Symbolic Devices

The definition and identification of problems for the purpose of gaining agenda status is, above all, about symbolic politics.[37] Relying on symbols and symbolic devices in political discourse is an appeal to shared values, preferably deeply held or fundamental values, and involves the attempt to manipulate those values in order to achieve political gain. With regard to civil justice reform, this is wonderfully illustrated by the Manhattan Institute's mission statement. As to setting the terms of the debate it says: "The rhetoric of liability reform must incorporate transcending concepts, like consumer choice, fairness, and equity, while simultaneously pointing out the opposition's indifference or opposition to these values. Across a wide cultural horizon today powerful new ideas like choice, empowerment, and voluntarism are capturing the public imagination; they can and should be brought into the debate about legal reform."[38]

The use of symbolic politics is also evidenced in the names chosen by many of the reform movement's public relations/lobbying organizations, for example, Illinois (or Indiana, Kansas, Nebraska) Project Justice. It is difficult to be against "justice," and the use of the term implies that justice is defined in practice by the agendas of these groups. Examples of similar organizations include the Truth and Fairness in Litigation Committee in Pennsylvania, the Ohio Basic Fairness in Litigation Coalition, and the Michigan Committee for Civil Justice Equity. Not to be left out of the symbolic battle, the opponents of the reform movement have also tried to wrap themselves in such values, witness the Trial Lawyers for Public Justice.

The concept of symbolic politics is about those matters people tend to accept uncritically, almost as a matter of common sense; this is what makes symbolic politics attractive and useful. It draws on deeply held, rarely questioned values that structure peoples' view of the world in which they live, and as a consequence, systematically collected empirical data are not likely to defeat claims that successfully tie themselves to such values and people's commonsense view of the world.[39] Such an appeal is, in essence, an appeal to emotion rather than reason, an attempt "to eliminate the mind and the critical faculties" from the evaluation process.[40] This can be described as the "tactical use of passion" in the political arena which provokes "feelings rather than thought."[41] Among the symbolic devices incorporated in this tactical use of passion are narrative stories, synecdoche (or anecdotes), and metaphors.[42] Each of these symbolic devices is used in the strategic representation of juries and the civil justice system as a compelling problem that may open a window of opportunity in the problem stream.

Stories of Decline. Among the most important symbolic devices used in defining policy problems is the use of a narrative structure. Such policy stories have "a beginning, a middle, and end, involving some change or transformation. They have heroes and villains and innocent victims, and they pit the forces of evil against the forces of good."[43] This seems to describe the rhetoric of reform quite well. It is full of lamented changes, good guys and bad guys, and innocent victims in distress and in need of rescue.

Reformers characterize the civil justice system as a system that has changed dramatically in recent years—and for the worse. Cast as villains are greedy plaintiffs' lawyers and undeserving plaintiffs out to make a quick buck.[44] One set of innocent victims are the defendants being sued by these greedy lawyers and undeserving plaintiffs, the companies or professionals who are simply "deep pocket" targets of various villains. More often, *we*—the general populace of hardworking and honest people—are the innocent victims. We are the ones who "pay the price" as the insurance industry public relations campaign says—we are the ones who cannot get adequate obstetrical care, whose children can no longer participate in high school sports, who can no longer turn to priests, ministers, or rabbis for spiritual comfort and advice, or we are the ones who will lose our jobs because American businesses are no longer competitive. We are the ones who pay Huber's "tort tax."

Two broad story lines, often intertwined, tend to dominate the defining of policy problems according to Stone. The first, and more important of the two, is a story of decline; and the second is a story of helplessness and control.[45] "The two stories are often woven together, with the story of decline serving as the stage setting and the impetus for the story of control. The story of decline is meant to warn us of suffering and motivate us to seize control."[46] Stone likens the story of decline to the biblical story of the expulsion from paradise. She says "it runs like this: 'In the beginning, things were pretty good. But they got worse. In fact, right now, they are nearly intolerable. Something must be done.' This story usually ends with a prediction of crisis."[47]

The idea of decline permeates the reform rhetoric: it forms the basic logic of the reformers' characterization of the civil justice system. Examples can be found in the writings of Peter Huber and George Priest who are concerned with the changes in the law itself, particularly with regard to liability. Each argues that fundamental changes in the law of liability have occurred since the 1960s and that the consequences of these changes have been disastrous. Writing in 1985 Priest said that: "Since 1960, our modern civil liability regime has experienced a conceptual revolution that is among the most dramatic ever witnessed in the Anglo-American legal system. Legal rules that had been entrenched for decades, and the attitudes and presuppositions that supported them, were suddenly repudiated and replaced by rules and presuppositions radically different."[48] In a 1987 article, he laid the blame for the "insurance crisis" of the middle 1980s on these changes. The story is one of good intentioned reforms gone awry causing all sorts of problems in the economy making the American people worse off, especially the poor.[49]

Peter Huber also characterizes changes in the law of liability as revolutionary and as evidence of a fall from grace that has had dire consequences. In the introductory chapter of *Liability,* he claims that "for all practical purposes, the omnipresent tort tax we pay today was conceived in the 1950s and set in place in the 1960s and 1970s by a new generation of lawyers and judges. In the space of twenty years they transformed the legal landscape, proclaiming sweeping new rights to sue."[50] In a section of that chapter entitled "From Consent to Coercion," Huber continues his story of the fall from grace and the wages of sin. In a remarkably short time he says, those who consciously designed this new system of rules "completely recast a centuries-old body of law in an entirely new mold of their own design . . . within two short decades they had achieved virtually every legal change that they had originally planned . . . compared with the cautious incrementalism with which the common law had changed in centuries past, an utter transformation over a twenty-year span can fairly be described as a revolution, and a violent one at that."[51]

Huber's paradise or golden age was one in which the law of contract ruled: "The revolution began and ended with the wholesale repudiation of the law of contract."[52] This was the fall from consent to coercion. The changes he condemns serve "only as an engine of social destruction," since undermining consent and contract in a tort-dominated system eventually undercuts other freedoms as well.[53] Huber paints a chilling picture of our fate as a nation should restoration to the old ways not occur:

> Americans have always taken for granted a structure of private legal rights that protects individual freedom and consensual economic relations. In Peru there is no functioning market for real estate, because the authorities refuse to administer a law of property that allows for most concepts of ownership or sale. . . . In some socialist and third-world countries, a similar paralysis, with similar roots in the repudiation of private law, grips the markets for consumer goods of every description. Anyone who cares to make the trip can see the results: squalid shanty towns with great numbers of people permanently frozen out of the market economy, black-market trading of desperately needed antibiotics that cannot be provided under the terms prescribed by law, starvation on a mass scale when the right of farmers to sell their produce as they wish is abolished. It is not that the individual citizens in these countries are less wise or industrious or compassionate than we are; they are prisoners of legal structure and social systems that systematically foil progressive self-help and generosity. Good law brings out the best in people, communities, and economies; bad law brings out the very worst.[54]

This is a story of decline of truly biblical portions, in Huber's view the consequence of the actions of well-intentioned but unrealistic utopians whose policies have backfired. Like all utopians who succeed politically, "they deliver only tyranny in practice."[55]

There are many other stories of decline in the rhetoric of reform. Chief Justice Warren Burger and former Vice President Quayle asserted that there had been an "explosion" of litigation and equated it with a societal decline. The widely distributed speeches of business leaders William McCormick and Robert Malott, discussed in chapter 1, were also structured as stories of decline, with the decline beginning in the 1960s. More recently, and in the same vein, is Walter Olson's book *The Litigation Explosion.* Another Manhattan Institute project, the logic of Olson's book is built on the idea of decline, and he explores each problem area in the civil justice system by explicitly comparing it to what is described as a better past when older ideas and institutions provided an orderly and harmonious system.

The second story line Stone finds prevalent in the politics of problem definition is a story of helplessness and control. This story line says that until now we had believed the situation was out of our control, something with which we simply had to live. Now, things have changed and we can see that in fact the situation can be controlled. "Stories about control are always gripping because they speak to the fundamental problem of liberty—to what extent do we control our own life conditions and destinies? Stories that purport to tell us of less control are always threatening, and ones that promise more are always heartening."[56]

This story line can be seen in the quote from Huber above and his chilling allusion to the spector of third world status. It is implicit throughout his book *Liability,* in Olson's *Litigation Explosion,* and in Priest's work—all of them making comparisons to a more orderly past, a legal order destroyed by well-intentioned but naive legal revolutionaries and utopians. Because of the changes wrought by these legal engineers, we have lost control over our legal system, and as a result it is out of balance and running amok with dire consequences. Indeed the "running amok" idea of a legal system out of control is at the heart of the reform rhetoric. It appears not only in the work of the "high theorists" of the reform movement. It underlies, for example, the frequent use of the term "litigation lottery" to describe the civil justice system, or the characterization of jury verdicts as unpredictable or biased, or the use of the term "skyrocketing" to describe recent trends in verdicts. The idea is clearly conveyed in the full title of Olson's book: *The Litigation Explosion: What Happened When America Unleashed the Lawsuit.*

The ideas of decline and lack of control work in combination to evoke a sense of impending disaster or crisis, and the story line tells us that something must be done—and done now. The civil justice system *must* be reformed the story tells us, and it can be reformed. There are solutions available, the problem can be remedied—there is hope. Said Huber: "The path we have been traveling is not inevitable, and there is yet time for a serious change in course."[57] The reform rhetoric speaks not of bold new experiments, but of taking us back to the way things were. Rather than speaking of experimentation, the reform rhetoric tells a comforting story of hope through restoration. The closing lines of Olson's *The Litigation Explosion* offer a combination of hope and restoration. He wrote: "we are most of us terribly vulnerable to the perils of litigation. Yet as a society, we are in no sense helpless to move against its evils. All it takes is the will. The will may not be here yet, but it is coming. When it does, we will again make litigation an exception, a last resort, a necessary evil at the margins of our common life."[58]

The fall from the grace of a better past, our ability to take control, and the chance for restoration are main story lines in the eight-part Aetna Insurance advertisement campaign noted earlier. This effort is set up as a series of fatherly chats with Aetna vice chairman William O. Bailey, and its key metaphors are "balance" and "restoration". As it appeared in *Time* magazine, the first advertisement sets the stage for the series by saying that while the original logic and purposes of our civil justice system are good, "the system's original purposes have become distorted with the passage of time."[59] It then goes on to outline the distortion—the system was originally created to balance individual rights and societal needs, but has strayed from this objective; it used to be efficient, but is now intolerably slow and costly; it used to make judgments on the basis of fault, now it makes them on the basis of who can pay; it used to compensate people fairly, but does no longer given the many big awards unrelated to the injuries suffered. There is still hope, this first advertisement says: "Americans have a demonstrated capacity to fix things that go wrong. We've been doing it for 200 years. . . . We *can* restore balance to this system. Public demand has put this on the agenda for change in state after state. I [Bailey] hope you will join me in working for meaningful reform of our civil justice system."[60] The second advertisement in the series deals with cost, the third with the issue of fault, the fourth with awards, the fifth and sixth with litigiousness, the seventh with delay and frivolous suits, and the final advertisement in the series discusses solutions, particularly in the products liability area.

The message this advertising campaign seeks to convey is clear. There are—allegedly—serious problems in the civil justice system, and they exist because the system has gotten out control. Its original purposes have been distorted, but if we work together we can gain control and restore the system to its prior state of grace. Support for the reformers' cause is not developed by detailed examinations of the present civil justice system and the system of the past followed by a reasoned argument for the superiority of the past. Support is constructed through the message conveyed by the story line—anxiety and despair generated as the effects of decline and distortion, and hope because of our ability to gain control and restore things to the true path which leads to security and well-being.

Anecdotes and Horror Stories. Another aspect of symbolic representation in the political process of defining problems to which Stone points us is synecdoche—"a figure of speech in which the whole is represented by one of its parts."[61] This is a form of symbolism frequently found in politics, "where examples are offered up as 'typical instances' or 'prototypical cases' of a larger problem. These typical cases then define the entire problem and frame the policy response."[62] A particularly useful tactic is to focus on an event or case dramatized as a horror story, as if it were merely one more representation of a larger and pervasive problem. Stone says such anecdotes are "a good organizing tool, because (they) can often make a problem concrete, allow people to identify with someone else, and mobilize anger."[63]

While the specifics of horror stories used in the reform rhetoric may vary, their structure is uniform. They portray Americans as pathologically litigious and juries as willing to inappropriately award millions of dollars at the drop of a hat, especially in medical malpractice and products liability cases. In particular, these tales are used to show five things: (1) many, if not most, money damage jury cases are frivolous and "strain credulity";[64] (2) most plaintiffs are undeserving, having been themselves the cause of their own injuries, to the extent the injuries are real; (3) juries are overly sympathetic to individual plaintiffs suing large corporations or other deep pockets, like physicians; (4) the defendant is not at fault; and (5) as a result of cases like this one the civil justice system has run amok. As we did in chapter 1, we must remind the reader that these stories are distorted versions of actual events, inaccurate, or simply fabrications.

One can see such themes in the tale of "Psychic and the CAT Scan" mentioned in the first chapter, one of the more infamous and most frequently recounted horror stories. The plaintiff is clearly not deserving of a $1 million award for what most sensible people would consider a fictitious injury—the loss of psychic powers. It is easy to assume that the jury which, as Olson notes in his telling of the story, deliberated for only 45 minutes, was simply oversympathetic to an individual suing a deep pocket defendant—here a physician.[65] Clearly any system that would allow this to happen has serious problems.

These themes appear in other frequently retold tales of the civil justice system such as: "The Pinto and the Horse," "The Ladder in the Manure," "The Drunk and the Phone Booth," and "The Fat Man and the Lawnmower."[66] Such tales, though brief, have great evocative power. Anthropologist Robert Hayden argues that "the continued success of the anecdotes is due to their reflection of American common sense: everyone *knows* that the legal system is faulty, and the anecdotes are simply further confirmation of this perception."[67] In their sheer outrageousness such stories summarize the reformers' allegations concerning the failings of the civil justice system and evoke a widespread feeling among people that a system permitting such bizarre happenings must need immediate and fundamental reform. Underlying this surface message, Hayden argues, there is another, deeper one—that the use of the civil justice system in such cases violates certain deeply held values in our culture, in particular individual responsibility and hostility to redistribution (especially when it involves gaining by chicanery rather than hard work).[68] In this sense we can see the story line of societal decline throughout these horror stories.

In using such anecdotes, the reform rhetoric has created a kind of crisis-oriented folklore surrounding the civil justice system. It is not unusual to see the same story appear five or six times in different places over the course of a year. In addition, rarely does an anecdotal recounting limit itself to a single story. More likely a group of such stories will be presented that collectively summarize most, if not all, of the alleged failings of juries and the civil justice system as a part of the overall tale of decline. For instance, a 1986 American Tort Reform Association solicitation letter had a group of five horror stories, including the "Fat Man," the "Psychic," and the "Drunk Driver."[69] Perhaps the largest collections of horror stories, and probably the most sophisticated use of them, are found in Huber's *Liability* and Olson's *Litigation Explosion*. The arguments of both books are built around the constant use of anecdotes as the primary means of describing the civil justice system in operation.

These stories are another aspect of the "tactical use of passion" that characterizes much of the reform rhetoric. Appealing to emotion rather than reason in a political battle over which ideas or image of the civil justice system will govern policy, they are vivid examples of what anthropologist F. G. Bailey calls the rhetoric of assertion.[70] As rhetorical devices, such stories demand assent. "They are peremptory, they assert truths that they present as inescapable, defying argument, so essentially true that they are beyond the need for corroborating evidence."[71] These stories are presented as authoritative statements of fact, often by people of prominence or people with special expertise (the head of a major corporation, the Vice President of the United States, or someone with very special professional training and expertise: "an M.I.T. trained engineer and a Harvard law graduate, has also taught at M.I.T. and formerly clerked for Supreme Court Justice Sandra Day O'Connor"—Peter Huber). Indeed, said Bailey, one of the tasks of assertive rhetoric is "to confer on values the status of facts."[72] He stated: "In rhetoric, to proclaim something a fact is to tell the audience that they have no alternative other than to give their assent, on pain of being excluded as crazy people."[73]

The rhetoric of assertion is also a judgmental or moral rhetoric in praising or condemning people and their intentions.[74] This is consistent with Hayden's idea that horror stories are successful because their message says that basic values are being violated. Each horror story is a mini-morality play. There is always the innocent victim—the defendant being forced to pay for something that was not its fault. And there is always an obvious villain—the plaintiff. The unscrupulousness of plaintiffs in these stories is palpable—a fat man with a heart condition suing the maker of a lawnmower when he should have known better than to overexert himself, or the woman with the fake injury of a loss of psychic powers suing her doctor, etc. Such plaintiffs, we are being told, are people without integrity or a sense of responsibility; they are simply dishonest.

There is still another level of villains and victims in these little morality plays. The reformers cast not only the hapless defendants as victims, but all of us. It is not just the defendants that pay, but as the insurance industry public relations campaign says: "we all pay the price." In other words, the unscrupulous plaintiffs cannot be seen simply as rogues to scoff at. Instead, they present a clear danger to the security and well-being of us all. As William McCormick lamented in his 1986 speech, "Day care centers all across the country are closing their doors"; "Non-profit organizations and local government boards are now having trouble finding anyone willing to serve"; "some manufacturers of life-saving products have quit" (such as anesthesia machines and even a drug to prevent sudden infant death syndrome); and "American vaccine makers are being driven out of the business."[75]

F. G. Bailey notes that in making moral judgments, the rhetoric of assertion very often includes a scapegoat, "A person or a category of persons against whom emotions can be aroused."[76] The scapegoats are juries, plaintiffs, and especially lawyers. From this perspective, Olson's *Litigation Explosion*—which explicitly blames lawyers for the "explosion" and its aftermath—is best seen not simply as an exercise in lawyer bashing, but as an explicit exercise in scapegoating. Vaccines and life-saving devices are not available—blame plaintiff's lawyers; American businesses are no longer competitive in the world economy—blame plaintiff's lawyers; not all women have access to adequate obstetric care—blame plaintiff's lawyers; and so on.

This type of moral judgment and scapegoating also incorporates blame shifting as a way of avoiding unwanted regulation and critical examination. For instance, in commenting on the reform rhetoric in the products liability arena, Kenneth Jost said: "The tort reformers' arguments also deflect attention from the real problems undermining U.S. competitiveness. When Chrysler President Lee Iacocca listed the U.S. automobile industry's problems while visiting Japan with President Bush in January, he made no mention of product liability. But with the product liability system as scapegoat, businesses can avoid hard questions about their own shortfalls in investment, marketing, research and worker training."[77] Placing the blame on a scapegoat is a way of disavowing any responsibility for something and focusing attention elsewhere.[78]

Another facet of these stories is that they seem impervious to criticism and claims that they are inaccurate, distorted, or even concocted. Accuracy and representativeness, however, are not necessarily relevant since the purpose of these horror stories is not to inform people by presenting neutral, systematic empirical data, but to evoke certain feelings and an image of the civil justice system that is decidedly negative in character. As Walter Olson said in responding to criticism that evidence of a litigation explosion was lacking—it's the stories that really matter, not the empirical data.[79]

Metaphors. Metaphor is yet another symbolic device used in representing juries and the civil justice system as a compelling problem. Metaphors are important because they can convey very powerful messages in the images that they create. Said Stone: "Metaphors are important devices for strategic representation. . . . On the surface, they simply draw a comparison between one thing and another, but in a more subtle way they usually imply a whole narrative story and a prescription for action."[80] The reform rhetoric frequently has made use of several very vivid metaphors—"explosion" or "explosive"; "skyrocketing" or "sky-high"; and "crisis." Each presents a clear and dramatic image regardless of the phenomenon to which it is attached.

"Explosion" has been a very powerful metaphor for describing the civil justice system and its constituent parts. Long before Walter Olson chose it as the title for his book, reformers had made use of the term "litigation explosion." Galanter found it used as early as 1970 by those concerned about the amount of litigation in the United States and the alleged change in litigiousness among the populace.[81] By the middle 1980s, the litigation explosion was an accepted and lamented fact.

The media latched onto the term in the mid 1980s. For instance, on June 6, 1986, *USA Today*'s editorial focused on the interrelationships among litigation, insurance, lawyers, and juries: "The insurance crunch has become a crisis with liability coverage. The explosion of litigation has choked court dockets. And too few lawyers tell potential clients that some cases are a waste of time."[82] At about the same time, the *Wall Street Journal* ran a four-part series on reform in the civil justice system entitled "Litigation Explosion."[83] The *Christian Science Monitor* ran a story on a news conference held by then Attorney General Edwin Meese and Commerce Secretary Malcomb Baldrige announcing a proposed products liability reform bill. The story reported: "the Reagan administration believes that there *is* an insurance crisis, and that it has been brought about in large part by an 'explosion' of huge liability judgments awarded by juries to injured plaintiffs."[84]

The explosion metaphor has also been used to describe increases in the size of jury awards. It is usually used in the form "explosive growth" or "explosive increase." A very prominent and influential example is the Reagan administration's *Report* which concluded that "the explosive growth in the damages awarded in tort lawsuits" was one of the primary causes of the "insurance crisis" of the middle 1980s.[85] The *Report* also included a section entitled "The Explosive Growth in Damage Awards."[86]

Another frequently used metaphor is "skyrocketing," a second term conjuring up an image of abrupt and rapid increase as well as one of events out of control. Perhaps the most common use of the term is to describe alleged changes in the size of jury awards or in the size of liability insurance premiums (increases which are in turn the result of increasing jury awards). The use of this metaphor in this context has also been with us for a while, appearing as early as 1962 in an article about jury verdicts in automobile accident cases.[87]

In the 1980s the media developed a fondness for this notion. A 1985 *Parade Magazine* article on medical malpractice reported, "Skyrocketing medical malpractice awards and fear of malpractice suits are driving our doctors to abandon their practices, worsening health care, inflating bills, and turning physicians and patients into adversaries."[88] A *Chicago Sun-Times* article on a proposed federal product liability law said, "Proponents say such legislation would combat skyrocketing insurance rates brought on by excess awards by juries in liability lawsuits."[89] The first article in the *Wall Street Journal*'s 1986 "Litigation Explosion" series noted, "Liability-insurance premiums are skyrocketing, and insurers blame enormous damage awards for the increase."[90] A slight variation on the theme is the use of "sky-high" as in a *U.S. News & World Report* cover story which carried the title, "Sky-High Damage Suits: The Impact on Consumers, Business and Professions."[91]

The skyrocketing metaphor has also found its way into three Supreme Court opinions written by Justice Sandra Day O'Connor in cases involving the issue of punitive damages. Her concurring/dissenting opinion in *Browning-Ferris Industries v. Kelco Disposal* opens with "Awards of punitive damages are skyrocketing."[92] In her dissent in *Pacific Mutual Life Insurance Co. v. Haslip,* Justice O'Connor described the size of awards in the following way: "Medians as well as averages are skyrocketing, meaning that even routine awards are growing in size."[93] Finally, in her dissent in *TXO Production Corporation v. Alliance Resources Corporation,* Justice O'Connor wrote, "as little as 30 years ago, punitive damage awards were rarely assessed and usually small in amount. Recently however, the frequency and size of such awards have been skyrocketing."[94]

The better and saner past, somewhere in the early 1960s or before, to which Justice O'Connor alludes in her comment above has become something of a metaphor as well. For many people, especially those that see themselves as social conservatives, the 1960s portray an image of moral decline and social experimentation of a kind that was threatening to traditional values. Moving this notion to the tort reform arena, the change for the worse that began in the 1960s is identified as being a result of "legal engineering" that occurred during that time. In *Liability*, Huber characterizes those he calls the "founders" of the current tort system as utopians, well-intentioned, but naive experimenters or revolutionaries who thoroughly undermined the old traditional ways.

The use of the 1960s as a metaphor is also found in Olson's book *The Litigation Explosion.* He structures his argument around an explicit comparison to older and better ways. On the very first page of his book, Olson says, "The trend proceeded gradually over decades and then quite suddenly moved into high gear in the late 1960s and 1970s. . . . Taken together, the changes amount to a unique experiment in freeing the legal profession and the litigious impulse from age-old constraints."[95] William McCormick (of Fireman's Fund Insurance Companies) used the rhetoric of the 1960s in a similar manner in his 1986 speech. He characterized the period of the 1880s–1960s as one of "historic stability" in comparison to the 1960s to today which he deemed the period of "the erosion of justice."[96] The use of the 1960s as a metaphor of decline makes it possible to effectively couple the severe erosion of the good old, traditional American civil justice system with the idea of a larger moral decline in American society as a whole.

What is perhaps the most important and powerful metaphor in the rhetoric of reform does not deal with change in the way the others do; instead, it presents an image of the consequences of change. It is the idea of "crisis." In ordinary discourse, crises are dire situations, something that happens which so disrupts normal social, political, or economic life that it demands an immediate and extraordinary response by public authorities.

The "crisis" that occurred during the middle to late 1980s was the "insurance or liability crisis." It involved the unavailability or unaffordability of liability insurance for businesses, manufacturers, municipalities, and professionals. The reason for this crisis according to the reformers was the civil justice system with its skyrocketing jury awards and other proplaintiff aspects motivated in part by ill-conceived underlying changes in the substantive law of liability.

Major news magazines regularly covered the crisis and its manifestations, introducing their coverage with titles selected to peak anxiety in their readership. An example is the cover story in the March 24, 1986 issue of *Time* entitled "Sorry, Your Policy Is Canceled." The article recounts a few horror stories about unavailability of obstetric services, park and recreational area closings, and business failure due to increasing insurance premiums, to highlight "a new national crisis."[97] The situation was summarized as follows:

> Given the litigious nature of American society these days, just about any kind of business, profession, or government agency is likely to be the target of a suit alleging malpractice or negligence resulting in personal injury. That makes liability insurance, the kind that pays off on such claims, just about as vital as oil in keeping the economy functioning. But in the past two years, liability insurance has become the kind of resource that oil was in the 1970s: prohibitively expensive, when it can be bought at all.[98]

The insurance crisis was the general or blanket term used to describe the problem of finding affordable and adequate coverage for a wide variety of concerns. The crisis image has also been used to address narrower interests. Consequently, although a "crisis" is supposed to be a unique, nonrecurring event, there has been a "product liability crisis," a "medical malpractice crisis," and even an "accountancy crisis." Each has its own stories of decline and restoration, its own horror stories, and its own accounts of "skyrocketing" or "explosive" insurance premiums and jury awards. While the particular substance may change, the form of the rhetoric stays surprisingly similar.

A malpractice crisis in the early 1970s triggered a round of civil justice reform in most states. A physician writing in the *Marquette Law Review* said in regard to this crisis: "The number of claims continued to rise, and by the 1970s physicians perceived the increase in the number and the size of claims as a threat that instigated job actions, strikes, and sit downs. It was called a crisis. . . . Physicians' premiums were skyrocketing, the number of claims was continually increasing, and this environment led to a 'siege mentality.' By 1975, the primary concern was the unavailability of liability insurance."[99] By the early 1980s the crisis rhetoric and reform process in this arena started all over again.

The claims about a products liability crisis and the political push for civil justice reform in that area also go back to the 1970s. For instance, according to the Report of the U.S. Senate Committee on Commerce, Science, and Transportation on the 1991 Product Liability Fairness Act: "In the mid-1970s, product liability was first recognized as a serious problem of interstate commerce which, in the view of many businesses and academic observers, had reached 'crisis' proportions and required federal response. This recognition came as a result of an increase in product liability claims and litigation and an increase in product liability insurance premiums."[100]

On another front, in 1992 the heads of the six largest accounting firms issued a joint statement on the "liability crisis" and its effect on the accounting profession. In language reminiscent of the middle 1980s, the statement began, "The tort liability system in the United States is out of control. It is no longer a balanced system that provides reasonable compensation to victims by the responsible parties."[101] Instead, the system forces innocent defendants to agree to coerced settlements or face even higher awards at trial while spending substantial amount of money to defend themselves against unwarranted claims.[102] "The flaws in the liability system are taking a severe toll on the accounting profession. If these flaws are not corrected . . . the consequences could prove fatal to accounting firms of all sizes. But a liability system seriously lacking in logic, fairness and balance is not just the accounting profession's crisis. It is a business crisis and a national crisis."[103]

No matter what the arena, the crisis is always described in graphic and threatening terms that bring matters into the everyday lives of ordinary persons. The crisis is not something abstract; it is concrete. The crisis is not remote or impending; it is immediate. The crisis does not just affect manufacturers and professionals; it touches the lives of every citizen.

Numbers

In addition to the symbols and symbolic devices used in defining situations as policy problems, Stone also asks us to examine the way numbers are used in this effort. Most discussions of public policy problems, she notes, "begin with a recitation of figures purporting to show that a problem is big or is growing."[104] The reason for this is that the best way to define some situation as a problem "in our profoundly numerical contemporary culture" is to measure it.[105] Measuring something makes it real, concrete, objective, and precise. Numbers, measures, or indicators, therefore, are symbolically very important and have played a critical role in the reformers' definition of a policy problem in the civil justice system. As Kingdon found, policymakers pay close attention to quantifiable issues.[106]

One of the keys to portraying some situation as a problem is being able to show change. According to Kingdon, "a steady state is viewed as less problematic than changing figures."[107] The idea is to find or create some measure or indicator that can summarize the behavior of the system in question, and then use it to demonstrate change for the worse. Kingdon found that policymakers considered a change in such an indicator or measure "to be a change in the state of the system; this they define as a problem."[108] In a similar vein, Stone argues that in the political context of policy debates, numbers are used to tell a story about change.

> Most obviously, they are the premier language for stories of decline and decay. Figures are invoked to show that a problem is getting bigger and worse. . . . Numbers are also important in stories of control and helplessness. . . . [S]tatistics have become the predominant form of identifying causal relationships and thus of identifying agents and factors of control. In both uses, numbers are invoked explicitly to tell the story. The author or speaker tells the audience, "The numbers show that my story is true."[109]

Numbers are also used to describe the extent or magnitude of a problem.[110] Debating magnitude "is one of the most prominent forms of discourse in public policy."[111]

In the political process of gaining access to the agenda, the use of numbers or indicators is highly problematic. While numbers may be symbols of precision, accuracy, and objectivity, decisions regarding which measure to use or how to construct a measure and what it means are all choices made, not by disinterested observers, but those with a political interest. For instance, in the context of civil justice reform a decision must be made about which measures to use as representative of the system's performance. This is especially problematic with regard to the civil justice system because there are no agreed upon summary indicators of performance; there is no equivalent to the unemployment rate or GNP. Furthermore, there is not even a consistent set of statistics regularly collected across states to use in constructing such a measure. In fact, some states do not even publish annual statistics on the level of court usage, and for many that do, only the most general figures are available. Virtually no states regularly compile figures on jury awards.[112] The situation for federal court activity is somewhat different in that more consistency exists across court jurisdictions, but problems arise from the distinctness of the federal system when compared to state courts.

A variety of measures have been used in the reform rhetoric, such as changes in the number of civil filings in state or federal trial courts. But this immediately raises a question as to whether figures for civil filings in trial courts—generally or just for torts or whatever—are reasonable indicators of what is going on in the system. Aggregate figures on the size of jury verdict awards or estimates of the cost of the civil justice system have been widely used. There are legitimate questions about what such figures can tell us. For instance, one recent study used aggregate figures on verdicts in a statistical analysis to draw conclusions about juror sympathy and the case selection decisions of plaintiffs' attorneys,[113] a dubious set of inferences at best. What are we to make of an increase in $1 million verdicts, especially if the figures are *not* in constant dollars? It is just as easy to say that such increases simply reflect increasing costs for services like medical care or higher wage rates as it is to say they reflect something wrong with the juries that make the awards. If a number is given to the cost of the civil justice system, how do we know if it is too high or too low? Lacking a reliable baseline, what can we say about change?

Nevertheless, numbers have played a pivotal role in the rhetoric of reform—take away the numbers and the arguments fall flat. Numbers have been, along with the horror story anecdotes, one of the main tools used in the strategic representation of the civil justice system as a system in chaos. This is the case despite the limited amount of data actually available and the question of how to interpret them. The horror stories discussed earlier always include the size of the dollar figure awards involved in the story. In fact, the impact of each story's message is dependent on the size of the jury award involved. A $1,000 award is only a curiosity and certainly not a threat or an indicator of a crisis; it is another thing altogether if the award is $1,000,000. The tale told in the story identifies the problem, and the size of the award, metaphorically, is an indicator of the size of the problem.

Equally dramatic and important are the figures used to describe the changes over time in the size of jury awards. These numbers lie at the heart of the story of decline and provide a concrete manifestation of the consequences of the changes in the substance of the law about which the high theorists of reform like Huber and Priest complain. These numbers make those more abstract criticisms real and understandable to a broad audience. Changes for the worse are described by showing an increase in the average or mean award for each year over some period of years, the message being that the increases in such a "typical" award show the decline of the system. These numbers are not used to empirically prove or verify the existence of a problem or crisis so much as they are used to illustrate what is already taken to be a fact. For instance, the Reagan administration's *Report* discussed changes in the size of awards in a section entitled "The Explosive Growth in Damage Awards."[114] It opens with the following two sentences: "Another area of great concern is the explosive growth in tort damages awards over the last decade. A few statistics will illustrate this point."[115]

To add a dramatic urgency to the message, change may be further described by noting not just the increase in the mean award itself, but in the percentage increase or by presenting a graphic or visual time series display. For instance, the *Report* presents figures to argue that the average (mean) medical malpractice verdict "increased from $220,018 in 1975 to $1,101,716 in 1985, a 363% increase. Average product liability jury verdicts during this same period increased from $393,580 to $1,850,452, a 370% increase."[116] Vice President Quayle's Council on Competitiveness noted figures on punitive damage awards that are even more dramatic: "A 1987 study by the Institute for Civil Justice, which examined 24,000 jury trials in Cook County, Illinois, found that the average punitive damage award increased, in inflation-adjusted dollars, from $43,000 in 1965–69 to $729,000 in 1980–84—a jump of 1,500%. In personal injury cases, the rise has been even more dramatic."[117]

The veracity of figures like these and the message they convey about the civil justice have been severely criticized for some time in the academic literature and elsewhere. They do illustrate one aspect of Kingdon's observations about the use of numbers and indicators in the political process of gaining access to the agenda. Constructing indicators or finding numbers to demonstrate a problem to which a favored solution can be attached "and getting others to agree to its worth become major preoccupations of those pressing for policy change. The need for such indicators can make people grasp for indicators with serious deficiencies."[118] Like Stone, Kingdon argues that numbers and indicators in the political process "are not simply a straightforward recognition of the facts. Precisely because indicators have such powerful implications, the methodology by which the facts are gathered and the interpretations that are placed on these facts become prominent items for heated debate."[119]

This is illustrated by the debate over the appropriate measure to use when making claims about changes in the size of jury verdicts. The reformers not only use, but aggressively advocate, the use of the arithmetic mean rather than the median as the appropriate measure to use in describing trends in the size of jury awards. The chosen measure is both politically and practically important because each of the two measures can give significantly different values to the "typical" award and hence present different images of trends. The reformers' position is politically expedient because mean award figures will always appear high and show the desired direction and magnitude of change over time. For example, as noted above the Reagan administration's *Report* presents average award figures to support its claims about explosive growth in jury awards, and the report's *Update*[120] vigorously defends the mean as the appropriate measure of central tendency.[121]

Regardless of the political considerations, as a technical matter, the median is more appropriate in this instance. According to Hubert Blalock, the author of a widely used textbook on statistics for the social sciences, the average is generally used in preference to the median, but not always.[122] There is an all-important difference between the two measures:

> *the mean is affected by changes in extreme values whereas the median will be unaffected unless the middle case is also changed. . . .*

> We may say, then, that *whenever a distribution is highly skewed,* i.e., whenever there are considerably more extreme cases in one direction than another, *the median will generally be more appropriate than the mean.* (emphasis in the original)[123]

The *Update* takes this difference and turns it on its head to make a fallacious argument in defense of the mean and against the median. In responding to its critics the *Update* argues:

> The use of the median data essentially obscures—to the point of non-recognition—the effects of "high-end" verdicts on the trend in jury awards. But, as noted, these "high-end" verdicts, while only a small percentage of all jury awards, represent a very large percentage of the total dollars awarded by juries. Accordingly, the median data substantially understate the growth of jury verdicts by eliminating or at least greatly obscuring the effect of the large awards.[124]

As this response makes clear, the mean is useful (indeed, necessary) to the reformers' attempt to show the "explosive" or "skyrocketing" growth in awards. If one uses the median, the response implies, there is little or no evidence of such growth.

Visual or graphic displays have also been widely used in the reform rhetoric to convey even more dramatic messages about change than the textual use of percentages of increase. Upward trends can effectively be demonstrated with little explanation or justification of the decisions that went into the measures being used. For instance, the *Time* cover story "Sorry, Your Policy Is Canceled" uses an eye-catching graphic to convey an unmistakable message. It is a graph showing changes in the number of $1 million-plus jury awards. Change is depicted by a thickly drawn arrow curving sharply upward, one that gets thicker as it shoots up to enhance the visual image.

Visual displays can do more than merely convey the message of change. They can also be used to tell the entire reform story of change, consequence, and causation. A 1985 story in *Business Week* entitled "Stopping the Bloodbath in Medical Malpractice"[125] provides a powerful example of this. It presented a three-panel visual display, the first panel of which graphically displayed the increasing size of the average medical malpractice verdict between 1974 and 1984. The second presented a graph of the increasing number of $1 million-plus awards. Each graph showed sharp increases, but there is more.

These presentations were not just simple line graphs; each was also a characterization. The first visual, entitled "Patients Win Bigger Malpractice Verdicts . . . ," presented a graph showing the increasing size of the average malpractice verdicts superimposed over the image of a person in a wheelchair holding a large stack of money in his/her lap. The second one, entitled " . . . And Awards of More than $1 Million Are Soaring . . . ," overlaid the graph on the figure of a judge rapping his gravel as if making a decision ordering these verdicts. The third visual in the article is entitled " . . . So the Burden of Insurance Losses Grows" and shows aggregate figures on medical malpractice losses (otherwise undefined). Rather than showing changes moving in an upward direction, this panel showed changes moving in a downward direction. The downward graph in this third visual is superimposed on a person in a business suit, presumably representing insurance companies, being bent downward as though being forced to carry a crushing burden.

This series of visuals presents a clear and unambiguous message: patients are getting substantially more money (stacks of it!), given to them by the courts (particularly in $1 million-plus awards), and as a direct consequence the burden on the physicians' insurance companies is growing. The contrast between the first and third visuals is especially important for the message of causation implied in the message. Where the first graph is arranged with the *x*-axis on the bottom in order to show an upward trend line for verdicts, the third graph is constructed upside down with the *x*-axis at the top so that it shows a sharp trend in costs with magnitude measured downward to reflect losses. Having increases in costs shown on an inverted graph is intended to convey the idea of dramatic losses by insurance companies in the context of dramatic gains by malpractice plaintiffs, implying that one is a direct consequence of the other—while one goes up the other automatically goes down.

The only thing intervening in this short but clear-cut story between these two visuals is the middle panel display. By its placement, this graphic is easily interpreted as representing the sole causal agent in a story of cause and effect for gains by some and losses for others. There are no other possible explanations for malpractice losses, there are no plausible alternative stories to explain insurance company losses. It nicely summarizes the basic logic of the reformers' argument. The only thing missing from the picture story is the role of plaintiff's lawyers, but that is covered in the body of the story in its highlighting of legislative efforts in California to limit contingency fees.

Visual representations of trends like these, while providing clear messages, need to be examined critically. The transformation of numbers into visual images can mask the problems inherent in the use of such numbers and measures. These images can be so compelling as to shut off any debate or questioning and remove the audience even farther from questions regarding the appropriateness of using the mean rather than the median, or whether different types of malpractice and products would show the same trends, or whether the patterns may be different in different parts of the country. The images can be made to appear so compelling that alternative explanations become impossible to envision.

Causality

The last aspect of strategic representation from Stone's scheme to examine is causality—ideas of cause and effect in the reform rhetoric. The glue that holds the reform rhetoric together is its causal theory that suggests that a particular set of dire negative consequences are the direct result of what has been happening in the civil justice system. It is this connection that gives force to the reform movement's argument. Persuading people, especially policymakers, of the veracity of this connection is crucial. The stories of decline, the anecdotes, the metaphors, and the numbers conveyed in the rhetoric of reform are all organized to tell a causal story connecting certain ills in society to the failures of the civil justice system. In politics, says Stone, "causal stories are strategically crafted with symbols and numbers and then asserted by political actors who try to make their versions the basis of policy choices."[126]

We have seen this causal connection asserted throughout our discussion of the reform rhetoric. It is there, for instance, in Huber's story of decline and the characterization of the insurance crisis and its related ills as the unintended consequences of a set of well-intentioned but misguided legal engineers. The connection is there in Olson's *Litigation Explosion,* where he argues that those changes in the law unintentionally and unknowingly unleashed the very worst in the nature of lawyers causing all sorts of problems. The connection is there in the speeches of business leaders Malott and McCormick and their respective juxtapositions of horror stories about jury verdicts and the loss of essential goods (e.g., vaccines) and services (e.g., medical care). It is there in journalistic accounts like the one in *Business Week* and its visual rendition of the causal story. Overall, the causal story is one of the "reforms" of the 1960s going awry with disastrous results.

This causal story is not so much about understanding how the world works as it is about assigning responsibility for the problems described.[127] Alternative sets of solutions are based on different perceptions as to where responsibility lies. For instance, with regard to the insurance crisis, the reform movement clearly blamed the civil justice system and called for fundamental reform as a result. The reformers' opponents (among them the trial lawyers' associations) offered an alternative view of responsibility and blamed the crisis on the insurance industry itself and its boom and bust business cycle. As a consequence, they called for greater regulation of the insurance industry. From this perspective, there was little or no connection between what happened in the civil justice system and the crisis of the middle 1980s.

As Stone observes, the "political conflicts over causal stories are . . . more than empirical claims about sequences of events. They are fights about the possibility of control and the assignment of blame."[128] This is what we have seen in the rhetoric of reform where empirical claims are used to direct blame at the law, legal institutions, and legal actors. The success of such causal stories is not judged necessarily by their veracity, but by their acceptance by the general public and by policymakers.[129] Such appears to be the case with regard to civil justice reform: by the late 1980s nearly every state had considered at least some form of civil justice reform.

Conclusion: Analyzing the Rhetoric of Reform

We have, up to this point, talked about the image of juries and the civil justice system presented in the reform rhetoric, and have done so in the context of the politics of ideas—the political struggle to gain access first to the public agenda and second to the decision agenda. The rhetoric's critics argue there is a substantial gap between the image portrayed in the rhetoric and what the best available evidence can tell us. This gap is much more a result of the political marketing of ideas tied to that political struggle over which image of the civil justice system will govern policy than it is a result of the limitations of the empirical literature. Viewed in this light, the interesting and troubling issue is not simply the fact that there is a substantial distance between rhetoric and empirical evidence, but that the image portrayed is accepted regardless of its veracity.

Two tasks are involved in analyzing the rhetoric of civil justice reform and the image it presents. The first is to explain the political character of that image along with the devices used to present that image as one people will accept. Chapter 2 has done this in a general way, and we will address this again in subsequent chapters for medical malpractice, products liability, and punitive damages. The second task is to critically examine the rhetoric's key claims as descriptions of reality.

This is done by comparing those claims to empirical evidence. The idea is not to debunk these claims, but rather to discern whether they have any basis in reality or are best seen as artifacts of a political battle. It is also important to know if the empirical evidence shows the existence of a reasonable alternative image and an alternative set of messages coming from patterns of activity in the civil justice system. In other words, the idea is not to "prove" the absence of problems and match rhetoric with rhetoric, but to show that an alternative picture is possible, one that may raise a host of questions revolving around a different set of issues.

Such a critical examination of the rhetoric's claims will ensure that there is in the marketplace of ideas regarding the civil justice system an alternative image grounded in empirical data. This is important because so much of the rhetoric presents its image as the authoritative and only reasonable portrayal. It is also important beyond the immediate political debates over the nature of the system's problems. It is important for a longer-term battle over the public mind in which rights of long-standing are in jeopardy, a battle that includes the intellectual, academic, and professional minds as well.

In examining the rhetoric's claims, it is not possible to do a comprehensive critical analysis because, as Saks and Sanders and Joyce pointed out, there is still much about the civil justice system for which the empirical evidence is thin or nonexistent. We will concentrate on just one area of controversy—juries and their verdicts—and draw from our own extensive research on jury verdicts in state trial courts. A detailed examination of this one area can be used as a case study of sorts for examining the reform rhetoric's claims, given the rhetoric's own focus on juries. Chapter 3 will present a basic overview of our jury verdict research and set the stage for the more detailed discussions in chapters 4, 5, and 6 on medical malpractice, products liability, and punitive damages, respectively.

CHAPTER THREE

Civil Juries: An Empirical Mapping

Pity the civil jury, lament Clermont and Eisenberg,[1] seen as the sickest organ of a sick system. Because they play a critical role in the civil justice system, juries have an important symbolic place in the rhetoric of reform. The rhetoric, we have seen, overstates and misrepresents that role—overstates it through a causal theory tying it to a wide range of social and economic consequences, and misrepresents it through the claims made about verdicts. Underlying this characterization of the jury's role is an image of a system out of balance or run amok with jury verdicts at the heart of it all—increasingly high plaintiff win rates and skyrocketing awards in a system that is no longer predictable, consistent, or fair. This is an image politically created and marketed in order to affect the public agenda. It is not part of a candid debate on the goals of the justice system geared toward constructing solutions in the light of good evidence and then empirically evaluating the effects of reforms.[2] Using data from our research on jury verdict activity, in this and the following three chapters we will present an alternative image.

This is not to say that we have found the kind of predictability and uniformity the reformers claim the system now lacks. Jury verdicts, as a general proposition, are not predictable and uniform in the aggregate, if for no other reason than the lack of fungibility among the cases going to trial. Differences in the cases themselves along with the variations in the makeup of juries and in the socioeconomic characteristics of the jurisdictions from which jurors are chosen all undermine broad-scale predictability and uniformity. Indeed, we found differences among sites in the mix of cases going to a jury trial, as well as variations among sites and types of cases in plaintiff win rates and award structure. Such variations should not be characterized as evidence of an irrational or chaotic system or one that has broken down, but rather as evidence of a system that is extremely complex and at best only partially understood. Complexity is inherent in a structure that is a highly decentralized collection of local subsystems with varying characteristics and legal rules. The fact that different substantive areas of litigation behave quite differently but in an orderly fashion within themselves adds to that complexity.[3]

Patterns and changes in jury verdicts can tell us a great deal about the civil justice system. Our purpose in this chapter is to present a general empirical discussion of verdicts in state trial courts of general jurisdiction in light of the claims found in the rhetoric of reform and to provide an empirical context for the next three chapters. It focuses on the *products* of jury decision making (who wins, how much they win, and so on) rather than the *process* of decision making (the internal dynamics of group decision making).[4] This chapter has three parts. The first part presents a conceptual scheme within which to discuss the importance of the products of jury decision making given the fact that the bulk of lawsuits filed are resolved short of formal adjudication. This scheme also provides a useful framework for examining the rhetoric of reform in later chapters. The second part briefly describes the data we utilize. The third part then discusses the general patterns and changes found in these data.

We will not present in this chapter, or the next three, sophisticated statistical analyses of our verdict data. There are two reasons for our decision not to pursue that course. First, the limitations of the collective understanding and knowledge of the products of jury decision making and of the litigation process are too limited (see chapter 1). Sophisticated statistical analysis presumes that we know enough to frame the kinds of questions about complex interactions this kind of analysis is used to answer. This lack of knowledge is aggravated by the rhetoric of reform with its politically constructed picture of juries and the civil justice system, a picture that persists at least in part because so little is actually known (see chapter 2). Second, the data we use on jury verdicts have very real limitations in what they can tell us and what can be inferred from them.[5] For instance, they tell us nothing about the internal dynamics of jury decision making, and they should not be seen as somehow representative of all verdicts nationally. Indeed, it may not be possible conceptually to construct a truly representative sample of all verdicts. Statistical techniques, no matter how sophisticated, cannot overcome such limitations of knowledge and data.

Our analysis of jury verdict data will be descriptive, what one commentator in looking at earlier work on our data described as "elegant description."[6] Our goal is to provide a series of simple but detailed descriptions of these data at progressively lower levels of aggregation. In the context of the politics of ideas, this is a situation that calls for simple techniques because the phenomena involved are so complex. With the minimal imposition of structure on our part we want to see what stories the patterns and changes in our jury verdict tell. The important stories—both theoretically and practically—are in the details.

Juries and the Disputing Process

As insurance executive William McCormick noted, "decided cases are only the tip of the iceberg; they directly affect thousands of other cases that get settled before going to trial, not to mention acting as a stimulant for even more lawsuits."[7] In other words, verdicts are important not just because of the results for the parties involved in the suit, but also because of the messages they send to others. Reformers like McCormick are especially worried about the messages they claim verdicts are sending to plaintiffs' attorneys and their potential clients, enticing them to file frivolous suits against deep pocket defendants in the hope of cashing in. There is a much more sophisticated version of the idea of juries as messengers in the law and society literature, one that places jury verdicts in a broader dispute-processing context.

In the law and society literature, this idea is usually associated with the work of Marc Galanter and what he has called the "radiating effects of courts."[8] Galanter argues that even though jury verdicts resolve only a small proportion of all civil disputes, they have a symbolic value and impact that extends well beyond their frequency.[9] Their importance lies in their role as "transmitters of signals rather as deciders of cases,"[10] and these signals contribute "a background of norms and procedures against which negotiations and regulation in both private and governmental settings takes place. This contribution includes, but is not exhausted by, communication to prospective litigants of what might transpire if one of them sought a judicial resolution. Courts communicate not only the rules that would govern adjudication of the dispute, but also possible remedies and estimates of the difficulty, certainty, and costs of securing particular outcomes."[11]

Two metaphors are often used to describe this idea of jury verdicts as transmitters of messages in the context of dispute processing: a pyramid and a shadow.[12] The pyramid is used to place jury verdicts, generally or in a particular area like medical malpractice or products liability, in the broader context of disputes by illustrating how few matters actually result in a jury trial. Jury verdicts are the pinnacle of the pyramid; at the base are those events, like a medical error or an automobile accident, that can cause an injury or the loss of something of value. In between the base and the pinnacle are a number of important processes which will help determine whether a dispute emerges and how it will ultimately be handled.

To move above the pyramid's base, an event must be perceived by someone as injurious. It is quite possible that the party actually injured will not recognize the event as being injurious; it is also possible to perceive an injury when none has actually occurred. If an injury is perceived, then the injured party must blame someone else for causing the injury for the matter to proceed up the pyramid. The injured party may, for instance, see the injury as the result of fate, his or her own carelessness, or just bad luck even though an outside observer might perceive the injury as the result of another's misdeeds. If blame is not assigned to someone other than the injured party, no dispute will emerge. If there is blame, then the injured party has a grievance. If this grievance is communicated to the alleged wrongdoer with the idea of obtaining some recourse, then the injured party has made a claim. It is possible for there to be a grievance but no claim. The injured person may not know how to communicate his or her grievance or have the resources to do so. Or, the injured person may simply feel that it is not worth the effort—for whatever reason—to pursue the matter. As Ladinsky and Susmilch found, some people may just decide to "lump it."[13]

A claim can be made in a variety of ways, formally and informally. It may be made through a private communication or the filing of a lawsuit. Once the claim is made, the matter may be resolved by the wrongdoer offering some acceptable form of compensation. If the claim is denied and no compensation is offered, the injured party then has a dispute which may or may not proceed farther up the pyramid. Even if there is a dispute, the injured party may choose not pursue the matter, perhaps again for lack of resources or due to a sense of hopelessness in obtaining any compensation. A claim may become a civil legal dispute if it involves rights or resources which can be granted or denied by a court.[14]

The empirical literature indicates that there is a substantial drop-off in frequency as one moves from the base of the pyramid to its pinnacle. The base of the pyramid for most areas of litigation—the number of potentially injurious events—is likely to be very wide. However, although the base is wide, it appears that for most events the person involved does nothing at all if for no other reason than the fact that most of these events involve trivial issues. The true frequency of events at this level is hard to gauge because these events are extremely difficult to observe systematically or even to estimate. The one area in which some attempt at an estimate has been made is medical malpractice.

In her 1985 book on medical malpractice, Patricia Danzon suggests that, on average, one in twenty hospital patients incurs an injury as a result of a medical error.[15] She based this estimate on a California Medical Association/California Hospital Association study of 20,864 inpatient charts from 23 California hospitals done in the 1970s. A similar study was done in New York State in the late 1980s as a part of the Harvard Medical Malpractice Study, and it found that one injury occurred for every 27 hospitalizations. Extrapolating the "New York population estimates to the nation as a whole implies that every year there are more than 150,000 fatalities and 30,000 serious disabilities precipitated by medical treatment in this country,"[16] said the project's director. According to the American Hospital Association, there were 33,566,557 hospital admissions in the United States in 1991. Using these figures, the one in 20 estimate from Danzon would translate to a total of 1,678,328 patient injuries nationwide, and the one in 27 estimate from the New York data would convert to 1,241,963 injuries.

Interestingly, these two studies also found that most of these events did *not* lead to a malpractice claim. The California hospital study showed that only 10% of the patients suffering an injury actually filed a claim. The Harvard study estimated that only one in eight (or 12.5%) of the injured patients filed a claim. To take the process one step farther, examinations of closed malpractice insurance claims indicate the few claims go all the way to a jury trial and that most claims are closed without any payment to the patient.[17]

A more general picture can be obtained from some of the findings of the Civil Litigation Research Project (CLRP) which surveyed (by telephone) approximately 1,000 households in 1980. According to Richard Miller and Austin Sarat, the survey found that 41.6% of the households reported having at least one grievance with $1,000 or more at issue during the three years preceding the survey. The survey found that 15.6% of these households reported at least one grievance in the tort area. Of these tort grievances, 85.7% led to a claim and 20.1% matured into dispute. Lawyers were contacted about 12% of the tort grievances, and slightly under 4% ultimately resulted in a court filing.[18] While virtually all of those households with tort grievances that reached the claim stage recovered something, very few (about 12%) received the full value of their original claim.[19]

A more recent study of accidental injuries conducted by the RAND Corporation's Institute for Civil Justice provides some additional evidence on the process of blaming and claiming.[20] It presents a picture quite at odds with the one animating the rhetoric of reform. This study involved a survey of "about 26,000 households by telephone, representing more than 70,000 individuals nationwide."[21] From the initial sample, the study then "interviewed about 2800 individuals, also by telephone. (The) hour-long interview provided a wealth of data . . . about how injured Americans view and use the tort liability system."[22]

Based on these interviews, Hensler et al. estimate that each year one in six American households experiences some economic loss as a result of an accidental injury.[23] Most of those injured, however, did *not* turn to the liability system for compensation—only about one in 10 do so.[24] Those most likely to pursue compensation were those involved in auto accidents, with about one-half of those injured in an auto accident pursuing compensation. These, however, were not the typical accidental injuries uncovered by the RAND study. The typical injury was a nonauto accident that occurred outside of work.

Among the study's most interesting findings was that for the typical accidental injury, "the injured person does not even consider the notion of seeking compensation from some other person or entity who might have been associated with the accident (for example, a product manufacturer or property owner), or if he does think about this possibility, he is unlikely to pursue it."[25] Overall, 19% of the respondents considered claiming, and 10% actually took some action. Only 7% of the respondents consulted an attorney, 4% hired an attorney, and 2% actually filed a lawsuit.[26] Among the most important factors in explaining these patterns of minimal claiming the RAND study found were the injured person's judgments about responsibility for the accident, norms of propriety or fairness, and the severity of the injury. "People fail to consider claiming because they believe that either no one or they themselves are responsible for the injury."[27] As the study concludes, this is a picture at odds with the characterization of an overly litigious society.[28]

In the final stages of this disputing process, only a very small percentage of those matters in which there is a court filing actually go to formal adjudication, meaning that the pyramid has as its pinnacle a sharp point rather than a wide tabletop. Most estimates place the percentage of filed tort cases that go to a trial at under 10%. The CLRP study, for instance, found that in the 10 courts it examined only 9% of the filings went to trial.[29] Studies of both medical malpractice and products liability also indicate that only a small proportion of filed suits proceed to trial.

In turn, most of this small proportion of tort suits that do go to a trial go to jury trials rather than bench trials. For instance, using a sample of all tort trials in 27 state trial courts of general jurisdiction over a three-month period in 1989, a National Center for State Courts study found that 85.3% of those trials were jury trials.[30] In a study of trials in the federal district courts occurring between 1979 and 1989, Eisenberg reported that 88.9% of the products liability trials, 92% of the medical malpractice trials, 86% of the automobile trials, and 84% of miscellaneous personal injury trials completed during this time period were jury trials.[31]

Though ultimately small in number, these jury trials cast a large shadow down the sides of the pyramid; they send signals down through the system. The meaning of these signals is dependent on the capabilities and resources of potential disputants to receive them and utilize them.[32] The fact that a message has been sent does not mean that it will be received or received correctly. These messages must also compete with other forms of normative ordering that "disseminate messages about norms, infractions, remedies and so on" (such as family, work group, and associations).[33] Disputant capabilities and alternative forms of normative ordering introduce a certain amount of variability into the effects of the messages sent. Variability also comes from the fact that "disputants do not encounter these messages floating freely, but rather in the context of a local legal culture."[34] These messages, however, help form the background of norms and procedures against which negotiations and regulation takes place. The negotiations used to resolve most matters take place in the "shadow of the law,"[35] and jury verdicts make up a substantial part of this shadow.

The Jury Verdict Data

The jury verdict data we will discuss are drawn from local jury verdicts reporters. These reporters are commercial, typically subscription, services which exist for the sole purpose of communicating the "going rate" in a given locale for particular types of cases along with other information such as the attorneys involved, expert witnesses, and so on. The "going rate" idea for civil cases is not unlike the idea of "going rates" in the plea bargaining process discussed in the criminal justice literature. In that arena, "going rates" define what a given case is worth, and these rates are relatively stable.[36] Learning the "going rate" process in a given criminal jurisdiction seems to be largely a function of being socialized into that local criminal justice system.[37] The "going rates" for different offenses are not listed or systematically collected and communicated. Feeley found that "prosecutors and defense attorneys tend to become inarticulate when pressed to specify how they evaluate the 'worth' of a case, they claim to know it intuitively."[38]

On the civil side, in contrast, information on particular types of cases is systematically tracked in many jurisdictions. In a system in which most matters are settled rather than tried such information is a very marketable commodity. Jury verdict reporters sell information to their subscribers with this in mind; most even offer conputerized search services. One publisher's marketing flier on its computerized search services states in part: "Offers time-saving RESEARCH of our published cases. You receive copies of comparable cases with pertinent information including attorneys, experts, injuries, fact summary, specials, settlement negotiations, and the verdict. . . . Save time and gain a powerful negotiating edge while we do the work!"

The reporters assume that negotiation and settlement takes place within a context formed by the jury verdicts for a particular type of case in a given locale. Interestingly, another reporter recently surveyed its subscribers to ask them whether they want the reporter to continue publishing the details of settlements along with verdicts. These details were published whenever available because the reporter "assumed that details of settlements can be of value as you prepare your cases. . . . If this information is of no value to you we will discontinue it. However, if most of our reorders would prefer that they continue to be printed we will be happy to do so."

The reporters we utilize are local rather than national in their coverage, most covering one or a handful of counties, although a few are statewide in scope (see Appendix 3.1 for a listing). As most local reporters are independently owned, serving the needs of a local audience, there is no single standard for their form and substance. Indeed, some of the local publishers are unaware of the existence of most other reporters outside of their state. In the reporters we use, information is consistently provided on the county in which the case was tried, the type of case, the names of the parties, a short description of the factual situation, the attorneys involved, the jury's verdict and award if one is given, apportionment of liability if relevant, and any compensatory, punitive, or multiplied damages. Some also provide the names of expert witnesses, pretrial demands and offers, components of the total award (pain and suffering, etc.), and detailed information on injuries.

Because of their interest in communicating "going rates" and related information, the publishers of these reporters go to some lengths to ensure the accuracy of their reports. They typically work from a combination of sources. Most will get their initial information on jury verdicts from court clerks, case files, attorneys, and local legal newspapers. After finding out about a verdict and obtaining the names of the attorneys involved, the publishers contact the attorneys asking for detailed information on the case and/or go directly to the case files. When there are discrepancies in information provided by opposing attorneys, for example, about pretrial demands and offers, those discrepancies are reported. Corrections and updates on previously published cases are also provided as required.

While none of the reporters we use claims to have 100% coverage of the verdicts in a given jurisdiction, a safe estimate of their coverage (based upon discussions with publishers, clerks, and users and comparisons with published court statistics) would be at worst 75% of the verdicts and at the very best 95% of the verdicts. Perhaps the broadest coverage—of 95% or more—is found in two Texas reporters, each of which works closely with the court clerk's office (and at one point, one of these publishers was the court clerk). It should be noted that we have not made use of all of the local reporters of which we are aware. We have not included data from reporters that are selective rather than inclusive in their coverage; nor do we include data from any national verdict reporters. Even for those reporters we do use, we do not use any data from their first year in business on the assumption that it took that first year for the publisher to set up a recording system and to develop a consistent reporting pattern.

The sites we include—82 sites covering over 100 counties in 16 states—are not a representative sample of all jurisdictions across the country; rather, they reflect a combination of regional balance and available source material. No sampling of verdicts was done within sites. We will use the data from these sites to present a picture of patterns and changes in jury verdicts in the context of the rhetoric of reform. In the next section, we will discuss plaintiff success rates and awards generally and for some particular categories of cases for the years 1988 to 1990. The idea is to present a snapshot of sorts of the recent past in a wide variety of locales. For a smaller subset of these sites, we will also discuss some basic trends and changes over a longer period of time.

General Patterns in Jury Verdicts

Plaintiff Win Rates and Awards

Among the most basic and widely made claims of the reform rhetoric are those dealing with the frequency of plaintiff success and the size of awards. The image offered is one in which high levels of plaintiff success and high awards are the normal or expected pattern nationwide. Table 3.1 presents a listing of all of the jurisdictions for which we collected jury verdict data, and for each site it enumerates the number of money damage jury verdicts, the overall plaintiff win rates, and the median and mean awards for those cases in which the plaintiff was awarded $1 or more for the years 1988–90. The award figures in table 3.1, and those throughout the remainder of the book, are shown in 1990 dollars, which reflects the last year for which we present data.

Perhaps the most immediate and simplest message conveyed in table 3.1 is one of variation. There is no single pattern for the sites included in the table; even within states there is variation. Most obviously and not unexpectedly, there is great variation in the numbers of jury verdicts among the sites. In some places—the lower population areas—there were few jury verdicts over the three-year time period. Seventeen of the sites—including the entire states of Alaska and Idaho—had fewer than 50 jury verdicts. At the other extreme are the major urban sites. Ten sites, all large jurisdictions with large cities, had 500 or more verdicts; and four of these—Los Angeles County, Cal., Cook County, Ill., Dallas County, Tex., and Harris County, Tex.—experienced over 1,000 verdicts during this three-year time period. One implication of the variation in just the frequency of verdicts is that conclusions drawn from any highly aggregated or purported national figures on verdicts will be driven by the handful of high-volume sites and will completely mask the rich variation we would expect from a highly decentralized civil justice system.

Consistent with this theme, table 3.1 shows that general plaintiff success rates also vary widely. They range from highs of 75.7% in Portage County, Oh. (just east of Akron), and 73.9% in Snohomish County, Wash. (just north of Seattle), to lows of 31.3% in Suffolk County, N.Y., 31.4% in Westchester County, N.Y., and 34.1% in Nassau County, N.Y., and Kalamazoo, Mich. As a general matter, plaintiffs do tend to succeed more than half of the time in most sites. The plaintiff success rates were below 50% in 20 sites, seven of which are in New York

Table 3.1 Plaintiff Success Rates and Median and Average Awards: All Jurisdictions, 1988–90 (*N* = 20,137)

Jurisdiction	*N*	Win Rate (%)	Median Award (1990 $)	Mean Award (1990 $)
Alaska	44	70.5	80,658	499,664
Arizona				
Maricopa	964	64.0	38,982	387,621
California				
Alameda	236	57.2	100,000	615,446
Fresno	68	55.9	215,116	666,116
Los Angeles	1,157	52.5	204,958	1,534,536
Sacramento	146	46.6	78,942	276,478
San Diego	312	43.3	175,000	1,390,045
San Francisco	368	58.4	78,225	335,035
Colorado				
Adams	86	57.0	66,000	363,253
Arapahoe	43	48.8	52,500	503,766
Boulder	82	62.2	46,750	155,941
Denver	443	55.8	52,500	462,988
El Paso	98	46.9	30,750	148,430
Jefferson	157	52.9	42,000	144,647
Georgia				
Cobb	113	54.0	35,000	178,070
DeKalb	218	53.2	30,825	276,227
Fulton	383	63.5	47,500	434,705
Idaho	30	70.0	108,150	281,599
Illinois				
Cook	1,877	56.3	32,550	631,525
DuPage	249	57.4	25,076	255,424
Kane	132	57.6	25,071	80,895
Lake	186	59.7	27,500	282,756
McHenry	37	59.5	39,180	96,046
Will	116	70.7	30,000	280,142
Winnebago	48	64.6	24,868	263,450
Kansas				
Johnson	141	54.6	20,000	116,346
Wyandotte	121	67.8	12,750	111,933
Michigan				
Genessee	83	50.6	57,500	194,149
Ingham	69	69.6	60,928	175,169
Kalamazoo	44	34.1	100,000	167,445
Kent	111	52.3	75,500	213,728
Macomb	134	37.3	78,188	204,757
Oakland	381	50.9	73,500	313,940
Washtenau	103	58.3	58,013	106,833
Wayne	882	51.4	106,400	616,909

(Continued)

Table 3.1 Continued

Jurisdiction	*N*	Win Rate (%)	Median Award (1990 $)	Mean Award (1990 $)
Missouri				
Clay	81	69.1	23,500	585,712
Jackson	588	61.6	27,500	335,447
Jefferson	78	62.8	12,600	127,038
Platte	12	58.3	30,640	60,082
St. Charles	87	63.2	13,000	90,728
St. Louis City	596	67.5	25,625	272,407
St. Louis County	447	57.9	20,000	75,029
Montana	196	50.0	89,042	361,372
New York				
Bronx	241	68.9	417,200	1,220,283
Erie	72	61.1	115,125	1,017,504
Kings	331	49.9	350,000	2,443,795
Monroe	63	58.7	66,000	269,317
Nassau	293	34.1	165,000	449,090
New York	557	54.6	348,400	1,474,847
Onondaga	80	47.5	104,750	1,099,125
Queens	205	40.0	242,500	1,421,394
Richmond	33	39.4	192,500	555,434
Suffolk	166	31.3	131,287	571,823
Westchester	121	31.4	104,500	904,225
Ohio				
Butler	40	70.0	24,313	101,112
Cuyahoga	336	63.1	34,650	379,093
Franklin	106	53.8	17,435	402,566
Hamilton	143	62.9	33,825	437,643
Lorain	41	48.8	49,989	305,850
Lucas	39	51.3	23,734	301,848
Montgomery	54	50.0	9,135	258,121
Portage	37	75.7	18,938	169,184
Summit	114	57.0	31,500	176,202
Oregon				
Clackamas	53	49.1	10,643	80,034
Lane	110	51.8	16,023	65,981
Marion	60	51.7	16,231	95,496
Multnomah	357	58.8	25,424	251,710
Washington	50	38.0	9,450	51,196
Texas[39]				
Bexar	742	49.9	35,650	572,493
Dallas	1,068	47.3	47,300	553,773
District 6	219	56.2	54,985	313,053
District 9	145	42.1	63,000	344,798
Harris	1,461	38.9	46,181	969,021
Travis	320	54.7	53,188	569,233

(Continued)

Table 3.1 Continued

Jurisdiction	*N*	Win Rate (%)	Median Award (1990 $)	Mean Award (1990 $)
Washington				
Clark	37	62.2	26,700	52,706
King	378	58.7	38,678	227,016
Pierce	106	65.1	50,000	230,670
Snohomish	46	73.9	48,137	427,242
Spokane	70	67.1	59,535	149,000
Thurston	27	51.9	71,316	167,022
Whatcom	31	61.3	35,750	151,553
Yakima	38	65.8	75,000	174,553

and four of which are in Texas. The largest proportion of the locales in table 3.1 had plaintiff success rates between 50% and 65% (48 of 82 or 58.5%); the rate exceeded 65% in 14 sites. Even among the largest sites the success rates varied widely—38.9% in Harris County, Tex., 47.3% in Dallas County, 52.5% in Los Angeles County, and 56.3% in Cook County. Some of the variation in plaintiff success rates may be due to basic differences in state law, such as negligence schemes or reliance on mandatory mediation for certain types of cases. This will not, however, explain the intrastate variations which may be a result of local legal cultures,[40] the socioeconomic characteristics of locales, or differences in the mix of cases going to a jury trial.

Wide variations are also evident in the award figures. We will utilize the median rather than the mean in describing awards because, as discussed in chapter 2, it is a better summary measure of central tendency in a situation in which there are a few extremely high awards. We have included the mean award figure here only for purposes of context. Median awards in cases in which the plaintiff was successful ranged from lows of $9,135 in Montgomery County, Oh. (Dayton), and $9,450 in Washington County, Ore. (just west of Portland), to $417,200 in Bronx County, N.Y. Montgomery and Washington Counties are both low-volume verdict sites with only 54 and 50 jury verdicts respectively over the three-year period. If we were to look only at sites with at least 100 verdicts over the three-year period, then the low end of the award range would be $12,750 in Johnson County, Kans. (just west of Kansas City, Mo.), and $16,023 in Lane County, Ore. (Eugene). Just over one-half of all of the sites (45 of 82 or 54.9%) have median awards of $50,000 or less, while 17 experienced median awards of $100,000 or more. Most of these 17 sites are in California (four sites) or New York (10 sites).

Some of the variations in award structures may be due to statutory differences in the amount in controversy subject to the jurisdiction of various courts. In California, for example, the lower courts—municipal and justice courts—have jurisdiction in civil matters involving amounts in controversy of up to $25,000. The Superior Courts, the trial courts of general jurisdiction, have concurrent jurisdiction, but arbitration is required for all matters involving $50,000 or less brought in those courts. The effect of these statutory requirements is to create a functional dollar amount floor for the cases going to the Superior Courts, and to produce a higher overall award structure for the California courts of general jurisdiction. The supreme courts in New York (general jurisdiction trial courts) also have no statutorily defined floor for civil matters jurisdiction, but the New York City civil court and the county courts in counties outside of New York City have concurrent jurisdiction for matters involving amounts in controversy of up to $25,000. Because low-end dollar amount matters may tend to go to these lower courts, we might expect somewhat higher medians in the New York sites as well. These jurisdictional matters, however, will not account for all of the difference between the sites in these two states and those elsewhere. For instance, if we were to drop all awards below $25,000 in Cook, Dallas, and Harris counties and then recalculate their respective medians using only awards of $25,000 or more, the revised figures put these sites more in line with California and New York ($162,316, $124,525, and $108,028 respectively). But the revised figures are still much lower than the New York and California sites with the highest medians—Bronx, Kings, New York, Queens, Fresno, and Los Angeles—all of which were in excess of $200,000. The explanation for the remaining differences is likely to be complex and tied to the types and mixes of cases that go to a jury trial in the respective sites as well as the local legal and socioeconomic environments.

Broad Categories of Cases: Harm to the Plaintiff

General figures such as those in table 3.1 serve a limited purpose. They provide us with a basic background, but little more because different categories of cases exhibit different patterns in plaintiff success rates and median awards. Categories of cases are not fungible: they have different histories and developments, deal with different realms of activity, and present different sets of opportunities and constraints as they proceed through the system to trial. The jury verdicts in our database can be categorized into four broad categories of cases based on the harm alleged by the plaintiff: bodily harm, financial harm, harm to property, and emotional or reputational harm. In this section we will examine the two harm categories—bodily and financial harm—which together comprised at least 75% of the verdicts in each of the 82 sites and 92.2% of all of the verdicts combined (69.9% bodily harm and 22.3% financial harm) between 1988 and 1990.

Table 3.2 presents data for the 82 sites on the percentage of verdicts in each of these two broad categories, the plaintiff success rate for each category, and the median award for each category. Again, the basic message is one of variation. While bodily harm cases comprised the largest percentage of verdicts in all but three sites (Cobb County, Ga. [suburban Atlanta], and Dallas and Travis [Austin] Counties in Texas), the percentages varied considerably, from 38.4% in Travis County, Tex., to 97.6% in Lorain County, Oh. (just west of Cleveland). In 13 sites, the percentage of bodily harm verdicts was 90% or more, and in another 18 sites the percentage was between 80% and 89.9%. In three states—New York, Oregon, and Washington—the percentage of bodily harm verdicts was 80% or more in all of the sites within those states for which we have data. By contrast, bodily harm made up less than one-half of the jury verdicts in only five sites. The four sites with 1,000 or more verdicts rendered during the three-year period between 1988 and 1990 also exhibited wide variation in the percentage of bodily harm verdicts: Los Angeles County—73.6%, Cook County—86.9%, Dallas County—40.4% and Harris County—75.8%. (Note the intrastate variation in the two Texas sites.)

While the percentages of verdicts accounted for by financial harm cases were generally lower, there was again substantial variation among the sites. In only one site—Dallas County—did financial harm verdicts make up as much as 50% of the verdicts. In 26 sites, the percentage was 10% or less, and in two of these sites no financial harm verdicts were reported (Lorain County, Oh., and Whatcom County, Wash. [Bellingham]).

Overall, plaintiffs were more successful in financial harm cases than in those involving bodily harm (60.6% v. 51.2%), and in most of the sites having verdicts in both categories, the success rate for financial harm cases equaled or exceeded that for bodily harm cases (52 sites or 63.4%). Success rates within each category, once again, varied considerably. For bodily harm cases the plaintiff success rate ranged from 27.4% in Macomb County, Mich. (north of Detroit), to 75.0% in Will County, Ill. (Joliet). Success rates in financial harm cases varied more broadly from 0% in Richmond County, N.Y., and Clark (Vancouver) and Thurston

Table 3.2 Distribution of Verdicts, Win Rates, and Awards by Harm (1988–90)

	Percentage of Cases		Win Rate (%)		Median Award (1990 $)	
Jurisdiction	(Bodily)	(Financial)	(Bodily)	(Financial)	(Bodily)	(Financial)
Alaska	50.0	40.9	72.7	66.7	99,930	82,335
Arizona						
Maricopa	62.2	32.4	64.3	65.2	32,903	60,858
California						
Alameda	61.1	29.2	53.8	66.7	77,545	153,643
Fresno	71.5	22.1	50.0	73.3	326,806	151,327
Los Angeles	73.6	19.5	49.1	61.5	157,779	381,982
Sacramento	71.2	24.0	48.1	45.7	64,793	423,539
San Diego	78.2	15.4	39.3	56.3	134,418	403,700
San Francisco	71.7	21.2	58.3	56.4	71,500	154,000
Colorado						
Adams	53.5	36.0	54.4	64.5	50,122	95,036
Arapahoe	60.5	20.9	50.0	55.6	55,000	30,269
Boulder	65.9	28.0	63.0	60.8	132,500	22,513
Denver	54.0	39.3	48.1	64.9	46,500	57,480
El Paso	69.4	26.5	39.7	65.4	19,425	53,982
Jefferson	52.9	40.1	43.4	60.3	43,550	37,171
Georgia						
Cobb	44.2	49.6	44.0	66.1	11,101	60,144
DeKalb	46.3	43.1	46.5	59.6	20,000	39,038
Fulton	52.0	39.4	53.3	72.9	58,300	47,629
Idaho	73.3	23.3	59.1	100.0	45,171	191,838
Illinois						
Cook	86.9	8.3	55.2	62.6	31,500	75,810
DuPage	71.1	22.5	53.7	67.9	16,500	74,675
Kane	84.1	7.6	57.7	60.0	26,400	61,229
Lake	65.1	23.7	58.7	61.4	23,646	76,380
McHenry	73.0	24.3	55.6	77.8	50,310	24,518
Will	82.8	14.7	75.0	47.1	30,000	50,444
Winnebago	75.0	18.8	69.4	55.6	31,763	24,472
Kansas						
Johnson	51.1	35.5	47.2	58.0	28,500	31,983
Wyandotte	62.8	24.0	65.8	72.4	25,157	10,500
Michigan						
Genessee	74.7	19.3	48.4	75.0	57,500	55,025
Ingham	49.3	36.2	61.8	80.0	113,400	41,711
Kalamazoo	68.2	20.5	33.3	22.2	133,650	*
Kent	57.7	34.2	37.5	68.4	134,935	64,150
Macomb	70.9	17.9	27.4	54.2	66,013	122,100
Oakland	63.5	31.0	43.8	66.1	83,585	65,025
Washtenau	61.2	31.1	50.8	68.8	58,450	62,738
Wayne	72.8	23.6	47.7	62.5	110,000	97,472

(Continued)

Table 3.2 Continued

Jurisdiction	Percentage of Cases		Win Rate (%)		Median Award (1990 $)	
	(Bodily)	(Financial)	(Bodily)	(Financial)	(Bodily)	(Financial)
Missouri						
Clay	53.1	37.0	72.1	60.0	57,750	28,216
Jackson	52.6	33.7	56.6	69.7	28,259	30,168
Jefferson	62.8	23.1	59.2	50.0	16,500	12,600
Platte	50.0	25.0	66.7	33.3	*	*
St. Charles	54.0	34.5	66.0	66.7	10,500	23,375
St. Louis City	69.3	18.6	70.9	64.0	30,000	16,500
St. Louis County	55.0	34.9	52.9	63.5	14,100	34,650
Montana	55.6	35.2	45.9	53.6	31,353	179,139
New York						
Bronx	94.6	2.5	68.9	66.7	435,680	*
Erie	87.5	9.7	63.5	28.6	229,000	*
Kings	93.4	3.3	49.2	54.6	367,500	457,306
Monroe	88.9	4.8	55.4	100.0	68,250	*
Nassau	92.5	4.4	33.2	46.2	190,750	57,000
New York	81.9	13.1	52.9	60.3	367,500	325,236
Onondaga	88.8	5.0	46.5	50.0	126,500	*
Queens	94.6	3.9	38.7	50.0	300,000	*
Richmond	93.9	6.1	41.9	0.0	192,500	N/A
Suffolk	92.2	6.0	30.7	30.0	165,000	*
Westchester	92.6	5.8	31.3	14.3	137,500	*
Ohio						
Butler	85.0	10.0	73.5	50.0	22,004	*
Cuyahoga	75.3	15.2	62.1	68.6	32,670	40,700
Hamilton	74.1	18.2	59.4	80.8	30,000	59,890
Franklin	73.6	20.8	55.1	50.0	19,950	17,435
Lorain	97.6	0.0	47.5	N/A	56,943	N/A
Lucas	79.5	10.3	48.4	50.0	12,453	*
Montgomery	94.4	3.7	49.0	50.0	9,135	*
Portage	81.1	13.5	73.3	80.0	18,938	*
Summit	78.1	14.0	57.3	68.8	30,000	23,500
Oregon						
Clackamas	86.8	3.8	47.8	100.0	14,926	*
Lane	84.5	7.3	53.8	37.5	12,465	*
Marion	85.0	5.0	51.0	33.3	14,537	*
Multnomah	84.9	8.1	58.8	55.2	24,206	41,298
Washington	90.0	6.0	35.6	66.7	9,409	*
Texas						
Bexar	54.2	31.0	41.0	60.0	33,700	38,158
Dallas	40.4	50.4	39.4	51.7	22,580	62,700
District 6	56.6	29.2	57.3	54.7	57,750	51,450
District 9	66.9	20.7	36.1	60.0	89,926	143,155
Harris	75.8	15.2	35.9	50.5	38,763	124,460
Travis	38.4	44.1	53.7	53.2	32,598	96,125

(Continued)

Table 3.2 Continued

	Percentage of Cases		Win Rate (%)		Median Award (1990 $)	
Jurisdiction	(Bodily)	(Financial)	(Bodily)	(Financial)	(Bodily)	(Financial)
Washington						
Clark	91.9	5.4	64.7	0.0	24,967	N/A
King	87.0	7.7	59.3	72.4	37,500	79,800
Pierce	85.8	6.6	65.9	42.9	42,000	*
Snohomish	80.4	13.0	73.0	66.7	35,000	*
Spokane	84.3	5.7	71.2	50.0	61,268	*
Thurston	96.3	3.7	53.9	0.0	71,316	N/A
Whatcom	90.3	0.0	60.7	N/A	35,750	N/A
Yakima	81.6	7.9	61.3	66.7	60,917	*

* Median not calculated; fewer than five winning cases.
N/A: not applicable because there were no cases or no plaintiff verdicts.

(Olympia) Counties, Wash., to 100% in Idaho, Monroe County, N.Y. (Rochester), and in Clackamas County, Ore. (east of Portland).

Turning to awards, medians generally tended to be higher for financial harm cases than for bodily harm cases. For the 56 sites with at least five winning verdicts in each category, 34 (or 60.7%) experienced a higher median in financial cases. The range for medians in both categories of cases is quite wide, but some of this variation may be the result of the jurisdictional differences as to amounts in controversy noted earlier, and some may be a function of the small numbers of winning verdicts in particular sites or the mix of case types within these broad categories. If we look only at the sites with at least 50 plaintiff physical harm verdicts, the range for median awards runs from below $20,000 in three sites—St. Louis County, Mo., Lane County, Ore., and DuPage County, Ill. (west of Chicago)—to over $300,000 in four sites. Three of these four are in New York, and the other is in California. If we take out the California and New York sites, the highest median in physical harm cases in sites with at least 50 successful verdicts is $110,000 in Wayne County, Mich. (Detroit); only three other such sites exhibit a median in excess of $50,000.

Among the 28 sites where there were 25 or more successful financial harm cases, the range for median awards ran from $16,500 in the city of St. Louis to over $300,000 in Los Angeles, San Diego, and New York County. (We used a lower threshold for analysis here because of the lower numbers of financial cases.) If California and New York sites are again removed, then only one county experiencing over 25 successful cases—Harris County, Tex.—had a median over $100,000. The aggregation of Montana counties also produced a median award in financial harm cases of over $100,000. In short, award structures varied greatly in these two broad categories of cases, but the especially high median awards which appeared mainly in California and New York may be attributable at least in part to differences in the jurisdictional scope of those courts.

The variations in win rates and award structures among sites generally and among the sites within various states which appeared in table 3.1 remain when broad case types are examined. In addition to variations in award structure resulting from statutorily dictated jurisdictional differences, we have seen that different categories of cases defined by underlying harm alleged are likely to have quite different award structures as well as different patterns in plaintiff success rates. However, there may be variations in the mix of different types of cases subsumed within the harm categories that affect plaintiff win rates and awards. It is useful, therefore, to take a deeper cut into the database and look more closely at particular types of cases.

Specific Types of Cases

It is not possible to canvass all types of cases within the broad categories of physical and financial harm to illustrate the differences in plaintiff success rates and award structures. Consequently, we will limit the discussion to four types of cases. Auto cases were selected for these purposes since they comprise a substantial proportion of jury verdicts in most jurisdictions and often a majority of the bodily harm cases. As a consequence, win rates and award structures in such cases will impact the overall picture of awards and success rates. One type of financial harm case—breach of contract—is included for comparison purposes as it comprises a substantial proportion of cases involving this type of harm. Breach of contract cases include landlord/tenant disputes, suits for payment due, and wrongful firing (excluding discrimination) matters. The other two types of cases appear less frequently but are highly visible and a focus of a great deal of controversy in the reform arena—products liability and medical malpractice. Table 3.3 presents data on the percentage of *all* verdicts within each site made up by each of the four types of cases and the win rate for each case type. These four types of cases make up 61.6% of the jury verdicts in the entire database.

There were 6,334 automobile jury verdicts during the three-year period 1988–90. They account for almost one-third of all of the jury verdicts in our 82 sites (31.5%). Among the sites, the percentage of automobile verdicts ranges from below 20% in nine jurisdictions

Table 3.3 Percentage of Verdicts and Plaintiff Success Rates in Selected Types of Cases (1988–90)

	Auto		Products		Medical		Contract	
Jurisdiction	Percentage	Win Rate (%)	Percentage	Win Rate (%)	Percentage	Win Rate (%)	Percentage	Win Rate (%)
Alaska	20.5	77.8	4.5	50.0	4.5	50.0	34.1	66.7
Arizona								
Maricopa	35.0	76.6	2.7	26.9	3.9	36.8	21.5	62.8
California								
Alameda	20.8	71.4	6.8	37.5	10.2	20.8	16.1	60.5
Fresno	27.9	73.7	8.8	50.0	7.4	20.0	20.6	71.4
Los Angeles	20.9	66.9	7.2	43.4	16.2	30.9	11.9	63.0
Sacramento	24.0	65.7	7.5	45.5	11.0	25.0	17.8	38.5
San Diego	21.5	68.7	4.5	21.4	17.9	30.4	11.2	54.3
San Francisco	17.4	78.1	14.9	54.5	5.2	26.3	10.6	69.2
Colorado								
Adams	27.9	58.3	3.5	66.7	3.5	33.3	22.1	68.4
Arapahoe	27.9	41.7	0.0	N/A	7.0	33.3	11.6	60.0
Boulder	32.9	74.1	7.3	33.3	9.8	62.5	23.2	63.2
Denver	23.7	61.0	3.2	35.7	7.7	25.5	30.0	67.7
El Paso	46.9	43.5	1.0	0.0	4.1	0.0	24.5	62.5
Jefferson	27.4	58.1	1.3	0.0	5.1	0.0	28.7	55.6
Georgia								
Cobb	29.2	48.5	0.0	N/A	8.8	20.0	30.1	61.8
DeKalb	29.8	60.0	1.4	66.7	9.2	20.0	29.4	54.7
Fulton	23.0	61.4	1.0	75.0	10.2	33.3	23.8	65.9
Idaho	30.0	66.7	6.7	0.0	10.0	66.7	16.7	100.0
Illinois								
Cook	47.3	58.4	6.3	48.3	14.4	39.3	6.7	59.5
DuPage	43.4	61.1	2.4	0.0	8.4	14.3	11.6	69.0
Kane	48.5	73.4	6.8	33.3	15.2	20.0	6.8	55.6
Lake	43.0	72.5	2.7	20.0	6.5	0.0	13.4	68.0
McHenry	48.6	66.7	2.7	100.0	8.1	33.3	16.2	83.3
Will	51.7	75.0	3.4	75.0	8.6	80.0	12.9	40.0
Winnebago	47.9	69.6	0.0	N/A	14.6	28.6	18.8	55.6
Kansas								
Johnson	30.5	58.1	0.0	N/A	6.4	11.1	21.3	73.3
Wyandotte	42.1	70.6	0.0	N/A	6.6	50.0	20.7	76.0
Michigan								
Genessee	25.3	57.1	3.6	33.3	14.5	25.0	14.5	75.0
Ingham	15.9	72.7	2.9	0.0	11.6	25.0	10.1	57.1
Kalamazoo	34.1	33.3	4.5	50.0	15.9	14.3	18.2	25.0
Kent	19.8	36.4	5.4	33.3	10.8	25.0	22.5	76.0
Macomb	14.2	47.4	6.7	11.1	19.4	7.7	12.7	52.9
Oakland	17.3	54.6	5.5	47.6	16.0	14.8	18.4	64.3
Washtenau	20.4	52.4	2.9	33.3	14.6	13.3	21.4	77.3
Wayne	17.8	54.1	6.3	37.5	17.7	28.2	15.9	60.0

(Continued)

Table 3.3 Continued

	Auto		Products		Medical		Contract	
Jurisdiction	Percentage	Win Rate (%)	Percentage	Win Rate (%)	Percentage	Win Rate (%)	Percentage	Win Rate (%)
Missouri								
Clay	22.2	94.4	4.9	50.0	9.9	12.5	24.7	60.0
Jackson	28.1	67.9	3.2	42.1	6.3	16.2	26.5	68.6
Jefferson	43.6	67.7	1.3	100.0	3.8	33.3	15.4	50.0
Platte	25.0	66.7	0.0	N/A	0.0	N/A	8.3	100.0
St. Charles	36.8	75.0	1.1	0.0	2.3	N/A	16.1	64.3
St. Louis City	33.4	76.4	3.9	52.2	9.4	39.3	14.9	65.2
St. Louis County	31.1	69.8	2.2	10.0	8.5	18.4	24.4	64.2
Montana	27.0	64.2	4.1	50.0	4.6	22.2	24.5	50.0
New York								
Bronx	28.6	71.0	3.3	50.0	8.7	66.7	2.5	66.7
Erie	26.4	84.2	2.8	100.0	15.3	27.3	6.9	20.0
Kings	26.9	50.6	1.5	20.0	21.5	47.9	2.7	44.4
Monroe	50.8	53.1	4.8	0.0	6.3	75.0	4.8	100.0
Nassau	33.8	43.4	3.1	0.0	21.5	38.1	3.8	45.5
New York	11.8	63.6	4.5	56.0	19.2	36.4	11.7	63.1
Onondaga	41.3	60.6	0.0	N/A	11.3	33.3	3.8	33.3
Queens	31.7	43.1	2.9	0.0	21.5	29.6	3.9	50.0
Richmond	33.3	36.4	0.0	N/A	15.2	60.0	3.0	0.0
Suffolk	40.4	43.3	1.8	0.0	19.9	21.2	6.0	30.0
Westchester	42.1	41.2	3.3	50.0	6.6	0.0	5.0	16.7
Ohio								
Butler	70.0	75.0	2.5	100.0	5.0	50.0	10.0	50.0
Cuyahoga	36.6	63.4	3.3	54.5	12.5	61.9	11.9	65.0
Franklin	49.1	63.5	3.8	25.0	7.5	50.0	17.0	38.9
Hamilton	43.4	69.4	3.5	40.0	7.0	40.0	13.3	79.0
Lorain	63.4	69.2	7.3	33.3	4.9	50.0	0.0	N/A
Lucas	48.7	47.4	2.6	100.0	7.7	33.3	10.3	50.0
Montgomery	68.5	59.5	1.9	0.0	16.7	33.3	3.7	50.0
Portage	62.2	82.6	2.7	0.0	5.4	50.0	10.8	75.0
Summit	40.4	76.1	2.6	33.3	14.0	6.3	11.4	76.9
Oregon								
Clackamas	66.0	60.0	1.9	0.0	3.8	0.0	3.8	100.0
Lane	58.2	59.4	1.8	0.0	5.5	66.7	5.5	50.0
Marion	66.7	55.0	0.0	N/A	5.0	66.7	3.3	0.0
Multnomah	51.0	64.8	2.8	20.0	4.5	56.3	5.0	55.6
Washington	68.0	47.1	0.0	N/A	6.0	0.0	4.0	50.0
Texas								
Bexar	27.0	53.5	3.1	26.1	3.2	25.0	22.9	63.5
Dallas	18.3	51.8	2.3	28.0	4.6	16.3	35.5	56.2
District 6	24.2	69.8	6.4	42.9	3.7	25.0	19.2	57.1
District 9	33.8	46.9	9.0	30.8	4.8	14.3	10.3	66.7
Harris	35.2	48.1	4.3	23.8	11.1	17.3	6.1	53.9
Travis	16.9	66.7	2.2	42.9	2.2	14.3	26.6	56.5

(Continued)

Table 3.3 Continued

Jurisdiction	Auto Percentage	Auto Win Rate (%)	Products Percentage	Products Win Rate (%)	Medical Percentage	Medical Win Rate (%)	Contract Percentage	Contract Win Rate (%)
Washington								
Clark	56.8	71.4	2.7	100.0	5.4	50.0	2.7	0.0
King	38.1	80.6	6.3	41.7	16.4	27.4	2.4	77.8
Pierce	48.1	80.4	3.8	50.0	9.4	20.0	3.8	25.0
Snohomish	50.0	87.0	4.3	50.0	8.7	75.0	6.5	33.3
Spokane	54.3	81.6	4.3	33.3	5.7	25.0	2.9	50.0
Thurston	40.7	72.7	0.0	N/A	14.8	0.0	3.7	0.0
Whatcom	35.5	90.9	3.2	100.0	16.1	40.0	0.0	N/A
Yakima	36.8	78.6	13.2	40.0	15.8	50.0	7.9	66.7
Overall	31.5	62.0	4.2	39.0	10.8	30.4	15.3	61.2

N/A: not applicable because there were no cases.

(including the high population density sites of San Francisco, Wayne, New York, and Dallas counties) to 70.0% in Butler County, Oh. (northwest of Cincinnati). The higher percentages of auto cases are clustered in the Illinois, Ohio, Oregon, and Washington sites, with lower percentages appearing in California, Michigan, and Texas. The reasons for these differences cannot be determined from an analysis of verdict data. In Michigan the lower percentages may be tied to the existence of the mandatory mediation programs that push out cases involving low-dollar claims, an effect also seen in California but attributable there to higher jurisdictional floors. Variation among the jurisdictions may also be the result of factors such as the settlement practices of automobile insurance carriers and plaintiff's attorneys.

The percentage of verdicts made up by contract cases is smaller than that for auto cases in most of the sites. In only 12 sites was the percentage of contract verdicts equal to or greater than that for auto accident verdicts. That group of 12 includes such larger sites as Denver, Colo.; Dallas, Tex.; Fulton, Ga.; New York, N.Y.; and Oakland, Mich. The range for the percentage of contract verdicts in any given site ran from zero in Lorain County, Oh., and Whatcom County, Wash., to 35.5% in Dallas County. Twenty sites had 5.0% or fewer such cases (most of those being in New York or Washington), while in only four sites 30.0% or more of the jury verdict caseload was composed of contract cases.

Products liability verdicts accounted for an even lower percentage of the jury verdicts in most sites. Only 4.2% of all of the jury verdicts in the 82 sites were attributable to products liability cases. In only two sites did products cases comprise as much as 10% of the verdicts: San Francisco (14.9%) and Yakima County, Wash. (13.2%). In 11 sites, there were no products verdicts during this three-year time period, and in another 53 sites products verdicts constituted only between 1% and 5% of the cases. In short, products verdicts were a small proportion of the jury cases, even in the sites with the highest numbers of total jury verdicts. In the four 1,000-plus verdict sites the percentages for products verdicts were: Los Angeles County, 7.2%; Cook County, 6.3%; Dallas County, 2.3%; and Harris County, Tex., 4.3%.

Medical malpractice verdicts were somewhat more prevalent than products cases although they never comprised as much as a quarter of the jury verdicts in any one site during this three-year period (N=2, 165). In 33 sites, medical malpractice verdicts accounted for 10% or more of the cases, and in three of these sites the percentage was over 20%. The highest percentage was 21.5% in Queens, Kings, and Nassau Counties, N.Y. The percentages of medical malpractice jury verdicts were generally highest in sites in California, Michigan, and New York.

Plaintiff success rates among these four types of cases were quite different. For automobile cases, the overall success rate was 62.0%, and the range among the various sites ran from below 40% in Kalamazoo County, Mich., Kent County, Mich. (Grand Rapids), and Richmond County, N.Y., to 94.4% in Clay County, Mo. (east of Kansas City), and 90.9% in Whatcom County, Wash. Most sites had success rates of 60% or higher (52 of 82), and 27 of these had success rates of 70% or higher. Only 15 sites had success rates lower than 50%. Of the 38 higher volume sites—those with 50 or more auto verdicts—success rates ranged from 41.2% in Westchester County, N.Y., to 80.6% and 80.4% in King and Pierce Counties in Washington. In the majority (25 or 65.8%) of these 38 sites, the plaintiff success rate was over 60%. Relatively high plaintiff success rates in this type of case are not unexpected given the prevalence of comparative negligence schemes.

Success rates for contract cases were also generally high, reaching 61.2% overall, although there were four sites in which there were no plaintiff verdicts in contract cases during this three-year period. Each of these four sites, however, experienced only one or two contract jury verdicts during this time. Of the 30 sites with 25 or more contract verdicts, success rates ranged from 38.5% in Sacramento County to 76.0% in Wyandotte County, Kans., and Kent County, Mich. Sacramento is the only site among the 30 with a success rate under 50%, although nine other sites had success rates under 60%. We might expect relatively high success rates in contract matters because the contracts themselves typically spell out in advance the respective rights and responsibilities of the parties. This would remove, perhaps, the somewhat more subjective issues of negligence found in tort cases and in fact reduce the matter to one of damages rather than assignment of fault.

Plaintiff win rates in products liability cases were lower than those in either auto or breach of contract cases; for all the sites combined the success rate was 39.0% for the three-year period between 1988 and 1990. Only 22 sites of our 82 sites experienced 10 or more products verdicts during this time period, and success rates in these counties ranged from 10% in St. Louis County to 56% in New York County. Only three other sites with this "higher" volume of products liability activity had success rates of 50.0% or higher: San Francisco, Cuyahoga County, Oh., and St. Louis City.

In spite of a higher incidence of such cases, success rates for medical malpractice cases tended to be even lower than those for products cases. The overall plaintiff success rate during this three-year period for such cases was 30.4%. Forty sites had 10 or more malpractice verdicts, and success rates in those jurisdictions ranged from zero in Lake County, Ill. (north of Chicago), to 80.0% in Will County, Ill. (Joliet). Only four of the 10-plus verdict sites had success rates of 50% or higher. In addition to Lake County, another 25 sites had success rates below 30%, and 13 of those experienced rates of 20% or lower. Even in the five highest volume sites (100 or more malpractice verdicts)—Los Angeles, Cook, Wayne, New York, and Harris Counties—success rates were relatively low, ranging between 17.3% in Harris County and 39.3% in Cook County.

Table 3.4 presents data on median awards for these four types of cases. A median is calculated only when there were at least five winning verdicts. Looking first at automobile cases, table 3.4 again shows substantial variation in the size of the median award among the 80 sites with five or more winning cases, ranging from $6,083 in Montgomery County, Oh. (Dayton), and $6,600 in Arapahoe County, Colo. (east of Denver), to $423,500 in Bronx County, N.Y. Most medians in this type of case, however, are modest with 60 of the 80 (75.4%) sites having median awards of $50,000 or less. Forty-three of these 60 experienced medians of $25,000 or less, and 10 had medians below $10,000—among them Cook County. Even if we look at the sites with the highest frequency of automobile verdicts, the median awards are low. For instance, 15 sites experienced more than 100 automobile jury verdicts during this three-year cycle, and the median award for

Table 3.4 Median Awards in Selected Types of Cases, 1988–90 (in 1990 $)

Jurisdiction	Auto	Products	Medical	Contract
Alaska	7,486	*	*	94,718
Arizona				
Maricopa	22,883	78,750	253,275	37,346
California				
Alameda	46,547	1,623,500	137,500	118,125
Fresno	303,796	*	*	140,235
Los Angeles	66,474	1,099,333	300,000	330,330
Sacramento	24,459	190,433	*	374,564
San Diego	80,795	*	214,270	367,500
San Francisco	30,125	247,060	173,250	78,681
Colorado				
Adams	32,801	*	*	24,673
Arapahoe	6,600	N/A	*	*
Boulder	34,500	*	283,500	21,328
Denver	22,825	330,000	544,950	54,414
El Paso	19,063	N/A	N/A	66,372
Jefferson	45,100	N/A	N/A	29,479
Georgia				
Cobb	10,250	N/A	*	45,440
DeKalb	14,000	*	*	36,288
Fulton	29,975	*	732,985	39,875
Idaho	12,850	N/A	*	211,619
Illinois				
Cook	9,108	266,430	412,205	57,156
DuPage	14,119	N/A	*	24,344
Kane	13,448	*	*	25,142
Lake	17,610	*	N/A	27,282
McHenry	18,425	*	*	24,518
Will	21,119	*	389,625	50,444
Winnebago	28,315	N/A	*	24,472
Kansas				
Johnson	9,790	N/A	*	25,375
Wyandotte	7,857	N/A	*	18,564
Michigan				
Genessee	51,000	*	*	46,000
Ingham	113,400	N/A	*	*
Kalamazoo	311,199	*	*	*
Kent	200,835	*	*	47,300
Macomb	50,000	*	*	108,084
Oakland	85,350	137,000	180,000	66,000
Washtenau	88,000	*	*	50,980
Wayne	96,600	745,500	333,000	58,350

(Continued)

Table 3.4 Continued

Jurisdiction	Auto	Products	Medical	Contract
Missouri				
Clay	16,000	*	*	6,585
Jackson	14,742	457,125	275,650	25,289
Jefferson	12,600	*	*	60,375
Platte	*	N/A	N/A	*
St. Charles	9,450	N/A	N/A	19,800
St. Louis City	10,251	574,875	311,306	14,114
St. Louis County	9,450	*	100,800	27,803
Montana	26,903	*	*	212,625
New York				
Bronx	423,500	*	605,000	*
Erie	141,750	*	*	*
Kings	367,500	*	742,088	*
Monroe	60,000	N/A	*	*
Nassau	108,150	N/A	500,000	70,000
New York	262,275	3,067,781	793,000	294,223
Onondaga	128,875	N/A	*	*
Queens	122,500	N/A	1,238,000	*
Richmond	*	N/A	*	N/A
Suffolk	105,000	N/A	220,000	*
Westchester	165,000	*	N/A	*
Ohio				
Butler	18,900	*	*	*
Cuyahoga	16,750	114,450	890,890	36,420
Franklin	13,491	*	*	8,500
Hamilton	23,100	*	*	36,750
Lorain	42,748	*	*	N/A
Lucas	9,350	*	*	*
Montgomery	6,083	N/A	*	*
Portage	19,500	N/A	*	*
Summit	27,000	*	*	43,327
Oregon				
Clackamas	16,852	N/A	N/A	*
Lane	11,117	N/A	*	*
Marion	12,439	N/A	*	N/A
Multnomah	18,230	*	533,500	18,974
Washington	9,184	N/A	N/A	*
Texas				
Bexar	20,475	368,825	644,391	36,847
Dallas	11,549	3,170,857	369,600	55,000
District 6	35,750	632,730	*	64,720
District 9	44,000	*	*	105,155
Harris	16,812	564,497	249,375	105,411
Travis	18,380	*	*	90,525

(Continued)

Table 3.4 Continued

Jurisdiction	Auto	Products	Medical	Contract
Washington				
Clark	22,250	*	*	N/A
King	28,629	215,000	245,700	79,800
Pierce	30,000	*	*	*
Snohomish	34,000	*	*	*
Spokane	15,750	*	*	*
Thurston	35,650	N/A	N/A	N/A
Whatcom	20,267	*	*	N/A
Yakima	24,150	*	*	*

* Median not calculated; fewer than five winning cases.
N/A: not applicable because there were no cases or no plaintiff verdicts.

these cases was under $25,000 in 12 (80%) of those sites. The highest median in automobile accident cases among these 15 sites was $96,600 in Wayne County, Mich. The Michigan and New York sites generally generated higher awards in vehicle accident cases.

Median awards for contract cases tended to be somewhat higher than those for automobile cases, but they were still relatively modest. In the 53 sites with five or more winning verdicts in contract cases, the medians ranged from $6,585 in Clay County, Mo., to $374,564 in Sacramento County. Eleven sites had medians over $100,000, and five of these were in California. One-half of the 53 sites had medians below $50,000, and 11 had medians below $25,000.

The median awards for products liability and medical malpractice were much higher despite their lower plaintiff success rates, with the highest award structure being found in the products liability cases. Only 18 sites had five or more winning products liability cases, and the median awards were spread over a very wide range—from $78,750 in Maricopa County (Phoenix), Ariz., to $3.2 million in Dallas County. In addition to Dallas County, three other sites had medians in excess of $1 million—Alameda, Los Angeles, and New York Counties. The reasons for the variations in median products liability awards seen here are likely to be complex, but as we will discuss later in chapter 5, much of this variation has to do with the severity of injury involved and the particular type of products liability case involved.

Twenty-seven sites had five or more winning medical malpractice verdicts, and again the median awards were spread over a very wide range. The medians ranged from $100,800 in St. Louis County to $1.2 million in Queens County, N.Y. Eighteen sites had median medical malpractice awards between $100,000 and $500,000. Again the reasons for the variations in these types of awards among the 27 sites are likely to be complex, but as will be discussed in chapter 4, much variation can be tied to the severity of the injury involved, the particular type of malpractice case, and the age of the injured person.

In short, discerning patterns in success rates and award sizes is a complicated task, even after disaggregating the verdicts into harm and case types. It is often the case that caseload mix and success rate help to explain overall award structures. It should be clear, however, that in jury trials plaintiffs do not regularly win large amounts across all types of cases. Many depictions of jury activity that suggest this are naive at best, and cavalier at worst. Perceptions of change across time are also an arena receiving much attention, and the next section will focus on this issue.

Jury Verdict Activity across Time

This section takes a different approach and looks at jury activity in several jurisdictions across time. We have 21 years (1970–90) of jury verdict data for 19 sites: six counties in California, seven counties in Illinois, three counties in Missouri, two counties in Kansas, and Dallas County in Texas. Four time intervals (one of six and three of five years) are used to smooth out year-to-year variations in order to examine any underlying trends.

The first issue to examine is whether, as the reform literature would have us believe, there are ever-increasing numbers of jury verdicts in these sites. As shown in table 3.5, the number of jury verdicts in California sites generally decreased during the 21-year time period, and in some counties rather dramatically. One underlying reason for this decrease in activity in the California Superior Courts is probably not a decrease in "litigiousness," but rather the rising statutory ceiling over time in the dollar value of cases that could be heard in the lower courts. This procedural change had the effect of decreasing the number of cases in the Superior Courts and pushing the median awards up. In Illinois, we see another pattern. While the number of jury verdicts in Cook County decreased, it increased in the other six counties, possibly as a result of major population increases in these "collar counties" during this period. Johnson County, Kans., had a not insubstantial increase in jury activity which peaked in the 1981–85 period and then declined in the 1986–90 interval. Wyandotte County, Kans., also experienced a peak in jury activity during the same time period. Two of the three Missouri Counties, Clay and Platte, saw minor fluctuations among the four time intervals, while Jackson experienced a general, but modest,

Table 3.5 Number of Jury Verdicts and Success Rates for Various Jurisdictions (1970–90)

	1970–75		1976–80		1981–85		1986–90	
Jurisdiction	*N*	Win Rate (%)	*N*	Win Rate (%)	*N*	Win Rate (%)	*N*	Win Rate (%)
California								
Alameda	801	52.8	523	55.6	355	55.5	373	52.8
Fresno	201	51.7	131	61.8	157	50.3	112	50.9
Los Angeles	3498	55.0	2518	58.5	1446	55.4	1962	51.9
Sacramento	615	56.9	558	57.5	347	54.2	210	48.6
San Diego	682	51.0	592	58.6	410	48.5	496	47.0
San Francisco	1676	57.1	811	61.4	668	59.7	724	55.7
Illinois								
Cook	5479	50.7	3847	49.6	4082	59.0	3334	58.3
DuPage	338	49.4	311	49.2	436	55.5	420	57.9
Kane	208	52.9	198	51.0	171	60.8	229	59.0
Lake	305	58.7	251	47.4	295	60.7	320	58.8
McHenry	38	47.4	50	38.0	61	54.1	55	56.4
Will	57	38.6	125	55.2	290	61.7	181	66.3
Winnebago	27	55.6	184	56.0	148	59.5	85	61.2
Kansas								
Johnson	146	49.3	203	53.7	310	53.2	247	53.0
Wyandotte	233	46.8	210	56.7	286	61.2	220	64.5
Missouri								
Clay	103	50.5	115	58.3	104	59.6	112	65.2
Jackson	829	46.4	832	47.8	894	55.5	904	61.7
Platte	11	63.6	29	51.7	47	59.6	22	68.2
Texas								
Dallas	2003	43.8	1712	49.0	2112	47.0	1933	46.1

increase over time. Jury verdict activity in Dallas displayed no particular pattern across the four time intervals.

Table 3.5 also provides data on plaintiff success rates for the four time intervals—and those rates fluctuated. In the six California counties, there was a fluctuation from interval to interval, but there was little evidence of increasing plaintiff success rates over time. In fact, the general pattern in the six California counties was one of slight increase from 1970–75 to 1976–80 followed by decreases in the following two intervals. The same is true for Dallas County where the success rate did not reach 50% in any of the four intervals. By way of contrast, in the Illinois, Kansas, and Missouri sites, there does appear to be an increase in plaintiff success rates over time. However, rather than indicating a softening of jury sympathy toward plaintiffs, another factor—change in the respective states' negligence systems—may be producing this shift.

Illinois changed from a contributory system to a pure comparative system in mid-1981. Legislation was passed in 1986 which again altered the system, moving it from a pure to a modified comparative scheme. The figures showing changes in the success rates in the Illinois counties from interval to interval might suggest that not only did the change in negligence systems have an effect, but changing from a contributory system to some form of comparative system may have had a much greater effect than changing from one form of comparative negligence to another. The plaintiff success rates in the Missouri and Kansas sites reinforce this notion. Kansas has had a modified comparative system since 1974. Missouri had a contributory system through 1983 and then moved to a pure comparative negligence system. The timing of these changes is mirrored in the success rate pattern.

Table 3.6 presents detail for those 19 sites on the median awards in jury cases in which plaintiffs were successful. With the exception of activity in the California jurisdictions, the galloping escalation in award sizes the reform rhetoric has led us to expect is not evident. In some sites, such as DuPage, Kane, Lake, Will, and Winnebago counties in Illinois, median award figures for the most recent interval have dropped from their 1970–75 levels. In other jurisdictions there have been increases, but the dollar levels are not the stuff of legend. In the non-California sites that have experienced increases, those increases for the most part do not evidence the straight line, ever-increasing pattern the reform rhetoric would suggest.

The movement in median award size in California verdicts may, to some degree, be a result of statutory changes in the jurisdiction of the municipal and justice courts as noted earlier. Over the relevant time period, these lower courts experienced a shift in the dollar ceiling for matters they were eligible to hear. In 1979 the jurisdictional limit for civil cases in the lower courts was raised from $5,000 to $15,000. In 1986, the limit was increased to $25,000. While the Superior Courts had no mandatory floor on the amount in controversy for cases which they could hear, the concurrent jurisdiction of the lower courts certainly drew much of the volume of the low end away from the Superior Courts. This process was further enhanced by the statutory provisions for mandatory arbitration. In 1979, as the jurisdictional ceiling rose in the lower courts, Superior Courts (with 10 or more judges) were directed to submit civil actions that involved amounts in controversy of up to $15,000 to arbitration (those Superior Courts with fewer than 10 judges could to do at their discretion). In 1981 the ceiling on arbitration cases in the Los Angeles (and the San Bernardino) courts

Table 3.6 Median Awards in Various Jurisdictions 1970–90 (in 1990 $)

Jurisdiction	1970–75	1976–80	1981–85	1986–90
California				
Alameda	34,741	36,000	79,200	119,700
Fresno	38,935	50,936	111,350	184,086
Los Angeles	39,750	53,183	104,580	162,969
Sacramento	37,212	32,940	61,750	87,773
San Francisco	44,100	39,100	84,011	78,681
Illinois				
Cook	14,641	11,556	12,600	29,150
DuPage	23,590	14,310	15,506	21,500
Kane	44,285	20,670	30,190	25,300
Lake	31,200	17,280	29,475	27,672
McHenry	10,725	18,636	19,650	33,005
Will	43,616	20,352	20,747	25,438
Winnebago	58,800	14,698	14,400	28,945
Kansas				
Johnson	14,700	11,289	11,291	15,750
Wyandotte	14,700	11,826	15,120	16,963
Missouri				
Clay	18,700	11,800	19,198	28,932
Jackson	14,535	13,027	14,405	23,246
Platte	44,100	10,800	16,401	30,640
Texas				
Dallas	13,583	13,785	23,864	38,500

was raised to $25,000, and in 1986 mandatory arbitration was dictated for all civil matters involving matters in controversy under $25,000 in all Superior Courts. In 1988 the amount was raised to $50,000. The median awards in the Superior Courts for which we have data would therefore be expected to rise after 1979 and again in 1986; and indeed this appears to be the case, not necessarily as a function of an increase in proplaintiff jury response, but rather as a reaction to administrative changes in the system.

Of course, much of the rhetoric complains of increasing plaintiff success and jury award size not in cases generally, but in particular kinds of cases. Rather than address this issue here in a cursory fashion, we will address it in detail in subsequent chapters which look specifically at three areas: medical malpractice, products liability, and punitive damages.

Conclusion

The general picture we have presented is one quite different from the one portrayed by the reform rhetoric both in terms of substance and perspective. The rhetoric of reform speaks in broad sweeping terms when talking about juries and jury verdicts. The important stories, however, are in the details. The story we have outlined in this chapter is, first, one of variability and, second, one of complexity. Viewed in the aggregate, plaintiff win rates and awards varied from state to state and among counties within states. The mix of cases going to a jury trial also varied. Complexity arises from the fact that patterns for victory and award vary among different types of cases, making any sweeping generalizations about jury verdicts overall highly problematic.

Chapter 3 provides context. The next three chapters pursue the stories found in a more detailed analysis of jury verdicts involving medical malpractice, products liability, and punitive damages, respectively. The themes of variability and complexity will be carried through these discussions. The more detailed analyses will show that there are logical and orderly patterns in these arenas—patterns quite different than those portrayed in the reform rhetoric.

APPENDIX 3.1 Jury Verdict Reporters

Alaska: *Northwest Personal Injury Litigation Reports,* Jury Verdicts Northwest, Seattle, Wash.

Arizona: Maricopa County: *The Trial Reporter of Central and Northern Arizona,* Phoenix, Ariz.

California: All counties: *Jury Verdicts Weekly,* Santa Rosa, Cal.

Colorado: All counties: *Jury Verdict Reporter of Colorado,* Littleton, Colo.

Georgia: All counties: *The Georgia Trial Reporter,* JAS Publications, Crestwood, Ky.

Idaho: *Northwest Personal Injury Litigation Reports,* Jury Verdicts Northwest, Seattle, Wash.

Illinois: Cook County: *Cook County Jury Verdict Reporter,* Chicago, Ill.; all other counties: *Urban Ring Jury Verdict Reporter,* Chicago, Ill.

Kansas: All counties: *Greater Kansas City Jury Verdict Service,* Prairie Village, Kans.

Michigan: All counties: *Michigan Trial Reporter,* JAS Publications, Crestwood, Ky.

Missouri: Clay, Jackson, and Platte counties: *Greater Kansas City Jury Verdict Service,* Prairie Village, Kans.; Jefferson, St. Charles, St. Louis counties and St. Louis City: *Jury Verdict Reporting Service,* St. Louis, Mo.

Montana: *Montana Law Week,* Helena, Mont.

New York: All counties: *The New York East Jury Verdict Reporter,* Moran Publishing Co., Islip, N.Y.

Ohio: All counties: *Ohio Trial Reporter,* JAS Publications, Crestwood, Ky.

Oregon: All counties: *Oregon Litigation and Arbitration Reports,* Jury Verdicts Northwest, Seattle, Wash.

Texas: Bexar County: *Soele's Trial Report,* San Antonio, Tex.; Dallas County: *Trial Report Service,* Garland, Tex.; District 6 and District 9: *East Texas Trial Reports,* Scurry, Tex.; Harris County: *The Blue Sheet,* Houston Trial Reports, Stafford, Tex.; Travis County: *Travis County Jury Verdict Reporter,* Austin, Tex.

Washington: All counties: *Northwest Personal Injury Litigation Reports,* Jury Verdicts Northwest, Seattle, Wash.

CHAPTER FOUR

Medical Malpractice

"The role of the jury in medical negligence cases ranks among the most contentious issues in contemporary debate about the merits of the tort system."[1] So writes psychologist and law professor Neil Vidmar in the opening of a recent law review article on jury awards in medical malpractice. W. John Thomas opened his recent critical examination of the malpractice debate in much the same way by observing: "Medical malpractice is perhaps the most controversial tort in the American legal system."[2] Because the use of juries in the medical malpractice arena has attracted some of the most severe and sustained attacks from the tort reform movement, it is an appropriate starting point for our detailed exploration of jury verdicts. An excellent example of this assault can be found in a 1991 *Stanford Law & Policy Review* article touting the American Medical Association's (AMA) reform package.[3] In that article attorneys Carter Phillips and Paul Kalk asserted that:

> The inequities and inefficiencies of the tort system result in large measure from reliance on juries. Juries are ill-equipped to resolve technical disputes or evaluate expert testimony. Moreover, because juries are not required to articulate reasons for their decisions, jury decisions provide no clear guidance to practitioners, patients, or their attorneys for the resolution of future claims. Perhaps most critically, they also provide no guidance to future juries.[4]

The image of juries and the civil justice system found in the malpractice reform rhetoric is perhaps best summarized by the assessment of Dr. Otis Bowen, Secretary of Health and Human Services during the second Reagan administration: "It has become more a lottery than a rational system."[5] An AMA official characterized the situation in a similar way when he complained of the system's unpredictability and the vagaries of juries.[6] In his view, "there are wide, irrational variations in both findings of liability and the amount of damages for similar cases."[7] According to this official, "the evidence from all of the objective studies done on medical malpractice shows that it is an irrational system."[8] The benefits of the jury system may not justify the time and expense.[9]

Underlying these conclusions is the deep-seated notion that juries are overly sympathetic toward plaintiffs and biased against physicians and other "deep pocket" defendants.[10] Vidmar quotes an AMA report as saying that "what makes the damage awards in professional liability lawsuits particularly disconcerting is the fact that *identical* injuries will command much higher recoveries in malpractice cases than in other tort suits."[11] He also quotes a study by the North Carolina Hospital Association as concluding: "Today, juries often make awards regardless of the 'fault' of anyone—out of sympathy for an injured person. . . . Too often, juries appear to award on [the] basis of emotion as opposed to facts and/or realistic evaluation of case circumstances."[12] These sentiments are no different than those of Jerome Frank's in the 1930s noted at the beginning of chapter 1.[13]

In the reform rhetoric, there is a "crisis" in the medical malpractice arena, and the verdicts and decisions of juries are crucial indicators of this crisis. Of course, other indicators are used, such as the increases in malpractice insurance premiums, but verdicts are especially symbolic. They are not only an indicator of the crisis, but also a cause of the various negative consequences that are used to describe the nature and seriousness of the crisis. Verdicts are used to link real or alleged problems in the cost and availability of health care to the legal system. Without an "explosion" of litigation and "skyrocketing" jury awards, the argument for reform falls flat. Verdicts, in short, show that the legal system no longer has any semblance of fairness and rationality, and so it—rather than the insurance system or the health care system—is in need of reform.

In this chapter, our guide will be the idea outlined in the conclusion to chapter 2, that analyzing the rhetoric of reform entails two tasks: first, examining the political character of its portrayal and the devices used to present it as one people will accept as a problem requiring immediate governmental action; and, second, critically examining its key claims by comparing them to the available empirical evidence. The first part of this chapter briefly explores the rhetoric of reform regarding medical malpractice and juries, and the legislative changes that have been made. The second and third parts critically examine the rhetoric's key claims. Utilizing the disputing pyramid idea introduced in chapter 3, the second part discusses the empirical evidence that can be used to outline the medical malpractice pyramid as a contrast to the rhetoric's portrayal. The third part continues this by presenting evidence from our own research on jury verdicts. It contains a cross-sectional examination of verdicts using data for the years 1988–90 as was done in chapter 3 as well as a longitudinal analysis using data from a smaller number of sites for the period 1970–90.

"More a Lottery than a Rational System": Rhetoric and Context

Strategic Representation

The image of juries and the civil justice system found in the rhetoric of malpractice reform is dramatic albeit timeworn. Typically, it is couched in terms of a crisis—crisis being, perhaps, the key metaphor in this arena—and it is built around a clear storyline of continual societal decline. The worsening contemporary situation is compared, implicitly or explicitly, to a better past. For instance, in his address to the 52nd Annual Meeting of the Central Association of Obstetricians and Gynecologists in 1984, Dr. Kenneth Vander Kolk took as his theme the title of the Peggy Lee song, "Is That All There Is?" He told his colleagues that "we practice in a cage of sorts, the bars of which are made from an alloy of legal scrutiny, legal harassment, legal endeavors, some legal expertise, and a good deal of legal omnipotence."[14] Physicians, he claimed, "are an easy prey for the hustling attorney who initiates a lawsuit."[15] Using 1954 as a point of comparison, Vander Kolk bemoaned the loss of innocence of an earlier time when an obstetrician-gynecologist's cost of business (including liability insurance) was dramatically lower. "There was practically no malpractice. There was no Medicaid, no Medicare, no health maintenance organizations, no preferred provider organizations, no diagnosis-related groups, and most patients paid in cash. These were the good old days."[16] In Vander Kolk's view, "no longer can anything less than a perfect result in patient care be considered to be act of God, as it was in 1954."[17]

We see in Vander Kolk's lament a story of decline from a better world for physicians, particularly those working in the field of obstetrics/gynecology (ob/gyn). The story's underlying theme is one of a loss of control and income in the face of an increasing amount of regulation and demand for outside accountability. Malpractice is a part of this predicament. The story of decline is also told—less figuratively—in reports of the increasing numbers of malpractice claims and lawsuits, the higher awards, and increasing malpractice insurance premiums. For instance, the Reagan administration's *Tort Policy Working Group Report* highlights changes in the size of the average malpractice jury award in a dramatic graph.[18] Using the graph to characterize the growth of awards as "explosive," the *Report* said that the average award "increased from $220,018 in 1975 to $1,017,716 in 1985, a 363% increase."[19] The *Report* also pointed to sharp increases in the number of malpractice insurance claims and lawsuits.[20] As a result, then Secretary of Health and Human Services Bowen noted in an address before an Institute of Medicine symposium that malpractice insurance premiums "skyrocketed."[21] In the middle to late 1980s, similar reports of dramatic increases in malpractice claims, lawsuits, awards, and insurance premiums appeared in the media, trade journals, and professional literatures.

What makes reports of such increases a part of the story of decline is their use in the political arena as evidence of a change in the civil justice system that has had serious and detrimental effects on the cost, availability, and quality of medical care. These consequences make the story work since they describe a "crisis" affecting everyone, not just physicians. More malpractice claims and lawsuits along with higher rates of plaintiff victory and higher awards have made malpractice insurance more expensive and less available. This is the first important causal connection made in the definition of this situation as a problem (and one that has been disputed since the crisis of the 1970s).[22] The malpractice insurance situation in turn affects the practice of medicine itself and the availability of medical services—the second important causal link (also disputed since the crisis of the 1970s).[23] The practice of medicine is affected, as the story is most often told, by the increasing amount of defensive medicine practiced which then drives up the cost of medical care. The availability and adequacy of medical care are also affected by increased cost as doctors limit their practices or leave certain specialties or do not train in them in the first place because of the fear of liability.

In addition to the story of decline, Vander Kolk's remarks point to another important aspect of the reform rhetoric—the focus on obstetrics/gynecology. When specific examples have been utilized in illustrating the crisis they are, more often than not, ones involving the availability of ob/gyn services. One rarely hears, for instance, about a crisis in American society engendered by problems in the availability of services by radiologists or orthopedic surgeons. The most vivid accounts of consequences tell of women in different parts of the country threatened with the loss of ob/gyn services or already without them. For instance, the 1986 *Time* magazine story noted in chapter 2 began with the horror story of women living on the island of Molokai in Hawaii who were completely without obstetrical services and had to travel to another island for the delivery of their babies. "The five Molokai doctors who once delivered babies have stopped doing so because malpractice insurance would cost them more than the total of any obstetrical fees they could hope to collect."[24]

Similar accounts appeared throughout the middle 1980s and into the early 1990s,[25] and the specter of an utter lack of obstetrical services has been a favorite topic of the reformers' public relations campaigns. It was the topic of one of the first advertisements in the Insurance Information Institute's 1986 campaign, "We All Pay the Price."[26] Entitled "The Lawsuit Crisis Is Bad for Babies," the advertisement shows someone holding an infant and says: "A medical survey shows one out of every nine obstetricians in America has stopped delivering babies. Expectant mothers have had to find new doctors. In some rural areas, women have had to travel elsewhere to give birth. How did this happen? It's part of the price of the lawsuit crisis."[27] On the very first page of his book *Liability*, Peter Huber claimed that "you cannot deliver a baby with medical assistance in Monroe County, Alabama" because of the "tort tax."[28] Walter Olson, in *The Litigation Explosion*, wrote that because of "the bad-baby litigation industry . . . the world of obstetrics and newborn care was devastated. Thousands of doctors, especially family doctors in rural areas, stopped delivering babies; by common estimates one-fifth of those in the field departed over a span of a few years."[29]

As a part of strategic representation with regard to malpractice, focusing on ob/gyn in telling a story of decline has special advantages. Because of the nature and severity of the injuries in some ob/gyn matters—the so-called "bad baby" cases—settlements and awards can be very high compared to those generated in other fields. Additionally, insurance premiums tend to be higher for ob/gyn practitioners. Consequently, if one wants to find "skyrocketing" premiums and "explosive growth" in awards, it is possible to do so in this arena. This is also a medical field in which there has long been evidence that identifiable parts of the population—in particular, the rural and urban poor—receive inadequate levels of care or no care at all.[30] This is traditionally discussed in terms of public health concerns about prenatal care, low-birth-weight babies, preventable complications of pregnancy and delivery, and infant mortality.

Additionally, if viewed with the idea of the politics of passion in mind, focusing on maternity and babies makes a story of decline all the more compelling. Taking, for instance, "The Lawsuit Crisis Is Bad for Babies" advertisement, the image presented—a picture of someone holding a newborn—appeals to the deepest emotional and almost instinctive levels. Who can be more innocent and helpless than a newborn, especially if the child is poor? The image almost defines the essence of innocence and helplessness. Those who harm children—especially infants—are seen as the epitome of callousness, if not outright evil. Innocence at risk demands our attention and action so that the evil at hand can be eradicated. There is great political advantage, then, in making malpractice reform a solution to long standing public health problems related to the ob/gyn field.

What is problematic about this characterization is not the issue of whether there are questions about the availability and adequacy of obstetrical care in some situations; but rather, whether the causes have been appropriately identified. The causal connection between problems in the availability of obstetrical services for some groups of women and what is allegedly occurring in the legal system is one made by assertion. The claim is made as if it were direct and obvious, and it is perhaps best seen in terms of F. G. Bailey's idea of the rhetoric of assertion as described in chapter 2. Perhaps the most symbolically and politically important attempt to make this causal connection is found in the efforts of the Institute of Medicine (IOM) in the late 1980s and its Committee to Study Medical Professional Liability and the Delivery of Obstetrical Care.[31]

The IOM along with the National Academy of Engineering and the National Research Council operates under the charter granted to the National Academy of Sciences by the Congress of the United States. It speaks with the authority of the federal government and with the prestige, certainty, and neutrality of science—characteristics quite important from the perspective of the politics of ideas. It is one thing for Dr. Vander Kolk to complain about the malpractice crisis and quite another for the IOM to define it as a major policy problem. Ideas framed in scientific or expert terms are precisely the kinds of ideas that have become a central part of the policy process, according to David Ricci. Ours is an era, he argues, in which expertise (or at least the appearance of expertise) has come to play an important role in the political process—an era in which there is uncertainty about traditional values and in which older party structures and patterns of voting behavior have eroded.[32]

The IOM committee focused on ob/gyn and the effects of the medical liability problem on the delivery of care and the policy implications of these effects.[33] There were two major reasons for this focus. First, even though there was a general concern with how professional liability issues might be affecting patterns of health care delivery and access to care, the ob/gyn situation was especially acute. Said the committee: "Preliminary evidence available to the committee indicated that obstetrical providers, compared with colleagues in most other specialties, appeared to be affected disproportionately."[34] Indeed, the committee described the liability problem—of increasing claims, insurance premiums, and so on—as being "most acute in obstetrics."[35] In short, the committee's focus on obstetrics was a result of this arena's distinction of supposedly being the worst case scenario. The second reason for the committee's focus on ob/gyn, interestingly, was that "the committee believed from the very beginning that the issues posed by professional liability in obstetrics in some ways could be representative of the issues posed by professional liability concerns to the health care system as a whole."[36] The worst case scenario, then, is also used to define what is typical or generally true. While this is a contradiction, there is much to be gained politically if the worst case scenario becomes accepted as a representative example.

As a part of its task, the committee commissioned a number of papers to explore the professional liability issue, sponsored three surveys, and "reviewed more than 50 surveys bearing on the medical malpractice problem in obstetrics."[37] Over one-half of these surveys were done by medical societies of their own members.[38] The committee also "held an interdisciplinary research symposium on June 20, 1988, with Secretary of Health and Human Services Otis R. Bowen, M.D., as the keynote speaker."[39] His address provided a political context for the symposium and for the two-volume report subsequently published by IOM. Bowen framed his remarks by opening with the idea of obstetrics being the worst case scenario—the arena hardest hit by malpractice claims with "skyrocketing premium costs" and where "verdicts or settlements for obstetrical cases can be in the million-dollar range, a figure that does not even count the hefty legal costs involved."[40] Within this framework—one accepted as obviously true—Bowen focused on his agency's ongoing concern with maternal care and infant mortality rates. Malpractice liability was a topic of interest for him because it is allegedly one of the problems that "stand in the way of the special initiative the HHS has under way to drive down infant mortality rates in this country. This initiative was undertaken because the steady decline in the nation's infant mortality rate showed signs of slowing down."[41] The causal message, then, is clear: the malpractice system is among those factors directly causing higher infant mortality rates, and so demands immediate governmental attention.

Generally speaking, Bowen presented the reform rhetoric's characterization of the malpractice system as an empirical certainty not requiring substantiation, and in so doing reflected the Reagan administration's perspective as well.[42] Presenting this partisan position as a part of an ostensibly academic symposium sponsored by the IOM gives it a special authority—the partisan portrayal gains the prestige, certainty, and neutrality of science. In effect, the reform rhetoric/Reagan administration's characterization is transformed. It is no longer a partisan viewpoint over which there can be disagreement in the political arena. We have no choice but to accept the portrayal because it is the judgment of the experts that it is a true one. Bowen is appropriating the authority of science and expertise to cut off debate. To question the proffered characterization would amount to questioning the IOM—indeed, to questioning science and technical expertise. As expressed in Bailey's idea of the rhetoric of assertion, "to proclaim something a fact is to tell the audience that they have no alternative other than to give their assent, on pain of being excluded as crazy people."[43]

The IOM committee followed Bowen's lead in its "Summary of Conclusions and Recommendations." Most of its remarks were devoted to the availability and adequacy of obstetrical care for women who are poor and/or living in rural areas, and to malpractice insurance for those providing obstetrical services to these individuals. The reform rhetoric's portrayal of juries and the civil justice system was simply accepted as a fact. The committee said, "in approaching the medical malpractice issue the committee was keenly aware that the U.S. civil litigation system generally has undergone explosive growth in certain kinds of tort liability in recent years. This growth has attracted wide attention because of dramatic, often breathtaking, jury awards and settlements."[44] The veracity of the causal connection to what has supposedly been happening in the legal system and the committee's focus were, of course, just assumed. All that was necessary were some illustrations.

The focus on the poor and/or rural residents seems to be a result of the fact that there was a preexisting literature on the problems of delivering medical care to these communities—all of which was independent of and predated the malpractice debate.[45] There is apparently no general literature specifically addressing problems in the delivery of obstetrical care per se. In short, the more specific problems of care for the poor and those living in rural areas and their literatures were appropriated for an entirely different policy purpose—to promote change in the civil justice system by offering malpractice reform as a solution for those problems.

One of the key devices used in the committee's summary to illustrate this causal connection was a graph taken from one of the papers commissioned by the committee.[46] This graph depicts two bars side by side, one indicating an estimate of almost 17,000 physicians practicing obstetrics in rural areas and the other showing an estimate of about 15,500. The purpose of this graph is not only to show changes over time—moving from the first bar to the second—but more importantly to identify the cause of what are described as changes with serious negative consequences. No specific timeline is indicated on the graph's x-axis; what is used instead is a before and after chronology: under the left-hand-side bar is the descriptor "Prior to Malpractice Crisis," and under the bar of lower magnitude is the label "Current." In this one neat picture, we can clearly see the effect and its sole cause.[47] The single causal element in this simple chronology is obvious in the descriptors used—the malpractice crisis. No more need be said or shown.

The IOM committee concluded that the tort system did not and could not adequately fulfill the goals of reasonable deterrence and appropriate compensation. Commenting on the effects of earlier reform efforts following the crisis of the 1970s, the committee noted that "the limited effectiveness of tort reform can be perceived from the data presented in . . . this report on the continuing problems of access to and delivery of health care generated by the medical malpractice problem." Consequently, the committee's recommended long-term solutions rejected further reform of the existing tort system, and argued instead for alternatives to that system. The alternative perspective—that limited effectiveness is a consequence of faulty assumptions about the legal system and the causal connections to medical care—was not considered.[48]

The report of the Institute of Medicine's committee is symbolically important from the perspective of the politics of ideas. It purports to provide neutral, expert, scientific proof for a crisis in the ob/gyn area whose cause is directly traced to the malpractice system. It elevates anecdotes and horror stories to the level of expert analysis and explanation. The characterization of malpractice and its consequences proffered by the most vocal and partisan reform advocates—the physicians' organizations—is presented as an empirical reality backed up by quantitative analysis that carries the prestige and authority of the Institute of Medicine and the National Academy of Sciences. In reality, however, the IOM report merely echoed the rhetorical claims of the reform advocates and the Reagan and Bush administrations. It never actually demonstrates the link between the problems in the ob/gyn arena and the malpractice system. Even though the problems facing women who are poor and/or live in rural have enormous emotional appeal, there is nothing beyond assertion that their predicament is in any way typical for the population of potential health care recipients or that it is inexorably tied to the workings of the tort system. Rather than an informed, methodologically sound empirical investigation, the committee's report is an attempt to attach a favored set of solutions to a preexisting set of problems.

Although images like these regarding medical malpractice may be powerful and the superficial persuasiveness of the underlying causal theory attractive, the accuracy of such claims has been challenged. Some of the criticism, of course, has come from those political interests opposed to reform. Serious questions have also been raised by academic researchers not tied to either side in the political debate, and the findings of these researchers will appear throughout the remainder of this chapter.[49] It is important to note that these commentators are not necessarily saying the malpractice system is flawless. Rather, they present a very different picture, one based on careful empirical research, which may point to a different set of problems. For instance, the authors of the Harvard Malpractice Study concluded that "our analysis of malpractice litigation data demonstrates that the problem is not a litigation surplus, but a litigation deficit. The gap between torts occurring in American hospitals and tort suits being filed in American courts is far greater than has ever been supposed."[50]

The authors of the Harvard study also pointed out another important characteristic of the debate over malpractice that must be kept in mind—that the debate is highly politicized. They said that it has been "well supplied with heated moralizing about medical malpractice, often conducted from starkly opposed perspectives and usually based on anecdotal evidence."[51] These divisions are found not just among the political combatants but also "in the scholarly literature, and not only with respect to medical accidents but also respecting the broader field of personal injuries from consumer products, motor vehicles, the workplace, and other sources."[52] W. John Thomas raised essentially the same idea in his critical examination of the malpractice debate in the *Temple Law Review*. His main point "is that adversarial dialogue between physicians and lawyers, rather than objective data, has informed the political and legislative debate over medical malpractice."[53] He argues that "neither physicians nor lawyers . . . have provided much data supporting or denying the existence of a 'malpractice crisis.' . . .

Rather, the medical and legal professional organizations have engaged in a long-term, heated debate, each locating the 'cause' of the crisis in the 'adversarial' professional community."[54] This adversarial dialogue and its rhetoric—the politics of ideas and the clash over which view of the world will govern policy—make it difficult to know what is happening in the malpractice system, especially when partisanship reaches into the scholarly literature.[55]

The character and tone of the reform rhetoric in the medical malpractice arena, interestingly, is not something new or unique to the contemporary debate. Kenneth Allen DeVille's book *Medical Malpractice in Nineteenth Century America* reports on a similar rhetoric. Allen opens one of his chapters with the following:

> In 1844, a writer for the *Boston Medical and Surgical Journal* warned that qualified physicians were "constantly liable to vexatious suits instituted by ignorant and unprincipled persons." In 1853, the *Western Journal of Medical and Physical Sciences* reported that malpractice suits "occur almost every month in the year and everywhere in our country." . . . As early as the 1840s, the frequency of suits in some parts of the country had filled doctors with a mixture of anger, panic, and confusion. The suits and the alarm increased as the decades passed. Frank Hamilton, a New York physician, claimed that between 1833 and 1856 "suits for malpractice were so frequent in the Northern states" that many men "abandoned the practice of surgery, leaving it to those who, with less skill and experience, had less reputation and property to lose. By 1860 John Elwell, a physician and a lawyer who wrote a book on the subject, could claim that "(t)here can hardly be found a place in the country where the oldest physicians in it have not, at some periods in their lives, been actually sued or annoyingly threatened."[56]

These remarks from DeVille's book should give us pause in looking at the current "crisis" and the rhetoric of reform. Many of the major themes found in the rhetoric have, it appears, been heard before—the fear and aggravation of malpractice suits, seen as frivolous; the idea of overlitigiousness in this area; the idea that the matter is so bad that nearly every physician has been the victim of such suits; and even the idea that the situation is driving physicians out of the business thereby threatening the availability and adequacy of health care services.

An Overview of Reforms

Through the 1970s and 1980s virtually every state enacted or at least debated some form of medical malpractice reform legislation, and much of that reform reflects the rhetoric's strategic representation. Writing in 1978—at the end of the first crisis in the middle 1970s—Sylvia Law and Steven Polan noted that "the most popular legislative response to the malpractice crisis has been to change the legal standards defining malpractice. These changes are premised on an assumption that it has become significantly easier for patients to prove medical malpractice, and that these changes in legal standards have had a significant impact on malpractice premiums."[57] Randall Bovbjerg, writing in 1989 at the end of the second crisis, concluded, in a similar vein, that both the crisis of the 1970s and the crisis of the 1980s were crises of insurance availability and affordability, "and most of the impetus for tort reform comes from problems in the insurance markets."[58] There were also other motivations, he said, such as a growing sense of dissatisfaction with the tort system generally or concern with the quality of health care, but insurance for physicians has been the primary one.[59]

In reviewing the malpractice reforms of the 1970s and 1980s, Bovbjerg saw four main issues underlying them. These issues, in turn, were portrayed as the causes of the insurance problems physicians faced—and they are a familiar part of the rhetoric of reform. First, the tort system was encouraging too many lawsuits because the law had become overly favorable to plaintiffs. Second, many of these suits were frivolous, and others took far too long to resolve.[60] Third, reformers complained about the competency of lay jurors and their sympathy for plaintiffs, a situation producing results that were seen as haphazard—like a game of chance or a lottery.[61] Finally, the system took too long and cost too much. Underlying the cost issue was the concern with contingency fees on the plaintiff side because "contingency fee arrangements can result in very large awards that seem disproportionate to the amount of effort involved."[62]

In terms of the malpractice reforms themselves, Bovbjerg categorized them into three broad categories. The first two were not aimed directly at the tort system itself. One category dealt directly with insurance. These measures were designed to maintain availability of adequate and affordable malpractice insurance and included such elements as the formation of insurance underwriting pools that existed outside of the commercial insurance markets, the imposition of limits on insurance cancellation, the identification of mandates for coverage, and the creation of special state-run patient compensation funds to handle the very large claims.[63] The other set of reforms not directly focused on the tort system were aimed at medical quality and dealt with such issues as peer review of health care providers, increased powers for disciplinary boards, reporting requirements on malpractice claims and disciplinary actions, and requirements for continuing medical education.[64]

The largest area of reform, however, concerned the civil justice system itself and the four issues noted above. Bovbjerg subdivided these reforms into four major groups based on the apparent legislative intent, and their reflection of the reform rhetoric's strategic representation is obvious. The first group addressed the issue of too many malpractice claims and lawsuits, and included the introduction of arbitration panels to settle matters before they reached a formal trial—the idea being that such panels would be less formal, less expensive, and quicker.[65] Limitations on plaintiff attorneys' fees were common, "since many medical observers blamed excessive contingency fees for encouraging unwarranted lawsuits and for depriving injured patients of a reasonable share of awards."[66] Most of the reform provisions dealing with contingency fees created a sliding scale for fees graduated by the size of the award.[67] There is no evidence of any legislation limiting the fees of defense attorneys. Some states enacted requirements for fee shifting in frivolous or fraudulent claims, and some mandated certificates of merit that required plaintiffs' attorneys to show that their suit was not frivolous. Related were pretrial screening panels to weed out nonmeritorious cases. Finally, in this first group of reforms, almost all of the states enacting such legislation shortened their statutes of limitations defining the amount of time an injured party has to bring suit after an injury.[68]

The second group of reforms addressed the size of awards—high awards being the result of jury bias, incompetence, and/or sympathy for the plaintiff. They included such elements as placing restrictions on *ad damnum* clauses or the amount of money sought in the initial complaint, with most simply restricting the amount to that necessary to meet jurisdictional requirement. "Their goal was two-fold: to limit the publicity obtainable by a malpractice claimant even before any evidence was presented and to limit potential or actual jury members' hearing about unsubstantiated general dollar amounts."[69] According to Bovbjerg, caps on awards "were probably the most significant reform in this area."[70] Most measures placed limits on noneconomic damages such as "pain and suffering" and ranged from \$250,000 to \$1 million.[71] Indiana took a different, more draconian approach and placed a \$500,000 cap on *all* damages.[72] Other reform measures mandated an offset against the award for collateral sources of compensation such as the injured party's own insurance or disability coverage. Modifications were made in the rules pertaining to joint and several liability that made one defendant—no matter what the degree of his/her negligence—financially responsible for the damages against any other defendant who could not pay. Limits were also placed on punitive damages, or they were prohibited altogether. Finally, periodic payments or structured awards were allowed in place of a single, lump-sum payment of the award.[73]

The third group of reforms dealt with reducing the plaintiff's chance of winning—the assumption being that the law had become too favorable to plaintiffs. Most of these measures sought to restrict the ability to sue and included a tightening of the doctrine of informed consent and the requirements for expert witnesses. Related to the issue of expert witnesses, some states also reasserted the traditional professional standard of care idea for judging negligence (rather than some lay standard). A fourth group of reforms was aimed at the functioning and cost of the judicial process in order to make it more timely and less expensive. Included were a variety of measures intended to encourage early settlement negotiations such as notice of intent to sue requirements, pretrial conferences, and mediation.[74]

The Question of Success

Not all of these reforms survived scrutiny in the state courts, and others were later repealed or allowed to expire.[75] The question of the success or effectiveness of those that have survived remains an open and important one. It has led some—like the IOM committee and the American Medical Association—to argue that more fundamental changes are needed because of the limited effectiveness of enacted reforms. Consequently, it is worth examining the effectiveness question since it has become an important part of the reform rhetoric. While not large, there is an empirical literature evaluating at least the reforms of the 1970s, and it finds few of the expected or promised effects. There have been, to our knowledge, no analyses of the effect of enacted reforms on the availability of ob/gyn services. The most widely cited evaluations of enacted reforms are aggregate, secondary statistical analyses of large data sets, and they focus on the civil justice–related reforms rather than those related to insurance or medical quality. For the most part, these studies have evaluated the success of enacted reforms by statistically analyzing their effects on patterns and changes in closed malpractice insurance claims.[76] Among them, the work of Patricia Danzon and of Frank Sloan are regularly used by reformers, and we will concentrate on them—first, summarizing their main findings, and, second, examining them as a part of the politics of idea and strategic representation.

Perhaps the most widely cited and influential studies are a series of analyses done by Danzon.[77] She found a variety of effects from the reforms—some intended and others perhaps not. For instance, in a 1985 book she stated that her statistical analyses of two nationwide data sets covering malpractice insurance claims closed in 1974 and in 1976 showed that reforms enacted in the middle 1970s designed to reduce large awards worked as intended.[78] However, the regulation of contingency fees for plaintiffs' attorneys, in her view, appears to have had some unintended consequences. Instead of simply reducing the fee and thereby increasing the net recovery for the claimant, these regulations "appear to have discouraged attorneys' efforts and hence have resulted in lower settlements, fewer cases litigated to verdict, and more cases dropped without payment."[79] Of course, for reformers these may be precisely the effects desired.

In a subsequent study, Danzon sought to evaluate the effects over time of the middle 1970s reforms using nationwide data for the years 1975 to 1984. Specifically, she analyzed state-level data on the frequency of malpractice claims and the size of payments.[80] She reported that her statistical analysis showed that both shortening statutes of limitation and allowing collateral source offsets reduced claim frequency; no other reform had such an effect. The presence of screening panels apparently had no systematic effect on claim frequency, but Danzon suggested that these panels may actually *encourage* more claim filings by reducing the claimants' costs. Binding arbitration, she found, appeared to increase the frequency of claims filed and of claims settled with a payment.[81] With regard to the size of payments for successful claims, she said that caps on awards reduced average payments to claimants as did collateral source offsets and arbitration.[82] Her analysis found no evidence that screening panels or limits on contingent fees reduced the overall size of payments.[83] Taken on their face, then, Danzon's analyses show a mixed set of effects on claim frequency and size. More importantly perhaps, she found that other factors having nothing to do with civil justice reforms, especially the degree of urbanization within a state, have as great or even greater effects on claim frequency and size than the specific reform measures.[84]

A 1989 study of the middle 1970s reforms by Sloan and colleagues also showed a mixed set of results. They statistically analyzed the effects of 21 different reforms on the probability of a claim being paid, the size of the payment, insurance company costs (primarily defense attorneys' fees) plus the payment, the number of months between the injury and the claim filing, and the number of years between claim filing and closure.[85] Their data for this analysis involved random samples of closed claims for 1975, 1976, 1977, and 1984 taken from two older studies.[86]

Sloan and his colleagues found only one significant relationship between any of the reforms and the probability of a claim being paid.[87] There was a *higher* chance of payment where a maximum time limit was placed on the statute of limitations. Five reforms—two involving pretrial screening, two involving award caps, and one involving cost shifting for frivolous claims—had significant relationships with the size of the claim payment. Award caps, cost shifting, and provisions allowing the results of pretrial screening to be admitted in a subsequent trial were all associated with lower payments—the intended relationship. Mandatory pretrial screening provisions were associated with higher payments.[88] Seven reforms had significant relationships with payment plus costs. Six were related to lower amounts of payments plus costs: provisions for arbitration agreements, cost shifting, caps on noneconomics awards, caps on total awards, collateral source offset, and the existence of joint underwriting associations to provide insurance for physicians. Again, mandatory pretrial screening provisions were associated with higher amounts for payment plus costs.[89]

Like Danzon, Sloan and his colleagues found that a variety of nonlegal factors were also very important in explaining the patterns and changes in their dependent variables. Where Danzon focused more on structural matters (i.e., urbanization, number of lawyers, number of physicians, etc.) in the aggregate (state-level data), Sloan and his colleagues were interested in characteristics of the claimant (sex and age), characteristics of the claim (where injury occurred, type of injury, and severity of injury), and the claimant's costs and losses. While the Sloan findings are too numerous to do justice to here, some are particularly noteworthy. Although only one tort reform had a significant relationship to the probability that a claim would be closed with a payment (and that one unintended), 21 nonreform items did. For instance, the most severe injuries were more likely to be closed with a payment as were injuries occurring in a doctor's office, misdiagnosis claims, ob/gyn claims, surgery claims, anesthesia claims, drug-related claims, monitoring-related claims, and blood-related claims. Males and claimants under the age of one year were less likely to receive an award as were those alleging only an emotional injury. Additionally, while claims closed in 1984 were less likely to receive a payment, these claims were significantly associated with higher payments, higher payments plus costs, longer times from injury to filing, and longer times from filing to closing.

Higher payments were significantly related to claimants in the 21–49 and 50–64 year-old age groups. Higher payments were also aligned with misdiagnosis claims, ob/gyn claims, surgery claims, blood-related claims, the most serious permanent injuries, higher medical expenses, and higher anticipated wage loss. Lower payments were significantly related to injuries occurring in a doctor's office and to less serious injuries.[90]

The reform rhetoric of the middle 1980s and the early 1990s argues that earlier malpractice reforms were insufficient, and as a consequence more drastic changes are needed. The academic evaluations we have just described are used in making this argument,[91] and so they too must be seen as an important part of the politics of ideas. While such studies can be criticized on technical grounds (i.e., the nature of the data used, the representativeness of the data, the measures and statistical techniques used, the years covered, etc.),[92] more can be learned from looking at them from the perspective of the politics of ideas. In the political battle over which image of juries and the civil justice system will govern policy, the message found in studies like these is the only thing of importance. Technical or methodological problems in the studies are rarely relevant.[93]

One of the major traits of studies like these that make them so useful in the political debate is their "scientific" character. This results from the fact that the studies have been done by experts (researchers with positions at major universities and/or institutes) rather than obvious partisans, and from the fact that the studies use large data sets, sophisticated statistical techniques, and the language of quantitative analysis rather than opinion or supposition. The "scientific" character of these studies allows them to be used as neutral and authoritative evidence. They are, however, something less, and this calls the veracity of their message into question. Two aspects of the studies indicate this—their operative definition of policy success and the way in which the findings regarding nonlegal factors were handled.

Viewed from the perspective of the politics of ideas, the choice of indicators or phenomena for use in defining "success" take on a special importance. Choosing an indicator for and a definition of success is not a simple, straightforward matter in such a highly politicized area of public and policy debate like this one. Writing in *Law, Medicine and Health Care*, lawyer and public health specialist Marshall Kapp noted that there are very real difficulties in defining what works in this arena—and it is politics that underlies these difficulties.[94] He said that "different constituencies, coming at this subject from different perspectives and with different interests, likely would list different indicators of 'solving' the widely perceived patient injury/liability claims crisis, and certainly would prioritize these indicia differently. . . . [P]olitical judgments always lie behind the choice of what to measure, and how to make and interpret the measurements."[95]

Choosing an indicator of success means, in practice, choosing a definition of *the* problem and a causal theory to explain it. The studies we have discussed see the most immediate problem as one involving malpractice claims, and they see legislative enactments as efforts to remedy this problem. They looked at changes in malpractice insurance claims (whether frequency, award size, etc., decreased) using indicators that presume the reform rhetoric's definition of the problem—too many claims, a plaintiff-oriented process, increasingly higher awards, and increasing costs and delay. These are the phenomena supposedly driving malpractice insurance premiums up and/or limiting the availability of insurance altogether. (In another study, Sloan analyzed the effects of reforms on insurance premiums.)[96] The rhetoric's characterization was accepted uncritically by the evaluation studies as was its causal theory. The policy problem for these studies has little or nothing to do with the nature of patient injuries,[97] the quality of health care, or the adequacy of compensation for injured patients.[98] Neutrality becomes problematic when the research is driven by the reform rhetoric's perspective, as does the message of these studies.

Even though Danzon and Sloan and his colleagues used statistical techniques that allowed them to assign number values for measuring the degree of success of enacted reforms, there are still problems in interpretation. Sloan and his colleagues, for instance, reported that "reducing the basic statute of limitations by a year lowered the mean delay [from injury] to filing by one-third of month."[99] Danzon reported that allowing collateral source offsets reduced awards by between 11% and 18%.[100] Interpreting or giving meaning to such apparently precise measures is, however, something of an open process. Just how much "success" is enough for a given reform to be judged effective? Do we have enough empirical evidence—beyond a statistical relationship—to confidently link changes in the law to changes or the lack of changes in the complex processes involved in the initiation and handling of malpractice claims? Can we actually explain the dynamics underlying such statistical relationships?

Problems of interpretation are also evident in the handling of nonlegal factors in the evaluation studies. The treatment of these factors is telling from the perspective of the politics of ideas because on their face they would lead one to look at alternatives to the reform rhetoric's perspective. What is important is what is missing—any substantive discussion of the findings with regard to nonlegal factors. Danzon, for example, found urbanization to be the most important variable in her 1985 analysis of the frequency of claims and the size of awards—far more important than legal factors. While this was noted, there was no attempt to pursue the implications of this finding or offer an explanation. She simply noted that "attempts to identify more precisely the characteristics of urban environments that influence claim frequency and severity were unsuccessful."[101] Her 1986 analysis, which again found urbanization the most important variable, did not pursue the matter either. Instead, that analysis focused on the precise, even though not substantial, effects of legal reforms.

Sloan and his colleagues found only one significant statistical relationship (an unintended one) between legal variables and the probability of a claim being closed with a payment to the injured patient. A number of significant relationships were found between nonlegal variables and the probability of payment. While there were some significant relationships between legal variables and the size of payment, the greatest effects were found with nonlegal variables—especially those dealing with the severity of injury. Yet, virtually no discussion of these findings was offered. There was a cursory discussion in three rather terse paragraphs introduced with the cryptic claim that "in general, the coefficients on the non-tort explanatory variables are plausible and lend considerable credibility to our findings on the tort variables."[102] The findings themselves were relegated to an appendix as if to say that the findings regarding different injuries, claimants, and types of medical situations are only of marginal importance.[103]

The findings regarding nonlegal factors are full of implications and questions begging for answers. If structural or socioeconomic factors are the most important ones for explaining what happens with malpractice claims in the aggregate, then there may be a need to rethink the idea of a generalized, nationwide problem. There would also be a need to explore the links between certain socioeconomic characteristics and patterns in the malpractice system. What is it about certain types of places or jurisdictions that leads to greater claim frequency and higher awards? Pursuing such a question, however, may mean having to look beyond the reform rhetoric's portrayal and causal theory. Possibly, legal reforms may make little difference not because they are inadequate, but because they may be largely irrelevant. In other words, legal reforms may be unsuccessful because the problem offered as a reason for their enactment and the causal theory underlying that problem may not exist as described.

If the characteristics of the injured patient, the injury itself, and the medical situation involved are key explanatory factors for patterns in malpractice claims, then we may need to rethink the idea of the malpractice system as a random or chaotic system driven by the vagaries of the legal system and those using it. Sloan and his colleagues found that the most severe injuries were more likely to be closed with a payment to the injured patient as were claims involving injuries occurring in doctor's offices, misdiagnosis claims, ob/gyn claims, surgery claims, anesthesia claims, drug-related claims, monitoring-related claims, and blood-related claims. What is it about these claims that leads to their being closed with a payment to the injured patient more often? Again, pursuing a question like this one may mean looking beyond the reform rhetoric's portrayal and causal theory, and it may mean exploring answers suggesting that legal changes like those enacted in the 1970s and 1980s may make little or no difference.

One possibility is that there is more demonstrable negligent injury in the situations just noted above. We can take one of them as an example, the often used example—ob/gyn. A 1985 study published in the *American Journal of Perinatology* explored the causes of injury in closed obstetric malpractice claims.[104] Underlying the study was a concern with increases in the number of obstetrics claims. Its operating presumption was that examining patterns in closed claims would provide data on the causes of the injuries involved, this information in turn to be used for risk management purposes and higher quality care. In short, this was an epidemiological analysis.

The authors—Julian et al.—found that identifiable risks to the patient were recognized by the physician and documented in the medical record just 54% of the time, and when recognized by the physician the risk was correctly managed only 32% of the time. They said, "The risks identified in these cases are common, recognizable problems of pregnancy with recognized standards of care. Physician performance was poor by any standard. . . . Management of risks in these cases suggests that standards of care were violated and as a result lawsuits were brought."[105]

In this study, then, a different problem was identified and defined than the one driving Sloan and his colleagues. For Sloan et al. the problem ultimately had to do with insurance for physicians and those things supposedly affecting it—especially claims by injured patients. For Julian et al.—the problem ultimately had to do with injuries and the quality of care. As a result, they point to a very different type of solution—risk management and improving the quality of care. This solution works at the base of the disputing pyramid—on the incidence of injuries, rather than on processes farther up the pyramid that involve responses to injuries that have already occurred.

Finally, the unintended consequences of some legislative enactments are also important, and pursuing them also requires looking beyond the reform rhetoric's portrayal and causal theory. Unintended consequences are important because efforts to explain them provide insight into just how the malpractice system may actually work. Perhaps the most interesting study in this regard is the series of analyses of Indiana's malpractice reforms done by Eleanor Kinney and her associates. Their findings point to something overlooked by the aggregate statistical evaluations like those of Danzon and Sloan that rely on the reform rhetoric's perspective—the process of handling claims and the behavior of key institutional actors in that process.

The Indiana reforms had three major parts: a comprehensive cap of $500,000 on all damages (raised to $750,000 for claims arising after January 1, 1990), mandated medical review before trial, and a state-run patient compensation fund to pay large claims.[106] The first part, of course, is the best known aspect of the Indiana reforms. The second two deal more with the process of handling claims. All claimants must go through a medical review panel before proceeding to trial, and this panel is intended "to provide an informal, early decision on liability, and thereby facilitate quick resolution of claims."[107] The panel has no role in setting damages, and the parties can settle at any time with or without panel review. The patient compensation fund pays all claims over $100,000, with the insurance carrier paying up to $100,000. The fund makes no determination on liability since liability will have been admitted or found by the time a claim reaches the fund. Few claims reached the fund after court proceedings as most were settled (of 410 claims examined in the study only 21 went to court).[108]

As a part of the study, monetary recoveries by injured patients in Indiana were compared with those from the neighboring states of Ohio and Michigan which did not have a cap on damages. The expectation was that large awards (those of $100,000 or more) would be higher in Michigan and Ohio because of the absence of a cap.[109] Using data from one malpractice insurance carrier that covered all three states, Gronfein and Kinney's analysis produced results they described as "strikingly counterintuitive."[110] They said: "The principal finding of this study was a considerable and unexpected difference among Indiana, Michigan, and Ohio in mean claim severity (size of payment) for large claims."[111] Payments were significantly higher in Indiana even when controlling statistically for sex, age, severity of injury, and allegations of negligence.[112] In addition, "a much higher percentage of Indiana claims (27.9%) were paid at the $500,000 cap than in either Michigan or Ohio, where the percentage of claims settled at or above $500,000 was only 12.3% and 14.1%, respectively."[113] In addition, "even though expressly designed to expedite the disposition of claims, large claims were not disposed of any more quickly than in either Michigan or Ohio."[114]

The reason for the unexpected differences between Indiana and its two neighbors, it was suggested, could be found in the incentive structure for insurance carriers created by the Indiana system. This incentive structure made the system work in practice like a no-fault system for large claims, even though this was not intended.[115] The incentive structure encouraged insurance companies (whose liability on a single claim is limited to $100,000) to settle large claims quickly with little consideration of the defendant's fault, thereby pushing the claim into the state-run patient compensation fund. This effectively limits the insurance carier's losses and costs. Kinney et al. noted that by law when the fund gets a claim it must assume the defendant's liability even if the insurance carrier gave it little consideration.[116] In addition, Kinney et al. found that medical review panels were used to assess defendant liability in less than one-half these large claims. When they were used, it tended to cause delay in the processing of the claim.[117]

Kinney and her associates concluded that these counterintuitive findings "should caution reformers, critics, and other observers to look more closely at the detailed aspects of how a system operates in practice before coming intuitively appealing conclusions about . . . the appropriateness of modifying the current medical malpractice system."[118] This conclusion highlights the point we made in chapter 1 concerning how little is actually known about the civil justice system in operation and just how important it is to recognize this dearth of knowledge. Kinney's conclusion also reinforces Malcolm Feeley's observation drawn from his study of criminal justice reforms regarding policies enacted with little or no concern for how the system actually works—those policies are doomed to fail.[119]

Kinney's conclusion again directs our attention to the politics of ideas. In particular it asks us to consider the effects of the intense political debate in this arena on the research enterprise itself. Examining how the malpractice system actually works would seem to be an obvious part of the research agenda, yet it is often ignored. The reason for this may be found, to some degree, in the political battle to determine which view of reality will govern policy in this arena. One aspect of this battle for the reformers has been influencing the academic literature so there will be "scientific" or "expert" materials to use in arguing for their favored view. Success in this effort comes when researchers accept the reformers' definition of the problem and causal theory as the defining logic of their research, as the Danzon and Sloan studies appear to have done. Accepting any particular perspective means that some topics will be considered relevant and important to study while others will not. From the reform perspective, the issues that concerned Kinney and her associates may not be all that relevant.

The Disputing Pyramid

There has been an increasing amount of empirical research on issues related to the policy debate in the medical malpractice arena. Drawing from this research and using the disputing pyramid idea introduced in chapter 3, we can get some empirical sense of the malpractice system. This will also provide a context for the jury verdict data to be presented in the next section. While most of the public debate on malpractice focuses on litigation and jury verdicts—perhaps because this is the most visible part of the process—the most important finding of this empirical literature shows that the bulk of the action takes place toward the bottom of the pyramid.

The Base of the Pyramid: Injuries

At the base of the medical malpractice disputing pyramid is the universe of medical events that have the potential for generating disputes between patients or families and health care professionals (or organizations) over the quality and effects of medical care. These events are the medical errors that result in patient injury and in turn may provide the basis for a claim against the physician or hospital. While medical error and other quality of care issues are rarely discussed in the rhetoric of malpractice reform, they are, however, a major concern of consumer's groups[120] and some plaintiffs' attorneys.[121] These constituencies have created their own rhetoric in opposition to the political movement for malpractice reform. Their rhetoric is often similar to that of the malpractice reformers from the perspective of the politics of ideas—it too is about strategic representation. It too plays the tactical use of passion with horror stories, evocative metaphors, and the like.[122]

The true frequency of events at the very bottom of the pyramid is hard to gauge because these events are extremely difficult to observe systematically. But as noted in chapter 3, the empirical literature suggests that the base of the pyramid is indeed quite broad. Patricia Danzon's 1985 book on malpractice estimated that on average one in 20 hospital patients incurs an injury as a result of a medical error.[123] She also noted that this figure probably underestimates the total universe of injuries.[124] The Harvard Malpractice Study found "that in New York in 1984 the incidence of adverse events suffered by hospitalized patients was 3.7 percent. Of these, 27.6 percent were due to negligence; that is, about 1 percent of all patients hospitalized suffered a negligent medical injury."[125] When these results are weighted to produce population estimates, the study's authors said that "among the 2.6 million patients discharged from New York hospitals in 1984 we estimate that nearly 99,000 suffered disabling injuries."[126] Of these, over 27,177 would be due to negligence in their estimation.[127] These quantitative studies based on hospital in-patient charts suggest that the raw frequency of patient injury is high. As noted in chapter 3, using the Harvard study's one in 27 estimate (one injury for every 27 hospital admissions) and 1991 American Hospital Association data on hospital admissions in the United States (33,566,557) there would have been approximately 1,241,963 patient injuries.

The Harvard study found the highest rate of negligence in situations involving death. One-half of the adverse events leading to death involved negligence—51.3%.[128] The study's authors deemed the implications of this finding striking: "If New York's adverse-event-related death total can be extrapolated to the U.S. population as a whole, one would estimate over 150,000 ratiogenic fatalities annually, more than half of which are due to negligence. Medical injury, then, accounts for more deaths than all other types of accidents combined, and dwarfs the mortality rates associated with motor vehicle accidents (50,000 deaths per year) and occupation-related mishaps (6,000 deaths per year)."[129]

Qualitative studies of medical work also suggest that error (though not necessarily negligence) and injury are widespread. In fact, these studies show that physicians and other health care professionals see their work as highly error prone.[130] This literature—based largely on ethnographic studies of medical work within hospitals—reports that error is frequent and inevitable because medical work is characterized by uncertainty.[131] Uncertainty in medical work has to do with the application of a general and imperfect body of knowledge to individual clinical cases by professionals whose skills and knowledge have limits (because they are, after all, still human). A 15-month, participant-observation study of the handling of error in two surgical intensive care units done under the auspices of the American Bar Foundation found that among those working in these units "error is seen as inevitable and even frequent. It is the result of the contingencies and uncertainties of what is believed to be an inexact science, of the unique characteristics and histories of individual patients, and of the organizational context in which medical work takes place. Error—or at least the potential for error—is pervasive, an artifact of medical work generally rather than just the work of physicians."[132] This is a reality recognized by health care professionals, and it animates the ways in which physicians are trained,[133] the way in which medical work is organized in hospitals, and even the design and physical layout of hospital units.[134] One also sees the recognition of this reality in hospital administration.[135]

Perhaps the best characterization of medical work and its contingent, uncertain nature was provided by medical sociologist Anselm Strauss and his colleagues in their book *The Social Organization of Medical Work* (1985). They drew the following analogy which they contrasted to precise, rational, scientific decision making:

> Managing illness trajectories is more like the work of Mark Twain's celebrated Mississippi River pilot [than precise, rational, scientific decision making]: the river was tricky, changed its course slightly from day to day, so even an experienced, but an inattentive pilot could run into grave difficulties; worse yet, sometimes the river drastically shifted in its bed for some miles into quite a new course. . . . The physician's and staff's management may be even more complex and the outcome of their work even more fateful than the pilot's. Some of the various contingencies may be anticipated, but only a portion of them may be relatively controllable, while some contingencies are quite unforeseeable, stemming as they do not only from the illnesses themselves but from organizational sources.[136]

Additionally, Strauss and his colleagues noted that the contingencies and uncertainties with which the medical pilots must deal stem not only from the limitations of medical science and personal skill, "but also from a host of work and organizational sources as well as from biographical and lifestyle sources pertaining to patients, kin, and staff members themselves."[137] While it is not possible to develop quantitative estimates of the amount of medical error or the amount of negligence on the basis of the findings of such qualitative or ethnographic studies, these studies are very important because they show that error and injury are widespread and inevitable due to the nature of the practice of medicine itself. Changing the malpractice system to make it harder for injured patients to claim compensation and harder to succeed when they do will not change this fact.

Moving up the Pyramid

Claiming. Despite a large universe of injury-causing medical errors, surprisingly few errors give rise to a dispute or even a claim, either because there is no negligence or because patients simply do not pursue the matter. As we can tell from the available evidence, only a small fraction of injuries lead to the actual filing of a malpractice insurance claim. Danzon, drawing from a California Medical Association/California Hospital Association study noted earlier, reported that "at most one in 10 negligent injuries resulted in a claim."[138] The Harvard study estimated that in New York State there was one medical malpractice claim for every 7.6 negligent injuries.[139] Unlike Danzon's study, however, the Harvard study also took into consideration the possibility that some proportion of the claims actually filed did not involve a negligent injury. The Harvard study examined the claims in its sample and made an independent judgment as to whether a claim involved a *negligent* injury or not.[140] Using its judgments on negligence, the Harvard study concluded that "the chances that a claim would be filed by a patient with an identifiable negligent injury was not 1 in 7.6, but rather only 1 in 50."[141]

The finding that most arguably negligently injured patients do *not* make a claim against a health care professional or institution is one of the factors that led the authors of the Harvard study to say "that the problem is not a litigation surplus, but a litigation deficit. The gap between torts occurring in American hospitals and tort suits being filed in American courts in far greater than has ever been supposed."[142] Richard Abel made the same argument regarding the tort crisis more generally in an essay entitled "The Crisis Is Injuries, Not Liability."[143] The question, then, is not—as phrased in the reform rhetoric—why so many injured patients pursue claims for compensation, but why so few do. A handful of studies have explored what injured patients do and whether their grievances are transformed into real disputes. May and DeMarco,[144] for example, surveyed patients in two southern Wisconsin communities who were dissatisfied with the medical care they received. They found that the most common response to patient dissatisfaction was to "lump it" (do nothing at all) or simply to change doctors. Only 25% of the patients contacted the offending physician directly, and only about 11% contacted a lawyer.

Another study by Allan Meyers also explored the common practice of "lumping it" in situations of patient injury. Like May and DeMarco, Meyers surveyed patients rather than relying on a retrospective examination of claims or hospital records. While noting the methodological problems of relying upon self-reports of injury, Meyers also points out a problem for retrospective archival studies in looking at the "lump it" phenomenon. He says that from the patient's perspective as to the perception of injury "there is no higher standard of validity than self-reports. Regardless of whether there is 'objective' evidence of iatrogenic illness or injury, there will never be a lawsuit unless someone believes that he or she or a close relative has been harmed."[145] Regardless of the existence of an injury, the disputing process will not and cannot begin until the patient *believes* he/she has suffered an injury.[146] It is possible that some percentage of injured patients "lump it" because they are unaware of the "injury" itself or do not connect a new physical problem with their medical treatment. Perception of injury and locating a cause are crucial elements in the emergence and pursuit of claims.

In a randomly selected sample of adult residents of Maine in 1986–87, Meyers found that 26% "of the respondents asserted that either they or a close relative had experienced at least one episode of harm as a result of medical treatment or treatment in a health care facility."[147] Most respondents reported that they discussed the injuries "with friends and relatives, especially those in their households. Relatively few discussed their experiences with attorneys, not many more than reported discussions with social workers, counselors, or clergy." Meyers also reported that "it appears from the content of the interviews that only one of those persons who contacted a lawyer initiated a suit."[148] As to why lawyers were rarely contacted, Meyers said that "responses reflect a combination of respondents' assessments that events were not serious (or not sufficiently serious, in respondents' judgments, to merit lawsuits), concerns about the costs of litigation, the low likelihood of favorable outcomes, and antipathy to lawyers."[149] Interestingly, Meyers comes to some of the same conclusions as the Harvard study. He notes: "Finally, and most significantly, the data suggest that we may have inaccurately or incompletely characterized the malpractice crisis. The crisis may be the high level of iatrogenic illness or injury for which people receive no compensation."[150]

A study by pediatrician Gerald Hickson and his colleagues took a different approach to the issue of why people file malpractice claims.[151] They interviewed families who had filed malpractice claims in Florida between 1986 and August 1989 in "bad baby" cases—claims in which the infants suffered injury or died. Their purpose was to examine the motivations for filing a claim and what allegedly was wrong with the medical care received. Hickson and his colleagues found that the reasons for filing a claim varied considerably, and a desire for money was not the only or even the main reason. Instead, they emphasized problems in physician-family communication, especially the perception of being deceived and/or ignored.[152] They noted:

> The desire for information, perception of being misled, anger with the medical profession, desire to prevent injuries to others, recognition of long-term sequelae, and advice by knowledgeable acquaintances, as well as need for money, appeared to contribute to families' decisions to file medical malpractice claims. This is not to say that financial concerns did not exist in households who fail to cite money as a reason for filing. It is important to consider the possibility, however, that economic losses and obtaining money may not be the only motivations for families who file suit.[153]

As in Meyers's study, Hickson and his colleagues found that discussing the situation with others was an important factor in the decision to file a claim. Unlike the more general Meyers study, Hickson and his colleagues found that the "most frequently reported reason families filed was that they had been advised or influenced to sue by someone outside the immediate family."[154] Like Meyers, however, they found that the someone was unlikely to be a lawyer. Most often, "the influential acquaintance was a member of the medical profession."[155]

Settling Claims. The disputing pyramid for medical malpractice shapes up as an odd edifice with a very broad base and relatively flat sides given that so few potential claims are actually made. The empirical literature indicates that patients who do pursue claims for malpractice are unlikely to pursue them as far as an actual trial. This means that most matters are settled—with or without a payment—short of formal adjudication. In some states this may mean settling at the stage of an arbitration panel or mediation, while in others it means settlement through informal negotiation. Studies of closed malpractice insurance claims show that as many as 90% of malpractice claims close without going to a trial. For example, a study of 2,896 closed claims from a single malpractice carrier in Wisconsin found that only 5.3% went to a trial.[156] Taragin and his colleagues, in a closed claim study of one New Jersey malpractice carrier, reported that 12% of the claims went to trial.[157] Another study of all closed claims in Minnesota, North Dakota, and South Dakota conducted by the Minnesota Commerce Department reported that only 3.0% of 3,689 claims went to a trial.[158]

While most claims are closed short of formal adjudication, patients do not generally come away with a monetary settlement. However, the range of experience regarding the rates at which claims close with payment is relatively broad. At the low end of this spectrum, a report produced by the Texas State Board of Medical Examiners found that during the middle 1980s only 20% of malpractice claims were settled with a payment,[159] and a Minnesota Commerce Department study reported that 27% of the claims were closed with a payment.[160] In their Wisconsin study, Grossman and her colleagues reported that only 31.8% of claims were closed with a payment, a success rate comparable to figures reported by the Missouri Division of Insurance for all closed malpractice claims for the years 1979–88. Of a total of 14,142 closed claims in Missouri during these years, 35.6% were closed with a payment.[161] In contrast, Taragin and his colleagues[162] found 43% of the claims closed with a payment in their study of data from one New Jersey carrier for the years 1977–91, and a 1980 nationwide study conducted by the National Association of Insurance Commissioners[163] found that 46% of malpractice insurance claims were settled with a payment. At the upper extreme, the Kinney study of Indiana closed claims noted that 68% were closed with a payment.[164]

The high-end figure for the percentage of claims closed with a payment in Indiana warrants a bit more attention because it raises an important issue. Kinney suggested the higher percentage may be a result of the Indiana reforms encouraging plaintiffs' attorneys to be more selective in the matters they handle[165]—a reasonable possibility but not the most likely one. A rather different possibility is that the reported higher percentage of claims closed with a payment is a characteristic of the major insurance carrier(s) in the Indiana market. Other carriers insuring physicians in the state could have a lower percentage of paid claims even within the same legal environment. In short, in studies using closed claims data the practices of individual insurance carriers involved are an important, though overlooked, factor. Indeed, even though insurance companies are major actors in the handling of claims and the resolution of disputes in the malpractice arena, they are rarely the subject of systematic research. This is especially important since the malpractice insurance market in many states is not very competitive, with one or two carriers dominating the market in a given state.

For instance, according to the General Accounting Office's *Medical Malpractice: Case Study on Indiana*, the Medical Protective Insurance Company of Fort Wayne, Ind. (MedPro), insured over 70% of the physicians in Indiana during the early to mid-1980s.[166] This means that the high percentage Kinney reported for the state was most likely the result of MedPro's experience, and indeed the data used in much of her work were from MedPro.

Since data on other carriers in Indiana are not readily available, we can not make direct comparisons regarding the rates of claims closed with a payment. We can, however, use data from the Grossman et al. Wisconsin study[167] to illustrate the importance of considering the claims handling patterns of the various insurance carriers. As noted, Grossman and her colleagues focused on a single carrier in Wisconsin for 1976–88 which closed 31.8% of its claims with a payment. This carrier administered a state-backed insurance plan which, at the time, covered the largest share of the market in Wisconsin.[168] MedPro, the carrier in the Kinney study, was also involved in the Wisconsin market during 1976–88. It closed 53.4% (687 of 1,287) of its claims with a payment working within the same legal environment as the state-backed plan. A third carrier in the Wisconsin market closed only 11.9% of its claims with a payment.[169] Although not as high as the payment rate in Indiana, the MedPro rate is high compared to the other two Wisconsin carriers. Perhaps MedPro generally closes claims with a payment at a higher rate than most other carriers. The reasons for the differences in percentage of paid claims among these carriers are unknown, but as another study will suggest, it is likely that the reasons have something to do with the carriers themselves—such as the way in which they handle and settle claims[170] or the types of risks insured.

Differences in payment rates also raises the question of how rational the system is. As noted earlier, some studies indicate that a portion of malpractice claims do not in fact involve negligence. The important question then becomes whether there is any rationality to the process of sorting out the claims that do not involve negligence. The reform rhetoric, of course, says that there are many frivolous claims and that there is no rationality in the process which sorts the frivolous from the legitimate. The issue is a difficult one to address because most claims are settled without formal adjudication, but one recent study attempted to do so. Taragin et al.[171] found that "in most of the malpractice cases included in our analysis, a physician was judged to have provided medical care that was defensible, and the plaintiff did not receive any payment. . . . For the small number of cases that required a jury verdict

(12% of all claims), only 24% resulted in payment to the plaintiff. . . . For the cases that were felt to be indefensible, the payment rate was 91%. . . . In contrast, in the cases where physician care was classified as defensible, the payment rate was 21%."[172]

The judgments on defensibility Taragin and his colleagues reported were the initial judgments of the insurance carrier itself as indicated in the claim file. The carrier's process worked as follows: first, the physician involved was contacted, and if he/she admitted error, the claim was labeled "indefensible;" second, if not, one of the carrier's claims personnel reviewed the case, and if this employee thought it was clearly medically defensible the case was labeled "no peer review, clearly defensible;" third, in the alternative, the claim was sent for peer review by a physician in the same specialty as the physician involved in the claim.[173] This reviewer then discussed the case with the carrier's claims personnel, the physician involved, and a defense attorney as a part of the evaluation. "Based on the standard of medical care currently practiced by physicians of similar training and experience in the community, the physician-reviewer classifies the claim as 'defensible' if standard care was provided, 'indefensible' if not, and 'defensibility unclear' if the reviewer is unsure."[174]

Taragin and his colleagues probed more deeply into the 21% of the claims initially labeled as defensible, but in which a payment was still made. They suggested that several factors may explain this, the first of which had to do with the timing of the process itself. The determination recorded in the file regarding defensibility was made very early in the process, and information from expert reviews and subsequent insurance carrier reviews that become available as the process continued may have shown the early judgment to be incorrect. This idea is "supported by the fact that 68% of the defensible cases that resulted in payment were settled before trial, in half of these before settlement was complete."[175] It also bolsters a second explanation offered by Taragin and his colleagues—that a physician-based review process may be biased in the physician's favor.[176] Additionally, because the physician involved had the right to refuse to settle and also because the insurance carrier itself was physician owned, "many of the defensible cases that resulted in payment were probably misclassified as defensible."[177] They conclude that "although we can only speculate on the number of cases that were inappropriately lost by the physician, our data suggest that inappropriate payments are probably uncommon."[178] In other words, this study suggests that while there may in fact be numerous claims made where there is no negligence, the sorting process involved in resolving those claims is anything but irrational. The Harvard study came to a similar general conclusion.[179] The New Jersey study also illustrates that a carrier's internal practices can affect the rate at which claims are closed with a payment.

Taragin and his colleagues reported on the size of the payment in claims which produced a monetary settlement—another important issue. Payments were made in less than one-half of all claims (43%), and the median dollar amount was $45,551 (in 1990 dollars). Fifty-two percent of the paid claims involved payments less than $50,000, and only 15% exceeded $200,000 (again in 1990 dollars). Grossman and her colleagues found that of 1,866 claims against individual physicians (as opposed to those against institutions), 35.2% were closed with a payment. The median payment in 1990 dollars was $27,198, and less than 5% exceeded $200,000.[180] They also reported the insurance carrier's costs for closed claims—a median of $3,309.[181] Kinney and her colleagues reported a median of $16,597 (adjusted to 1990) from their Indiana closed claims study.[182]

Multiple Pyramids and Medical Settings

Even in the academic literature, much of the discussion of malpractice is fairly general, as though claims were an undifferentiated mass of interchangeable individual parts. In reality, of course, claims emerge from a wide variety of medical situations and specialties, and they are anything but fungible. Each medical setting may have its own unique disputing pyramid with different amounts of medical error, different kinds of injury, different patterns in claiming, and different patterns in claimant success and awards. People seek medical treatment for a wide variety of ailments and injuries, and they may receive care from different kinds of health care professionals for those varying problems. Additionally, these different health care professionals offer different—often distinct—types of treatment geared to the nature of patient's problem. This is reflected, most obviously, in the distinct specialties into which the medical profession divides itself. And beyond the specialties within the mainline medical profession, there are also those offering treatment based on other philosophies of medicine, such as chiropractic and osteopathy.

Because of the differences in ailments and treatment arenas, we should not expect the same malpractice incident and claim patterns across all medical settings, and the empirical literature confirms this.[183] For instance, in their Wisconsin study Grossman and her colleagues found that of 1,751 claims against individual health care professionals, physician–no surgery (19.1%) occurred most frequently.[184] This was the case in Missouri in the late 1980s as well.[185] Over 40% (41.2%) of the claims examined in the Wisconsin study involved one of the surgical specialties, with three of them accounting for at least 10% of 1,751 claims each: orthopedic surgery (12.0%), ob/gyn (10.0%), and general surgery (10.0%). Together, these three specialties made up nearly one-third of the claims, a pattern similar to that reported for Missouri[186] and for Indiana.[187]

As seen in table 4.1, which is adapted from Grossman and her colleagues, claims arising from different settings have different rates of claimant success (closed with a payment), different levels of injury incurred,[188] and different levels of payment. The table includes those categories of health care professionals in the Wisconsin study for which there were 10 or more claims closed with a payment. Claimants were most often successful in their claims against podiatrists and plastic surgeons, receiving a payment in over one-half of the claims. Claimants were least successful against physicians–no surgery, and they were also less successful against the three most frequently appearing surgical specialties—orthopedic, ob/gyn, and general surgery.

The injuries suffered by claimants varied in their severity among the different categories of health care professionals in the Wisconsin study. Four categories were characterized by relatively high percentages of death claims (exceeding 20%), with thoracic surgery producing the highest percentage (36.8%). In three others, by way of contrast, less than 5% of the injuries involved a death, with plastic surgery generating no claims involving death. Physician/minor surgery, general practice/surgery, general surgery, vascular surgery, and podiatrics were characterized more by temporary injury than by permanent injury or death. Neurological surgery, ob/gyn, and plastic surgery were characterized more by permanent injuries.

Payments for injuries attributable to the different categories of professionals also varied considerably. In the Wisconsin data, median payments ranged from a low of $16,350 for podiatrics to a high of $151,284 for neurological surgery. Podiatrics claims tended to involve temporary, less severe injuries while neurological surgery claims were more likely to be for permanent and very severe injuries. Grossman and her colleagues noted[189] that of the 16 neurological surgery cases closed with a payment, nine involved the two most severe levels of

Table 4.1 Physician Categories (with 10-plus Successful Claims): Claimant Success, Injury Severity, and Payments*

Category	*N*	Claimant Success Rate (%)	Injury: Temporary (%)	Injury: Permanent (%)	Injury: Death (%)	Median Payment (1988 $)
Physician—No Surgery	334	29.9	38.6	26.6	29.6	22,800
Physician—Minor Surgery	144	36.1	48.6	30.6	17.4	18,575
General Practice—Surgery	257	35.8	49.0	30.4	19.1	19,950
Surgery—General	174	34.5	53.4	29.3	16.7	19,110
Surgery—Thoracic	38	36.8	36.8	26.3	36.8	68,700
Surgery—Vascular	35	40.0	51.4	37.1	8.6	24,640
Anesthesiology	100	43.0	42.0	34.0	23.0	38,500
Surgery—Neurologic	44	36.4	34.1	56.8	6.8	151,284
Surgery—Obstetrics/ Gynecology	174	35.1	37.9	46.6	13.2	38,500
Surgery—Orthopedic	210	33.3	53.3	41.0	4.8	28,000
Surgery—Plastic	46	54.3	41.3	58.7	0	26,080
Nurse—Anesthetist	33	33.3	33.3	39.4	27.3	19,980
Podiatry—Surgery	82	58.5	73.2	23.2	2.4	16,350

* Adapted from Grossman et al., 1992, table 4.

permanent injury.[190] Generally speaking the higher payments tended to be found in the more specialized surgery categories, which in turn were characterized by a larger percentage of permanent injuries or death.[191] The exception was plastic surgery which had the highest percentage of permanent injuries (58.7%) and a relatively modest median payment of $26,080 in 1988 dollars. The reason for this exceptional situation is the absence of death claims and the fact that very few claims involved the most severe levels of permanent injury.[192]

While much more could be said of these Wisconsin data, we have used them only for illustrative purposes. They suggest that the malpractice system is a complex but orderly one, with the possibility of different disputing pyramids for different medical settings. This means that no single setting—like ob/gyn—can be used to represent the system as a whole, that problems as well as solutions may be setting-specific, and that any enacted reforms are likely to have varying effects across settings. To begin to understand the malpractice system it is important to know about the mix of malpractice claims and the patterns among the ingredients of the mix. This idea will frame much of our discussion in the next section where we turn to the pinnacle of the pyramid—jury verdicts, the one part of the pyramid that has been the rhetorical focus of much of the political debate.

Jury Verdict Patterns

General Background: 1988–90

Jury verdicts are at the heart of the political debate over medical malpractice. This makes them important politically despite the fact that so few matters reach the disputing pyramid's pinnacle. They are also important as a practical matter because of their influence on the earlier stages of the disputing process. Again, as Galanter puts it, the importance of juries lies not so much in the frequency of their use but in their symbolic value as "transmitters of signals rather than as deciders of cases."[193] Jury verdicts cast a large shadow down the sides of the pyramid. The actions of juries in the malpractice arena help set the range in which negotiation and settlement takes place. Verdicts in a given jurisdiction can, for instance, influence both the malpractice insurance carrier's decision to settle and the amount of any payment.

On the other side, the actions of juries will influence a plaintiffs' attorney's decision whether or not to handle a particular claim. Verdicts will also affect the attorney's strategy regarding the claim he/she has taken on, including the settlement demand and the decision whether or not to actually risk a jury trial. Galanter has argued, in this regard, that the jury's principal contribution "to dispute resolution is providing a background or norms and procedures against which negotiations . . . take place."[194] The problem for the reformers, of course, is the set of messages they perceive verdicts as sending into the community at large and into the malpractice arena in particular.

One straightforward way of sorting out these messages is to describe patterns and changes in malpractice verdicts. Table 3.3 presented data from 82 jurisdictions for 1988–90 on the percentage of all verdicts made up by medical malpractice matters and the plaintiff win rate in these cases (the *number* of malpractice verdicts in each site can be obtained by multiplying the total *N* found in table 3.1 by the malpractice percentage found in table 3.3). In the discussion of these data in chapter 3, we noted that malpractice cases never comprised as much as one-quarter of the jury verdicts in any site. If we look solely at the numbers of malpractice verdicts, we find that 39 sites had 10 or more reported malpractice verdicts, and only 11 had 50 or more. The highest numbers, not surprisingly, were found in major urban centers. Cook County was the highest (270), with only Los Angeles, Harris, Wayne, and New York counties experiencing 100 or more verdicts.

Contrary to the picture portrayed by the reform rhetoric, table 3.3 showed that plaintiffs were not likely to win malpractice jury cases. Overall, plaintiffs prevailed in 30.4% (658) of the 2,165 malpractice verdicts in 1988–90. This compared to a 32.4% win rate reported for jury verdicts in 1981–85 for 45 of these sites.[195] Plaintiff success rates varied considerably among sites. For instance, of the five sites with more than 100 malpractice verdicts the win rate ranged from 17.3% in Harris County, Tex., to 39.3% in Cook County

Awards for malpractice cases, as table 3.4 showed, were relatively high. No site in which there were at least five winning verdicts had a median award of under $100,000 (in 1990 dollars), the lowest being $100,800 in St. Louis County. At the other end of the range, only Queens County experienced a median over $1 million. Of the 27 sites with five or more winning verdicts, eight had medians between $100,000 and $250,000, nine more were between $250,001 and $500,000, six were between $500,001 and $750,000, and only two were between $750,000 and $1 million. While these median award figures are relatively high, we must keep in mind that plaintiffs were infrequent winners. If we express awards as expected awards—the median award multiplied by the win rate[196]—the figures are more modest. Half of the 27 sites had expected awards under $100,000, and only Cuyahoga County, Oh., had an expected award over $500,000 ($551,461).

The severity of injury suffered was an important factor for awards. Both plaintiff win rates and median awards varied according to the severity of the injury involved in a relatively orderly way. This is important for understanding the "messages" being sent by the actions of juries, and it is something not addressed by the reform rhetoric. Not all malpractice cases, as the earlier discussion of closed claims pointed out, involve the same types of injury, and they are not equally divided across levels of injury. Generally speaking, more severe injuries result in higher jury awards and plaintiff win rates. Table 4.2a presents win rates and median awards along with the frequency distribution for different injury levels in the sites with 10 or more malpractice verdicts using the nine-point scale described in Appendix 4.1.

Forty-three percent of the verdicts involved injuries in the middle of the scale—temporary major (level 4) and permanent minor injuries (level 5). Relatively few verdicts involved either the least or most severe nonfatal injuries. Slightly over a fifth of the cases stemmed from injuries producing a death. Win rates and awards were lower for the less severe injuries, and they were substantially higher for the most severe injuries. At the most severe level of permanent injury (level 8), the win rate was

Table 4.2 Severity of Injury: Frequencies, Win Rates, Awards for Sites with 10-plus Verdicts, 1988–90 (N = 1,926)

4.2a Nine-Point Severity Scale

Injury Level	(Code)	N	Percentage	Win Rate (%)	Median Award* ($)
Emotional only	(1)	60	3.1	26.7	134,375
Temporary insignificant	(2)	35	1.8	20.0	21,000
Temporary minor	(3)	109	5.7	18.3	64,523
Temporary major	(4)	393	20.4	28.0	105,000
Permanent minor	(5)	442	22.9	30.5	245,000
Permanent significant	(6)	259	13.4	33.6	605,000
Permanent major	(7)	119	6.2	34.5	3,179,000
Permanent grave	(8)	94	4.9	51.1	4,720,000
Death	(9)	404	21.0	28.7	599,570
Unknown	—	11	0.6	—	—
Total		1,926	100.0		

4.2b Collapsed Severity Scale

Injury Level	N	Percentage	Win Rate (%)	Median Award* ($)
Minor injury	646	33.5	27.6	193,008
Major injury	865	44.9	33.1	519,992
Death	404	21.0	28.7	599,570
Unknown	11	0.6	—	—
Total	1,926	100.0		

* Median awards in 1990 dollars.

just over 50% with a *median* award of $4.7 million. Part of the reason for such a high median in these cases was the age of the plaintiff. The median age for injury level 8 cases was one year compared to a median of 40 years for all cases; these are the so-called "bad baby cases" in which future medical and other costs tend to be very high.

We can collapse the nine-point injury scale into three general categories: minor injury (levels 1, 2, 3, and 5), major injury (levels 4, 6, 7, and 8), and death. Table 4.2b presents win rates and median awards for these collapsed injury categories. The largest percentage of verdicts involved major injuries, 44.9%. Plaintiffs won one-third of these cases, with a median award of $519,992. One-third of the verdicts involved minor injuries. Plaintiffs won these cases less frequently, 27.6%, and the median award was lower, $193,008. Death cases accounted for a smaller percentage of verdicts, 21.0%, and plaintiffs won these cases at a rate similar to that for minor injury cases. The median award for death cases, however, was substantially higher at $599,750.

These general patterns cannot be explained easily. Any explanation would require not only an analysis of the verdicts, but also analyses of prior aspects of the dispute-handling process. This is best illustrated by a comparison to data from closed claims studies with regard to the distribution of different levels of injury. Again, table 4.2a shows that the largest percentage of verdicts in our data set fell into injury levels in the middle of the nine-point scale or involved a death. Closed claims studies show a different distribution, with the largest percentages of claims falling into the less serious, minor levels of injury. For instance, the 1980 National Association of Insurance Commissioners (NAIC) study of malpractice claims nationwide reported that the largest percentage of claims, 32.7%, involved injury level 3, temporary minor injuries.[197] In their Wisconsin study, Grossman and her colleagues[198] also found that nearly one-third of claims involved level 3 injuries. In table 4.2a, only 5.7% of the verdicts fell into this level of injury.

The difference is more stark if presented in terms of the collapsed injury categories of table 4.2b. Almost 45% of the verdicts in our data set involved major injuries, compared to only 18.8% of the claims in the NAIC study.[199] One-third of the verdicts involved minor injuries, compared to 62.8% of the claims in the NAIC study.[200] If a working hypothesis were to be stated for future investigation, it would be that major injuries are more likely to go to trial than minor injuries. A full explication of this pattern would require more than an analysis of those matters going to a jury trial. An investigation of those claims that do not reach the pinnacle of the dispute resolution pyramid along with an exploration of the process or processes that take some kinds of claims to a trial at a higher rate than others would be needed.

Medical Settings

The earlier discussion of medical settings argued that malpractice claims are not an undifferentiated mass. Using the logic of epidemiology, we cannot assume that all claims are fungible, meaning that in interpreting the general patterns in table 4.2 we must keep in mind that each medical setting may have its own characteristics, unique dispute resolution pyramid, and patterns in win rates and awards.[201] It is important, then, to disaggregate malpractice verdicts and organize a more detailed examination around the medical settings from which they emerged.[202] This somewhat broader approach makes more sense than trying to rely exclusively on the specialty of a physician-defendant. It is often the case that the setting will be the specialty of a physician defendant, but not always. Defendants are not always physicians; a hospital or clinic or a

Table 4.3 General Medical Setting: Frequencies, Win Rates, Awards for Sites with 10-plus Verdicts, 1988–90 (*N* = 1,926)

General Setting	*N*	Percentage	Win Rate (%)	Median Award* ($)
Surgery	1,196	62.1	29.3	385,000
Minor/No surgery	566	29.4	29.7	500,000
Hospital	91	4.7	40.7	131,250
Non-MD	59	3.1	39.0	214,270
Others	14	0.7	21.4	—
Total	1,926	100.0		

* Median award in 1990 dollars.

non–board certified physician may also be the defendant. This approach to medical setting is patient and injury centered, being based upon the ailment or problem involved and the kind of treatment sought.

The first question to ask at this level of analysis concerns the distribution of medical settings in the verdict data. Studies of closed claims,[203] as we saw earlier, indicate that claims are not evenly distributed across all medical settings and medical specialties. Table 4.3 shows that the same is true for our 1988–90 data for the general medical setting. Over 60% (62.1%) of the verdicts involved an injury emerging from a surgical setting. Nearly 30% (29.4%) involved injuries generated in a minor/no surgery setting, with another 4.7% produced in a hospital or other institutional setting.[204] Only 3% involved a non-MD setting, such as chiropractic. Plaintiff win rates for the two largest general settings are nearly identical at about 29%; the rates for the hospital and non-MD settings are higher at about 39%–41%. Median awards, however, are lower for the two smaller settings and higher for the two larger settings. The highest median is $500,000 for no/minor surgical settings cases.

The different settings do not share similar profiles when we look at the cause of the injury involved. Figures 4.1a and 4.1b show breakdowns by cause of injury for surgical and no/minor surgical. The figures use general categories taken from the malpractice literature.[205] The most frequent cause of injury for surgical settings, not surprisingly, was related to a specific procedure, 42.4%. Over one-third (35.6%) of the verdicts involved an injury caused by errors in the medical management of the patient—the overall planning and handling of patient care, including the use and management of medications. Injuries caused by

Figure 4.1a
Surgical Settings:
Cause of Injury

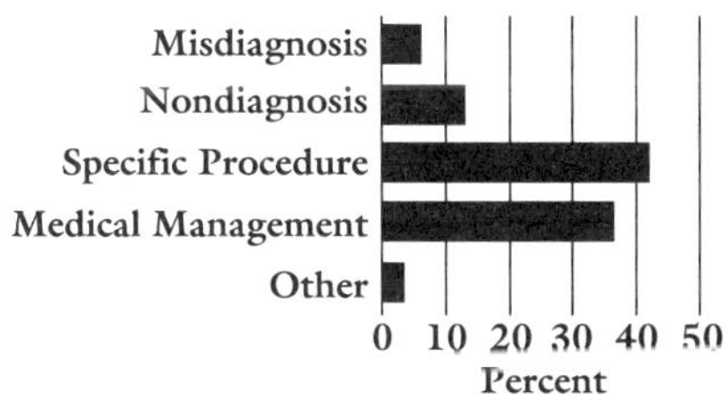

Figure 4.1b
No/Minor Surgery Settings:
Cause of Injury

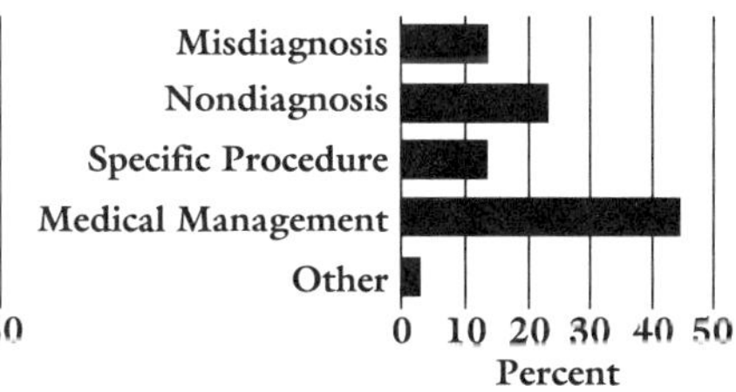

FIGURES 4.1a–4.1b Cause of Injury Within Settings for Malpractice Verdicts

diagnostic problems (either nondiagnosis or misdiagnosis) made up a smaller proportion of the verdicts.

Plaintiff win rates did not vary much within surgical settings by cause, ranging from 25.2% for nondiagnosis to 29.4% for specific procedure. Median awards did vary, with lower figures for misdiagnosis ($207,350) and specific procedure ($251,475) and higher figures for nondiagnosis ($459,750) and medical management ($402,440). Win rates were somewhat more variable for no/minor surgical, ranging from 20.4% for nondiagnosis to a high of 34.6% for specific procedure (the same low and high categories as for surgical). Median awards, again, were lower for misdiagnosis ($445,625) and specific procedure ($325,500) and higher for nondiagnosis ($550,000) and medical management ($510,000). In both general settings, then, plaintiffs did not win often, but when they did, the award structures were higher for injuries caused by nondiagnosis or failures in medical management.

Surgical Settings. Each of these two general settings can be broken down further into more specific settings. Table 4.4 unpacks the general surgical setting and includes those specific medical settings that accounted for at least 1% of *all* of the 1,926 malpractice verdicts in the sites with 10-plus verdicts. It presents the number of verdicts in each setting, the win rate, and the median award (table 4.4a) along with the percentages of each setting in different categories of injury severity (table 4.4b). Only two of the 11 settings included in table 4.4 accounted for as much as 10% of all verdicts: ob/gyn (16.9%) and orthopedic (13.6%). Surgery-general produced 9.3%. Only one other setting, emergency (6.0%), accounted for more than 5% of all cases.

Table 4.4 Specific Settings within Surgery Comprising More than 1% of All Verdicts, 1988–90 (N = 1,196)

4.4a Frequencies, Win Rates, Awards

Setting	*N*	Percentage of All	Win Rate (%)	Median Award* ($)
Colon/rectal	21	1.1	23.8	†
Emergency	116	6.0	27.6	323,176
General	180	9.3	28.9	448,520
Neurological	57	3.0	22.8	1,100,000
Ob/gyn	326	16.9	34.6	738,544
Opthalmology	45	2.3	28.9	435,390
Orthopedic	261	13.6	28.7	247,500
Otolaryngology	29	1.5	13.8	†
Plastic	58	3.0	32.8	136,500
Thoracic	24	1.2	20.8	†
Urology	58	3.0	37.9	190,000
Other	21	1.1		
Total	1,196	62.0		

* Median award in 1990 dollars.
† Five or fewer winning verdicts.

4.4b Severity of Injury by Setting and Frequency (Settings with more than Five Winning Verdicts)*

Setting	Minor Injury (%)	(*N*)	Major Injury (%)	(*N*)	Death (%)	(*N*)	Levels 7 and 8 (%)	(*N*)
Emergency	23.3	(27)	35.3	(41)	41.4	(48)	6.0	(7)
General	29.4	(53)	48.9	(88)	21.7	(39)	9.4	(17)
Neurological	26.3	(15)	63.2	(36)	10.5	(6)	29.8	(17)
Ob/gyn	22.7	(74)	60.7	(199)	16.3	(53)	23.0	(75)
Opthalmology	31.1	(14)	66.7	(30)	2.2	(1)	6.7	(3)
Orthopedic	52.1	(136)	39.1	(102)	8.4	(22)	4.6	(12)
Plastic	63.8	(37)	34.5	(20)	1.7	(1)	0	—
Urology	36.8	(21)	54.4	(31)	8.8	(5)	1.9	(1)

* Percentages for each setting add to 100% reading across (minor+major+death); levels 7 and 8 are included in major injury.

The three most frequently appearing surgical settings in the verdict data—ob/gyn, orthopedic, and general—are usually also among the most frequently appearing surgical settings in closed claims studies.[206]

Plaintiff win rates varied considerably among the settings—from 13.8% for otolaryngology to 37.9% for urology;[207] most were between 20% and 30%. Of the three most frequently appearing settings, ob/gyn had the highest win rate at 34.6%. The other two, orthopedic and general, were nearly identical at 28%–29%. Median awards also varied over a wide range, from a relatively modest $136,500 in plastic surgery to $1.1 million in neurological. Ob/gyn was the only other setting with a median award over $500,000.

Having seen that awards, as a general proposition, increase with the severity of injury, we might expect the higher award settings in table 4.4a to be the ones with higher percentages of the more severe injuries. Table 4.4b uses a collapsed version of the nine-point severity scale to present the percentage breakdown for each setting with more than five plaintiff verdicts by injury category. It also includes the percentage of verdicts in each setting in the two most severe nonfatal injury levels—levels 7 and 8.

Over one-half of the cases in two settings, orthopedic and plastic, involved minor injuries. Under 5% of the cases in orthopedic were levels 7 and 8 injuries, and none of the plastic surgery cases were in this range. Both of these categories had relatively low award medians, under $250,000. While just over one-half of the urology cases, the other low median award setting, involved major injuries, only one of those was in either a level 7 or 8 category and the plaintiff lost. Additionally, even for major injury cases, the median award was relatively low, $174,000.

In contrast, the two highest award settings in table 4.4—neurological and ob/gyn—had relatively high percentages of major injury injury cases. The percentages were 63.2% for neurological and 60.7% for ob/gyn. More importantly, these two settings had, by far, the highest percentages of cases involving injury levels 7 and 8—29.8% and 23.0% respectively. For no other setting did the percentage in these two levels reach 10%. Median awards for major injury cases were high in these two settings—$1,582,154 for neurological and $890,850 for ob/gyn. The highest awards tended to be in injury levels 7 and 8; both settings having median awards over $4 million in these injury categories. Interestingly, the setting with the highest percentage of verdicts involving major injuries generally, ophthalmology (66.7%), did not have a relatively high median award. This setting included few injury level 7 or 8 cases—only three—and plaintiffs won none of them. Plaintiffs did win nine of the 30 major injury cases in this setting, with two awards exceeding $1 million, the highest being $2.9 million. The median major injury award was $453,390.

While both neurological and ob/gyn had high percentages of major injuries—especially the most severe injuries—underlying their higher award structures, the patterns were different in terms of the causes of these injuries. The largest percentage of verdicts for neurological were caused by a specific procedure, 59.6%; another 22.8% were caused by problems in medical management. For ob/gyn, the largest percentage of verdicts involved injuries caused by problems in management—43.6%, and 37.4%—were caused by a specific procedure. If we wanted to look for the cause of injury for the very highest awards, we would find it in specific procedures in major injury cases for neurological. These cases had a median award of $1.1 million. For ob/gyn, we would find the highest awards in major injury verdicts involving problems in medical management. The median award for these cases was $3.2 million. The median was $4.7 million for injury level 7 and 8 cases where the cause was medical management, and these are primarily the so-called "bad baby" cases. In no other grouping of ob/gyn verdicts by cause and severity did the median award reach $1 million.

Minor/No Surgery Settings. Table 4.5 breaks down minor/no surgery into more specific settings, again those accounting for at least 1.0% of *all* of the 1,926 malpractice verdicts in the 10-plus verdicts sites. Like table 4.4, it presents the number of verdicts in each setting, the win rate, and the median award (table 4.5a) along with the percentages of each setting in different categories for severity of injury (table 4.5b). Six settings plus an "other" category are included in table 4.5a, but only one setting accounted for even 5% of all verdicts, internal medicine (15.7%). The next highest percentage involved pediatrics (3.6%).

Plaintiff win rates varied considerably—from 16.7% for family practice to 50% for radiology and 48.9% for psychiatry. In contrast, the highest win rate for the surgical settings in table 4.4a was 37.9% for urology.[208] Median awards in table 4.5a ranged from $123,200 for radiology to $1.1 million in pediatrics and in neurology, with the other medians being below $500,000. The two high-award settings, neurology and pediatrics, both had the largest percentage of their cases in the major injury category. For pediatrics, over 60% of the verdicts involved major injuries with nearly one-third of pediatric verdicts involving level 7 or 8 injuries. This was the highest percentage of level 7 and 8 injuries found in any of the settings in table 4.4a or in table 4.5a, and the median age of the plaintiff in these cases was less than one year. The largest percentage of pediatric major injury cases, in turn, involved injuries caused by problems in medical management, 46.5%. (One-half [50.7%] of all pediatric verdicts involved problems in medical management.) Plaintiffs won seven of 20 pediatric major injury cases involving problems of medical management with a median award of $8.25 million. Of those 20 cases, 15 involved level 7 or 8

Table 4.5 Specific Settings within Minor/No Surgery Comprising More than 1% of All Verdicts, 1988–90 (N = 566)

4.5a Frequencies, Win Rates, Awards

Setting	N	Percentage of All	Win Rate (%)	Median Award* ($)
Family practice	30	1.6	16.7	†
Internal medicine	303	15.7	26.1	435,000
Neurology	27	1.4	29.6	1,094,000
Pediatrics	69	3.6	36.2	1,114,043
Psychiatry	45	2.3	48.9	271,250
Radiology	18	0.9	50.0	123,200
Other	74	3.8		341,250
Total	566	29.3		

* Median award in 1990 dollars.
† Five or fewer winning verdicts.

4.5b Severity of Injury by Setting and Frequency* (Settings with more than Five Winning Verdicts)

Setting	Minor Injury (%)	(N)	Major Injury (%)	(N)	Death (%)	(N)	Levels 7 and 8 (%)	(N)
Internal medicine	26.4	(80)	31.7	(96)	41.9	(127)	8.3	(25)
Neurology	33.3	(9)	40.7	(11)	25.9	(7)	14.8	(4)
Pediatrics	15.9	(11)	62.3	(43)	21.7	(15)	31.9	(22)
Psychiatry	42.2	(19)	31.1	(14)	26.7	(12)	6.7	(3)
Radiology	44.4	(8)	50.0	(9)	5.6	(1)	22.2	(4)

* Percentages for each setting add to 100% reading across (minor+major+death); levels 7 and 8 are included in major injury.

injuries, and plaintiffs won five of the cases with a median award of $11.5 million.

The small number of neurology cases—especially the small number of cases in which plaintiffs were successful (8 of 27)—makes it difficult to examine these cases much detail. We can note that eight of the 27 cases involved injuries caused by a nondiagnosis; three cases involved level 7 and 8 injuries, and three were death cases. Ten of 27 involved problems in medical management, with one-half involving minor injuries and only one involving level 7 or 8 injuries (and the plaintiff lost this case). The small number of cases prevents any detailed discussion of the anomalous situation of radiology—a high win rate (50%), with half of the verdicts involving major injuries, and a very modest median award, $123,200. The largest percentage of these verdicts had their cause in a specific procedure with plaintiffs winning just over one-half of these cases (six of 11 specific procedure matters).

The more numerous internal medicine cases presented a different picture with a relatively low percentage involving the most serious injuries (8.3% in levels 7 and 8), and a relatively high percentage of death cases (41.9%). Most internal medicine cases primarily involved injuries caused by medical management (45.2%) and by nondiagnoses (27.1%). Misdiagnoses were involved in 13.5% and specific procedures in 12.5%. Plaintiffs won most frequently in misdiagnosis cases (14 of 41, 34.1%) and tended to receive the highest awards, exhibiting a median award of $511,250. Plaintiffs won seven of 15 major injury misdiagnosis cases with a median award of $462,000 and six of 16 death misdiagnosis cases with a median award of $945,190. Only four misdiagnosis cases involved level 7 and 8 injuries, and plaintiffs won only one of them. Plaintiffs were successful in 41 of 137 (29.9%) cases in which the cause of injury involved problems in medical management with a median award of $412,602. The largest number of these were death cases (58 of 137), and plaintiffs won 31.0% (18) with a median award of $339,988. Another 38 of the medical management cases involved major injuries. Plaintiffs were successful in 36.8% (14) of these with a median award of $567,997. Thirteen of these 38 cases involved level 7 and 8 injuries, with plaintiffs winning 42.2%. The median award for the six winning level 7 and 8 cases was $1.9 million.

Patterns such as the ones we have described for surgery and minor/no surgery settings suggest that there is order in the malpractice system. Contrary to the reform rhetoric's characterization, the malpractice system does not appear to be a "bizarre lottery."[209] While the patterns vary in terms of injury cause, injury severity, plaintiff win rates, and awards among different settings, the patterns within specific settings can be quite clear. If we look at verdicts as transmitters of messages, those messages may go beyond information relevant to handling disputes over injuries caused by medical negligence. Patterns in verdicts can tell us important things about the matters that actually go trial, such as the distribution of different medical settings among cases going to a jury trial. Within settings, patterns in verdicts can tell us about the seriousness of the injury involved and the alleged cause of the injury in addition to how often plaintiffs win and how much they are awarded when they do.

In short, they can inform us about, as one recent study of closed malpractice claims in the medical literature put it, the epidemiology of error.[210] In this sense, patterns in verdicts offer messages about the base of the disputing pyramid—the types and causes of injuries. It is important to know, for instance, that over one-half of all the verdicts in our database (55.5%) came from just four medical settings: ob/gyn, internal medicine, orthopedic surgery, and general surgery. It is important to know that for the largest percentages of the first three settings (which together account for 46.2% of the verdicts) the alleged cause of injury involved problems in medical management: 43.6%, 45.2%, and 40.6% respectively. And it is important to know that the largest percentage of the most severe injuries among these three settings—and hence the highest awards—are found in cases involving problems in medical management.[211] Patterns like these, to borrow from the Kravitz et al. epidemiology study of medical error using closed claims, "may hold lessons the medical profession ought to learn" and may help in "identifying important problems in medical practice and . . . suggesting solutions."[212] Patterns in verdicts and in closed insurance claims are useful "because they highlight the types of problems that result in negligent injury and demonstrate the relative importance of different error types among cases consequential enough to prompt legal action."[213] Patterns in verdicts, then, may offer a message suggesting that targeted efforts at quality assurance may be as or even more appropriate than fundamental legal reform aimed at the process of handling disputes after injuries occur.

Temporal Patterns: 1970–90

An essential part of the reform rhetoric's strategic representation of the malpractice system is the portrayal of change. It speaks of increasing numbers of cases and skyrocketing awards resulting from the avarice of undeserving plaintiffs and their unscrupulous lawyers, inappropriate and biased jury verdicts, and so on. The consequences of these changes in the legal system are ultimately suffered by ordinary members of society who can no longer get adequate health care. The rhetoric gains much of its appeal from its portrayal of change as a story of decline. The social consequences, as we saw earlier, are couched in terms of the direst situations—often symbolized by the plight of women unable to obtain obstetrical services. The rhetoric emphasizes the ob/gyn arena because it is supposedly representative of a broad pattern of increasing numbers of lawsuits, plaintiff win rates, and awards across all types of malpractice cases. While this characterization is certainly useful for political purposes, the reality of patterns over time appears to be much more complex. In this section, we will explore patterns in malpractice verdicts between the years 1970 and 1990, organizing the discussion around the same four time periods used in the discussion of temporal patterns in chapter 3.

General Patterns. The simple question with which we begin is whether we will find aggregate patterns over time anything at all like those found in the reform rhetoric. To answer this question, we need to look at sites that have had some number of malpractice verdicts between 1970 and 1990. This in itself is something of a problematic task because of the low numbers of verdicts within each time period, especially when the data are disaggregated. Of the 19 sites for which we have 21 years of data, eight had at least 100 malpractice verdicts over the course of those years.[214] Given the low rate of plaintiff success in malpractice cases, the numbers of winning cases are much lower. Only two sites had more than 100 winning malpractice verdicts, and none had an overall plaintiff win rate as high as 40%.[215] To explore patterns over time, we will focus on the three counties with the highest numbers of cases: Los Angeles, Cook, and San Francisco. These sites also had the highest numbers of winning cases and the highest win rates. The lower numbers of verdicts in the other sites within each time period, particularly the lower numbers of cases in which plaintiffs won, make it difficult to talk about temporal patterns with any confidence. For instance, there were only four plaintiff wins in Jackson for 1970–75 and only four in Sacramento for 1986–90. While the lower number of verdicts prevents the use of Dallas for many purposes, where possible we will use it to help provide perspective (from another major urban center) for the other three sites.

Table 4.6 provides aggregate data on plaintiff win rates and median awards for Los Angeles, Cook, San Francisco, and Dallas Counties across the four time periods. The most obvious conclusion to be drawn from these figures is that there were no consistent, general patterns shared by the four sites. Win rates did not follow any simple pattern, nor were they high. No win rate reached as high 45%, and in fact most were below 35%. These win rates, however, were higher than those in Dallas where the win rate fluctuated between 16.9% and 21.4%. Los Angeles, the site with the greatest number of verdicts, had a surprisingly stable win rate over time (surprising in light of what might be expected based on the reform rhetoric). In Cook, the win rate dropped sharply in 1976–80 and then steadily rose to just under the 1970–75 level. The reason for that sharp decline is difficult to pinpoint. Illinois had enacted a major malpractice reform package in 1975, but the state supreme court quickly declared its key provisions unconstitutional.[216]

Table 4.6 Patterns in Win Rates and Awards: 1970–90

	1970–75			1976–80			1981–85			1986–90		
Site	*N*	Win Rate (%)	Median Award* ($)	*N*	Win Rate (%)	Median Award* ($)	*N*	Win Rate (%)	Median Award* ($)	*N*	Win Rate (%)	Median Award* ($)
Los Angeles	287	33.4	165,800	393	33.1	206,170	305	31.1	189,000	305	31.8	273,710
Cook	59	42.4	171,836	98	25.5	270,600	141	33.3	254,745	383	40.7	347,563
San Francisco	101	33.7	163,274	59	28.8	83,475	38	39.5	226,800	37	27.0	212,480
Dallas	32	18.8	148,654	42	21.4	18,043	42	21.4	70,560	83	16.9	313,719

* Median awards are in 1990 dollars.

Illinois again enacted reform in the middle 1980s, only to have the state supreme court find that some, but not all, of the key provisions were unconstitutional.[217] California also enacted a major reform package in the middle 1970s, the major provisions of which were found to be constitutional by the state supreme court.[218] The Los Angeles win rates, as noted, stayed stable. The San Francisco win rates fluctuated—dropping in 1975–80, rising in 1981–85, only to drop again in 1986–90.

None of the counties shows a pattern for median awards consistent with the reform rhetoric's characterization. For malpractice awards taken as a whole, there was no general pattern of skyrocketing awards. In Los Angeles County, the site with the highest number of verdicts, the median award oscillated between $165,800 in 1970–75 and $273,710 in 1986–90 within a pattern of slight upward direction. The pattern for Cook was somewhat different—rising in 1976–80, drifting downward slightly in 1981–85, and then rising again to $347,563—the highest median in table 4.6. In San Francisco, the median award followed a pattern different than that in either Los Angeles or Cook. It dropped sharply in 1976–80, rose even more sharply in 1981–85, and drifted slightly downward in 1986–90.[219]

Figures 4.2a–4.2c present a more detailed picture of patterns in awards over time. The graphs in these figures are arranged so that the bottom of the bar in a given time period represents the 25th percentile for awards and the top of the bar the 75th percentile. The two lines in each of these graphs are for the median and mean awards, the upper line being the mean and the lower line the median. The graphs show, most obviously, that while the patterns for each of the counties were distinct, there was one important similarity—the most dramatic changes were at the higher end of the scale as represented by the means and 75th percentiles rather than across all verdicts generally.

Cook (figure 4.2b) exhibited the highest award structure. While there were no dramatic increases over time in the 25th percentile and

Figure 4.2a: Los Angeles

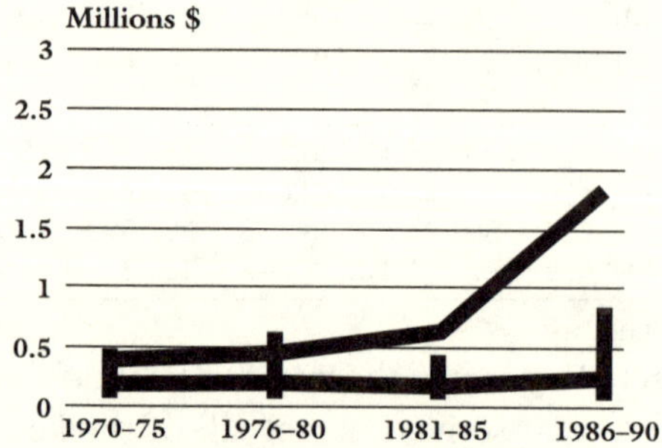

Figure 4.2b: Cook

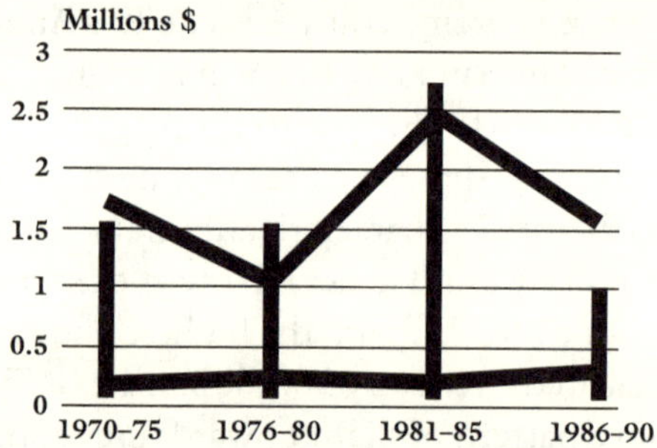

Figure 4.2c: San Francisco

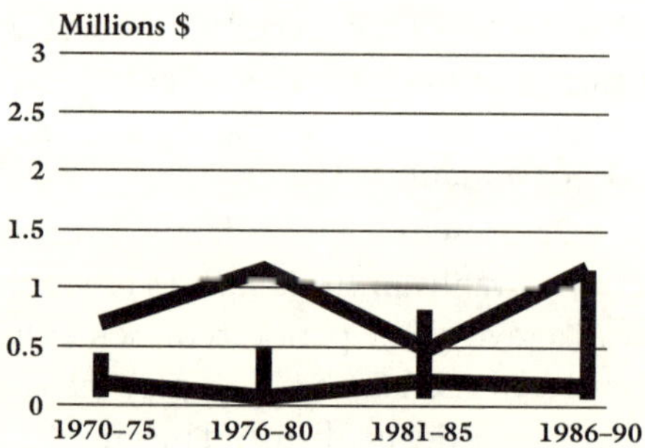

FIGURES 4.2a–4.2c Award Structure (1990 dollars)

Note: top line is mean, bottom line is median

the median award (at its highest, the 25th percentile reached $79,200 in 1976–80), the 75th percentile increased sharply from $1.6 million in 1976–80 to $2.8 million in 1981–85. In 1986–90 it decreased even more sharply to $987,857. The mean followed a different pattern, decreasing from $1.7 million in 1970–75 to $1.1 million in 1976–80, increasing to $2.5 million in 1981–85, and then decreasing again in 1986–90 to $1.6 million. The reasons for this pattern are likely to be very complex, but one potential factor can be ruled out—the effect of punitive damages. Legislation enacted in 1985 abolished punitive damages in malpractice suits,[220] but even before this punitive damages were a rarity. Between 1970 and 1985, punitive damages were awarded in only three of 97 plaintiff verdicts in Cook.

The pattern in Los Angeles was quite different. The median, 75th percentile, and mean award were lower than those for Cook with the exception of the 1986–90 mean award ($1.9 million in Los Angeles). The one dramatic increase depicted in figure 4.2a occurred in the mean award which moved from $631,834 in 1981–85 to $1.9 million in 1986–90. Much of this increase was a result of a small number of very high awards. Six of the 97 plaintiffs' verdicts in 1986–90 exceeded $10 million. All six involved permanent grave injuries (injury level 8), and five of the six involved problems in medical management (the sixth involved a specific procedure). Five of the six injured parties were less than one year old at the time of the injury, and the sixth was between one and two years old. In other words, these were "bad baby" cases. If these six verdicts are removed, then the 1986–90 mean award drops to $685,795.

California's 1975 malpractice reforms did include a limitation on noneconomic damages ($250,000), but the high awards pushing the Los Angeles mean upward in 1986–90 were awards primarily for economic damages. "Bad baby" cases can produce very high awards because of the cost of long-term or even lifetime care. Still, it is possible that the 1975 cap on noneconomic damages helped to keep the Los Angeles award structure relatively stable before 1986–90. San Francisco, in contrast, exhibited a less stable pattern than Los Angeles. While the median award went up and down, the 75th percentile increased, especially after 1976–80. It reached $1.2 million in 1986–90, when there were only 10 winning verdicts—three of them over $1 million, with the highest being $8.2 million. The greatest variations in the award structure in San Francisco occurred in the mean award, but this was due to small numbers of winning verdicts (34, 17, 15, and 10 across the four time periods).

Medical Settings. While aggregate patterns in awards and win rates such as those just described are likely to draw most of the attention in the policy debate, the key to understanding what is happening in the malpractice system is found in the patterns and changes within different medical settings. There is no reason to think that different medical settings would follow the same patterns over time or be affected by enacted reforms in the same way. As a result, no general or specific setting can represent all types of malpractice matters. The crucial question asks what kinds of changes will be found within the major general settings—surgery and no/minor surgery—and within the higher frequency specific settings within each of the general settings, especially ob/gyn, orthopedic surgery, general surgery, and internal medicine. Contrary to what might be expected from the political debates, we found no dramatic changes within settings. With respect to verdicts, at least, the malpractice system appears to be a relatively stable one. But against this relatively stable background, there were some very important subtle shifts.

Figures 4.3a–4.3c show patterns over time in general settings for Los Angeles, Cook, and San Francisco Counties. For each, the largest proportion of verdicts came from the surgical setting—at least half of the verdicts in each county for each time period. As a point in contrast, the percentage of all malpractice verdicts made up by the surgical setting was lower in Dallas, dropping below 50% in 1976–80 and 1981–85 (45.2% and 45.2%) and reaching no higher than 55.4% (in 1986–90). In the other three sites, the percentage dropped below 60% only twice—58.2% in Cook for 1981–85 and 59.4% in San Francisco for 1986–90. These figures show no marked changes in the percentage of verdicts coming from the surgical setting. In Los Angeles, which had the highest surgical setting percentages, there was stability with a slight downward drift in 1986–90 when the percentage was 62.6% (71.1%, 69.7%, 70.2%, 62.6%). In Cook, the percentage ranged between 64.4% and 58.2%, with a slight downward shift from 1970–75 to 1981–85 (64.4%, 62.2%, 58.2%) and then a move upward to 62.1%. In San Francisco, the percentage drifted upward—61.4%, 64.4%, 65.8%, and then dropped down in 1986–90 to 59.4%.

In Los Angeles and Cook, the second largest percentage of verdicts in each time period came from the no/minor surgery setting. The Los Angeles percentage fluctuated between 17.8% and 20.4% for the first three time periods and then increased to 29.2% in 1986–90, as the percentage from the surgery setting decreased slightly. In Cook, the pattern was one of slow increase over time—22.0%, 24.5%, 27.0%, 31.3%—while the percentage from the surgery setting was slipping downward through the first three time periods. In San Francisco, the percentage from the no/minor surgery setting stayed stable for the first

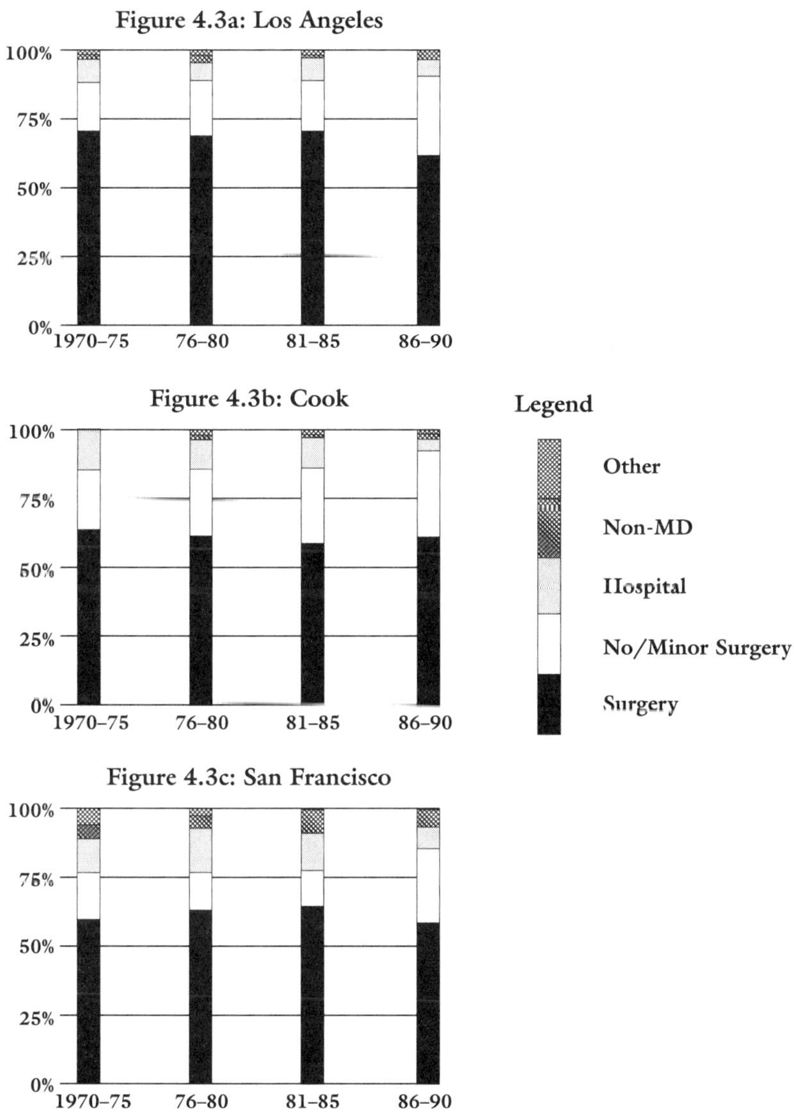

FIGURES 4.3a–4.3c General Medical Setting

three time periods (11.9%, 13.6%, 13.2%), and then increased to 27.0%. In 1976–80, the hospital setting accounted for more verdicts than no/minor surgery (16.9% v. 13.6%), and an equal amount in 1981–85 (13.2% for each setting). After 1976–80, the percentage from the hospital setting decreased to 8.1% in 1986–90. The percentage from the hospital setting in Cook decreased from 13.6% to 5.0% across the four time periods, and in Los Angeles it fluctuated between 8.7% and 5.9%.

While no marked changes occurred in these three counties with regard to general settings, they shared shifts toward slightly fewer verdicts from the surgery setting and slightly more from the no/minor surgery setting. Patterns for plaintiff win rates within the surgery setting differed among the three counties, but only Cook showed a pattern of increasing win rates within this setting. After dropping from 42.1% in 1970–75 to 16.4% in 1976–80 (despite the fact that the state supreme court struck down reforms aimed at curbing what were thought to be too many frivolous suits), the win rate increased to 25.6% and then to 43.7%. The win rate in Los Angeles for the surgery setting stayed within a narrow range—between 28.8% and 31.9%. The win rate in San Francisco, where the numbers of cases were smaller, fluctuated over a wider range (from 21.1% to 36.0%), but showed no directional trend.

In Los Angeles, the most fertile ground for discussion because of the larger number of cases, there was no dramatic increase in the median award for cases arising in the surgery setting. Over the four time periods, it went from $172,250 to $236,635 to $208,800 to $275,000. There were no dramatic changes with regard to the patterns in the more specific settings within surgery, the severity of injury involved, or the cause of injury. There was, for instance, no dramatic increase in the percentage of surgery verdicts from the ob/gyn setting. The percentage increased from 20.6% of the surgery verdicts in 1970–75 to 29.9% in 1976–80, and then drifted downward to 25.1% in 1986–90.[221] There was no pattern of increasing plaintiff win rates in ob/gyn verdicts; the rate fluctuated between 37.8% and 39.3% over the first three time periods and then slipped to 33.3% in the last time period. The median award for ob/gyn cases showed little increase over time, going from $243,675 to $164,000 to $239,000 to $267,850.[222]

What is more important are the subtle shifts that occurred against the relatively stable patterns in the surgery setting in Los Angeles. Although a specific procedure was the most prominent cause of injury in the surgery setting, the percentage declined somewhat over time from a high of 50.4% of surgery setting verdicts in 1976–80 to 43.0% in 1981–85 and 41.9% in 1986–90. The percentage of verdicts with a problem in medical management as the cause of injury increased over the same years from 27.0% to 31.8% to 37.7%. This shift is important because the surgery setting verdicts involving medical management as a cause of injury tended to have higher awards than those involving a specific procedure. Over time the general pattern for median awards in verdicts with medical management–caused injuries moved upward from $172,250 to $270,000 to $229,250 to $432,000. The median award for verdicts with specific procedure–caused injuries peaked in 1976–80 at $173,850. When the medical management–caused injuries were major injuries, the award structure was even higher—$187,525 to $265,248 to $566,000 to $1,771,875. Additionally, while they were few in number, in medical management–caused injuries that were the most severe—injury levels 7 and 8—awards were higher still. For three such cases in 1970–75, the median award was $290,700 ($202,800, $290,700, $2,099,500); for three in 1976–80, it was $1,413,000 ($265,248, $1,413,000, $1,780,000); for three in 1981–85, it was $1,475,060 ($648,000, $1,475,060, $3,780,000); and for seven in 1986–90, it was $9,183,158.[223]

The shift toward a somewhat higher percentage of verdicts with management–caused injuries was not a phenomenon found consistently across all specific surgery settings. Overall, the emergency medicine setting had the highest percentage of management–caused injuries, 50% (47 of 94 verdicts). The percentage dropped from 53.8% in 1970–75 to 47.4% in 1976–80 and to 42.3% in 1981–85. It rose again in 1986–90 to 56.5%. Most of these emergency medicine verdicts, however, did not involve major injuries (nine of the 47 management–caused injuries). The ob/gyn setting had the next highest percentage of management–caused injuries—43.9% (100 of 291 verdicts)—and over time the percentage went from 52.4% to 28.0% to 51.8% to 54.2%. An increase did come in the percentage of ob/gyn verdicts with management–caused *major* injuries—26.2% to 14.6% to 28.6% to 41.7%. Accompanying this increase was a change in the median age of the injured person in management–caused major injury verdicts in ob/gyn. It dropped from 35.0 years in 1970–75 to 1.5 years in 1976–80 to one year or less in 1981–85 and 1986–90. Again, these are the so-called "bad baby" cases, and median awards in these cases, though few in number, increased over time—from $202,800 for five winning verdicts to $322,600 for three verdicts to $566,000 for five verdicts to $9,146,609 for nine verdicts.[224]

Los Angeles, Cook, and San Francisco shared a shift toward slightly more cases from the no/minor surgery setting. Patterns for win rates for this general setting differed among the counties, but none had a pattern of increasing win rate. In fact, for Cook the rate declined over time from 46.2% to 41.7% to 39.5% to 35.0%. In Los Angeles the rate fluctuated between 23.3% and 33.8% (25.5% to 33.8% to 23.3% to 31.5%). The win rate in San Francisco, where the numbers of cases were much lower, fluctuated over a very wide range with no directional trend. In each of the counties, the largest percentage of no/minor surgery verdicts came from the internal medicine setting. With the exception of Cook in 1970–75 (38.5%), the internal medicine setting accounted for at least 40% of the no/minor surgery verdicts in each of the counties.

Focusing again on Los Angeles because of its greater number of verdicts, the median award for no/minor surgery verdicts declined over the first three time periods—from $421,250 to $318,000 to $178,475. It rose to $363,770 in 1986–90. There were some changes in the severity of injury. The percentage of verdicts involving minor injuries dropped from 31.4% in 1970–75 to 23.8% in 1976–80 and then rose again to 28.3% and to 30.3%. The percentage involving major injuries increased from 31.4% in 1970–75 to 38.8% in 1976–80 and then stayed relatively stable (40.0% and 37.1%). The percentage involving the most severe major injuries—levels 7 and 8—rose slightly: 7.8% to 11.3% to 10.0% to 15.7%.

The highest awards for no/minor surgery verdicts in Los Angeles tended to be in cases involving major injuries, especially injury levels 7 and 8, and most especially injury level 7 and 8 cases arising from the pediatric setting. The numbers of verdicts in the pediatric setting, however, were too low to assess patterns over time. There were only six pediatric verdicts involving injury levels 7 and 8. All involved injured children of less than two years of age, and all but one were generated by medical management–caused injuries (the last involved and problem in diagnosis). Five of the six awards were in excess of $1 million, all of them involving management–caused injuries, with the highest award being $15 million (the sixth award was the diagnosis–caused injury, $360,000).

Summary

The messages offered by these patterns in malpractice verdicts over time are not consistent with the picture portrayed by the reform rhetoric. These patterns suggest not a system that has devolved into chaos or some other degenerate state, but an orderly system that did not change in any major way over the 21-year period. Still, there were important shifts within this system that underlied some of the patterns for the high end of the award structure. These shifts involved cases with major injuries (especially the most severe levels of injury), medical management–caused injuries, and younger people. Such shifts cannot be simply explained as the result of increasingly generous or biased juries, or of even increasingly greedy lawyers. They reflect the dynamics of activities farther down the disputing pyramid—activities about which little is known. We do not know, for instance, what changes have occurred at the pyramid's base and in the number of injuries. We do not know if plaintiffs' attorneys have changed the way in which they decide to handle a matter or what kinds of matters to handle. Are plaintiffs' attorneys, for instance, seeking out more management–caused, severe injury matters, or has the way such matters are handled changed so that more of them are brought to trial? We do not know what changes may have occurred in the way malpractice insurance carriers handle the defense and settlement of these claims.

In chapter 2 we offered the general argument that the portrayal of juries and the civil justice system animating the politics of reform is best understood as strategic representation in a political struggle over which image of reality will govern policy.[225] This argument can be applied more specifically to medical malpractice as part 1 of this chapter shows. Consistent with commentators like Michael Saks and Joseph Sanders and Craig Joyce, this chapter shows there is a substantial gap between the claims of the reform rhetoric and the available empirical evidence.

The extant literature along with our own research on jury verdicts presents a very different picture than the reform rhetoric's strategic representation. There is evidence suggesting that, rather than being chaotic, the malpractice system is orderly, stable, and dauntingly complex. This picture shows medical injury—even negligently caused medical injury—to be frequent. Yet, most injured patients do not file a claim, they "lump it." Most claims that are filed are closed without formal adjudication, and most appear to be closed without any payment to the injured patient. Those closed with a payment typically do not involve large payments. In those matters that do go to a trial, plaintiffs do not win often. Also, while jury awards can be large, the larger awards tend to involve younger plaintiffs with severe, permanent injuries.

Two things need to be said in light of the difference between politically motivated rhetoric and our best sense of reality. First, the lack of veracity in the rhetoric's strategic representation does not necessarily mean that the malpractice system is operating flawlessly or even adequately. Alternative images may point to different problems. For instance, as noted earlier, the authors of the Harvard Malpractice Study found that most negligently injured patients do not make a claim, meaning that they go uncompensated. Rather than a litigation surplus, they spoke of a litigation deficit. This is one of the reasons why they argue for the use of a workers' compensation–like system for the malpractice arena, one that imposes some form of strict liability for medical injuries.[226] The predicament of injured but uncompensated patients is underscored by the findings of a variety of studies that suggest that medical error, patient injury, and substandard care are not rare occurrences.[227]

Second, policies that do not have at least some grounding in the way things work in practice are unlikely succeed. Additionally, they may engender a variety of unintended consequences with their own dynamics and costs. This is clearly seen in the empirical evaluations of Indiana's reform efforts.[228] The response to the idea that the malpractice reforms of the 1970s and 1980s did not measure up to expectation is revealing. Rather than questioning or reevaluating the characterization of juries and the civil justice system guiding reform, the response has been the call for more fundamental changes since the lack of success is taken as an indicator of the depth of the problem.

Conclusion: The "Vagaries" of Juries

We opened this chapter by quoting psychologist and law professor Neil Vidmar, and we want to close by briefly describing some of his findings on juror decision making in the malpractice arena. Unlike most of the research discussed in this chapter—our own included—Vidmar's findings come from experimental research. Where our discussion has focused largely on the patterns in aggregate data of various kinds and whether those patterns are consistent with reform rhetoric's portrayal, Vidmar's experimental findings directly address one of the central tenets of the rhetoric's portrayal—the vagaries of juries. Vidmar's novel research focuses on assessments of noneconomic damages (like "pain and suffering"), especially with regard to the "deep pockets" hypothesis (the claim that lay juries make decisions solely or largely on the defendant's ability to pay). He specifically chose this focus because it goes to the very heart of the reform rhetoric's negative characterization of juries in the medical malpractice arena and the idea that lay juries are biased and somehow incompetent in comparison to expert decision makers. Two reports of his research are important for our purposes.

In one study, Vidmar conducted an experiment using a sample of "147 veniremen waiting to be called for jury selection in the Wake County (Raleigh), North Carolina state court"[229] to test the "deep pockets" hypothesis in malpractice cases. The experiment was designed to see if the "pain and suffering" damages would be different for the same physical injury occurring in different situations. The situation differed according to the cause of injury: medical malpractice or an automobile accident, the idea being that doctors and hospitals are "deep pockets" and lay juries—which are allegedly biased against deep pockets—will award higher amounts for the same injuries when they are defendants. The experimental situations also differed according to the number and type of defendants. Those situations covered malpractice with one defendant, with two defendants, and with a hospital defendant, and an automobile accident with one defendant, two defendants, and corporate employer defendant. The jurors were then randomly assigned to one of these six experimental situations and given materials to use in making a decision. These materials told each juror that liability had already been established and economic damages stipulated. The only decision remaining was on "pain and suffering."

Vidmar's experiment found "no support for the deep pocket hypothesis or the psychological dynamics that are posited to be behind it."[230] The cause of the injury—malpractice or automobile injury—did not make a difference in the size of the "pain and suffering" award given. He concluded that "there is no support for the hypothesis that jurors would be prejudiced against medical providers in comparison to motor vehicle operators or to corporations who are legally responsible for them . . . (and) there was no general support for the hypothesis that the number or type of defendants makes a difference."[231]

A companion study investigated the question of whether the size of jury awards for noneconomic damages are appropriate.[232] Underlying this study was the reform rhetoric's claim that such lay jury awards are too high and that professionals (such as judges or arbitrators) who are less biased and emotional, and presumably more expert or competent, would give lower awards. This experiment used a single malpractice case and presented it to a sample of jurors and to a sample of experienced lawyer-arbitrators in order to compare their assessments of noneconomic damages. There were 89 jurors, 47 veniremen awaiting jury duty in Durham, North Carolina, and 42 veniremen awaiting duty in Greensboro, North Carolina. Twenty-one lawyer arbitrators from North Carolina made up the other experimental group. They were "arbitrators for various personal injury, contract, and labor disputes. . . . Eighteen were senior members of the North Carolina bar; five had previously been judges in the North Carolina superior courts. Only one indicated that his law practice was predominantly plaintiff-oriented, and nine indicated a predominantly defense-oriented practice."[233]

Vidmar and Rice found that their "data lend no support to the widely held view that jurors are more generous than judges or arbitrators in awarding non-economic damages. Moreover, the data do not support the view that the reasoning of laypersons in calculating the award is substantially different from that of legally trained persons."[234] They did find greater variability in awards among individual jurors as compared to individual professionals, but as they noted, the question is what happens when a jury decides, not just an individual juror. To address this, they randomly drew 100 12-person juries from the responses of the 89 individual jurors and then took the median award of each of the 100 experimental juries. Vidmar and Rice found that there was *less* variability among these awards than among the professionals' awards. They noted that the implication of this finding "is that more stable estimates of non-economic damages would be obtained from a 'jury' than from single arbitrators or judges."[235] In addition, they point out that in the absence of any absolute standard for judging human suffering or metric for converting suffering into dollar figures, there are important advantages in using juries drawn from a community's citizens. A jury's decision "may have the advantage of providing a sense of procedural justice and legitimacy to the award."[236]

As Vidmar noted, experimental findings as these cannot be simply generalized. But he pointed out that when the findings of experimental research on juries and aggregate research on juries point in the same direction, we gain confidence in both. His experimental findings run counter to the reform rhetoric's portrayal and are consistent with the patterns found in aggregate data on jury verdicts. We might add that when the findings of research using very different methodologies find little or no support for the reform rhetoric's characterization of juries in the malpractice system, there is especially good reason for skepticism about the definition of the policy problem and the solutions proffered for solving it.

APPENDIX 4.1 Nine-Point Injury Scale

Severity Level Code	Description
1	No Physical Injury (emotional only, e.g., fright)
2	Temporary Insignificant Injury (e.g., lacerations, bruises, contusions)
3	Temporary Minor Injury (e.g., broken ankle, infection)
4	Temporary Major Injury (e.g., burns, back injury, drug side effect)
5	Permanent Minor Injury (e.g., loss of fingers)
6	Permanent Significant Injury (e.g., loss of limb, one eye, deafness, loss of one kidney or lung)

7	Permanent Major Injury (e.g., paraplegia, blindness, loss of two limbs, brain damage)
8	Permanent Grave Injury (e.g., quadraplegia, severe brain damage, injury requiring lifelong care)
9	Death

Adapted from NAIC, 1980, at 10.

CHAPTER FIVE

Products Liability

Like medical malpractice, products liability has been a highly visible and hotly contested part of the civil justice reform debate. Proposals to federalize this traditional area of state law have been on the Congressional agenda since 1977,[1] and the effort to get on the federal agenda goes back even earlier into the 1970s.[2] The use of a "crisis" characterization to describe products liability also dates back to the 1970s. For instance, the report of the U.S. Senate Committee on Commerce, Science, and Transportation on the 1991 Products Liability Fairness Act[3] noted that "in the mid–1970s, products liability was first recognized as a serious problem of interstate commerce which, in the view of many businesses and academic observers, had reached 'crisis' proportions and required a Federal response."[4] And as Victor Schwartz, long-time reform advocate/policy entrepreneur, wrote in a 1978 article, "In 1975, an apparent crisis arose in the field of product liability. Many manufacturers alleged that product liability insurance had become unavailable or unaffordable."[5]

Among the primary causes of this "crisis" are the frequency of products liability suits and the proplaintiff proclivities of juries. Said the Reagan administration's Tort Policy Working Group, "(t)he growth in the number of product liability suits has been astounding."[6] With regard to jury verdicts in these suits, the *Report* characterized them as "explosive."[7] Underlying these harmful phenomena, the argument goes, are changes in the law relating to products liability, especially the development of the doctrine of strict liability. These changes are characterized as overly proplaintiff, so much so that the system is said to be badly out of balance. As the discussion of the views of reform high theorists Peter Huber and George Priest in chapter 2 indicated, some commentators characterize the underlying changes in the law in even more dramatic terms—as a revolution, taken with that term's most negative and threatening connotations. For Huber at least, the ultimate consequences of this revolution are indeed chilling—the likely destruction of our way of life. In the concluding chapter of his book *Liability*, Huber characterized the revolutionized law "as an engine of social destruction."[8]

The decisions and verdicts of juries are crucial indicators of the crisis. While other indicators are used to draw our attention to the negative consequences of the changes in the law itself—from the "costs" of the liability system to the number of lost jobs to lost tax revenues—products liability filings and jury verdicts are the most important in linking those consequences to the legal system. Verdicts are especially symbolic because they provide concrete evidence of the problems caused by the changes in the law relating to products liability. Without an "explosion" of litigation and "astronomical"[9] jury verdicts, the complaints about the changes in the law become abstract or theoretical and hardly worth the attention of policymakers. Verdicts with "astronomical" awards provide the causal link between issues like the loss of jobs, declining competitiveness, or the decline of certain industries and the legal system. Verdicts, in short, show that the legal system is badly "out of balance" and in need of reform so that balance can be restored.

In this chapter we first will briefly explore the rhetoric of reform regarding products liability and juries. As we did with medical malpractice, we will then discuss the empirical evidence that can be used to outline the disputing pyramid for products liability. We will present evidence from our own research on jury verdicts in three sections. The first of these data-oriented discussions broadly examines products liability verdicts for 1988–90. The second section looks at these verdicts in more detail based on the situations or settings in which the injury occurred. The final section examines patterns in verdicts over time using data for 1970–90.

"Let's Restore Balance": Rhetoric and Context

Strategic Representation

There is a rich rhetoric of reform in the products liability arena. It is built around a story of decline that is told through the recounting of the negative consequences of the products liability system for American society and economy. In chapters 1 and 2, we reviewed in some detail the kinds of consequences that have been ascribed to the failure of the products liability system. At the extreme is Peter Huber's picture of consequences, one that is truly biblical in proportion and leads to the demise of American society as we know it.[10] Somewhat less dramatic descriptions tell of products—typically important or needed ones—either not developed or no longer available,[11] or like the characterization presented by the Washington Legal Foundation, depict reform as needed "for the sake of the living standards of present and future generations."[12]

This rhetoric has long included horror story anecdotes of outrageous jury verdicts, verdicts which in the words of business leader/reform advocate Robert Malott "strain credulity."[13] These stories typically tell of greedy (and perhaps dishonest) plaintiffs and their attorneys suing hapless and innocent companies in situations where the plaintiff was probably to blame for his or her own injuries. Juries then decide in favor of these plaintiffs, awarding very large sums of money, thus illustrating the failings of the products liability system.

Numbers, particularly those describing the size of the jury verdicts in these horror stories, have also been a prominent part of this rhetoric. The size of the award is, symbolically, an indicator of the size of the problem. Cases with small awards, no matter how bizarre the factual situation or outcomes may seem, are a curiosity but not evidence of a fundamental problem. Large, very large awards are another matter. Reports of extremely high average awards in products liability cases, such as those reported by the Reagan administration's Tort Policy Working Group,[14] for example, are used as indicators of the severity of the situation. Other large numbers besides those describing jury verdicts have also been used as indicators of the seriousness of the problem. Perhaps the best example is Peter Huber's infamous and widely cited $300 billion estimate of the indirect cost of the system.[15]

Perhaps the key metaphor in the reform rhetoric for products liability is the idea of balance. Reports on jury verdicts and the like are offered as proof of imbalance in the system, an imbalance which is leading to the decline of American society and economy. As a political metaphor, balance is very attractive and powerful, allowing reformers to cast their desired changes not as something revolutionary or coldly self-serving, but rather as a means of restoring balance to the system. The metaphor is especially powerful when used in the context of things legal because it brings to mind our culture's most enduring symbol of justice—the blindfolded woman holding aloft her balanced scales—

with justice being equated with fairness.[16] A system out of balance is unfair, unjust because it favors one side over the other. The scales of justice have been tipped. The system is deemed to be out of balance because it allegedly favors plaintiffs over defendants. This imbalance is built into the law relating to products liability (especially, but not only, the doctrine of strict liability) and is evidenced by the verdicts rendered by juries. These verdicts, in turn, affect the more informal settlement processes that handle the much larger number of product-related claims that never reach a jury trial. As we noted in chapter 2, William McCormick observed: "there is enormous leverage on these recent court cases—they directly affect the thousands of other cases that get settled before going to court, not to mention acting as a stimulant for ever more lawsuits."[17] In so doing, verdicts tip the scales of justice even more.

The balance metaphor has been a part of the reform rhetoric for a number of years. It has regularly appeared in the titles of articles, essays, and speeches by those arguing for reform. For instance, Robert Malott, then chairman and chief executive officer of FMC Corporation and a frequent voice for reform, titled a 1983 *Harvard Business Review* article "Let's Restore Balance to Product Liability Law."[18] William McCormick, then chairman and chief executive officer of Fireman's Fund Insurance, used the metaphor in a widely circulated 1986 speech entitled "The American Tort System: A Time to Rebalance the Scales of Justice."[19] Restoring "balance and fairness to our civil justice system" was a major theme of the 1987 Aetna Insurance Company public relations campaign noted in chapter 2.[20] The idea appears again in the title of a proposed piece of federal legislation—the Product Liability Fairness Act.[21]

Litigation and jury verdicts, as we noted, are primary indicators of imbalance in the products liability system. Writing in that 1983 article Malott said that over the previous three decades, "product liability law has changed dramatically," and true to the story of decline the change has been for the worse.[22] From his perspective, the "pendulum has swung too far in favor of the injured product user, imposing on manufacturers and distributors enormous and inequitable costs that are ultimately passed on to society as a whole."[23] According to Malott, "the most graphic evidence of this escalating exposure is the rapid growth in the number of product liability suits being filed and in the amounts of damages awarded."[24] Later in the same article he also claims that under the strict liability scheme currently governing products liability, "the size and number of product liability awards have increased greatly, and they have every indication of continuing to grow at astronomical rates."[25]

Malott pursued the same themes in a widely distributed 1985 address to the Northwestern Corporate Counsel Institute in Chicago and offered some examples of that "graphic evidence." He recounted three products liability horror stories. The first was of two men who sued the manufacturer of a commercial laundry dryer which exploded when they tried using it to dry their hot air balloon and "ended up winning nearly $900,000 in damages." The second involved an overweight man with a history of coronary disease who suffered a heart attack while trying to start a Sears lawnmower and sued Sears, winning $1 million dollars plus $500,000 in prejudgment interest. The third story was that of a two-year-old child being treated in the hospital for bronchial spasms who suffered brain damage from a drug overdose. In this case, even though the hospital staff exceeded the amount prescribed by the physician and recommended by the drug manufacturer, the child's parents still won a $22 million jury verdict against the manufacturer which included $13 million in punitive damages.[26] Malott presents these horror stories—"cases of absurdly generous liability awards"—as both true and typical, although as we noted in chapter 2 these stories are anything but true and typical.

The balance metaphor has another level of meaning when the rhetoric addresses the consequences of imbalance in the products liability system. These consequences reach far beyond the legal system. Some are general and broadscale in nature, such as American industry's loss of competitiveness in the world market, which lead to a lowering of our standard living. Others are more direct and more specific like lost jobs, foregone products, and higher prices for products generally[27] or in particular industries.

For instance, the Huber and Litan–edited volume discussed in chapter 1, *The Liability Maze*, is devoted to evaluating the costs and benefits of the products liability system. Huber and Litan concluded that as a general proposition, any linkages between this system and consumer safety are weak,[28] suggesting little positive benefit to society. With regard to innovation (and by implication competitiveness, etc.), they noted that the case studies included in their book "identify some concrete instances of the liability system's negative impact on innovation. General aviation appears to have suffered broad systemic effects. . . . In several industries—most notably some types of pharmaceuticals and small aircraft—the combined effects of uncertainty and high awards seem to have discouraged the research, development, and marketing of entire categories of products."[29] Similar arguments about the costs and benefits of the products liability system appeared as major themes in the 1991 report of the Senate Committee on Commerce, Science, and Transportation in its favorable recommendation on the Product Liability Fairness Act.[30] Indeed, *The Liability Maze* was a major source cited in that favorable recommendation,[31] and the committee also had the benefit of Huber's summary of its major findings in his testimony before them.[32]

Still other claims about consequences of the products liability system, like those discussed in chapters 1 and 2, were much more emotional in their appeal and were very much the tactical use of passion.[33] These are the claims aimed at instilling fear and apprehension. For example, a fact sheet prepared by Vice President Quayle's press office as a companion piece to his 1991 address before the American Bar Association stated that "1 out of every 7 companies indicates it has laid off employees because of liability issues."[34] Malott's 1985 speech noted that "10 of the 13 U.S. firms making football helmets have had to stop production due to runaway jury awards."[35] For Malott, "the most pernicious example" of the imbalance in the products liability system is "the decline in the production of the DPT vaccine, which is used to prevent diphtheria, tetanus, and pertussis—commonly known as whooping cough—among young children. The reason: excessive liability costs."[36]

McCormick's 1986 speech played to similar emotions and fears. He too used the DPT vaccine as a consequence as well as the decline in the manufacturing of "life-saving products" like anesthesia machines and "a drug designed to prevent sudden infant death syndrome-crib death."[37] Writing in the prestigious journal *Science*, Richard Mahoney and Stephen Littlejohn (chairman/CEO and public affairs director, respectively) of the Monsanto Company concentrated on the health care–related industry as one of the hardest hit areas. They quoted the American Medical Association regarding the negative impact of the product liability system on "potentially life-saving medical technologies."[38] In particular, they drew attention to declines in the area of contraceptives and vaccines as well as in medical equipment such as a suitcase-sized kidney dialysis unit and anesthesia machinery.[39] The cause of this—"strict liability and huge jury awards, bloated by the uncontrolled imposition of punitive damages."[40]

Doctrine: "An Engine of Social Destruction"

Huge, bloated, explosive, or astronomical jury awards are indicators of the problem in the products liability system which ultimately can be traced, the reform rhetoric says, to underlying changes in the law related to products liability. These changes, which represent nothing less than a "revolution," primarily have to do with the doctrine of strict liability. Regardless of the rhetorical characterization, there is no disagreement over the fact that significant changes have occurred in the law relating to products liability. Perhaps the most important of these was a shift away from a cause of action grounded in contract to one grounded in tort, a shift that seemed to follow changing socioeconomic conditions and technology.

The traditional doctrine of privity of contract limited the liability of sellers of products to only the immediate purchaser, because the seller's obligation was a contractual one running to the purchaser and not to third parties or bystanders. This doctrine is generally traced to the 1842 English case of *Winterbottom v. Wright*,[41] which was a leading case both in England and the United States during the remainder of the nineteenth century. Briefly, the case involved a suit brought by a coach driver (Winterbottom) who was injured when his coach broke down because of a latent defect. Winterbottom's employer, Wright, contracted with the Postmaster-General to provide horses and drivers for coaches used to carry the mail. Wright had also entered into a contract with the Postmaster-General to provide the coaches to carry the mail and keep them in good and safe condition.

Winterbottom sued Wright claiming the coach's defect caused the accident. His claim was rejected because Wright had no contractual obligation to Winterbottom; Wright's only obligation was to the Postmaster-General. In his opinion Lord Abinger said: "There is no privity of contract between these parties; and if the plaintiff can sue, every passenger, or even any person passing along the road, who was injured by the upsetting of the coach, might bring a similar action. Unless we confine the operation of such contracts as this to the parties who entered into them, the most absurd and outrageous consequences, to which I can see no limit, would ensue."[42]

The privity requirement in products cases in the United States was removed in the 1916 New York case *MacPherson v. Buick Motor Co.*[43] That case involved an accident caused by a defective wheel on a Buick automobile—a wheel made by another manufacturer. Buick sold the car to a retail dealer who, in turn, sold it to MacPherson. In his opinion,

Judge Benjamin Cardozo argued that the manufacturer of the finished product had a duty, irrespective of contractual obligations, to ensure that the product was carefully made if that product was a dangerous one. Said Cardozo: "If the nature of a thing is such that it is reasonably certain to place life and limb in peril when negligently made, it is then a thing of danger. Its nature gives warning of the consequences to be expected. If to the element of danger there is added knowledge that the thing will be used by persons other than the purchaser, and used without new tests, then, irrespective of contract, the manufacturer of this thing of danger is under a duty to make it carefully."[44] An automobile can be such a thing of danger, and by design and purpose it will be used by persons other than the first purchaser, so Buick had a duty to make sure that the car's wheels were free of defect. Cardozo's reasoning consciously took into consideration the changing conditions of society and technology. He said: "Precedents drawn from the days of travel by stage coach do not fit the conditions of travel today. The principle that the danger must be imminent does not change, but the things subject to the principle do change. They are whatever the needs of life in a developing civilization require them to be."[45]

MacPherson initiated a major change in the law of products liability, and by the mid–1960s every state accepted the *MacPherson* rule. According to Epstein et al.,[46] "the court in but a single step both rejected the privity doctrine *and* embraced a theory of strict liability for defective products." In the 1960 case *Henningsen v. Bloomfield Motors*,[47] the New Jersey Supreme Court ruled that a sales contract could not be used to disclaim all warranties and liability except to the original purchaser. The court held that there was an implied warranty of merchantability that extended beyond the original purchaser. Epstein et al. noted that the court based at least part of its reasoning on "modern economic social conditions."[48] The extension of implied warranty was a development the New Jersey court "found absolutely necessary given the web of contracts adopted by large manufacturers to insulate themselves from liability under the sales act."[49]

In 1944 strict liability was extended beyond the ideas of warranty and contract in *Escola v. Coca-Cola Bottling Co.*[50] In that case the plaintiff was injured by an exploding soda bottle. Even though no specific act of negligence was shown, the California Supreme Court upheld the a judgment for the plaintiff relying on the doctrine of *res ipsa loquitur*. More important for the future development of the law in this area was Justice Roger Traynor's concurring opinion in which he laid out the rationale for a more general idea of strict liability. He said that "it should now be recognized that a manufacturer incurs an absolute liability when an article that he has placed on the market, knowing that it is to be used without inspection, proves to have a defect that causes injury to human beings."[51] This liability should hold, Traynor said, regardless of negligence because "public policy demands that responsibility be fixed wherever it will most effectively reduce the hazards to life and health inherent in defective products that reach the market."[52] Manufacturers can do this where the public cannot, and manufacturers are responsible for the product reaching the market. Additionally, manufacturers are better equipped to handle the costs of injury than the injured party. "The cost of an injury and the loss of time or health may be an overwhelming misfortune to the person injured, and a needless one, for the risk of injury can be insured by the manufacturer and distributed among the public as a cost of doing business."[53] Traynor believed that the prevention of injuries caused by defective products was in the public's interest, and holding manufacturers liable—regardless of negligence—was one way to accomplish this end and to keep dangerous products off the market.

Traynor reviewed these issues again in the 1962 case *Greenman v. Yuba Power Products, Inc.*,[54] this time writing for a unanimous California Supreme Court. Rejecting the defendant's arguments based on breach of warranty, Traynor clearly placed the manufacturer's strict liability in tort rather than contract. The manufacturer's liability "is not assumed by agreement but imposed by law, and the refusal to permit the manufacturer to define the scope of its own responsibility for defective products make it clear that the liability is not one governed by the law of contract warranties but by the law of strict liability in tort."[55] Strict liability ensures that the costs of injuries "are borne by the manufacturers that put such products on the market rather than by the injured persons who are powerless to protect themselves."[56] All the injured party now needed to do was to show that the injury occurred while the product was being used for the purposes for which it was intended.

The evolution of the law regarding products liability ultimately led to the authoritative treatment of strict liability in the American Law Institute's 1965 Restatement (Second) of Torts. Section 402A of the 1965 Restatement adopted an idea of strict liability in tort that holds regardless of any contractual relationship between the original seller of the product (the manufacturer) and the injured party. In its comments, §402A notes that by placing a product on the market, the manufacturer assumes a special responsibility toward any member of the consuming public injured by the product. The public has the right to expect that manufacturers will stand behind their goods. Echoing Traynor's viewpoint, §402A states "that public policy demands that the burden of accidental injuries caused by products intended for consumption be placed upon those who market them, and be treated as a cost of production against which liability insurance can be obtained."[57]

The manufacturer still has a number of defenses available including nondefectiveness, assumption of risk, unforeseeable misuse, and that the product is unavoidably unsafe. In addition, comparative negligence may apply in some jurisdictions. The plaintiff must still show that the product was defective when it left the seller, that it was unreasonably dangerous, that the product's defect caused the plaintiff's injury, and that the product reached the consumer without substantial change. Epstein et al. argued that in meeting these requirements, plaintiffs—even with strict liability—do not have an easy task.[58]

This overview of the major changes in the law related to products liability has been brief, but it does present a context for the rhetoric of reform in this arena. Much of the rhetoric, especially the horror stories, makes sense against the background of these changes. It is the idea of strict liability itself that ultimately is identified as the problem, and much of the rhetoric is geared toward arguing that the system it defines is fundamentally out of balance because it overwhelmingly favors plaintiffs over defendants. It rejects out of hand the rationale underlying the case law from *McPherson* onward. Again, jury verdicts are a crucial indicator of this imbalance. In the next section we will discuss the empirical evidence that outlines the disputing pyramid for products liability, and in the following section we will present evidence from our own research on jury verdicts.

The Disputing Pyramid

As is the case with medical malpractice, jury verdicts in the products liability arena represent only the pinnacle of the disputing pyramid. Unlike the situation with medical malpractice, there is not much of an empirical research literature on which to draw in trying to provide even an outline of the pyramid for products liability. While there is a rich theoretical literature which includes some sophisticated statistical analysis of highly aggregated data, there is, for example, nothing comparable to Harvard Medical Malpractice Study, the NAIC study, or the various detailed studies of hospital charts and closed claims for different places and/or types of claims. There are studies of products liability filings and verdicts, and one major study utilizing closed insurance claims data,[59] but little that will help us begin outlining the pyramid by providing data that helps describe its base.

The Base of the Pyramid: Injuries

Because of the bewildering array of products that can cause injury, property damage, or financial loss and the varying settings in which products are used, it is impossible to devise a reasonable estimate of the amount of product-related harm in a given year. For personal injuries alone, it is possible that the raw numbers could be very large. For instance, in its 1981 report,[60] the U.S. Consumer Product Safety Commission estimated "that Americans annually suffer approximately 36 million consumer product-related injuries that require medical treatment or result in some limitation of normal activity." The CPSC's 1990 report gave an estimate of 29 million personal injuries.[61] These figures provide no indication of the number of product-related injuries in settings outside the private consumer setting, and the CPSC reports do not distinguish between accidents that were not just product related, but were product caused. Additionally, they do not provide information regarding whether the injured party pursued any claim against the product's manufacturer.

Some figures are available on occupational injuries and illnesses—the U.S. Department of Labor reported that during 1990 approximately 6.8 million job-related injuries or illnesses occurred.[62] Some injuries or illnesses may have been product related or even product caused, but again there is no way to estimate how many. (For example, the highest number of these job-related injuries involved workers in eating and drinking places, unlikely sources for a large percentage of product-caused injuries.)[63] George Priest and Kip Viscusi both have used such problematic aggregate national accident figures to argue that there is no apparent connection between the number or rate of accidents and the "explosion" of products liability litigation—that products liability litigation is increasing while accidents are not. Both Priest and Viscusi rely on federal court filings, although Priest also uses verdict data from state courts in Cook County, Ill. and San Francisco County, Cal.[64] For instance, Viscusi says:

> With litigation on the rise and court awards escalating as well, a natural inference might be that society is becoming increasingly risky. More specifically, one might conclude that the products we use are presumably more hazardous since they are generating considerably more litigation. Such a conclusion is not borne out by the accident statistics, which indicate that

product safety has been improving throughout this century—the safety trends over the 1977–1987 decade, which includes the period in which the products liability crisis emerged, all fail to suggest a reason for the explosion in litigation.[65]

Viscusi attributes the explosion and escalating awards to a greater demand for safety translated into lawsuits by a products liability system more favorable to plaintiffs.[66] Priest comes to the same conclusion.[67]

Our discussions in chapters 3 and 4 with regard to the disputing pyramid and claiming by injured people suggests that the arguments and conclusions of Priest and Viscusi should be viewed with skepticism. There is much that may—or, more importantly, may not—occur that will affect the transformation of a product-related injury into a lawsuit and help determine whether a filed lawsuit will go all the way to a trial. Additionally, there are alternative interpretations of accident statistics and the figures of filed lawsuits. Some interpret the kinds of figures Priest and Viscusi use quite differently and do not see the "problem" they do. For instance, Richard Abel argues that the "problem" is the reverse of the one Priest and Viscusi see. According to Abel there are too many injuries and not enough claims or lawsuits.[68] Rather than claiming or suing being characterized negatively, from his perspective, within the existing socioeconomic system "asserting tort claims and helping others to do so is a vital civic duty."[69] Although Abel has strongly stated his political opposition to much of the contemporary legal system (including torts), it is his belief that as long as this system persists, tort law should be used vigorously.[70] "Increasing the frequency of claims is imperative . . . if tort law is to perform its undisputed functions. The failure of victims to claim erodes the norm against injuring others, allows anger and resentment to fester, leaves the most disadvantaged victims uncompensated and often impoverished, and tolerates—indeed encourages—dangerous behavior."[71]

Moving up the Pyramid: Claiming

There are many factors that may affect what goes on near the bottom of the pyramid after an injury or some other harm has occurred. Unfortunately, we are aware of no empirical work akin to the May and DeMarco[72] or Meyers[73] studies noted in chapter 4 exploring processes at this level. One recent and more general research effort focusing on accidents does, however, provide at least some suggestive evidence regarding product-related injuries. The study—*Compensation for Accidental Injuries in the United States*[74]—was conducted by the

RAND Corporation's Institute for Civil Justice, and it presents a picture of blaming and claiming on the part of accidental injury victims quite at odds with the one animating the reform rhetoric. The study involved a survey of "about 26,000 households by telephone, representing more than 70,000 individuals nationwide."[75] From this initial sample, the study "interviewed about 2800 individuals, also by telephone. [The] hour-long interview provided a wealth of data about the economic, social, and psychological experience of becoming injured and about how injured Americans view and use the tort liability system."[76]

Among the types of accidental injuries covered in this study were product-related injuries that occurred at work as well as those that occurred in nonwork settings. The largest percentage of all accidental injuries—almost 40%—were slips and falls. "Thirty percent involved a product such as a tool, a household appliance, or sports equipment. The products most often involved were toys, sports equipment, household and personal items, and industrial hand tools and equipment."[77] The study found that the highest frequency of product-related injuries occurred at work. The availability of workers' compensation, the researchers posited, may have diminished the likelihood of a liability claim as a result of the injury.

In general, the RAND study found that most of the injured people in the study did *not* turn to the liability system for compensation—the rate was only about one in 10.[78] Those most likely to pursue compensation were those involved in auto accidents; about one-half of those injured in an auto accident pursued compensation. In the typical injury—a nonauto accident occurring outside of work—"the injured person does not even consider the notion of seeking compensation from some other person or entity who might have been associated with the accident (for example, a product manufacturer or property owner), or if he does think about this possibility, he is unlikely to pursue it."[79] In other words, there is little blaming and little claiming.

Regarding product-related injuries, those injured at work were more likely to make a claim against manufacturers or product sellers than those injured in nonwork situations.[80] They were also more likely to think about claiming. Twenty-four percent of the individuals injured at work at least *thought* about making some kind of liability claim, while only 8% of those injured in a nonwork situation did. This compares to a figure of 67% for auto accidents (except those that were single-vehicle accidents and in which the injured party was the driver).[81] Still, in general the vast majority of those suffering product-related injuries did not even consider a liability claim.[82]

The percentages became even smaller when the RAND study looked at the individuals who actually took some action. Of those experiencing product-related injuries at work, 7% actually took some action, 6% consulted a lawyer, and 4% hired a lawyer. Again, for the nonwork product injuries the percentages are smaller still: 2% took some action, 1% consulted a lawyer, and 1% hired a lawyer.[83] Within these two categories of product-related injuries, the individuals suffering more serious injuries were more likely to take some action than those with minor injuries. The study found that of those suffering serious workplace injuries, 41% considered a liability claim, 16% took some action, 14% consulted a lawyer, and 9% hired a lawyer. For serious nonwork product injuries, the percentages were 20%, 7%, 5%, and 3% respectively. In contrast, of the individuals who experienced serious injuries caused by an auto accident, 100% considered a liability claim, 89% took some action, 70% consulted a lawyer, and 57% hired a lawyer.

The findings of the RAND study, then, indicate that individuals suffering product-related injuries are not at all likely to pursue a liability claim or even consider it. This *suggests* that the products liability disputing pyramid, like that for medical malpractice, may be one with a wide base and relatively flat sides—one consistent with Richard Abel's perspective.

The RAND research also explored the question of why people claim, a particularly interesting question given that so few do so.[84] The study found that most of those with product-related injuries occurring in a nonwork setting blame themselves and so attribute no fault to the manufacturer. "Three-quarters of those injured in product-related nonwork accidents . . . say that their own behavior was mostly the cause of the injury."[85] This lack of attribution of causation to manufacturers, the study says, may help to explain the low rate of claiming for such injuries. In product-related work injuries, employers were the most likely other to be seen as the cause of the injury. Still, just over one-half (54%) of those with product-related work injuries said that their own behavior was mostly the cause of the injury.[86] By way of contrast, of those injured in auto accidents, 75% said another person was mostly the cause of the injury.[87] In general, then, the study found that those who attribute the cause of their injury to other people are more likely to consider a liability claim, more likely to take some action, and more likely to consult and/or hire a lawyer.[88] Underlying this process, the study concluded, were norms of responsibility and fairness.[89]

As we saw with medical malpractice, the available evidence indicates that those who do pursue claims for compensation are unlikely to pursue them as far as a trial. Most matters are settled—with or without a payment—short of formal adjudication. In chapter 4, we noted that closed claims studies for medical malpractice show that as many as 90% of malpractice claims close without going to trial. The most systematic analysis of closed products liability claims is found in Viscusi's *Reforming Products Liability.* He analyzed data from the Insurance Services Office's 1977 Products Liability Closed Claim Survey which included information on 10,784 claims from 23 insurance companies closed between the later half of 1976 and mid–1977.[90] Viscusi found that 19% of the claims were dropped and that 95% of the remaining claims settled before or during the trial. Overall, 4% of the 10,784 claims went to a verdict.

Two other sources support the idea that few products liability claims mature into full court adjudication. The Missouri Division of Insurance reports periodically on closed products liability insurance claims as it does for medical malpractice. Between 1981 and 1990, the Department's reports include data on 20,060 closed claims, less than 3% of which went to a trial and verdict.[91] Recent reports from the Texas State Board of Insurance covering products liability claims closed with a payment of $10,000 or more indicate that no more than 3% of the claims closed between 1988 and 1990 went to a trial and verdict.[92]

Both the Missouri reports and the Viscusi study indicate that products liability claims close with a payment at a higher rate than malpractice claims. In Missouri, 54.9% of the products claims closed with a payment,[93] and Viscusi reports that 78.4% of the claims in the insurance industry data closed with a payment.[94] The success rate for malpractice claims tends to be below 40%. Despite the relatively high success rates for products liability, the amount of the payment for most claims is low. Viscusi reports that the preponderance of claims settled short of a verdict settled with payments under $10,000.[95] The Missouri data are consistent with this pattern. In the early 1980s, the bulk of the paid claims in Missouri (2,288 of 3,128 or 73.1%) closed with a payment less than $2,000.[96] For 1988–90, most paid claims closed with payments of less than $2,500 in unadjusted dollars (2,203 of 3,012 or 73.1%), and the *average* payment was $12,667 ($13,350 in 1990 dollars).[97]

Finally, before turning to our jury verdict data, a brief look at products liability filings in the federal courts is needed. Although our interest is in state court verdicts, claims about federal court litigation have been a major part of the reform rhetoric.[98] The major assertions surround the idea of a "litigation explosion" in products liability after 1974. The Tort Policy Working Group, for instance, reported a 785% increase in products liability filings in the federal courts between 1974 and 1985.[99] Two other studies offer an alternative interpretation of the changes in filings.[100]

Those two studies, one done by the GAO and the other by Terry Dunworth at RAND, made two important points regarding changes in the frequency of federal court filings after 1974 and the idea of an "explosion." The first point turns on the choice of 1974 as a baseline for measuring the explosion. Specific identification of products liability cases was begun by the Administrative Office of the U.S. Courts in 1974, but products liability classifications were in fact not universally made by the District Courts until 1976. Consequently, using 1974 as a baseline guarantees a pattern indicating a sharp increase.[101] Second, claims based on aggregate filing figures lead to the conclusion found in the rhetoric of reform that the explosion of products liability litigation is a general or systemic one. Both the GAO and Dunworth studies point out that a significant proportion of the increase in filings that did occur was due to the growth in suits involving only three products: asbestos, Dalkon Shield, and Bendectin. The GAO study showed that asbestos cases accounted for 40% of the growth in federal products liability filings between 1974 and 1985, Dalkon Shield accounted for 12%, and Bendectin for 5%.[102] With over one-half of the growth of filings involving just three products, it is difficult to speak of a generalized explosion of litigation.

Dunworth presented additional evidence indicating that important patterns were occurring within particular types of product litigation. He found that a limited number of business entities were named as defendants in a substantial number of filed cases. For example, 80 lead defendants were named in about half of the 85,694 products cases filed in the federal courts between 1973 and 1986.[103] In terms of specific business sectors the data were even more telling. Twenty of the 494 companies named in federal asbestos suits were lead defendant in 90% of the filings.[104] Two of the 434 companies named in pharmaceutical suits were lead defendants in 60% of the filings.[105] Five of the 616 companies named in motor vehicle suits were the lead defendant in 60% of the filings.[106] These findings suggest that the products liability system—federal or state—is much more complex than the reform rhetoric's portrayal, and that claims based on aggregate data are highly problematic.

Jury Verdicts: 1988–90

General Background

In chapter 3 we saw that during the three-year period between 1988 and 1990 products liability cases accounted for only 4.2% of all of the jury verdicts in the 82 sites for which we have verdict data (see table 3.3). There were no products verdicts during this period in 11 sites and products cases as a percentage of all verdicts exceeded 10% in only two sites: San Francisco (14.4%) and Yakima County, Wash. (13.2%). In the majority of the sites, products cases comprised between 1% and 5% of the verdicts. The percentages of products verdicts in the four sites with more than 1,000 verdicts overall were: Los Angeles County, 7.2%; Cook County, 6.3%; Dallas County, 2.3%; and Harris County, Tex., 4.3%. In short, products cases were a small proportion of all verdicts, even in the sites with the highest numbers of total verdicts.

For medical malpractice verdicts, we saw in chapter 4 that in general both win rates and awards varied by the severity of injury involved (see table 4.2). Table 5.1 shows that this pattern holds generally for products liability with respect to median awards, but not plaintiff win rates. However, when the injury levels alleged in products cases are collapsed into the broad categories of minor and major injuries, we find that the major injury category does have a higher win rate than the minor injury category (47.3% v. 33.3%) and a higher median award ($496,750 v. $200,000). It is also worth noting that for all but one of the specific injury levels (level 6), as well as the broader minor and major categories, median awards for products liability verdicts are higher than those for malpractice. The possible reasons for this are many, not the least of which is the higher rate of punitive damage awards in products liability compared to medical malpractice (8.6% v. 2.5%). But before we could say that this is indeed *the* explanation for a higher award structure, the similarities and differences for other types of damages would also need to be examined. Unfortunately, our source materials do not consistently report on the various types of damages awarded by juries in large part because in many jurisdictions the actual verdicts themselves are not broken down in detail.

Settings

Where do products liability cases come from? In other words, in what situations or settings do the injuries that give rise to products

Table 5.1 Severity of Injury: Frequencies, Win Rates, Awards for Sites with 10-plus Verdicts, 1988–90

Injury Level[1]	(Code)	(*N*)	Percentage	Win Rate (%)	Median Award (1990 $)
Emotional only	(1)	7	1.0	28.6	—
Temporary insignificant	(2)	29	4.3	34.5	39,024
Temporary minor	(3)	55	8.2	29.1	130,391
Temporary major	(4)	119	17.7	36.1	175,000
Permanent minor	(5)	188	27.9	34.6	357,000
Permanent significant	(6)	123	18.2	57.7	561,750
Permanent major	(7)	22	3.3	50.0	4,622,792
Permanent Grave	(8)	11	1.6	45.5	6,314,995
Death	(9)	76	11.3	44.7	2,000,000
Property/Financial		44	6.5	31.8	243,810
Totals		674	100.0	40.2	372,978

Personal Injury Only

Injury Level[2]	*N*	Percentage	Win Rate (%)	25th Percentile ($)	Median ($)	75th Percentile ($)
Minor injury	279	44.3	33.3	59,000	200,000	554,897
Major injury	275	43.7	47.3	123,498	496,750	1,924,664
Death	76	12.1	44.7	448,875	2,000,000	3,269,857
Totals	630	100.0	40.8	117,125	385,889	1,472,605

[1]See Appendix 4.1 for detailed examples of each injury level.
[2]These are the same categories used in chapter 4.

liability claims occur? This is an important threshold question to ask because differences among settings are the key to logic and order in the products liability system. This is the same general—or roughly epidemiological—approach used for the discussion of medical malpractice in chapter 4 where the more detailed examination of verdicts was organized around the medical setting from which they emerged. In the products liability arena, different settings define distinct subsystems, each with its own set of unique characteristics. Cases emerging from different settings involve different industries and products as well as different types of injuries. Because of these distinct characteristics of each setting, products cases arising in the different settings demonstrate different patterns in success rates and award structures, as well as different trends over time.

Looking at the settings from which products cases emerge also directs our attention to the relationships between parts of the products liability system and other systems of injury compensation and safety regulation in a way not possible with medical malpractice. While a variety of commentators point to the inadequacies of the systems for licensing and disciplining health care professionals when examining the malpractice issue—the "bad apple" argument[107]—in products liability the development and evolution of litigation activity in some settings may be closely tied to the existence and efficacy of other systems of injury compensation and regulation. Failures in these alternative compensation and regulatory schemes may push certain types of matters into the civil justice system in ways not found with malpractice cases.[108]

Table 5.2 sets out the allocation of products verdicts among the five largest settings for those sites with 10 or more products verdicts during the 1988–90 period (see tables 3.1 and 3.3 for the total frequencies for all sites—all verdicts and products verdicts respectively). Eighty-six percent (582) of the 674 verdicts from these 22 sites arose in one of five settings—work, home, vehicle, recreation, or medical. The work setting was by far predominant, accounting for just over one-half (52.7%) of these products verdicts. The vehicle and home settings together generated another 25.9% of the verdicts. The percentage of verdicts from the home setting, 15.7%, seems relatively low in light of much of the reform rhetoric which leads one to the conclusion that the great bulk of products cases arise from the misuse of consumer goods by individual consumers. Even if the recreation setting verdicts are combined with those arising in the home setting, the percentage is still low in light of this rhetorical characterization.

Perhaps more importantly, table 5.2 also shows the wide variability in the distribution of products cases across settings among sites generally and among those within states. Work cases were the largest proportion of products liability verdicts in all but one site (San Diego County), and in 12 of the 22 sites they made up over one-half of the products verdicts. Still, the percent of verdicts emerging from this setting varied from 21.4% in San Diego to 85.5% in San Francisco. Four sites had no reported vehicle product cases (San Francisco, Denver, Texas District 6, and King), while in San Diego and St. Louis City over 20% of the product verdicts fell in this setting. The percentage of home setting cases ranged from none in St. Louis County and 4.0% in Dallas to over 30% in Bexar County, Tex., and Oakland County, Mich. Medical and recreation cases made up smaller proportions of the products verdicts, with those in the medical setting exceeding 10% only in those sites with fewer than a dozen products verdicts overall. In 12 sites there were no medical cases, and eight experienced no recreation cases.

Table 5.2 Products Liability Cases by Setting for Sites with 10-plus Verdicts, 1988–90

Jurisdiction	*N*	Work	Vehicle	Home	Recreation	Medical
Arizona						
Maricopa	26	58.3	7.7	11.5	3.8	7.7
California						
Alameda	16	62.5	12.5	12.5	0.0	0.0
Los Angeles	83	48.2	16.9	14.5	4.8	3.6
Sacramento	11	63.6	9.1	9.1	9.1	0.0
San Diego	14	21.4	28.6	28.6	7.1	0.0
San Francisco	55	85.5	0.0	5.5	1.8	1.8
Colorado						
Denver	14	57.1	0.0	7.1	0.0	0.0
Illinois						
Cook	118	54.2	8.5	20.3	4.2	1.7
Michigan						
Oakland	21	47.6	9.5	33.3	9.5	0.0
Wayne	56	60.7	10.7	12.5	3.6	3.6
Missouri						
Jackson	19	52.6	15.8	15.8	0.0	0.0
St. Louis City	23	43.5	21.7	21.7	4.3	4.3
St. Louis County	10	60.0	10.0	0.0	0.0	10.0
New York						
New York	25	64.0	16.0	8.0	0.0	0.0
Ohio						
Cuyahoga	11	36.4	9.1	18.2	0.0	18.2
Oregon						
Multnomah	10	40.0	10.0	20.0	20.0	0.0
Texas*						
Bexar	23	30.4	8.7	39.1	13.0	0.0
Dallas	25	32.0	12.0	4.0	8.0	0.0
District 6	14	57.1	0.0	14.3	0.0	0.0
District 9	13	46.2	7.7	7.7	15.4	0.0
Harris	63	34.9	11.1	19.0	11.1	4.8
Washington						
King	24	70.8	0.0	12.5	0.0	4.2
Overall	674	52.7	10.2	15.7	5.0	2.7

* See chapter 3 for counties in District 6 and District 9.

Among the five settings there were differences in plaintiff win rates and award structures. Table 5.3 shows that win rates ranged from 49.0% in work setting cases and 48.6% in recreation cases to 16.7% for those in the medical setting. Although the work setting includes the largest proportion of the verdicts and exhibits the highest win rate, the award structure is not the highest. Vehicle cases have the highest award structure by far with a *median* award of $2.1 million (1990 dollars) compared to the next highest median, $379,434, in the

Table 5.3 Plaintiff Win Rates and Size of Awards by Setting for Sites with 10-plus Verdicts, 1988–90

Setting	*N*	Win Rate (%)	25th Percentile ($)	Median ($)	75th Percentile ($)	Mean ($)
Work	355	49.0	143,850	379,434	1,048,725	1,101,806
Vehicle	69	40.6	499,375	2,110,625	6,146,766	5,474,353
Home	106	23.6	24,106	150,000	1,050,000	887,938
Recreation	34	48.6	38,711	103,950	912,500	1,615,055
Medical	18	16.7	*	*	*	*

* No award figures are reported for the medical setting because there were only three verdicts in which the plaintiff was successful.

work setting. Home and recreation verdicts exhibited more modest award structures.

Settings and Severity of Injury

Products liability cases, as table 5.1 showed, involve a broad range of injuries. Table 5.4 shows that different settings are characterized by different injury profiles. Using the collapsed scale for injury severity, table 5.4 sets out the breakdown of injury levels within the three primary settings in which products cases arise: work, vehicle, and home. Home setting cases primarily involved financial or property harm and minor personal injuries. Work setting cases were more likely to be characterized by major personal injuries and death, although only a relatively small proportion of these involved the most severe levels of injury (levels 7 and 8). Major injuries and death also accounted for the largest percentage of verdicts in the vehicle setting; but unlike the situation for the work setting verdicts, a substantial number of the vehicle verdicts involved the two most severe levels of major injury (levels 7 and 8). While only 2.8% of all work cases (6.0% of major injuries) alleged the most severe levels of major injury, 21.7% (46.9% of major injuries) of vehicle cases involved such injuries. Both the work and vehicle settings exhibited relatively high win rates for major injuries (work, 55.4%; vehicle, 50.0%). The higher awards for major injuries, and especially for those involving the two most severe levels of major injury (see table 5.1), help to explain the moderately high award structure for work setting verdicts and the even higher structure for the vehicle setting cases. The lower award structure found in the home setting verdicts is understandable in light of the higher percentage of minor injuries and the low win rate in the major injury cases (25.8%).

Table 5.4 Settings and Injury Levels for Sites with 10-plus Verdicts, 1988–90

	Work		Home		Vehicle	
Injury	Percentage	(*N*)	Percentage	(*N*)	Percentage	(*N*)
Minor	40.8	(145)	51.9	(55)	31.9	(22)
Major	47.3	(168)	29.2	(31)	46.4	(32)
Death	10.4	(37)	7.5	(8)	18.8	(13)
Property/Financial	1.4	(5)	11.3	(12)	2.9	(2)
Totals	99.9	(355)	99.9	(106)	100.0	(69)
Levels 7 and 8	*2.8*	*(10)*	*1.9*	*(2)*	*21.7*	*(15)*

Settings and Industries

If the settings in which products cases arise represent persistent, orderly subsystems within the products liability arena, we would expect them to be characterized by unique sets of industries and products. To place the data on products cases into a coherent framework, we use, as have other studies,[109] the Standard Industrial Classification Manual (SIC). The SIC organizes manufacturing businesses into 20 divisions identified by a two-digit code (e.g., Fabricated Metal Products, SIC 34), then divides each of those 20 divisions into a number of industry groups based upon the general types of products manufactured and identified by a three-digit code.[110] The SIC structure further subdivides these industry groups into industry numbers based on specific types of products and categorized by a four-digit code.[111]

Table 5.5 sets out the distribution of products cases by manufacturing division within setting. Only 11 of the 20 divisions individually generated as much as 1% of the products verdicts in the 22 counties with 10 or more products verdicts during the three-year period 1988–90. Together these 11 divisions accounted for 95.9% of the cases. Three-fifths of the products cases were generated by just three industry divisions: Stone, Clay, Glass, and Concrete Products (SIC 32); Industrial and Commercial Machinery (SIC 35); and Transportation Equipment (SIC 37). The largest percentage of verdicts, 31.5%, involved Industrial Machinery, an unsurprising finding given the predominance of work setting cases. Nor, for the same reason, is it unexpected that Stone, Clay, would make up the second largest percentage, 15.1%, of verdicts. Almost 90% (89.2%) of the 102 Stone, Clay cases were asbestos cases.

Table 5.5 SIC Division by Setting for Sites with 10-plus Verdicts, 1988–90

SIC Industry Code	Work (*N*=355)	Vehicle (*N*=69)	Home (*N*=106)	Recreation (*N*=35)	Medical (*N*=18)
20 Food	0.3	0	15.1	0	0
22 Textile Mill Products	0.6	0	0	0	0
24 Wood Products	2.5	0	2.8	0	0
25 Furniture	2.5	1.4	0.9	2.9	0
26 Paper Products	0	0	0.9	0	5.6
28 Chemicals	3.4	0	9.4	0	38.9
29 Petroleum Refining	0	0	0.9	0	0
30 Rubber	1.7	4.3	1.9	2.9	0
31 Leather	0.3	0	0	5.7	0
32 Stone, Clay	25.6	1.4	5.7	0	0
33 Primary Metal Industry	0.6	0	0	0	0
34 Fabricated Metal	7.9	0	14.7	22.9	0
35 Industrial Machinery	43.7	1.4	20.8	2.9	0
36 Electronic Equipment	2.0	4.3	17.9	2.9	5.6
37 Transportation Equipment	5.4	81.2	0	25.7	0
38 Instruments	1.4	1.4	3.8	2.9	50.0
39 Miscellaneous Manufacturing Industries	0.3	2.9	4.7	28.6	0
Other	2.0	1.4	0	2.9	0

Table 5.5 shows that each setting is characterized by a different set of industries, and two patterns emerge. First, the cases arising in three of the five most frequently appearing settings—vehicle, recreation, and medical—are characterized by a very narrow range of industries. Slightly over 80% of the vehicles cases involved Transportation Equipment (SIC 37), with another 8.6% equally divided between Rubber and Miscellaneous Plastics Products (SIC 30) and Electronic Equipment (SIC 36). Recreation setting cases are clustered in three divisions—Transportation Equipment, Fabricated Metal (SIC 34) and Miscellaneous Manufacturing Industries (SIC 39), a division which includes sporting and athletic goods. Two divisions accounted for nearly all of the products cases arising in the medical setting: Measuring, Analyzing, and Controlling Instruments (SIC 38) and Chemicals and Allied Products (SIC 28).

The second pattern is that work and home cases were characterized by a broader array of industries, although most are clustered within a few divisions. Within the work setting, two divisions generated slightly over two-thirds of the cases: 43.7% involved Industrial Machinery (SIC 35), and 25.6% involved Stone, Clay, Glass and Concrete Products (SIC 32). Nearly all of the latter were asbestos cases. The home setting was also characterized by a wide array of industries, but without the level of concentration found in the work setting. Only four industry divisions accounted for as much as 10% of the home cases, and none of these produced more than 21% of the verdicts. The relative diversity of industries involved in products cases arising in the home setting reflects the broad range of products by which a consumer may be injured at home.

To this point, we have emphasized the importance of the settings in which cases emerge to show that there are orderly, intelligible patterns in products liability verdicts. The next portion of our discussion takes the analysis a step farther by examining patterns in injury levels, industries, win rates, and awards within each of the three largest settings.

Verdict Patterns within Injury Settings

Work Setting

The work setting accounted for slightly over half of the products liability verdicts in our database for the three-year period 1988 to 1990 (see table 5.2). Forty-one percent (40.8%) of these verdicts involved allegations of minor injury, with the largest proportion of these being permanent minor injuries such as the loss of a finger (114 of 145, 78.6%). Forty-seven percent (47.3%) of the products-related work cases involved major injuries, and the largest proportion of these were permanent significant injuries (99 of 163, 60.7%). Seventy of the 99 permanent significant injuries involved one product, asbestos. Ten percent (10.4%) of the work cases involved a death, and again asbestos products generated a substantial portion of these matters (15 of 37). In only 1.4% of the products-related work cases were either financial or property damages the sole harms alleged.

Overall, plaintiffs won 49.0% of the work cases, and the median award was $379,434. As shown in table 5.6, the win rate was higher for major injury work cases than for those involving minor injuries, and the plaintiff success rate in death cases was nearly equal to that for major injuries. However, the highest win rate for products-related work cases occurred in death cases involving asbestos. Plaintiffs were successful in all but one of the 16 asbestos cases involving a death (see table 5.7). The award structure for minor injury work cases was lower than that found in major injury or death cases, and while the median for major injury cases was not much higher than that for minor injuries (see table 5.6), the differences between the two means suggest that the major injury cases produced a greater number of high awards. The highest

Table 5.6 Settings: Plaintiff Win Rates and Size of Awards by Injury Category for Sites with 10-plus Verdicts, 1988–90

	Minor Injury	*Major Injury*	*Death*
		Work	
	(*N*=145)	(*N*=168)	(*N*=37)
Win rate	40%	55.4%	54.1%
Median award	$322,850	$ 367,500	$1,184,936
Mean award	638,566	1,149,789	2,073,510
		Vehicle	
	(*N*=22)	(*N*=32)	(*N*=13)
Win rate	27.3%	50.0%	46.2%
Median award	$671,000*	$2,633,925	$3,011,265*
Mean award	69,216*	6,335,957	7,961,880*
		Home	
	(*N*=55)	(*N*=31)	(*N*=8)
Win rate	21.8%	25.8%	25.0%
Median award	$ 56,452	$ 970,500*	**
Mean award	397,527	1,756,608*	**

* Calculated on a base of less than 10 awards.
** Median not calculated; fewer than five winning cases.

award structure was in the death cases, where even the median award exceeds $1 million.

While the highest plaintiff win rate occurred in death cases involving asbestos, these cases are not the reason for the high award structure for work setting death cases generally. The median award for death/asbestos cases was $451,500. The higher award death cases were scattered across a number of different industry types. Table 5.7 presents data on the most frequently appearing industry areas in each of the injury categories for work cases. Its purpose is primarily illustrative rather than exhaustive in order to show two things. First, it shows what kinds of products produce the largest proportions of cases within each injury category. Second, it presents data on win rates and median awards for these industry areas.

Table 5.7 shows that the minor injury category was dominated by products from one industry area to a degree not seen for the other two categories. Over 60% of the verdicts involved products within the Industrial Machinery area—more than twice as high a percentage as that in either major injury or death. Within Industrial Machinery, products from three specific industry groups appeared most frequently, as the boxed material in table 5.7 for minor injuries shows. Both win rates and median awards varied considerably among these three industry

Table 5.7 Work Setting: Industries, Plaintiff Win Rates, and Size of Awards by Injury Level (Partial Data)

SIC	Industry Code	*N*	Percentage	Win Rate (%)	Median ($)
				Minor Injury	
34	Fabricated Metal	14	9.7	21.4	**
35	Industrial Machinery	91	62.8	41.7	339,350
353	Construction and Materials Handling Equipment	29	20.0	41.8	265,089
354	Metal Working Equipment	24	16.6	33.3	487,619*
355	Specialized Industrial Machinery	18	12.4	50.0	715,000*
				Major Injury	
32	Stone, Clay, etc.	71	42.3	69.0	500,000
35	Industrial Machinery	51	30.4	41.2	273,000
353	Construction and Materials Handling Equipment	26	15.5	38.5	257,125
354	Metal Working Equipment	9	5.4	55.6	650,000*
355	Specialized Industrial Machinery	9	5.4	44.4	**
3292	Asbestos	70	41.7	68.6	466,853
				Death	
32	Stone, Clay, etc.	16	43.2	93.8	451,500
35	Industrial Machinery	10	27.0	20.0	**
353	Construction and Materials Handling Equipment	6	16.2	16.7	**
3292	Asbestos	16	43.2	93.8	451,500

* Calculated on a base of less than 10 awards.
** Median not calculated; fewer than five winning cases.

groups, but the small numbers of winning cases in two of the groups (eight for Metal Working Equipment and nine for Special Industrial Machinery) make it difficult to offer possible explanations. To pursue feasible explanations, we would also need information on how and why such matters move into the civil justice system despite the existence of workers' compensation—information not yet available.

Major injury cases involved a different combination of products than did minor injuries. Like death cases, major injury cases were largely generated by products from Stone, Clay, and Industrial Machinery industries. As with the death cases, one particular product stands out; all but one of the Stone, Clay major injury matters were asbestos cases. Plaintiffs won these cases at a very high rate, although not as frequently as was the case for death cases involving asbestos. The awards, however, were somewhat higher for the major injury asbestos cases, but not substantially so.

Plaintiffs won major injury Industrial Machinery cases at the same rate as they won minor injury cases involving these products. In general, however, they won less money. The lower median award for major injury Industrial Machinery cases may be a result of the fact that there were few that involved serious major injuries. Only four involved injury level 7 (two of which plaintiffs won) and none involved injury level 8—the most severe levels of injury which tend to generate especially high awards. Most of the Industrial Machinery major injury cases (31 of 51) involved less severe temporary major injuries (e.g., back injury) which tend to have lower awards (median $257,125). When an Industrial Machinery case involved a death, the plaintiff did not fare well, winning infrequently.

The threshold patterns we have described in this rough "epidemiology" of the work setting raise an important question about the message being transmitted by jury verdicts. While the political debate claims that patterns in jury verdicts reflect a civil justice system "out of balance," we are drawn to a different potential message. The fact that the work setting accounts for the largest proportion of products verdicts in our data combined with the kinds of products involved (and the unusually high win plaintiff rates for some products) points to the possibility of problems or failures in other systems of injury compensation or safety regulation. Most obviously, there is the workers' compensation system, the means through which one would expect most workplace injuries to be handled. Even a cursory literature review, however, will uncover the problems a number of states have faced with workers' compensation that may have a direct effect on the products liability system.[112]

For example, California, one of the states from which we have jury verdict data, has long been criticized for the inadequacies of its workers' compensation system.[113] The benefit schedule has been identified as inadequate, and adjustments in compensation scales over time have been infrequent. When reforms were finally made in 1989, the California system's benefits ranked among the lowest in the nation.[114] In addition, an unusually low fee schedule for applicants' attorneys in the California system may discourage attorneys from handling workers' compensation claims, especially those involving more complicated permanent injuries—claims that are more costly to prepare.[115] Problems such as these may have an important effect on the *process* of handling disputes arising out of workplace injuries. Problems in schemes for promoting workplace safety—such as the Occupational Safety and Health Administration (OSHA)—may also have an important effect—not on the process of handling matters but on the frequency and nature of workplace injuries at the very bottom of the disputing pyramid. This too is an area about which there has been much criticism. The failures of OSHA, for example, have been widely discussed and analyzed.[116]

Vehicle Setting

The patterns for vehicle cases are quite different than those for work cases, suggesting that the two settings are distinct subsystems. The vehicle setting is less about minor injuries than it is about major injuries and death. It is dominated by one SIC division to a degree not found in the work setting. Eighty-one percent (81.2%) of the vehicle cases involved Transportation Equipment products, with no other division accounting for more than 4% of the cases. Transportation Equipment produced no less than 75.0% of all cases in each injury category (75.0% of the major injury cases, 86.4% of the minor injury cases, and 92.3% of the death cases). More specifically, a majority of cases at each injury category involved motor vehicles and passenger car bodies (SIC 3711).

The win rates and award figures for vehicle cases in the different injury categories were presented in table 5.6. In comparison to the work setting, win rates for vehicle cases were somewhat lower—especially for minor injury cases. Awards, however, were substantially higher. The greatest difference between the awards in these two settings is for major injury cases, where the *median* award for vehicle cases was $2,633,925—more than seven times higher than median for work major injury cases and more than twice as high as the *mean* for work cases.

A key factor in the higher award structure for major injury cases is that vehicle setting cases involve more of the most serious injuries than work setting cases, especially injuries like paraplegia and quadraplegia (injury levels 7 and 8, respectively). Ten of the 24 Transportation Equipment major injury cases (41.7%) involved the two most severe levels of injury, and there were five in each. In contrast, as we saw above, only four of 51 Industrial Machinery major injury cases (7.8%) involved the most severe injuries (all level 7). Plaintiffs won half of the injury level 7 and 8 cases involving Transportation Equipment with awards ranging from $1 million to $6.3 million.

Like the patterns for verdicts in the work setting, those in the vehicle setting direct attention to other systems of compensation and regulation that may involve the process of claiming and the handling of disputes as well as the frequency and nature of injuries (the very bottom of the disputing pyramid). Most obviously, questions may be raised concerning the scope and coverage of automobile insurance.

While this would be the first source of compensation for vehicle-related injuries, the actual medical and long-term care costs for the injuries that underlie most vehicle setting awards (especially major injury and death) are likely to exceed the limits of most automobile insurance policies, assuming there is any coverage at all.[117] The problem is illustrated by comparing vehicle setting products liability verdicts to the ordinary automobile accident cases in our data (see chapter 3). Vehicle setting cases "cost" more than the typical automobile case. Where the median award for all vehicle setting cases was $2.1 million (see table 5.3) for the 22 sites with 10-plus products liability verdicts, the highest median among these sites for automobile accident cases was $262,275 in New York County (see table 3.4). Eighteen of those 22 sites had automobile medians below $50,000, 13 were below $25,000. Higher stakes may help push some parties into the products liability system to seek additional compensation, but, unfortunately, this too is an area with no empirical literature to turn to for insight. Like the work setting, there are also questions on the injury side about the effectiveness of the safety regulation. As with the safety regulation of workplace safety, the regulation of automotive safety has been only partially successful, perhaps because it too has been an area subject to a great deal of political pressure.[118]

Home Setting

Much of the rhetoric of reform—especially the horror stories—focuses on what we characterize as home setting cases. As we saw earlier in this chapter, the picture portrayed here is one of innocent defendants being sued by greedy plaintiffs (who themselves are often the cause of their own injuries) winning most of the time and winning very large awards. The reality of home setting verdicts in our database presents a starkly different picture than might be expected.

The home setting verdicts were characterized more by minor injuries than major injuries, and there were few death cases. The home setting generated a higher percentage of minor injuries (51.9%) than either the work (40.8%) or vehicle (31.9%) settings, and a lower percentage of major injuries (29.2%) compared to the other two settings (47.3% and 46.4% respectively). Only two of the home setting cases involved the two most severe levels of major injury. Table 5.6 shows that plaintiff win rates for each injury category in the home setting were the lowest of all three settings. The highest was only 25.8% for major injuries, compared to 50.0% for vehicle and 55.4% for work setting major injuries. For minor injuries, the category in which the largest proportion of home cases fell, the win rate was the lowest in table 5.6, 21.8%. Awards for home cases also tended to be relatively low; the median for all home setting cases was $150,000 (see table 5.3). For minor injuries, the median award was only $56,452 (table 5.6); for major injuries the median was $975,500, but there were only eight winning cases in this category.

The home setting was different from work and vehicle in that a broader array of industries was involved. Four SIC industry divisions each produced at least 10% of the home cases, with only one accounting for as much as 20%: Food and Kindred Products (SIC 20), 15.1%; Fabricated Metal (SIC 34), 14.7%; Industrial Machinery (SIC 35), 20.8%; and Electronic Equipment (SIC 36), 17.9%. These four divisions collectively comprised slightly over two-thirds of the home verdicts (68.0%).

The small numbers of home setting verdicts in any one industry division limits what can be said about them. Three of the divisions noted above—Food and Kindred Products, Fabricated Metal, and Industrial Machinery—primarily generated minor injury cases, while Electronic Equipment products were more likely to produce major injury cases. Plaintiffs, however, won only one of nine Electronic Equipment major injury cases. In general, plaintiffs won most often in Food and Kindred Products cases (seven of 15) and least often in Industrial Machinery cases (two of 22). Most of the Industrial Machinery cases (15 of 22) involved lawnmowers and similar equipment, and most (11) were minor injury cases. Given the widespread use of horror stories involving lawnmower injuries by reform advocates, it is worth noting that plaintiffs won *none* of these cases. In addition, there were seven ladder cases in the home setting (another horror story favorite), two involving wooden ladders (SIC 2499), and five involving metal ladders (SIC 3499). Plaintiffs won only a single ladder case, one in which the injury was caused by a metal ladder and the plaintiff was an attorney.

It is difficult to neatly characterize home cases in comparison to work and vehicle cases because of their diversity and the low frequencies in any particular categories once the verdicts have been disaggregated. At most, we can say that win rates and awards tend to be lower in comparison to those in the work and vehicle settings, and the injuries tend to be less serious. Unlike our experience with the work and vehicle setting cases, the patterns here do not obviously direct our attention to possible failures in some other systems of compensation, except perhaps for the more serious injuries where concern might focus on the limitations and availability of private health insurance. Interestingly in this regard, the RAND study of accidental injuries discussed earlier in this chapter noted that even though claiming for all but automobile accidents is infrequent, for those who do claim, one of the most important reasons was the need to pay expenses.[119] As to safety regulation and the frequency of injury (the bottom of the pyramid), concern might turn to the consumer product safety arena, again an area of regulation with marginal or mixed success and one that suffered political attack in the 1980s.[120]

Summary

The discussion of products liability verdict activity from 1988 to 1990 suggests the existence of a products liability system quite different from the one found in the reform rhetoric. It is an orderly but complex system made up by distinct parts. It is, however, a system about which little is known. The verdict data raise many questions about this system in operation, but there is little empirical literature to consult for assistance in answering them. This only reinforces the conclusions of commentators like Michael Saks and Joseph Sanders and Craig Joyce discussed in chapter 1 about how little is known about the civil justice system in operation. Still, our discussion provides a context for the reform rhetoric as part of the politics of ideas. It points out, at the very least, that there can be an alternative picture of the products liability system in the marketplace of ideas.

There is a final matter we want to briefly address here before moving on to an exploration of patterns in verdicts over time. We concluded the discussion of medical malpractice in chapter 4 with a summary of the findings of Neil Vidmar's research on jurors in malpractice cases. While there are no directly comparable studies of jurors in products cases, Professor Valerie Hans has done similar research of jurors in tort cases in which businesses were defendants—including products liability matters.[121] Like Vidmar's, her findings provide an important adjunct for the jury verdict data we have presented.

Interviews with 141 jurors regarding the way in which jurors evaluated the tort liability of businesses and corporations showed the following:

> Rather than revealing jurors willing or eager to impose on business the costs of plaintiffs' injuries, our findings show that jurors were suspicious of the legitimacy of plaintiffs' claims and concerned about the personal and social costs of large jury awards. Despite insistence on product safety and high expectations of business, jurors were generally favorable toward

business, skeptical more about the profit motives of individual plaintiffs than of business defendants and committed to holding down awards.[122]

Like Vidmar, Hans also looked at the "deep pockets" hypothesis. She found that a minority of jurors thought it appropriate to consider a business or corporate defendant's financial resources. "A much more common position was that the organization's assets should not be and were not relevant to the liability and award decisions."[123] Like Vidmar's findings that some jurors held physicians to a special, higher level of responsibility,[124] Hans found that some jurors held businesses and corporations to a higher level of responsibility than individual defendants.[125] Said Hans: "these findings indicate that juries do approach cases with corporate defendants differently from cases with individual defendants. But the different treatment appears to reflect an expected and distinctive standard of behavior for business corporations—a 'reasonable corporation' standard—rather than a deep-pocket explanation."[126]

Verdict Patterns over Time: 1970–90

The reform rhetoric, as we discussed earlier, characterizes products liability activity over time in much the same way as it does medical malpractice—in the direst terms. It speaks of ever-increasing numbers of cases and upward spiraling award structures as the results of inappropriate jury decisions in combination with expanding definitions of liability, greedy lawyers, and so on. The rhetoric says that patterns of increase in the frequency of suits, win rates, and awards can be found across products liability cases generally. This characterization of change gives the story of decline its force and is a key part of the reformers' strategic representation of the product liability system as one in need of fundamental change. While this characterization is useful for political purposes, the reality of the situation is much more complex.

General Patterns

To explore change in jury verdicts, we will focus on settings as we did with the 1988–90 data. This approach suggests that the important temporal patterns will be found within settings and that these patterns may not be the same across settings. A similar idea can be found in Marc Galanter's discussion of case populations and congregations. He argues that different populations and congregations of cases (congregations being a subdivision within a given population) have their own "careers." Galanter notes that "there is no uniform or general movement in which

Table 5.8 Counties with 100-plus Products Liability Verdicts: 1970–90

Site	*N*	Winning Cases
Los Angeles, Cal.	699	283
Cook, Ill.	522	216
San Francisco, Cal.	202	98
Alameda, Cal.	132	48
Dallas, Tex.	123	39
Sacremento, Cal.	101	35

every type of litigation increases or decreases; different kinds of cases increase or decrease at different rates. Yet there is order over time in the occurrence of a particular kind of case."[127] The question for our purposes is what kinds of patterns we will find within settings for products liability verdicts over time and whether we will find the order to which Galanter alludes.

As was the case with medical malpractice, few of the 19 sites for which we have 21 years of data experienced substantial numbers of products liability verdicts during that time period. Only six of these sites had 100 or more products verdicts. Table 5.8 shows that four of the six were in California. To explore patterns over time, we will use the three counties with the highest numbers of cases: Los Angeles, Cook, and San Francisco. The lower number of cases in the other three sites, particularly the lower number of cases in which plaintiffs were successful, makes it difficult to talk about temporal patterns with any confidence. For instance, when we disaggregate the cases by setting and time period, we find that in one of the four time periods used in our analysis, Dallas had only four work setting cases in which plaintiffs were successful.

Basic data on plaintiff win rates and awards over time in the three higher frequency counties are shown in table 5.9. One of the important conclusions emerging from these data is that there were no consistent, general patterns shared by all three sites. Win rates did not follow any simple pattern, nor were they high. Only in San Francisco did the win rate reach 50%—in the second two time periods. We will see shortly, however, that this was due primarily to the influx of one type of case within the work setting—asbestos cases—rather than some broader change. The 54.5% and 52.3% win rates in 1981–85 and 1986–90 for San Francisco represented an increase from the 42.0% and 42.4% win rates in the first two time periods. Win rates in Cook dropped after the first time period and then increased through the next three reaching 48.1%. In Los Angeles, there was still another pattern—stability in win rates over the first two periods followed by an increase and then a decrease to the previous level.

Table 5.9 Win Rates and Median Awards (1990 $): 1970–90

	1970–75			1976–80			1981–85			1986–90		
Site	*N*	Win Rate (%)	Median Award ($)	*N*	Win Rate (%)	Median Award ($)	*N*	Win Rate (%)	Median Award ($)	*N*	Win Rate (%)	Median Award ($)
Los Angeles	150	38.7	118,070	155	38.7	469,345	245	45.3	537,600	149	36.2	758,079
Cook	115	40.0	187,200	112	33.0	238,500	114	35.1	330,990	181	48.1	290,952
San Francisco	50	42.0	124,800	33	42.4	204,300	33	54.5	451,623	86	52.3	210,000

Los Angeles appears to have the kind of pattern over time with respect to award structure that the reform rhetoric claims to be the case in general. The median award in Los Angeles increased over time, reaching $758,079 by 1986–90. This is different from the pattern for medical malpractice verdicts in Los Angeles as seen in chapter 4. In that arena, there was no comparable increase in median awards,[128] and the award structure generally was much lower. While the median award for products reached $758,079 in Los Angeles for 1986–90, the median for malpractice was $273,710. Cook and San Francisco had very different patterns for median awards in products cases, with the median increasing through 1981–85 (at levels lower than in Los Angeles) and then going down. The patterns for median awards in malpractice cases in Cook and San Francisco were quite different from those for products cases (see table 4.6).

Figures 5.1a–5.1c explore temporal patterns in the award structures for the three counties in more detail. Each graph is arranged so that the bottom of the bar in a given time period represents the 25th percentile for awards and the top of the bar the 75th percentile. The two lines in the graphs are for the median and mean awards, the upper line being the mean and the lower line the median. We immediately see that the patterns for each of the counties are distinct, but with one important similarity. For all three, the most dramatic changes came in the 75th percentile and the mean awards—the higher end of the award structure.

Los Angeles (figure 5.1a) had the highest award structure. Both the 25th percentile and the median increased over time, reaching $193,356 and $758,079 respectively, by 1986–90. The 75th percentile and the mean tracked each other closely, rising in 1976–80, dropping in 1981–85, and rising again to just over $2 million in 1986–90. This reflects a growing number of relatively high awards. Of the three counties, Los Angeles comes the closest to the picture portrayed by the reform rhetoric. In Cook (figure 5.1b) the pattern was different. The median

Figure 5.1a: Los Angeles

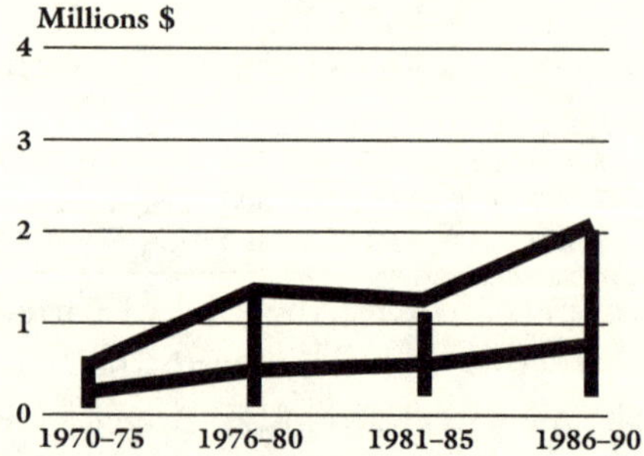

Figure 5.1b: Cook

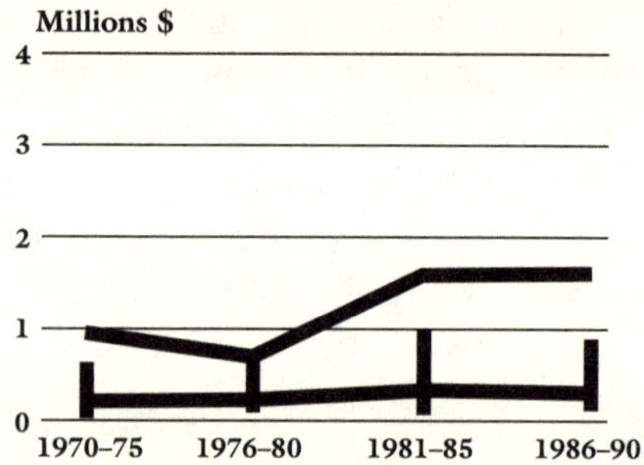

Figure 5.1c: San Francisco

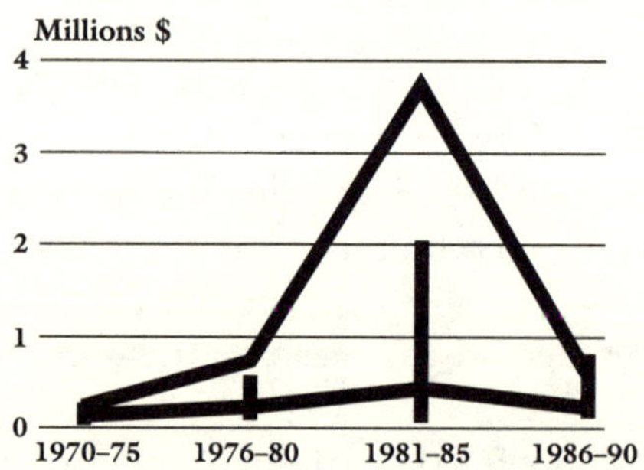

FIGURES 5.1a–5.1c Award Structures (1990 dollars)

Note: upper line is mean award; lower line is median award

award rose to $330,990 in 1981–85 and then declined to $290,952 in 1986–90. The 75th percentile was also at its highest in 1981–85, reaching $988,410, and declined afterward to $905,750. The mean followed a somewhat erratic pattern of decline, rise, and then essentially leveled off at approximately $1.6 million. The difference between the 75th percentile and the mean in Cook reflects a relatively small number of large verdicts against a backdrop of generally lower awards.

San Francisco (figure 5.1c), with its relatively smaller number of cases, presents an altogether different picture. The median award followed a pattern similar to that in Cook of increasing through 1981–85, and then decreasing in 1986–90. Unlike the situation seen in Cook, however, the mean and 75th percentile awards in San Francisco show dramatic increases in 1981–85, reaching $3,702,010 and $2,058,574, respectively. This was followed by equally dramatic decreases in 1986–90. Part of the reason for these changes is the smaller number of verdicts in San Francisco generally, coupled with one extremely high award in 1981–85. This one award was for $46,879,260 (in 1990 dollars), and it was made in a *non-personal injury* case in which a business entity was the plaintiff. Without this case the mean and 75th percentile for 1981–85 would be $1.2 million and $1.3 million respectively. While this would produce a less dramatic picture than the one depicted in figure 5.1c, the basic pattern of a substantial increase in 1981–85 for the mean and 75th percentile followed by a decrease in 1986–90 would remain. The underlying cause for this dramatic pattern in award structure is found in the mix of cases in San Francisco and in particular the influx of asbestos cases, cases that do not yield very high awards. In general, the key to understanding aggregate patterns in win rates and awards, such as those in table 5.9 and figures 5.1a–5.1c, is to be found in the mix of cases going to jury trial. It is to this consideration that we turn next.

Settings

The three counties experienced different mixes of products liability cases as figures 5.2a–5.2c show. In Los Angeles, there was a clear pattern over time. The proportion of verdicts emerging from the work setting increased steadily from 33.3% in 1970–75 to 53.0% in 1986–90, and the proportion of verdicts generated by the vehicle setting decreased from 34.0% in 1970–75 to 13.4% in 1986–90. The proportion of home setting cases stayed stable over time—between 11.0% and 14.2%. Win rates for work setting cases changed little—drifting over the four time periods from 42.0% to 40.0% to 40.3% to 38.0%. In the vehicle setting, the trend in plaintiff success rates was one of steady increase in the first three time periods (31.4% to 41.7% to 51.9%), followed by a decrease in 1986–90 to 40.0%. The different patterns for these two settings make broadscale claims about increasing jury favoritism for plaintiffs problematic. And as we shall see shortly, it is unlikely that increasing plaintiff favoritism will explain the pattern in vehicle cases.

Median awards in Los Angeles for all three settings increased over time, but most dramatically in the vehicle setting. In 1970–75, the median award in these cases was $196,840, and in 1976–80 it jumped to $965,319. By 1981–85, the median award increased to just over $1.3 million, and it increased again in 1986–90 to $3.3 million. Hence, while becoming a proportionately smaller part of the products liability picture in this site, vehicle cases were characterized by increasing awards and win rates alike. Consequently, vehicle cases made up a disproportionate share of the top 25% of the award structure in Los Angeles—consistently a larger proportion of the top 25% of awards than of all products verdicts.

Vehicle setting verdicts in Los Angeles, therefore, help to explain the pattern over time at the high end of the award structure in figure 5.1a. Underlying this was a shift in the severity of injury involved in the vehicle cases going to a jury, a shift toward more severe personal injuries. Major injuries made up a larger proportion of vehicle cases over time, reaching nearly two-thirds of those cases in 1986–90 (65.0%).[129] More importantly for patterns in awards, the two most severe levels of nonfatal injury (levels 7 and 8) made up an increasingly larger proportion of personal injury vehicle cases over the four time periods (6.1%–14.3% to 33.3%–36.8%). Plaintiffs won major injury vehicle cases (50.7%) more often than vehicle cases involving minor injury (34.0%) or death (44.4%), and they were most successful (54.8%) in cases involving levels 7 and 8 major injuries. The median award for vehicle setting major injury cases was $1,552,500, and for cases with levels 7 and 8 injuries it was $5,625,000.

Though a smaller percentage of all Los Angeles verdicts, home setting cases also showed a shift toward major injury and away from minor injury. By 1986–90, just over one-half of the home cases involved major injuries (52.6%), and plaintiffs won more often in these cases (48.1%) than in minor injury home setting cases (31.4%). The pattern for work setting cases, in contrast, was quite different. During no time period did major injury cases make up the largest proportion of these verdicts; the percentage comprised of major injuries changed little, staying between 34.0% and 39.5%. Additionally, the two most severe levels of major injury (levels 7 and 8) made up only a small proportion of personal injury work cases (5.7% overall). Minor injuries consistently accounted for at least one-half of the verdicts (between 50.8% and 54.4% over the

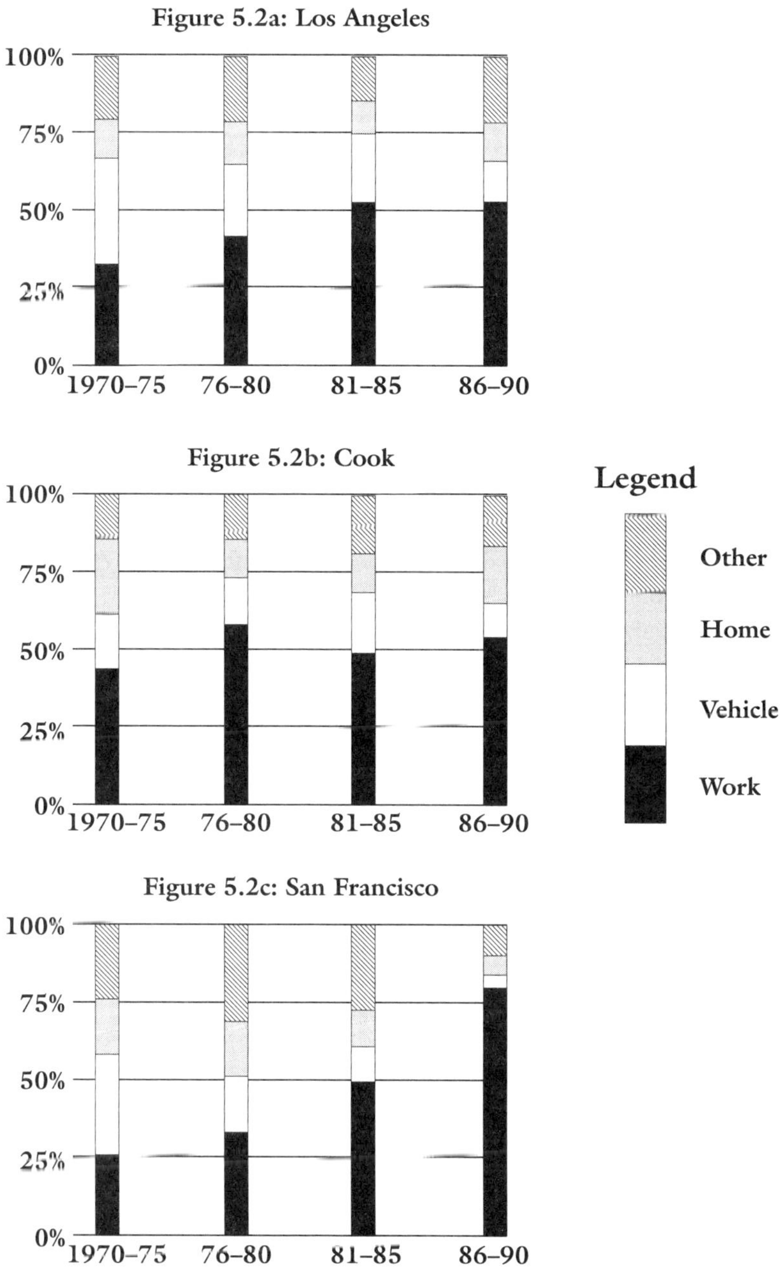

FIGURES 5.2a–5.2c Settings, 1970–90

four time intervals). Plaintiffs generally won more often in major injury cases than in minor injury cases, but the difference was not great (43.8% v. 39.2%). Over time, the minor injury plaintiff win rate rose slightly reaching 39.5% in 1986–90, while the major injury win rate dropped from just over 50% in the first two periods to 39.2% and 37.9% in the last two periods. Additionally, plaintiffs did not win often in the few injury level 7 and 8 cases (only five of 18 cases or 27.8%).

Median awards for work setting cases in Los Angeles rose as did those for vehicle setting cases, but not as dramatically, perhaps as a result of the differences in the severity of injuries involved as just noted. The median award for work setting cases increased modestly from $303,750 in 1970–75 to $378,090 in 1976–80, and then jumped to $531,720 in 1981–85 and to $974,912 in 1986–90. The median for vehicle cases was more than three times as high during the 1986–90 interval. The award structure pattern for major injuries in work cases was also different. There was a substantial increase in the median award in work setting cases involving major injuries from $129,200 to $756,000 in 1976–80, followed by a decrease to $583,538 in 1981–85. In 1986–90 the median in these cases escalated to $1,575,000. For major work injury cases overall, the median award was $562,275 compared to $1,552,500 for all vehicle setting major injury plaintiff verdicts.

Changes in work setting cases, then, may help explain some of the change in the median and the lower end of the award structure for Los Angeles seen in figure 5.1a, while changes in the vehicle setting explain those in the high end of the structure and the mean. A conclusion that juries became more generous or sympathetic over time[130] is too simplistic, and making inferences from jury verdict data about the motives of jurors is a dangerous business. The products liability system of 1986–90 in Los Angeles was quite different from that of 1970–75. The proportion of verdicts originating in the work setting increased, while the proportion of verdicts coming from the vehicle setting decreased. Cases from the home setting consistently represented a small proportion of the verdicts. The work and vehicle settings themselves changed, as we saw, with regard to win rates and awards. Additionally, while the percentages accounted for by minor and major injuries in the work setting stayed relatively stable, an important change occurred in the vehicle setting as major injuries increased and minor injuries decreased.

The reasons for the within-setting changes in Los Angeles are complex, and the explanations for each setting are likely to be quite different. Unfortunately, these explanations cannot be fully uncovered using verdict data; other factors would need to be investigated. For instance, for the work setting, it would be necessary to examine the operation and efficacy of the state's workers' compensation system as well as the regulation, under OSHA and the state equivalents, of workplace safety along with the relationship of these structures to the products liability system. There are also compensation and safety regulation systems connected to vehicle setting cases to consider, but the shift over time toward major injuries and away from minor injury may point us to even other factors. It may be that plaintiffs' attorneys handling vehicle cases have become more selective in the cases they choose to handle or take to a jury. Although the literature is thin on this subject, there is some empirical indication of such systematic selection processes. The risks and incentives of the contingency fee system (in which the attorney usually finances cases like these, which are costly, up front) may have pushed attorneys toward cases that they believed had the greatest chance of success and the highest award potential.[131] In the vehicle setting, this would mean major injury cases.

Finally, there is the largely uncharted process of negotiation and settlement that disposes of most product liability matters. How are these matters settled, and in particular how do liability insurance carriers or the large, self-insured manufacturers handle such matters? These are key players in the process. Changes in the negotiation process are something we know virtually nothing about, yet they are important for attaining a more comprehensive understanding of the patterns and changes in the products liability system.

While the patterns and changes in products liability verdicts in Los Angeles raise a host of questions, the patterns in San Francisco raise additional ones. Like Los Angeles, San Francisco experienced an increase in the proportion of verdicts arising in the work setting and a decrease in those generated by the vehicle setting (home setting cases also decreased, from 18.0% in 1970–75 to 5.8% in 1986–90). As figure 5.2c shows, however, the changes were far more dramatic. By 1986–90, work cases accounted for 80.2% of the products verdicts in San Francisco, while vehicle cases comprised only 3.5%. The primary reason for this change was the influx of asbestos cases brought by workers starting in 1981–85. By 1986–90, two-thirds of all products jury verdicts in San Francisco were asbestos cases (58 of 86 or 67.4%). There was no comparable influx of such cases in Los Angeles, although asbestos cases did increase with time (none in 1970–75, one in 1976–80, nine in 1981–85, and eight in 1986–90).[132] In addition, the win rate for asbestos cases was much higher in San Francisco (65.1%) than in Los Angeles (38.9%). Awards for asbestos cases in San Francisco, however, were not very high, which helps to explain the decrease in the award structure in 1986–90 (see figure 5.1c). The median award for the 36 winning asbestos cases in 1986–90 was $210,000.

The differences between these two California sites point to the importance of factors unique to the place or jurisdiction. The San Francisco Bay area has long been a major port and shipbuilding area, much more so than Los Angeles County, and therefore the occurrence of relatively large numbers of asbestos cases should not be surprising. It is possible, of course, that there was indeed a roughly comparable number of asbestos cases *filed* in Los Angeles County, but that they did not go to a jury trial at the same rate as such cases in San Francisco. Even so, the important point remains—that there are critical differences produced by factors unique to the place, whether it be the local legal culture and the way certain cases are handled or geography and economy which may generate different kinds of cases.

Cook County (figure 5.2b) exhibits yet another pattern, again highlighting the importance of factors related to the place itself. Unlike the two California sites, the work setting has always been the predominant setting in Cook County, and there is no simple pattern of an increasing proportion of work cases accompanied by a decreasing proportion of vehicle cases. At its lowest point during the four time periods, the work setting accounted for 44.3% of the products cases (in 1970–75). The percentage increased to 58.0% in 1976–80, decreased to 49.1% in 1981–85, and then increased again to 54.1% in the final period. Vehicle cases also fluctuated over time—between 19.3% and 10.5% of all products cases. The proportion of home cases declined initially from 24.3% in the first interval to 11.6% in 1976–80 and rose thereafter to 17.7% in 1986–90. In Cook, then, there appears to have been a products liability system that did not change dramatically with regard to setting as was the case in the California sites, but rather one that fluctuated within relatively broad boundaries.

There were also differences within settings in Cook County distinct from those in the California sites. For instance, there was no shift toward major injury in the vehicle setting cases along with higher win rates and awards over time. Perhaps the most notable feature in the vehicle cases in Cook is that plaintiffs won infrequently. Overall, the win rate was 16.7% (13 of 78 cases), and in none of the four time periods did the win rate reach as high as 30% (the highest was 26.3% in 1986–90, and the lowest was in 1981–85). Additionally, it was not until 1986–90 that there was a $1 million-plus vehicle setting verdict (in 1990 dollars). In fact, the highest reported award before 1986–90 in the vehicle setting was $243,000. This pattern is in sharp contrast to the one found in Los Angeles. We would search in vain for an explanation of these differences between sites using verdict data alone. Unfortunately, these differences again take us beyond the extant empirical literature.

Differences in temporal patterns for products liability verdicts, together with the patterns for medical malpractice verdicts discussed in chapter 4, reinforce some crucial points made in chapter 3. First, jury verdicts as a general proposition are not predictable and uniform in the aggregate, if for no other reason than the lack of fungibility among the cases going to trial. Differences in the cases themselves, along with the variations in the socioeconomic characteristics of specific jurisdictions, undermine broadscale predictability and uniformity. Over time in the three sites, we found differences in the mixes of products liability cases going to a trial, as well as variations among sites in plaintiff win rates and award structures. Rather than being evidence of an irrational, chaotic, or out-of-balance system, what we found is a system that appears to be extremely complex, yet orderly. To return to Galanter's observation, "there is no uniform or general movement in which every type of litigation increases or decreases; different kinds of cases increase or decrease at different rates. Yet there is order over time in the occurrence of a particular kind of case."[133]

These findings highlight, once again, the conclusions of commentators like Michael Saks and Joseph Sanders and Craig Joyce discussed in chapter 1 regarding just how little systematic, reliable knowledge we have available about important parts of the civil justice system. Our results raise a variety of questions, but often there is a scant literature to turn to for possible answers. The findings with regard to temporal patterns, however, help to provide a context for the rhetoric of reform—for the politics of ideas. As we noted at the outset of this discussion of products liability, ideas about change have been a key part of the rhetoric, and these ideas have been widely and aggressively marketed with some success in the face of an empirical literature unable to provide an alternative picture. The discussion in this chapter presents an alternative picture of the products liability system, one quite different from that in the reform rhetoric. Our hope is that this alternative will not simply lead one to be skeptical of the reformers' proffered policy changes, but rather that it provokes critical thought about the agenda-setting process itself, the politics of ideas, and the devices used to create images as a part of the struggle to determine which vision of the world will govern policy.

The reformers create their image, in large part, from their perceptions of the messages being sent by juries in deciding products liability verdicts. The decisions and verdicts of juries are used as crucial indicators of "crisis." As a conclusion to this chapter, we would like to briefly explore an important message emerging from the findings we have discussed—the relevance of other systems of injury compensation and safety regulation that overlap the products liability arena. In short, before we kill the messenger, let's read the message.

Conclusion: Don't Kill the Messenger till You Read the Message

The patterns we have just described suggest a products liability system—at least that portion of it that reaches a jury trial—quite different from the rhetoric of reform. It is a system characterized first and foremost by cases involving products encountered in the workplace, and then by vehicle-related products and products generally encountered in the home. Each of these areas is subject to a variety of continuing regulatory or safety programs. Workers' compensation is perhaps the most obvious for workplace injuries, but there is also the federal Occupational Safety and Health Administration (OSHA) and its state-level counterparts. The products involved in the vehicle and home settings are also the subject of governmental interest through agencies such as the National Highway Traffic Safety Administration, the Federal Trade Commission, the Food and Drug Administration, and the Consumer Product Safety Commission. One message being sent by patterns in jury verdicts may be less about the civil justice system and more about about failures of other systems of compensation that affect the way injuries and any resulting claims are handled and about failures of systems for safety regulation that may affect the frequency and nature of injury. To explore this, we will briefly discuss this concept by focusing on such activity in the work setting, the area that produces the largest proportion of products liability verdicts in our database.

Work Setting: OSHA

OSHA has been the most prominent of the agencies in the workplace safety arena, largely because of its policy role. Created in 1971 in response to concerns about a rapid growth in recorded job accidents in the 1960s,[134] OSHA's primary weapon is its ability to "set mandatory occupational health and safety standards applicable to business affecting interstate commerce."[135] While OSHA has in fact promulgated thousands of industry standards related to health and safety, critics have argued that many of these standards, particularly those created in the administration's early days, were inappropriately focused on readily visible safety hazards or were simply arcane exercises addressing such issues as the shape of toilet seats, the precise height of fire extinguishers from the floor, or the availability of portable toilets for cowboys.[136] Critics have also been concerned with OSHA's enforcement efforts and their efficacy in producing significant improvements in the workplace. In his examination of the history of OSHA inspection patterns, Kip Viscusi notes that in its early years OSHA placed much of its emphasis on the inspection of low-risk industries and small firms.[137] In later years this focus changed with inspections of larger firms producing violations at the same rate as was found in small firms. However, Viscusi believes that even that redirection is insufficient given the large number of workers affected by large firm activity.[138]

Regardless, Viscusi argues that improved targeting for OSHA inspections could not be effective unless accompanied by appropriate incentives for compliance. He concludes that the penalty levels imposed in the early 1970s were too low to have an effect on business decisions to invest in compliance or in rectifying existed job hazards.[139] In examining OSHA activity between 1971 and 1975, he noted that the average number of standards violations cited per inspection was 3.7 and the average penalty per violation was $25.68. Factoring in the odds of being subject to inspection, the average OSHA penalty per establishment was $7.58 between 1971 and 1975 or $1.52 annually.[140] Looking at longer term data for the period 1973 to 1983, Viscusi claims that OSHA regulations reduced all work injuries by 2.6%, injuries and illnesses causing lost days of work by 2.6%, and the rate of total lost work days by 6.1%.[141] While finding that the percentage reduction in injuries is largest for the most severe injuries, he concludes that because the number of inspections and penalties assessed was low, OSHA has had at best a moderate effect on workplace health and safety.[142]

In addition, other critics have focused on the specific standards OSHA has set. For instance, a Ford administration task force examined the standards pertaining to machine guards and handheld power tools, and found that the standards set applied to only 15% of the various types of machines then in use.[143] Other commentators have emphasized the influence of political pressure and interest group activity on OSHA, especially during the Reagan years. The point of such political activity was to affect enforcement by altering the rules governing decisions on which companies will be inspected, the circumstances determining the particular inspection procedures used, the instances in which penalties will be assessed, the amount of negotiation allowed over the size of the penalty, the numbers and types of cases sent for criminal prosecutions, and the levels of staffing and the selection of inspectors.[144]

Much of this political effort was successful from the point of view of the Reagan administration and the business community. In the early 1980s, OSHA sought to work more cooperatively with industry and to move away from enforcement through punishment and deterrence. OSHA altered its screening procedures to exempt a broad range of workplaces from programmed inspections, and it actively downplayed dollar penalties for noncompliance. Greater emphasis was placed on corporate willingness to remedy cited violations, and less on follow-up inspections and nonabatement penalties. In addition, limitations were placed on the discretionary authority of agency field officers.[145] As a result of this philosophy of cooperation with industry, there was a 78% drop in the dollar amount of penalties assessed between 1980 and 1982.[146] The shifts in OSHA policies put in place in the early 1980s were viewed positively by industry, but others argued that the changes further weakened an already ineffective program.[147] The general consensus appears to be that overall, OSHA has not had a substantial, positive effect on workplace safety.

Work Setting: Workers' Compensation

The history of workers' compensation is well known. Workers' compensation schemes were devised as a response to concerns about workplace injuries and the remedies available to workers in the legal system. Focusing on causation rather than fault, these schemes assign absolute liability to employers for the costs of work-related injuries, thereby providing for rapid compensation and a means to avoid the confrontational aspects of a tort against an employer. The employers' liability is limited by fixed schedules of benefits defining the levels of compensation for different injuries in the form of medical costs and lost wages. Almost 90% of American workers are covered by state workers' compensation schemes or a federal equivalent such as FELA.[148] As a point of comparison, Viscusi noted that in 1987, workers' compensation claims were over 1,000 times as large as the total penalties levied by OSHA.[149]

While the corporate sector complains about its rising costs for workers' compensation,[150] the coverage of benefits under such plans may be insufficient, pushing claimants into the courts seeking recovery for the full costs of their injuries.[151] Students of the workers' compensation system, like Weiler and Viscusi, have argued that the system's handling of serious and enduring injuries and its handling of occupational diseases are both inadequate. Weiler, for instance, noted that it is generally recognized that "the workplace makes a significant contribution to diseases . . . which are the major sources of disability and death among the working-age population. . . . However, while WC has long had to grapple with the problem of occupational diseases . . . this no-fault system has been notably unsuccessful in delivering compensation to all the victims of such workplace diseases."[152] Weiler describes the struggle of workers' compensation to determine liability for disease an "intractable problem."[153] Among the occupational diseases he refers to is asbestosis among asbestos workers.[154]

Viscusi, in his analysis of products liability closed claims insurance data, found that job-related products claims tended to involve more severe injuries or death and that they were more likely to got to a trial than products matters generally.[155] More serious injuries and death involve larger dollar amounts or greater stakes, perhaps beyond the benefits of workers' compensation. He argues that "the greater stakes of job-related claims decrease the claimant's propensity to drop a case by boosting the expected pay off from litigation."[156] Interestingly, Viscusi found that many of these job-related products claims were not brought by the injured worker. Instead, "almost one-fourth of all job-related products liability claims are the result of subrogation actions in which employers or insurers are seeking reimbursement for their payment of worker losses."[157]

Consistent with Viscusi's findings, Weiler noted that for the most serious injuries, benefits in a large majority of states are still not adjusted regularly for inflation. "Since by definition these disabilities will continue for a long time, the real value of the pensions is inevitably eroded."[158] This is consistent with the criticisms of the California workers' compensation system noted early in this chapter.[159] Among serious injuries, Weiler characterizes the predicament of a worker who suffered a permanent partial disability (such as the loss of a limb or its use) as "one of the more difficult problems confronting present-day WC."[160] Here the individual may be able to return to work, but perhaps not to the same job with the same wages, and so on. The individual may then receive a partial pension. Weiler pointed out, however, that empirical studies showed this system "provided reasonably adequate wage replacement only in the first two to three years of a disability."[161] And for a small number of workers whose limited impairment precluded reemployment, the partial pension left them drastically undercompensated forcing them "to subsist on public or private systems of insurance or assistance."[162]

Weiler's and Viscusi's findings provide evidence for a potential link between the failings and problems of a compensation system on products liability. As Viscusi argues, "since job-related claims are an important component of the total products liability burden, in terms both of number of claims and of their magnitude, any comprehensive program for tort liability reform must examine the workers' compensation-products liability linkage."[163] One could also turn to studies of regulatory programs relevant to the vehicle and home settings, and find additional evidence for links to the products liability system.[164]

Findings such as Weiler's and Viscusi's on workers' compensation along with those on OSHA in conjunction with the data discussed in this chapter illustrate vividly the importance of an idea we raised at the end of chapter 2. That idea was the need to show the existence of a reasonable alternative to the politically created image found in the reform rhetoric and that such an alternative can raise a host of questions revolving around a different set of issues requiring different kinds of policy responses. This, in turn, highlights both the practical and theoretical importance of the politics of ideas and the definition of "problems"—that the policy process is indeed about which view of the world will govern policy.

CHAPTER SIX

Punitive Damages[1]

Punitive damage awards are the last of the three most visible targets of tort reform and a major subject in the reform rhetoric. As with medical malpractice, discontent with the concept of punitive damages has a long history. In 1873, for instance, a member of the New Hampshire Supreme Court characterized them in the following terms: "The idea is wrong. It is a monstrous heresy. It is an unsightly and unhealthy excrescence, deforming the symmetry of the body of the law."[2] Still cited today by those critical of the doctrine of punitive damages, this judicial protest illustrates both the age and the tone of the debate.[3]

Contemporary reformers confidently claim that the doctrine has specific and demonstrable negative effects reaching crisis proportions.[4] They have typically cast these effects as a major cause of the "insurance crisis" of the 1980s and other ills in the 1990s, and target punitive damages for substantial change if not outright abolition.[5] Four straightforward, empirical propositions underlie these claims: punitive damages are routinely awarded, they are awarded in large amounts, the frequency and size of those awards have been rapidly increasing, and these phenomena are national in scope.[6] Mirroring the claims about jury verdicts in the medical malpractice and products liability arenas, these assertions regarding punitive damages and their effects speak of a truly sorry state of affairs in which businesses are destroyed and jobs lost, the development of useful and even essential products is deterred, and so on. It is a state of affairs in which greedy plaintiffs and their contingency fee attorneys are enriching themselves at the expense of the economic health and well-being of America.

Despite a recent body of empirical studies challenging the reformers' claims about punitive damages, they remain a critical part of the reform argument. In addition to their use in legislative efforts on both the state and federal levels,[7] these claims have also been used prominently in constitutional litigation before the U.S. Supreme Court seeking the abolition of punitive damages. Indeed, the Supreme Court has heard four major challenges to the constitutionality of punitive damages between 1988 and 1994.[8] This sequence of cases initially dealt with the issue of the appropriateness of punitive damages generally and moved on to consideration of the size of the punitive damage award involved in a specific case and the appropriate standards for judicial review of that award.

In this chapter we will provide a brief overview of the doctrinal debate over punitive damages along with a discussion of the strategic representation of punitive damages found in the contemporary rhetoric of reform. This will be followed by discussion of our empirical data on patterns in the frequency and size of punitive damages for the years 1988–90 and changes over time in select jurisdictions.

"A Monstrous Heresy . . . [A]n Unsightly and Unhealthy Excrescence": Rhetoric and Context

The Doctrinal Debate

Because punitive damages cut across so many areas of litigation, it is worth examining the contours of the long-running doctrinal debate itself as background for current policy discussions. The debate focuses on two issues: whether the purposes of the doctrine are appropriate, and whether they are being met. Examination of the purposes of punitive damages must begin with a recognition of the doctrine's substantial history. Its common law origins generally are traced to two 1763 English cases arising from the same underlying cause of action. In *Wilkes v. Wood*[9] and *Huckle v. Money*,[10] appellate courts upheld jury awards of damages in excess of actual damages.[11] These cases established a form of monetary civil punishment, not necessarily proportional to the actual injury, to fulfill a sense of outrage resulting from affronts to the honor of an individual.

Punitive damages have a history of almost equal duration in the United States. *Coryell v. Colbaugh*,[12] an action for breach of promise to marry decided in 1791, is one of the earliest cases that refers to punitive damages. The court instructed the jury "not to estimate the damages by any particular proof of suffering or actual loss; but to give damages for *example's* sake, to prevent such offences in [the] future."[13] The court stated that "such a sum . . . would mark [the jury's] disapprobation, and be an example to others."[14]

Today, an award of punitive damages is predicated on behavior by the defendant that can be characterized as malicious, willful, wanton, oppressive, or outrageous. State statutory provisions generally emphasize the punishment or deterrence rationales, or both, for punitive damages. Dorsey Ellis, one of the doctrine's leading academic commentators, identified seven objectives for punitive damages that he gleaned from judicial opinions and related commentary:

1. Punishment of the defendant;
2. Specific deterrence, to prevent the defendant from repeating the offense;
3. General deterrence, to prevent others from committing similar offenses;
4. Preservation of the peace;
5. Inducement for private law enforcement;
6. Compensation to victims for otherwise uncompensable losses;
7. Payment of the plaintiff's attorney's fees.[15]

Current state statutory provisions generally emphasize the punishment or deterrence rationales, singly or collectively, for punitive damages. However, the propriety of such objectives and their efficacy has been severely criticized. The punishment rationale, for example, is criticized for duplicating criminal punishment without the procedural safeguards of criminal law.[16] The burden of proof in the civil system, proof by a preponderance of the evidence, is less rigorous than that required by criminal law, proof beyond a reasonable doubt.[17] Other procedural safeguards inherent in criminal but not civil procedure include the right to counsel and the role and size of juries. Those who find the procedures for assessing punitive damages inadequate argue that juries are not equipped to assess appropriate damages after hearing evidence on the defendant's wealth and motives. These critics assert that juries are overly affected by the presence of an injured plaintiff.[18]

Critics also argue that deterrence is an inadequate rationale for the imposition of punitive damages. Some opponents believe that there is insufficient evidence to prove that deterrence is actually accomplished.[19] Others believe that jurisdictions using this rationale fail to clarify the entities to be deterred.[20] Another concern is that even if deterrence is a legitimate goal, the individual plaintiff is not the appropriate recipient of what becomes a windfall award.[21] Additionally, the prospect of punitive damages might prompt a "race to the courthouse" in which those plaintiffs arriving first deplete the funds available to compensate all wronged parties.[22] To resolve these and similar problems, the doctrine's critics propose the use of caps on awards and ratios of punitive damages to compensatory damages.[23] The most radical of the critics argue for the abolition of punitive damages altogether.[24]

Proponents of punitive damage awards defend against such criticisms in several ways. They rebut the argument that punishment is an inappropriate purpose for a civil remedy by reasoning that not all outrageous conduct is criminal in nature, making civil remedies necessary and appropriate.[25] Proponents address the critics' procedural concerns with examples of increasing numbers of jurisdictions that have adopted a "clear and convincing" standard of proof rather than the preponderance standard.[26] Some also argue that a burden of proof lower than the criminal standard is appropriate in cases where the defendant has a comparative advantage in access to evidence, such as those involving medical malpractice and products liability.[27] Additionally, proponents argue that trial court control and appellate review are adequate safeguards against potential jury abuse. They also point to the lack of systematic empirical evidence that juries are excessively plaintiff oriented.

Proponents of punitive damages also defend the deterrence rationale. Much of this rationale's criticism presumes that punitive awards are made in excessive amounts, suggesting not deterrence but overkill. The proponents counter that no systematic evidence exists to support opponents' claims about excessive awards. Thus, without such evidence, allegations that juries are incapable of fairly considering the character of the defendant's misconduct, the extent of the plaintiff's injury, and the wealth of the defendant to determine an appropriate award are mere speculation. Moreover, proponents of the doctrine argue that placing caps on awards or imposing ratios of punitive to compensatory awards would take away the threat of high damages necessary for effective deterrence.[28]

Marc Galanter and David Luban have offered perhaps the most sophisticated recent defense of punitive damages.[29] It is a defense based on practical necessity and normative principle. In terms of practical necessity, Galanter and Luban's argument is simple. Punitive damages provide the only practical means of sanctioning large and flourishing economic actors in the face of weak administrative controls and the limits of criminal justice. Because potentially severe monetary sanctions are involved, they say that punitive damages "are perhaps the most important instrument in the legal repertoire for pronouncing moral disapproval of economically formidable offenders."[30] They characterize the practical value of punitive damages most vividly in the following: "High punitive damage awards hit *homo economicus* where it hurts: an eye for an eye, a tooth for a tooth, and bottom line for a bottom line. It is poetic justice."[31]

Galanter and Luban argue that criminal penalties fail against such offenders because these cases would be seldom prosecuted due to the cost and complexity of investigations. Where criminal penalties are used, "corporate criminal offenders are not severely punished when they are convicted" allowing corporations to simply treat potential fines as a cost of doing business.[32] Similar problems plague administrative schemes for controlling wrongdoing by such actors. Punitive damages *and* the contingency fee system, Galanter and Luban argue, offer the only practical means of controlling the wrongdoing in question. Together they provide injured parties and their lawyers a financial incentive to investigate and pursue egregious and morally shocking civil wrongs. The contingency fee system is a necessity if punitive damages are to have any practical value. Whatever one may think of plaintiffs' lawyers and the contingency fee system, say Galanter and Luban, without them "we would end up with something much worse. That, of course, is wrongdoing that goes merrily along on its illegal and devastating way because nobody is around to blow the whistle."[33]

Practicality does not in and of itself provide a principled justification for punishment in general or punitive damages in particular. Galanter and Luban find one in a retributivist justification for punishment based on the work of legal philosopher Jean Hampton.[34] Hampton's approach is appealing because it combines retribution with norm projection and deterrence as justification for punishment, *and* because it provides a way to scale punishment. This last matter is especially important in the context of the debate over punitive damages. "A retributivist scales punishment to the heinousness of the offense, and that is not measured by the magnitude of the harm."[35]

The underlying ethical principle here is that all people are of equal moral value and that it is wrong to treat them otherwise. From this perspective, a wrongdoer has explicitly or implicitly "asserted a kind of undeserved mastery and superiority over the victim. In other words, the wrongdoer has expressed a falsehood about the world of value. The purpose of punishment is to reassert the truth of the relative value of wrongdoer and victim by inflicting a publicly visible defeat on the wrongdoer—what we shall term an 'expressive defeat.' The magnitude of punishment must reflect the magnitude and, if possible, the nature of the asserted inequality between wrongdoer and victim."[36] The more heinous the wrong—because it expresses more contempt for the victim—the more decisive must be the defeat for the wrongdoer. In this way the victim's worth can be reasserted. In publicly punishing the wrongdoer, society also is acting to deter others from committing similar egregious wrongs in the future and to express commitment to the value of persons.

This principled approach provides a moral justification for a variety of specific modes of punishment, and Galanter and Luban believe it is an especially good justification for punitive damages. In fact, with its emphasis on how people are treated and a sense of honor based on equal moral value they argue that this "theory fits the historical rationale for punitive damages quite closely, better perhaps, than it fits the historical rationale for criminal punishment."[37] It would allow for relatively high punitive awards depending on the wrong involved. In some situations it may even *require* especially high awards if the social goals of punishment, norm projection, and deterrence are to be served. If the wrong is egregious and the wrongdoer is a formidable economic actor, the award would have to be high enough to capture the attention of upper management and not be treated as just a cost of doing business. It also must be high enough so that the "expressive defeat" is credible to both the wrongdoer and the public—credible enough for the wrongdoer to be seen as having been shamed.

Given this, Galanter and Luban argue against specific caps on punitive damages as well as any scheme limiting punitive damages to some multiple of compensatory damages. The limits of punitive damages are based on the heinousness of the wrongful act, not the victim's monetary losses. To help ensure this, Galanter and Luban suggest that juries be required to provide a reasonable rationale for the size of the punitive award. This would also serve the goals of norm projection and deterrence by providing a public statement on the wrongdoing being punished.

Finally, it is worth noting that the most vocal and active proponents for the reform and/or abolition of punitive damages are the actors Galanter and Luban are most concerned about. The proponents of reform, as we have seen throughout this book, tend to be the kind of formidable economic actors who—as a practical matter—can be punished only through the imposition of punitive damages. From Galanter and Luban's perspective, reform of punitive damages would put them effectively beyond punishment. Viewed this way, the rhetoric of reform can be seen as the attempt by formidable economic actors to cast themselves not as actual or potential wrongdoers but as victims, and to cast victims and their lawyers as wrongdoers.

Strategic Representation: "Astronomical Figures That Boggle the Mind"

Commentators have debated the appropriateness of punitive damages for some time. During the past decade or so, however, the traditional arguments have been transformed as the debate has become more and more political in nature. Proponents of change have used all of the devices discussed in chapter 2 in presenting a strategic representation of punitive damages as a key part of a story of decline telling about a civil justice system run amok. Their arguments are geared toward convincing the public and policymakers of the veracity of the four empirical propositions noted earlier. All of the claims about the harmful effects of punitive damages—effects that outline the story of decline—presume the accuracy of those propositions. The presumption is that if these propositions accurately describe the punitive damages system, then all of the alleged harmful effects automatically and necessarily occur.

A series of materials assembled by a Washington, D.C., public relations firm,[38] and widely distributed to editors of a variety of publications during the late 1980s and early 1990s, provides a revealing illustration of strategic representation with regard to punitive damages. Titled *Punitive Damages Update*, the materials were assembled as a "service of a number of corporations and organizations supporting tort reform."[39] Among the most interesting of those materials is a "press kit," dated April 12, 1989,[40] and mailed to targeted journalists the week prior to oral arguments before the Supreme Court in *Browning-Ferris Industries v. Kelco Disposal Co.*[41]—an Eighth Amendment challenge to the constitutionality of punitive damages.

The press kit utilized both horror stories and aggregate data to characterize the punitive damages system as one so seriously flawed and threatening as to require fundamental change. Under the guise of presenting background information for those journalists reporting on *Browning-Ferris*, it communicated the basic claims that underlie the reformers' characterization: punitive damages are awarded routinely and with increasing frequency, in a wider variety of cases, in larger and larger amounts, and without any apparent pattern.[42] The image presented is a disturbing one of a system out of control. As a result of this situation, the press kit states, essential goods and services such as medical services and vaccines are becoming more expensive or even unavailable.[43] Additionally, research and development in American industry are being halted or discouraged, thereby making American businesses less competitive in the international market and threatening jobs. Consequently, the press kit says, the punitive damages problem is a direct threat to economic stability.[44] This characterization of a system out of control is at the very heart of the "slice-of-death" appeal to fear and anxiety, and fundamental civil justice reform appears to be the only method to alleviate those feelings.

Among the materials the press kit uses to substantiate such claims are two commentaries written by Richard J. Mahoney, chairman and chief executive officer of Monsanto.[45] Both rely prominently on horror stories, as does a third Mahoney commentary, coauthored with Stephen E. Littlejohn, the public affairs director for Monsanto, that appears in a late 1989 issue of *Science*.[46] This third piece is touted in a December 15, 1989 press release mailed by *Punitive Damages Update*.[47] Mahoney's three essays are similar in tone and message, but each is directed to a different audience.[48] Mahoney seeks to justify reform and garner support for the cause by generating fear and anxiety about reduced or curtailed innovation, research, and development in American industry. He links reduced or curtailed research and development to the availability of essential health care services and technologies, to economic stability and prosperity, and in the *Science* article, to the professional well-being of scientific and technical professionals.[49] Punitive damages according to the *Science* article, "constitute the driving force behind this problem, and both judges and legislators should aim at bringing them under control with legal reforms."[50] The Mahoney pieces are worth examining in detail because they illustrate the politicization of the punitive damages debate and provide the most sophisticated and persuasive examples of the reformers' efforts at characterization. This examination emphasizes the Mahoney and Littlejohn article because the fact that it was published in *Science*, arguably the most prestigious American scientific journal, gives their arguments substantial credibility and force.

To illustrate the negative effects of punitive damages, Mahoney tells horror stories, including one involving his own company. Monsanto, he says, canceled a program to develop an asbestos substitute because of the threat of punitive damages. The Monsanto employee directing the ill-fated project is quoted as saying that "seven-figure jury awards on claims without merit are enough to send shivers down anyone's spine."[51] Mahoney also complains repeatedly of a civil justice system that "makes it too easy for lawyers to persuade the jury . . . to enrich plaintiffs and contingent fee lawyers with multi-million-dollar windfalls."[52] He refers to a "statistically proven relationship between the punitive damages award and the relative wealth and unpopularity of the defendant."[53] Such damages, he argues, "were . . . virtually unknown" in the past but are now "almost commonplace with multi-million dollar awards occurring monthly."[54]

Two of the three Mahoney articles present the following stories about actual punitive damage cases:

> After the longest running trial in America's history, a jury in Belleville, Ill., last year awarded one dollar to each of 65 plaintiffs as nominal damages for alleged personal injuries in a case involving one of my company's products—orthochlorophenol crude—which is used to make wood preservatives. Then, in a burst of tortured reasoning, the jury awarded $16 million in punitive damages to the plaintiffs.
>
> More recently, Monsanto's G. D. Searle subsidiary was assessed $7 million in punitive damages in a St. Paul, Minn., case involving the Copper 7 intrauterine device that not only has Food and Drug Administration approval, but also a long history of safe use and substantial medical acclaim.[55]

The *Science* article, aimed at an audience more interested in research and development, presents a third story as representative of jury awards of punitive damages:

> One case exemplifies the problem with punitive damages. Lederle Laboratories, a pharmaceutical company, followed Food and Drug Administration (FDA) instructions to the letter in producing and marketing a polio vaccine, only to have a Kansas jury hand down an $8 million punitive damage verdict against it. The reason: The lay jury decided that the firm should have used a less effective vaccine, essentially overruling FDA doctors, scientists, and policymakers who had told the firm to do otherwise.[56]

This story is immediately preceded in the article by the presentation of "hard data" presumably intended to show that large, even multimillion dollar, punitive damage awards are routine. In Cook County, Illinois, according to Mahoney and Littlejohn, the average punitive damage award in personal injury actions from 1980 to 1984 was $1,934,000.[57]

Once the punitive damages problem is "proven," the essays then describe the alleged adverse effects that punitive damages have on health care and economic well-being: there is "a profound negative impact on the development and utilization of potentially life-saving medical technologies."[58] Pharmaceuticals have been severely affected. According to the *Science* article, the American Medical Association has concluded that basic biomedical research is deteriorating, and small companies are delaying or foregoing innovative product releases.[59] Similarly, the National Academy of Sciences has allegedly found that because of the high cost of vaccine-related injuries, many manufacturers may not "pursue the derivation or distribution of a vaccine to prevent AIDS."[60] Furthermore, the article cites another medical authority for stating that the United States is now losing its leadership role in the area of contraceptive technology.[61] Thus, it would appear that punitive damages are a threat to public health and necessary medical care.[62]

The alleged adverse impact also extends to the country's economic well-being. Mahoney says that the cases he recounts are "known only too well by major American companies, costing everybody in lost jobs, new and improved products, and international competitiveness."[63] Indeed, "American manufacturers are falling behind in key industries and major product groups."[64] In addition, research laboratories, such as the Lawrence Livermore Laboratory in California and the University of Wisconsin at Madison, are allegedly reluctant to transfer discoveries to the marketplace because of liability concerns.[65] This claim, no doubt, is intended to show the readers of *Science* that the punitive damage problem is one to which they must pay attention.

Finally, there is the question of how to characterize the punitive damages debate itself. For Mahoney, it is a simple matter of balancing the interests of undeserving plaintiffs and greedy trial lawyers against the public good. In two of his essays he portrays the issue in the following way: "Who loses with these reform proposals? Only plaintiff lawyers and their already compensated clients who have hit the punitive damages jackpot. But the whole country wins with important gains in jobs, new and improved products, international competitiveness—and a fairer legal system for all."[66]

Mahoney intends to create a state of mind and a characterization of the situation that leads to one conclusion: "Clearly, reforms in punitive-damages law are vitally needed by the entire nation."[67] He claims that our collective well-being depends on changes in the punitive damage system and that those who support his reforms will affirm that the nation's future depends on the continued pursuit of innovative scientific knowledge. For Mahoney, current punitive damage rules "stifle the forward progress of innovation."[68]

Horror stories in the punitive damages debate, exemplified by the Mahoney pieces, have great evocative power despite their problematic accuracy. They imply that Americans are overly litigious, that juries are willing to award millions of dollars in compensatory and punitive damages on a whim, especially in areas such as products liability and medical malpractice, and that plaintiffs' attorneys abuse the contingency fee system for their own enrichment. The approach's evocative power comes from its appeal to latent prejudices about undeserving plaintiffs and ambulance-chasing attorneys, and from its generation of anxiety concerning the alleged effects of the punitive damage problems, such as the unavailability of vaccines and life-saving drugs or essential medical services.[69] In appealing to such prejudices and anxieties, the horror stories direct attention away from alternative explanations that may justify large punitive damage awards and portray defendants as something other than the innocent victims of greed—including Monsanto.[70]

Reformers present aggregate data on punitive damage verdicts, the second major type of evidence used in the political debate, as more precise and scientific proof of the problem's scope. Their data provide the broader context that makes the horror stories so convincing. Such "hard data" are meant to serve as symbolic benchmarks, much like the figures for monetary losses or deaths after a natural disaster, by which people will shape their perceptions of punitive damages and the civil justice system.[71] These benchmarks arouse concern and evoke a belief that the civil justice system is reaching a crisis stage.[72] Mahoney and Littlejohn's use of "hard data" from Cook County and California is a good illustration.[73]

The *Punitive Damages Update* press kit includes a section summarizing the findings of a study on punitive damage awards in Cook County and San Francisco conducted by the RAND Corporation's Institute for Civil Justice (ICJ).[74] According to the press kit, the study found:

> The average punitive damage award in Cook County increased in inflation-adjusted dollars from $43,000 in 1965–69 to $729,000 in 1980–84—a 1,500 percent increase.
>
> In San Francisco, the average punitive damage awards jumped from an average of $95,000 in 1964–69 to $381,000 in 1980–84—a 300 percent increase.
>
> The average *personal injury* punitive damage award in Cook County increased from $14,000 in 1965–69 to $1,934,000 in 1980–84—13,700 percent increase.
>
> Business/contract punitive damage awards in Cook County during the same period went from $97,000 to $624,000, a 543 percent increase in inflation-adjusted dollars.[75]

These findings are presented with little or no context and no satisfactory explanation of the source of the data, the method of data collection, or the proper method of interpreting the data.[76] Regardless of these weaknesses in the data, such astronomical figures for the rate of increase in awards present to the reader an apparently clear message that a crisis exists. Used in this way, aggregate data, like horror stories, appeal to emotion and anxiety rather than to reason. When used together with horror stories, aggregate data can create a convincing characterization that calls for the abolition or severe limitation of punitive damages.[77]

Because the "hard data" are a key part of the reformers' argument, the data also demand closer scrutiny. The findings of the ICJ study, presented in the press kit, are the most widely cited data in the punitive damage debate.[78] The ICJ collected data on jury verdicts in both Cook County and San Francisco using local jury verdict reporters,[79] although the Cook County data typically receive emphasis. Both sides of the debate cite the ICJ data with equal confidence, thus demonstrating the problematic nature of the findings.[80] The reformers, however, use the data more frequently and more manipulatively than the defenders of punitive damages. The most prominent use of the ICJ data in the political debate is found in the Reagan administration's *Report of the Tort Policy Working Group* (*Report*)[81] and in a subsequent update (*Update*) of the *Report*.[82] In both documents, the Reagan administration unequivocally supported the reform movement[83] and argued for severe limitations on punitive damages, if not their outright abolition.[84]

The *Report* discusses punitive damages in the context of noneconomic damages and their contribution to the alleged explosive growth in the size of awards generally. The *Report*, like Mahoney's essays, places special emphasis on personal injury cases. According to the *Report*:

> Such non-economic damages are inherently open-ended and subjective, and, therefore, easily susceptible to dramatic inflation. Of interest in this regard is a recent preliminary study by the Institute for Civil Justice which indicates that the average punitive damage award in Cook County, Illinois, increased from $63,000 in 1970–74 to $489,000 in 1980–84. Of particular interest is that the average Cook County punitive damage award in personal injury cases increased from $40,000 in 1970–74 to $1,152,174 in 1980–84.
>
> This explosion in damage awards, particularly in the case of non-economic damages, is vastly in excess of the rate of inflation over the comparable period. For whatever reasons, tort damage awards have suddenly soared in the United States without any apparent justification.[85]

Accompanying this passage is a chart using ICJ's Cook County data showing that the *average* personal injury punitive damage award increased from $40,000 (in constant dollars) in five cases in 1970–74 to $271,000 in six awards in 1975–79 to $1,152,000 in twenty-three awards in 1980–84.[86] In a footnote, the *Report* adds that the ICJ's "analysis of punitive damage awards in San Francisco also showed an increase in such awards, though of lesser magnitude than in Cook County."[87]

Differences in the presentation of the ICJ data in the press kit and the *Report* illustrate the problematic nature of these findings and their use. The two sources adopt different time periods in their respective discussions, the press kit using 1965–69 and 1980–84[88] and the *Report* using 1970–74 and 1980–84.[89] The press kit examines punitive awards overall as well as separately, divided into personal injury cases and business or contract cases.[90] The *Report* focuses on personal injury cases in which the numbers are much more dramatic,[91] as does Mahoney.[92] Additionally, discrepancies exist between the figures in the press kit and in the *Report*. The press kit cites an average punitive damage award in Cook County of $1,934,000 in 1980–84 for personal injury cases,[93] while the *Report* uses a figure of $1,152,174.[94] The press kit reports an overall punitive damage award in Cook County of $729,000 in 1980–84,[95] and the *Report* cites an average of only $489,000.[96] Because neither the press kit nor the *Report* provides any background for the data used or for the ICJ study from which the data are taken, the reason for the differences remains unknown.

The *Update* also presents ICJ punitive damages data, and it provides an additional illustration of discrepancies in the evidence and of the problematic nature of "hard data" in this debate. According to the *Update*, "[t]he available data indicate that in the last decade the size of punitive damages awards has undergone almost explosive growth, particularly in personal injury cases."[97] The *Update* states that the ICJ data for Cook County show "that the average personal injury punitive damage award grew from $28,000 in 1970–74 to $1,934,000 in 1980–84, a 6,900% increase."[98] This information conflicts with figures presented in the *Report*, which indicate that the average award increased from $40,000 in 1970–74 to $1,152,174 in 1980–84.[99] The discrepancy is noted without commentary in a footnote in the *Update*.[100] Explaining such discrepancies, however, is not the important issue in this context. What is important is that the discrepancies exist and that they receive no discussion that would allow the reader to make a judgment as to the veracity of the new figures. If the reformers' goal were to present an accurate picture of the punitive damages system, the discrepancies would be noted and explained so that the reader can understand why the award figure increased. From a symbolic perspective, however, the veracity of the "hard data" used is less important than the general message they are intended to send.[101]

A final problem with the reformers' use of the ICJ data concerns the logic of generalization. The ICJ data are from two case studies, with the Cook County data typically receiving emphasis. Case studies have one important limitation. They cannot be used to assess the general incidence or frequency of some phenomenon within a population of sites.[102] A case study does not represent a legitimate sample and cannot serve as the basis for statistical generalization. Yet the reformers present the ICJ data as a representative sample and use the data to make what are, in effect, statistical generalizations about the frequency and size of punitive damage awards nationwide.[103] One amicus brief in *Pacific Mutual Life Insurance Co. v. Haslip*[104] even claimed that the ICJ data comprise "[a] comprehensive analysis of jury verdicts in the United States."[105] Such generalizations are inappropriate and unfounded no matter how politically expedient they may be.

At first glance, the horror stories and aggregate data seem to provide persuasive evidence for the reformers' arguments. In fact, however, they provide little, if any, reliable evidence about the law in action with regard to punitive damages. They have been used to create a state of mind in the furtherance of a political agenda and should be interpreted accordingly. This does not mean that the reformers have been unsuccessful.

Justice O'Connor's dissent in *TXO Production Corp. v. Alliance Resources Corp. et al.*,[106] the third in a series of four recent Supreme Court decisions dealing with due process challenges to punitive damage awards, presents an embodiment of the success reformers have had in communicating their picture of a civil justice system in distress. This was a common law slander of title action in which a West Virginia jury awarded Alliance $19,000 in actual damages and $10 million in punitive damages, an award upheld by the Supreme Court. Justice O'Connor began her dissent by chastising the Court's majority for failing to keep their "promise that punitive damage awards would receive sufficient constitutional scrutiny to restore fairness in what is rapidly becoming an arbitrary and oppressive system."[107] She chided the Court for failing to provide some standards or guidelines that courts may use in their jury instructions to guide jurors in assessing appropriate levels of damages.

This guidance is necessary because "jurors are not infallible guardians of the public good. They are ordinary citizens whose decisions can be shaped by influences impermissible in our system of justice. . . . Arbitrariness, caprice, passion, bias, and even malice can replace reasoned judgment and law as the basis for jury decisionmaking."[108] Justice O'Connor suggested that the jury was quite likely unduly influenced by the fact that TXO was not only a deep pocket defendant, but an out-of-state deep pocket defendant.

Her concluding paragraph is a concise restatement of the reformers' position on punitive damages. It reads as follows:

> As little as 30 years ago, punitive damages awards were "rarely assessed" and usually "small in amount" (Ellis, 56 *S. Cal. L. Rev.*, at 2). Recently, however, the frequency and size of such awards have been skyrocketing. One commentator has observed that "hardly a month goes by without a multimillion-dollar punitive damages verdict in a product liability case (Wheeler, 40 *Ala. L. Rev.* 919 (1989)). And it appears that the upward trajectory continues unabated. The increased frequency and size of punitive damage awards, however, has not been matched by a corresponding expansion of procedural protections or predictability. On the contrary, although some courts have made genuine efforts at reform, many courts continue to provide jurors with skeletal guidance that permits the traditional guarantor of fairness—the jury itself—to be converted into a source of caprice and bias.[109]

Patterns and Changes in Punitive Damage Verdicts

"Almost Commonplace with Multi-Million Dollar Awards Occurring Monthly": Patterns 1988–90

Frequency. To provide some perspective on the allegations regarding the frequency with which punitive damage awards occur, this section examines the incidence of punitive damage award injury verdicts during the time period between 1988 and 1990. (The Washington State counties used in earlier chapters are excluded from this analysis as punitive damage awards are not allowed at common law in that state.) Table 6.1 displays the total number of punitive awards, the percentage of all reported money damage jury verdicts that include an award of punitive damages, and the percentage of successful cases (those in which the jury awarded the plaintiff at least one dollar) in which an award of punitive damages was made. (Total number for each county can be found in table 3.1.) From these figures, two simple but important conclusions emerge.

The first is that in general, juries do not award punitive damages in a large percentage of money damage cases. Thus, it appears that punitive damage awards may not in fact be routine or "almost commonplace." The second is that a great deal of variation exists among the sites in terms of the number and rates of punitive damage awards suggesting that sweeping statements about national trends used to instigate reform should be viewed with a great deal of skepticism.

Overall, there were 19,404 civil jury verdicts in the counties in table 6.1, 864 or 4.5% included a punitive damage award. Such awards were made in 8.3% of the cases in which plaintiffs were successful. Although changes over time will be addressed later in this chapter in some detail, it is worth comparing the figures in table 6.1 with the findings from an earlier study we conducted covering the early 1980s. Using the somewhat more limited database from the earlier study,[110] we found that 4.9% of all verdicts included a punitive damage award as did 8.8% of all successful verdicts.[111] Reducing our 1988–90 database to the same sites used in the earlier study yields a punitive damage rate of 4.8% for all jury verdicts and one of 9.1% for successful verdicts during this time period. This quick look at the aggregate punitive damage award activity suggests, again, the need for a certain degree of skepticism with regard to claims about the increasing frequency of such awards.

Returning to table 6.1, we can examine the variation in punitive damage rates that occurred among the various sites. Only six experienced 50 or more punitive damage awards during this period, and four of those were in Texas: Los Angeles County, Cal.; Jackson County, Mo.; Dallas County, Bexar County (San Antonio), Harris County (Houston), and Travis County (Austin), Tex. Regardless of the raw numbers, the percentage of verdicts that included a punitive award was generally modest. The punitive damage rate for all money damage cases (successful and unsuccessful) ranged from 0% in Fresno County, Cal.; Platte County, Mo.; Kalamazoo, Macomb, and Washtenau Counties, Mich.; Bronx, Nassau, and New York Counties, N.Y.; Portage, Montgomery, and Lorain Counties, Oh.; and Washington County, Ore., to 15.9% in Travis County, Tex.

The punitive damage rates are higher when calculated as a percentage of successful verdicts. Putting aside those counties which experienced no punitive damage awards during this three-year time period, the rate ranges from 0.5% in Oakland County, Mich., to 29.1% in Travis County (Austin), Tex. Looking at only those sites with at least 10 punitive damage awards during this period, the rate varies from 1.4% in Cook County, Ill., to the 29.1% figure in Travis County. The Texas

Table 6.1 Reported Punitive Damage Jury Verdicts (1988–90)

Jurisdiction	Number of Punitive Awards	Percentage of All Verdicts	Percentage of Successful Verdicts
Alaska	2	4.5	6.5
Arizona			
Maricopa	45	4.7	7.3
California			
Alameda	19	8.1	14.1
Fresno	0	—	—
Los Angeles	58	5.0	9.6
Sacramento	3	2.1	4.4
San Diego	17	5.4	12.6
San Francisco	11	3.0	5.1
Colorado			
Adams	8	9.3	16.3
Arapaho	3	7.0	14.3
Boulder	3	3.7	5.9
Denver	32	7.2	12.9
El Paso	5	5.1	10.8
Jefferson	12	7.6	14.5
Georgia			
Cobb	5	4.4	8.2
DeKalb	15	6.9	12.9
Fulton	37	9.7	15.2
Idaho	6	20.0	28.6
Illinois			
Cook	15	0.8	1.4
DuPage	9	3.6	6.3
Kane	4	3.0	5.3
Lake	3	1.6	2.7
McHenry	2	5.4	9.1
Will	1	0.9	1.2
Winnebago	1	2.1	3.2
Kansas			
Johnson	7	5.0	9.1
Wyandotte	1	0.8	1.2
Michigan			
Genessee	1	1.2	2.4
Ingham	1	1.4	2.1
Kalamazoo	0	—	—
Kent	1	0.9	1.7
Macomb	0	—	—
Oakland	1	0.3	0.5
Washtenau	0	—	—
Wayne	11	1.2	2.4

(Continued)

Table 6.1 Continued

Jurisdiction	Number of Punitive Awards	Percentage of All Verdicts	Percentage of Successful Verdicts
Missouri			
Clay	5	6.2	8.9
Jackson	50	8.5	13.8
Jefferson	4	5.1	8.2
Platte	0	—	—
St. Charles	5	5.7	9.1
St. Louis City	17	2.9	4.2
St. Louis County	20	4.5	7.7
Montana	9	4.6	9.2
New York			
Bronx	0	—	—
Erie	2	2.7	4.5
Kings	4	1.2	2.4
Monroe	2	3.2	5.4
Nassau	4	1.4	4.0
New York	10	1.8	3.3
Onondaga	2	2.5	5.3
Queens	0	—	—
Richmond	0	—	—
Suffolk	2	1.2	3.8
Westchester	1	0.8	2.6
Ohio			
Butler	1	2.5	3.6
Cuyahoga	14	4.2	6.6
Franklin	5	4.7	8.8
Hamilton	3	2.1	3.3
Lorain	0	—	—
Lucas	3	7.7	15.0
Montgomery	0	—	—
Portage	0	—	—
Summit	2	1.8	3.1
Oregon			
Clackamas	1	1.9	3.8
Lane	1	0.9	1.8
Marion	1	1.7	3.2
Multnomah	7	2.0	3.3
Washington	0	—	—
Texas			
Bexar	80	10.8	21.6
Dallas	114	10.7	22.6
District 6	16	7.3	13.0
District 9	10	6.9	16.4
Harris	88	6.0	15.5
Travis	51	15.9	29.1
Total	864	4.5	8.3

sites are the only ones where the punitive damage rate exceeded 20% between 1988 and 1990.

In summary, contrary to the reform rhetoric, punitive damages were not routinely awarded during the 1988–90 period in the sites we examined. In only one of the 74 sites did the punitive damage rate ever exceed one-quarter of all successful cases or 15% of all money damage verdicts. It is also important to note that there was substantial variation among the sites, suggesting the possibility that there is not a consistent national pattern.

Reformers assert that even if punitive damage awards are not routine in general, they are commonplace in certain types of cases. For example, personal injury cases purportedly attract frequent punitive damage awards, particularly those cases involving "deep pocket" defendants (especially medical malpractice and products liability).[112] There are two ways to examine the distribution of punitive damage awards among different types of cases. The first analyzes the distribution of the total number of punitive damage awards across various categories of cases, and the second examines the punitive damage rate within each of these categories. This distinction is critical because each of these two alternatives presents a different portrait of the punitive damages system. The picture portrayed by the first approach would suggest that the reformers are correct in some of their key allegations. The picture emerging from the alternative approach implies an altogether different conclusion.

Table 6.2 displays the breakdown of punitive damage verdicts by category of case for the 22 sites that had 10 or more punitive damage cases during the three-year period 1988–90. It groups jury verdicts into four broad categories of cases based on the type of harm involved in each case. The first category includes all cases in which the primary harm alleged was physical (e.g., auto, assault, slip and fall, medical malpractice). The second category includes all cases in which the primary harm was financial (e.g., breach of contract, fraud, misrepresentation, business interference). The third grouping is of all cases in which the primary harm is to property, and the fourth category includes all cases involving emotional harm or damage to reputation.

The picture presented in table 6.2 shows that most punitive damage awards occur in cases involving either physical or financial harm. Few arise in those cases involving property damage or emotional or reputational harm. These data would also seem to lend some support to the reformers' assertion that physical harm cases attract punitive damage awards. In 15 of the 22 sites 20% or more of the punitive

Table 6.2 Breakdown of Punitive Damage Jury Verdicts by Harm Category: 1988–90 (Sites with 10-plus Punitive Verdicts)

Jurisdiction	Physical (%)	Financial (%)	Property (%)	Emotional (%)
Arizona				
Maricopa (45)	30.4	63.0	4.3	2.2
California				
Alameda (19)	21.1	57.9	0.0	21.1
Los Angeles (58)	20.7	58.6	3.4	15.5
San Diego (16)	18.8	68.8	0.0	12.5
San Francisco (11)	27.3	45.5	9.1	18.2
Colorado				
Denver (32)	15.6	71.9	6.3	6.3
Jefferson (12)	33.3	66.7	0.0	0.0
Georgia				
DeKalb (15)	13.3	53.3	20.0	13.3
Fulton (37)	29.7	56.8	2.7	10.8
Illinois				
Cook (15)	46.7	13.3	13.3	20.0
Michigan				
Wayne (11)	63.6	18.2	0.0	18.2
Missouri				
Jackson (50)	28.0	46.0	16.0	10.0
St. Louis City (17)	41.2	23.5	17.6	17.6
St. Louis County (20)	10.0	40.0	15.0	35.0
New York				
New York (10)	50.0	10.0	20.0	20.0
Ohio				
Cuyahoga (14)	28.6	35.7	7.1	28.6
Texas				
Bexar (80)	26.3	37.5	28.8	7.5
Dallas (114)	14.9	70.2	9.6	5.3
District 6 (16)	37.5	37.5	25.0	0.0
District 9 (10)	10.0	80.0	0.0	10.0
Harris (113)	26.5	34.5	22.1	16.8
Travis (51)	9.8	58.8	25.5	5.9

damage awards occurred in cases of this type. It should also be noted however that in 11 sites 50% or more of the punitive damage awards were made in cases involving financial harm.

The percentage of punitive damage awards in cases in which the primary harm was physical ranges from a low of 9.8% in Travis County, Tex., and 10% in St. Louis County and District 9, Tex., to a high of 63.6% in Wayne County (Detroit), Mich., where there were only 11 punitive damage awards during the three-year period, 1988–90. The range of punitive awards in financial harm areas exhibits wide variation. It extends from a low of 10% in New York County (where there were only 10 punitive awards) to a high of 80% in District 9 in Texas (where again the total number of punitive damage awards was low).

When presented in this manner, these data appear to support the widespread belief that punitive damage awards occur with some frequency in cases involving physical harm. Thus, it would seem that the reformers' focus on physical harm cases as a key ingredient of the punitive damage "problem" is appropriate. However, although on its face a sensible method of examining the incidence of punitive damage awards, the approach taken in table 6.2 may not be the most appropriate one. It distorts perceptions of punitive damage patterns because it is strongly influenced by the makeup of the jury docket in a given jurisdiction. The number of cases on the jury docket relative to other types of cases determines the magnitude of the percentage in table 6.2 for a given case type, not the *rate* at which punitive damages are awarded. If, for example, there is a large number of physical harm cases on the jury docket, it is likely that the *number* of physical harm punitive cases will comprise a relatively high percentage of all punitive damage awards, even if the *rate* at which such awards are made in physical harm cases is quite low. The rate at which a jury awards punitive damages is the more important issue with regard to the frequency of punitive damage awards. Information regarding how often punitive damage awards occur in particular types of cases is necessary to draw any conclusions about their frequency.

Table 6.3 presents data on punitive damage award rates for the sites included in table 6.2. The figures for physical harm cases are significantly lower in table 6.3 than they are in table 6.2. The punitive damage rate is generally quite low and fluctuates within a very narrow range—from 0.8% in Cook County to 12.7% in Bexar County. Indeed, it exceeds 5% in only nine of the 22 sites, and exceeds 10% in only three sites. Contrary to what might be expected based on the rhetoric of reform, punitive damage awards appear to be far from commonplace in cases involving claims of physical harm. Higher punitive damage rates are found in financial harm cases, ranging from a low of 2.1% in Cook County to 44.4% in District 9, Tex.

The two types of cases often focused upon in the reform debate as primary sources of punitive damage awards—medical malpractice and products liability—are included in the physical harm category. A look at the incidence of punitive damage awards in these two types of cases does not produce a sense of great calamity. Table 6.4 draws data from

Table 6.3 Punitive Damage Rates for Successful Cases by Case Category: 1988–90 (Sites with 10-plus Punitive Verdicts)

Jurisdiction	Physical (%)	Financial (%)	Property (%)	Emotional (%)
Arizona				
Maricopa	3.6	14.2	10.5	11.1
California				
Alameda	5.1	23.9	0.0	50.0
Los Angeles	2.9	24.5	10.0	31.0
San Diego	3.1	40.7	0.0	33.3
San Francisco	2.0	11.4	16.7	18.2
Colorado				
Denver	4.3	20.0	16.7	28.6
Jefferson	11.1	21.1	0.0	0.0
Georgia				
DeKalb	4.3	14.3	42.9	33.3
Fulton	10.4	19.1	7.2	30.8
Illinois				
Cook	0.8	2.1	4.6	25.0
Michigan				
Wayne	2.3	1.5	0.0	18.2
Missouri				
Jackson	8.0	16.7	21.1	45.5
St. Louis City	2.4	5.6	10.3	33.3
St. Louis County	1.5	8.1	15.0	70.0
New York				
New York	2.1	2.3	22.2	20.0
Ohio				
Cuyahoga	2.6	14.3	7.1	66.7
Texas				
Bexar	12.7	21.7	40.4	60.0
Dallas	10.0	28.8	23.9	54.6
District 6	8.5	17.1	23.5	0.0
District 9	2.9	44.4	0.0	100.0
Harris	7.5	34.8	27.5	63.3
Travis	7.6	40.0	46.4	50.0

the same counties used in table 6.1 and presents information on the punitive damage rate for successful medical malpractice and products liability cases. Neither type of case accounts for a large proportion of the verdicts; medical malpractice cases comprise 10.6% of the verdicts, and products cases make up 4.2%. As table 6.4 indicates, plaintiffs were not generally successful in these cases, and they rarely received punitive damage awards when they were successful. The punitive damage rate for successful cases involving medical malpractice claims is 2.5%, and

Table 6.4 Punitive Damage Rates: Medical Malpractice and Products Liability

	N	Success Rate (%)	*N* with Punitive Award	Punitive Rate in Successful Cases (%)
Medical malpractice	2,064	30.6	16	2.5
Products liability	809	37.6	26	8.6

8.6% for those involving products liability claims. These rates are nearly identical to those we reported in our earlier study of 1981–85 jury verdict data—2.9% and 8.9% respectively.[113] Interestingly, plaintiff success rates are also similar to those reported in the earlier study—32.4% for malpractice and 39.2% for products liability compared to 30.6% and 37.6%, respectively, in table 6.4.

Award Structures. Although it may be the case that the incidence of punitive damages is generally modest, another question raised in the reform debate goes to the issue of the size of punitive damage awards. The reformers allege that these awards are generally so outrageously large—awards that "boggle the mind"—that they go beyond the punishment or deterrence objectives of statutory provisions. Table 6.5 presents data on the median award for all of the sites in tables 6.2 and 6.3—those with more than 10 punitive damage awards for the period 1988–90. It shows the median punitive damage award, the median total award (including both the compensatory and punitive damage award) in successful punitive damage cases, and the median total award for all jury verdict cases during that three-year period (all in 1990 dollars).

The median total award in punitive damage cases exceeded the overall median award for each site. However, in many of the sites, the median punitive damage award itself is not a figure that is likely to be a cause for great concern or to "boggle the mind." Half of the 22 sites had a punitive damage median below $50,000, and five had experienced medians under $30,000. Still, five sites—Los Angeles County, San Diego County, Wayne County, District 9 in Texas, and Harris County—had medians above $100,000 during this three-year period, suggesting that there are some places where punitive damages awards were relatively high. It should be noted that awards in Los Angeles, San Diego, and Wayne Counties are generally high, each having an overall median exceeding $100,000. Two of these five sites had relatively few punitive awards (Wayne, 11; Texas District 9, 10),

Table 6.5 Median Awards in 1990 Dollars (Sites with 10-plus Punitive Verdicts)

County	Median Punitive ($)	Median Total in Punitive Cases ($)	Median Total in All Cases (%)
Maricopa, Ariz.	52,500	152,500	38,982
Alameda, Cal.	78,750	297,000	100,000
Los Angeles, Cal.	275,000	563,607	204,958
San Diego, Cal.	165,000	473,550	175,000
San Francisco, Cal.	23,100	82,500	78,225
Denver, Colo.	51,250	298,875	46,750
Jefferson, Colo.	35,000	67,350	52,500
DeKalb, Ga.	26,250	42,630	30,825
Fulton, Ga.	35,000	77,000	47,500
Cook, Ill.	31,500	89,250	32,550
Wayne, Mich.	124,150	499,125	106,400
Jackson, Mo.	45,100	71,050	27,500
St. Louis City, Mo.	26,250	42,500	25,625
St. Louis County, Mo.	10,125	37,760	20,000
New York, N.Y.	44,250	101,900	348,400
Cuyahoga, Oh.	15,000	89,751	34,650
Bexar, Tex.	62,813	199,875	35,650
Dallas, Tex.	53,750	142,087	47,300
District 6, Tex.	48,700	87,675	54,985
District 9, Tex.	220,000	329,561	63,000
Harris, Tex.	110,000	377,528	46,181
Travis, Tex.	68,802	131,550	53,188

and a third had only a handful more (San Diego, 16). In both Los Angeles and Harris, the punitive damages rates for physical harm cases were relatively low (see table 6.3). The rates for financial harm cases were higher, but the highest rates were for cases involving emotional harm.

"Skyrocketing": Patterns over Time

Frequency. Perhaps the most dramatic and evocative of the reformers' allegations is their claim that the frequency and size of punitive damage awards have changed dramatically in recent years. Proponents of reform assert that awards are skyrocketing to unprecedented levels.[114] We will examine this concern by looking at punitive damage award activity in sites from four different states over a 21-year time period—Cook, Dallas, Jackson, and Los Angeles Counties. Figure 6.1 presents trend data on punitive damage rates (percent of successful

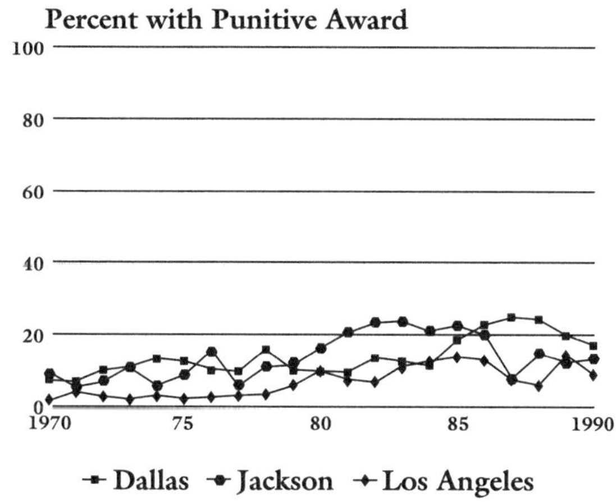

FIGURE 6.1 Punitive Damage Rates: 1970–90

cases with a punitive award) for three of these sites—Dallas, Jackson, and Los Angeles Counties—for the period 1970–90. Cook County is not included in this figure because the punitive damage rate was so low. It fluctuated within an extremely narrow range, between 0.6% in 1971 and 4.1% in 1978, and exceeded 2% in only eight years.

There are several different patterns evident in figure 6.1. In Dallas County, the punitive damage rate fluctuated within a relatively narrow range between 1970 and 1984. During these years the rate ranged from 7.1% in 1971 to 16.1% in 1978. After 1984, the rate steadily increased reaching 25.0% in 1987 and then declined to 17.4% in 1990. In Jackson, the pattern was different. Between 1970 and 1978, the punitive damage rate fluctuated again within a relatively narrow range—from a low of 5.5% in 1971 to a high of 15.5% in 1976. It increased steadily after 1978, reaching a peak of 23.7% in 1983. The rate fell sharply to 7.9% in 1987, jumped to 15.0% in 1988, and dropped slightly in 1989 and 1990. Punitive damage activity in Los Angeles County exhibited yet another pattern. The punitive damage rate remained low in the first part of the time line, not exceeding 5% until 1979. In the following years the rate fluctuated with no clear trends between a low of 6.0% in 1988 and a high of 14.4% in 1989.

A comparison of the punitive damage rates in these three counties presents an interesting picture. It belies the perception of a consistent national trend of ever increasing rates of punitive damage awards. The rate seems to have peaked between 1979 and 1983 in Jackson, between 1985 and 1988 in Dallas, and between 1983 and 1985 in Los Angeles. Clearly, this picture is one of diversity and local variation; a national trend may not in fact exist. There may be only local trends in which some areas have increasing rates, some have decreasing rates, and still others—like Cook County—experience no significant change at all. To begin exploring possible reasons for these variations, we next look at punitive damage rate patterns over time in broad types of cases.

Figure 6.2a presents punitive damage rates in physical harm cases for Cook, Dallas, Jackson, and Los Angeles Counties over the 21-year period 1970–90, using the same four time periods used in previous chapters. The most striking aspects of this depiction are that the rates are low and, with the exception of Dallas in the last two time intervals, there is a lack of real variability within the four sites. During this 21-year period, there were 106 punitive damage verdicts in physical harm cases in Cook, 78 in Dallas, 37 in Jackson, and 83 in Los Angeles, translating to 21-year overall punitive damage rates for physical harm cases of 1.4%, 6.9%, 4.4%, and 1.7% respectively.

A look at the underlying year-to-year variation in these sites highlights the absence of clear trends. In Cook, the punitive damage rate for physical harm cases never exceeded 3.4% (the rate for 1978). In Dallas, the rate fluctuated within a tight band between 1970 and 1985. It ranged from 0% in 1970 to 15.0% in 1985 when there was a marked increase. The punitive damage rate then climbed to 20.6% in 1986 and 22.0% in 1987, only to drop substantially in subsequent years. In Jackson County between 1970 and 1979 the punitive damage rate did not exceed 3%; in fact, there were six years during this period in which there were no punitive awards in these types of cases. Between 1980 and 1990 the rate fluctuated between a low of 2.4% in 1987 and a high of 10.5% in 1990. In Los Angeles County the punitive damage rate in physical harm cases did not exceed 4.5% during the entire 21-year period.

Figure 6.2b, which presents data on punitive damage rates for financial harm cases in the four counties, exhibits quite a different picture than that seen in figure 6.2a. In addition to displaying higher punitive damage rates generally, the variability within and between the sites is more marked. That the incidence of such awards in financial harm cases is higher than those in physical harm cases is confirmed by the overall rates for the entire 21-year period: Dallas, 15.3%; Jackson, 21.0%; and Los Angeles, 32.2%. In Cook County, the overall rate was only 5.5%.

Figure 6.2a
Bodily Harm Cases

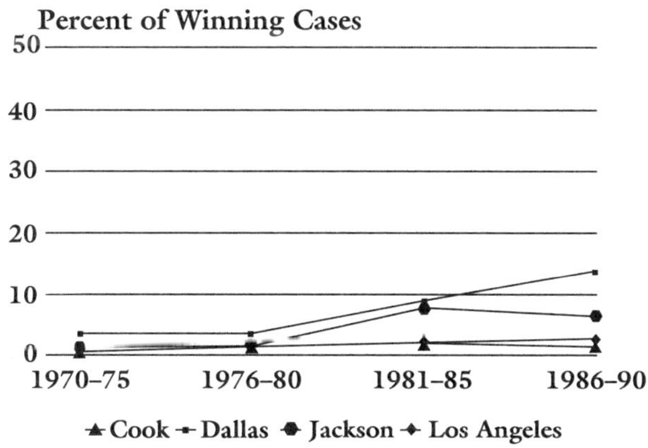

Figure 6.2b
Financial Harm Cases

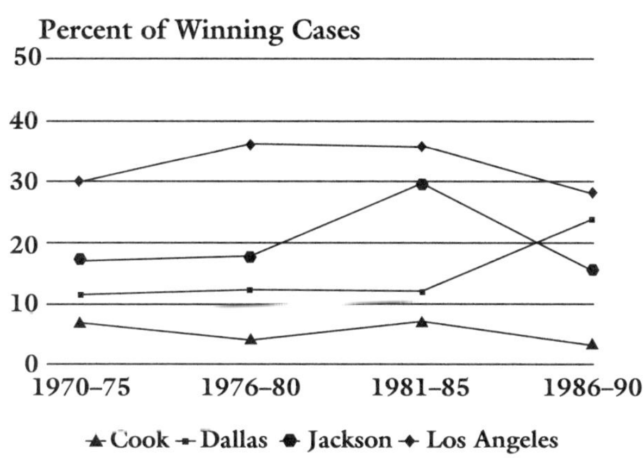

FIGURE 6.2 Punitive Damage Rates

The year-by-year rate analysis again produced no precise, consistent patterns. The punitive damage rate for financial harm cases in Dallas stayed relatively flat for quite a substantial period of time. Between 1970 and 1984 (with the exception of a spike in 1978 to 25.3%), the rate fluctuated between a low of 5.4% in 1980 and a high of 14.3% in 1975. After 1984, the punitive damage rate increased steadily reaching 32.5% in 1988 and then declined in 1989 and 1990. In Jackson, the punitive damage rate in financial cases varied a great deal between 1970 and 1979, experienced a relative period of growth, and then declined after reaching a high of 44.4% in 1985. The rate in Los Angeles exhibited no particular trend, but rather there was a great deal of variability over time with only one short period of consecutive increase—between 1977 and 1981. The rate in Cook also varied, but reached as high as 10% in only one year in which there were more than five punitive awards (1985).

The highest rates for punitive damages are found in emotional/reputational harm cases. In many years, the rate in some sites was as high 100%, but unfortunately the low numbers of successful cases each year make it impossible to discuss long-term patterns. In Jackson, plaintiffs obtained a successful verdict in 101 emotional/reputational harm cases during the 21-year period. Plaintiffs were awarded punitive damages in 57 of those cases for a punitive damage rate of 56.4%. In Dallas, plaintiffs won in 126 emotional/reputational harm cases and were awarded punitive damages in 55 (43.7%). In Los Angeles, there were 166 successful cases of this type, and in 62 (37.3%) punitive damages were awarded.

The findings regarding punitive damages in these counties for different broad categories of cases parallel those outlined earlier in this chapter for the 1988–90 cross-sectional data. Plaintiffs were least likely to receive a punitive damage award in physical harm cases. In fact, punitive damage awards have always been relatively rare in such cases in these four counties. Plaintiffs were more likely to receive a punitive award in financial harm cases, but punitive damages were still far from routine in such cases. Plaintiffs were most likely to receive a punitive award in emotional/reputational harm cases, but as just noted, the small numbers of such cases prevent any discussion of temporal patterns. Neither physical nor financial harm cases demonstrated any consistent, dramatic trends over time in their rates. With the exception of Dallas in 1986 and 1987, figure 6.2a shows relatively low, stable rates for physical harm cases. The patterns are more varied in figure 6.2b for financial harm cases, but there was no indication of a consistent upward trend in rate across these counties. Cook's rate stayed low and stable. Jackson's rate for financial harm cases fluctuated with no consistent trend—it went up and then down. In Dallas, there was some evidence of an upward trend in the late 1980s following a relatively stable pattern through the 1970s and early 1980s (although at the very end of the period the rate began dropping again). Los Angeles, on the other hand, had a general trend of decline after the early 1970s.

In short, there is no evidence in these sites of skyrocketing punitive damage rates for either of the two largest of the broad categories of cases. Even if we look at punitive damages within the two highly controversial areas of medical malpractice and products liability, there is again no evidence in these sites of rapidly increasing punitive damage rates. For instance, the largest number of punitive damages awards in these two substantive areas occurred in Los Angeles (eight in malpractice and 11 in products liability). The punitive rates for malpractice in Los Angeles were 1970–75, 2.1%; 1976–80, 1.5%; 1981–85, 3.2%; and 1986–90, 1.0%. For products liability the punitive rates were 1970–75, 3.5%; 1976–80, 4.5%; 1981–85, 3.6%; and 1986–90, 1.9%.

Award Structures. The reformers' other principal claim concerning punitive damages is that the size of these awards has risen to unprecedented levels. They imply that most punitive awards are in six-figure amounts or even higher. Using our 21 year database for the four counties we can examine typical award sizes to explore the common allegation that punitive damage awards have risen to unforeseen levels. Figure 6.3 presents data on patterns and changes in median punitive damage awards in Cook, Dallas, Jackson, and Los Angeles Counties for the period 1970 to 1990. Again, the patterns displayed are not what might be expected. In Cook, the median dropped in 1976–80 from $18,145 to $12,000 and then rose to $28,750 in 1986–90. In Jackson County, the median punitive damage award fluctuated within a relatively narrow range and followed no particular trend over time. Median punitive awards were generally modest, not reaching $30,000. In Dallas County, the pattern of punitive damage awards was somewhat different, but it was not dramatic either. The median rose gradually to $40,000 in 1986–90. More specifically, in the 1970s the median punitive damage award fluctuated within a narrow range, between a low of $10,290 in 1973 and a high of $33,700 in 1970. Beginning in 1980, the median punitive award varied more widely, rising to an all-time high of $94,690 in 1984, falling back down to below $31,000 for 1985 through 1987 and then moving upward again. Punitive damage awards in Los Angeles County followed a different pattern, one of sharp increase in comparison to Cook, Dallas, and Jackson. Median awards were, for the most part, substantially higher here than in the other sites, and we see the kind of general trend that the reformers confidently claim is occurring on a national basis. But there is no reason to presume Los Angeles was somehow representative of all jurisdictions, or even of all large, urban jurisdictions as figure 6.3 suggests.

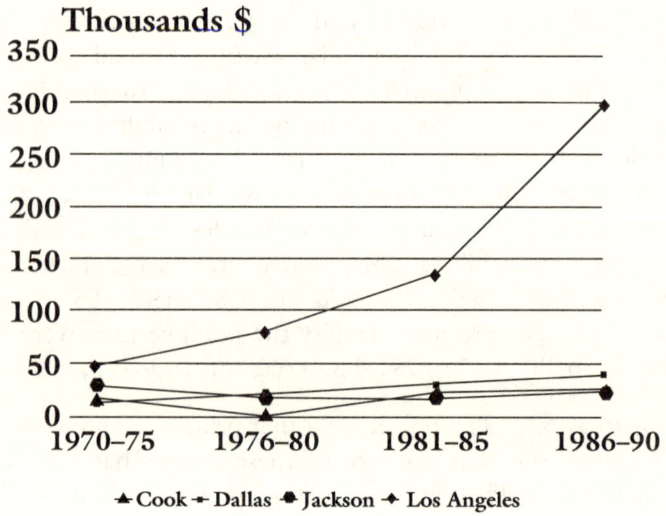

FIGURE 6.3 Median Punitive Damage Award

Figures 6.4a through 6.4d present the patterns and changes in the punitive damage awards structure for these counties in greater detail. They present the interquartile range for punitive damage awards along with the median. In each, the vertical bar shows the distance between the 25th percentile and the 75th percentile when awards are ordered from the lowest to the highest. It shows the middle 50% of punitive awards as the line cutting through the boxes. If the size of punitive awards generally has increased dramatically over time, not only should the median skyrocket, but the 25th and 75th percentiles should as well. It is important to note the difference in scale between figures 6.4a–6.4c (Cook, Dallas, and Jackson)—which have a maximum value of $300,000—and figure 6.4d (Los Angeles)—which has a maximum value of $1.2 million.

Figure 6.4a shows the award patterns for Cook County, and it displays a pattern in which the median at first drops slightly and then gradually increases to $28,750 in 1986–90. There is a similar, but more dramatic pattern for the 75th percentile. Between the first and second period it dropped sharply followed by a sharp increase after 1976–80. The 75th percentile reached $287,813 in 1986–90.

Figure 6.4b presents the interquartile range for punitive damage awards in Dallas. It shows that while remaining modest, the median award moved upward gradually. It goes from $13,365 in 1970–75 to

Figure 6.4a: Cook

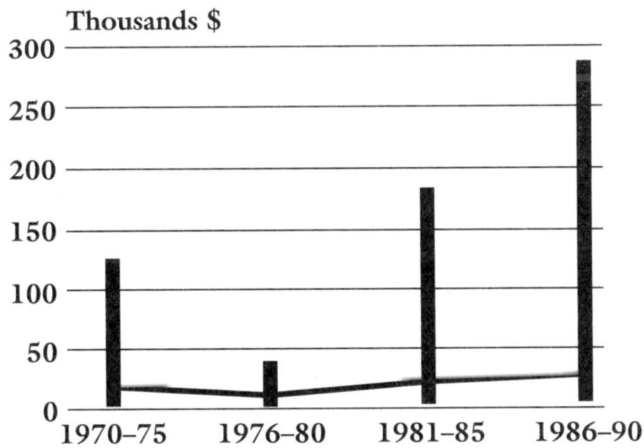

Figure 6.4b: Dallas

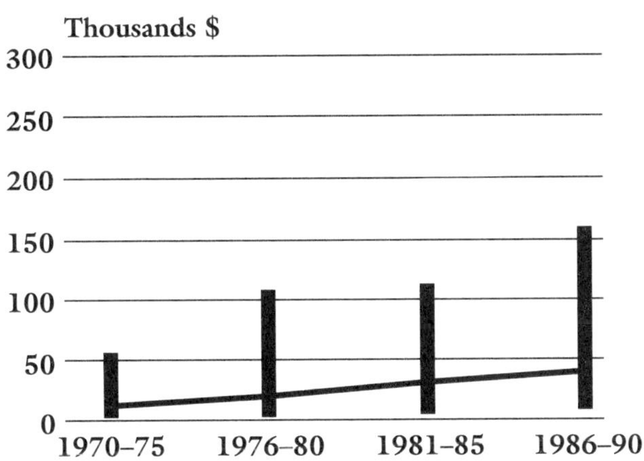

FIGURE 6.4 Punitive Damage Award

75th percentile—top of bar
25th percentile—bottom of bar
median—line through bars

$40,000 in 1986–90. The shift in the 25th percentile was also slight, remaining under $6,000 for the first two time periods, shifting to $7,200 in 1981–85, and reaching $10,000 in 1986–90. As with Cook, a more dramatic change occurred in the 75th percentile and in the

Figure 6.4c: Jackson

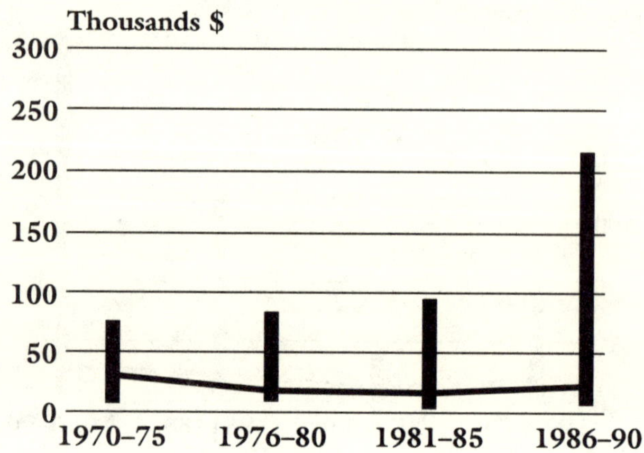

Figure 6.4d: Los Angeles

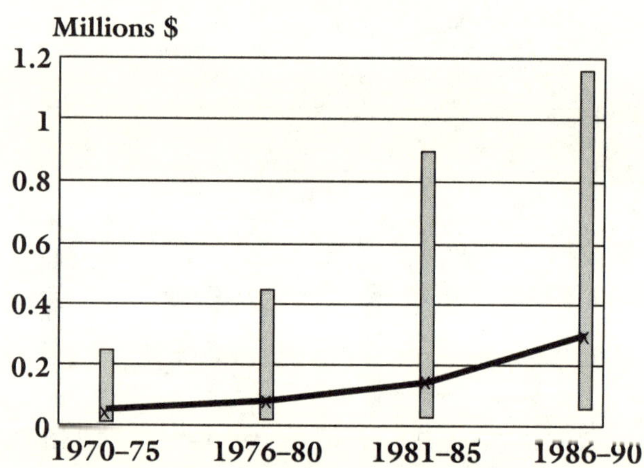

FIGURE 6.4 Punitive Damage Award ***(continued)***

75th percentile—top of bar
25th percentile—bottom of bar
median—line through bars

widening distance between the 25th and 75th percentiles. The 75th percentile increased from $55,605 in 1970–75 to $106,905 in 1976–80. It increased only slightly in the third time period, then rose to $156,875 in 1986–90. Thus, the pattern of punitive damage awards in

Dallas, as presented in figure 6.4b, was not a simple one of dramatic increase over time generally, but rather one of modest increase in the median and 25th percentile and a more major change in the top 25% of the award distribution.

Figure 6.4c, for Jackson, presents a modest pattern. Unlike the steady, if unspectacular, upward trend in Dallas, the median punitive award in Jackson "peaked" in the first time period at $29,400, dropped to below $17,000 for the 1976–80 and 1981–85 periods, and rose again to only $22,000 in 1986–90. Again, the most dramatic change occurred in the 75th percentile. While there was a slight upward shift in the distance between the median and the 75th percentile from the first to the third time intervals, a major jump occurred in the 1986–90 period.

Punitive damage awards in Los Angeles in Figure 6.4d present a strikingly different pattern, so different that a significantly higher scale is required to describe it. The 25th percentile increases upward throughout the cycle from $4,898 in 1970–75 to $55,930 in 1985–90. The median punitive damage award increases at a greater rate, moving from $47,625 in 1970–75 to $297,500 in 1986–90. Once again, however, the most dramatic change occurred in the high end of the award spectrum as the distance between the 25th and 75th percentiles increases in a major way over the four time intervals.

This series of figures presents some interesting and important similarities and contrasts. In Dallas, Jackson, and Cook, increases in the 25th percentile and median over time were quite modest or nonexistent. In Los Angeles, the magnitude of the change in the median award was substantially greater than in the other three sites—being nearly equal to or greater than the 75th percentile in the other sites. Regardless, the principal changes in the punitive damage award structure occurred at the upper end of the award spectrum in all four sites. This is dramatically illustrated by figure 6.5 which presents patterns in the mean punitive award—and which requires a *much* higher scale to do so. There were, in effect, two punitive damage systems in these sites. One changed little, except in Los Angeles, and it is comprised of the bulk of the cases. The second involved only the small proportion of cases with the highest awards, and here the change could be substantial.

To explore this second, more dramatically changing punitive damage system, we will examine the types of cases that account for the highest 25% of the award structure. The reformers' claims about patterns in punitive awards would lead to the expectation that this second system of unusually high awards is increasingly comprised of physical harm cases,

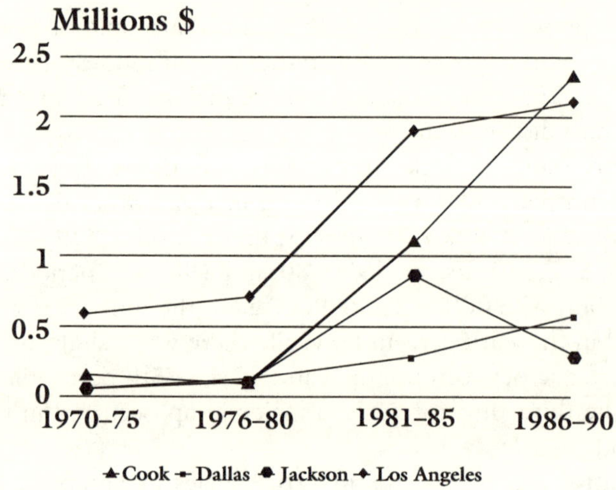

FIGURE 6.5 Mean Punitive Damage Award

particularly products liability and medical malpractice cases. This was not the situation in Dallas, Jackson, or Los Angeles Counties, although it was in Cook where the overall award structure is relatively low.

Table 6.6 shows the composition of the top 25% of the punitive damage award distribution for Cook, Dallas, Jackson, and Los Angeles Counties using the same case categories as in tables 6.2 and 6.3. The table presents the percentage of punitive damage cases in each category, with the total number of punitive damage cases for each time period in parentheses. For three of the four counties, for all four time periods, at least 50% of the high-award punitive damage cases involved financial, not physical harm. Cook is the exception, and it was only in 1970–75 that financial harm cases comprised a larger component of the punitive damage cases than did physical harm cases.

A more detailed examination shows that in Dallas, a substantial proportion (60.2%) of the high-end punitive damage awards occurring in financial harm cases were attached to cases involving fraud. In Jackson County, while 19% of the high-end financial harm cases involved fraud, another 19% occurred in cases involving a unique Missouri service letters statute which allowed individuals to sue former employers in certain situations.[115] In Los Angeles County, insurance bad faith cases were more prevalent than fraud cases under the umbrella of financial harm: 31.9% of the high-end punitive damage cases in this county occurred in insurance bad faith actions, while 17.4% arose in fraud cases.

Table 6.6 Breakdown of Highest 25% of Punitive Damage Award Distribution: Dallas, Jackson, and Los Angeles: 1970–90

	Types of Harm Alleged*			
County	Physical (%)	Financial (%)	Property (%)	Emotional (%)
Cook				
1970–75 (*N*=7)	28.6	57.1	0	14.3
1976–80 (*N*=9)	44.4	22.2	11.1	22.2
1981–85 (*N*=17)	64.7	23.5	0	11.8
1986–90 (*N*=11)	72.7	9.1	0	18.2
Dallas				
1970–75 (*N*=24)	8.3	79.2	8.3	4.2
1976–80 (*N*=24)	8.3	66.7	12.5	12.5
1981–85 (*N*=35)	14.3	80.0	0	5.7
1986–90 (*N*=49)	16.3	71.4	6.1	6.1
Jackson				
1970–75 (*N*=7)	14.3	57.1	0	28.6
1976–80 (*N*=12)	0	66.7	0	33.3
1981–85 (*N*=28)	17.9	57.1	3.6	21.5
1986–90 (*N*=19)	21.1	57.9	10.5	10.6
Los Angeles				
1970–75 (*N*=12)	16.7	58.3	0	25.0
1976–80 (*N*=18)	16.7	61.1	0	22.2
1981–85 (*N*=38)	2.6	84.2	0	13.2
1986–90 (*N*=26)	7.7	84.6	0	7.7

* Percentages for each time interval add to 100% reading across (physical + financial + property + emotional).

Physical harm cases comprised a much smaller percent of the high-end punitive damage award spectrum in these three counties: 12.9% in Dallas, 14.1% in Jackson, and 10.6% in Los Angeles. Of the 17 physical harm cases falling into the top 25% of the punitive award structure in Dallas, four were products cases and two were medical malpractice cases. Five of the 10 high-end physical harm cases in Jackson County were products cases; none were medical malpractice punitive cases. In Los Angeles County five of the 10 physical harm cases with punitive damage awards in the top 25% of the award spectrum were products cases and three involved medical malpractice. Products and medical malpractice cases therefore comprised only 4.6% of all of the high-end punitive award verdicts in Dallas, 7% in Jackson, and 8.5% of those in Los Angeles.

Cook County was quite different in that physical harm cases accounted for the largest percentage of the top 25% of the punitive damage award structure. Almost three-quarters (74.3%) of these verdicts involved physical harm. However, the predominance of physical harm cases at the upper reaches of the award structure should not be surprising given that a very large percentage of all of the punitive damage awards in Cook fell in physical harm cases and only a very small percentage involved financial harm. This reflects the composition of the Cook jury docket which is heavy on physical harm cases and light on financial harm. Between 1970 and 1990, 86.4% (14,461 of 16,743) of the cases involved physical harm compared to 6.4% for financial harm (1,071). Most of these cases, however, did not involve malpractice or products liability (there were four of each among the 26 physical harm cases in the top 25%). The remainder of the high-end punitive cases were scattered across a variety of issues, with the largest number—four—involving assault or intimidation.

In summary, financial harm cases accounted for the largest proportion of cases in the top 25% of the punitive damage award distribution in three of the four counties for which we have data. Nonetheless, as figures 6.4a–6.4d show, Cook with its predominance of physical harm–based punitive awards did not experience the most dramatic changes in punitive damage award structures. The most dramatic changes were in Los Angeles, where financial harm cases appear to have been the driving force. Table 6.6 shows that there was an increase over time in Los Angeles in the percentage of the top 25% of the punitive awards attributable to financial harm matters and a decrease in those involving physical harm. To the extent there was an important general trend in Los Angeles regarding the size of punitive awards, it involved financial harm cases. At the same time that these matters were making up, in Los Angeles, larger proportions of both punitive damage cases overall and the top 25% of the award structure, the size of the attendant punitive awards was also increasing. The median punitive award in financial harm cases for Los Angeles increased from $101,110 in 1970–75 to $143,750 in 1976–80 to $245,550 in 1981–85 to $476,000 in 1986–90. The 75th percentile increased from $476,580 to $1.3 million to $2.5 million and then slipped to $2.1 million. In contrast, the median punitive award for physical harm cases in Los Angeles went from $26,500 to $23,000 to $57,600 to $19,040. The 75th percentile exceeded $100,000 only in 1981–85. For the most frequently appearing financial harm case with punitive damages in Los Angeles—insurance bad faith—the punitive award structure was even higher. After the 1970–75 period, the median punitive award for these cases did not drop below $800,000.

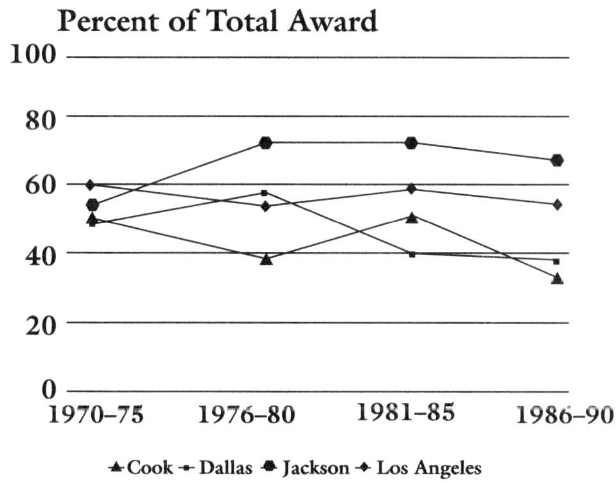

FIGURE 6.6 Punitives as a Percent of Total Award

Punitives in Relation to Other Damages. One issue remains regarding changes in punitive awards—their relationship to compensatory damages. This issue has two aspects to it, both of which have been long debated: the percentage of the total award made up by punitive damages and the ratio of punitives to all other damages. The rhetoric of reform suggests that punitive damages are typically awarded in amounts that far exceed underlying compensatory damages. These large punitive damage awards have a deleterious effect on businesses and service providers that goes beyond appropriate punishment or deterrence and clearly are just windfalls for plaintiffs and their lawyers. Furthermore, this disparity between compensatory and punitive damages is allegedly increasing over time. Figure 6.6 shows the percentage of the total award represented by punitive damages for Cook, Dallas, Jackson, and Los Angeles Counties. It presents these data as a median percentage for the same time periods used in figures 6.4a–6.4d.

Figure 6.6 shows that in Jackson County, where the typical punitive damage award was relatively low, the percentage of the total award represented by punitive damages was higher than that in the other counties for all four time periods except Los Angeles in the first time period. The percentages in Jackson ranged from a low of 56.0% to a high of 75.0%, in Dallas from 40.0% to 60.0%, in Cook from 35.0% to

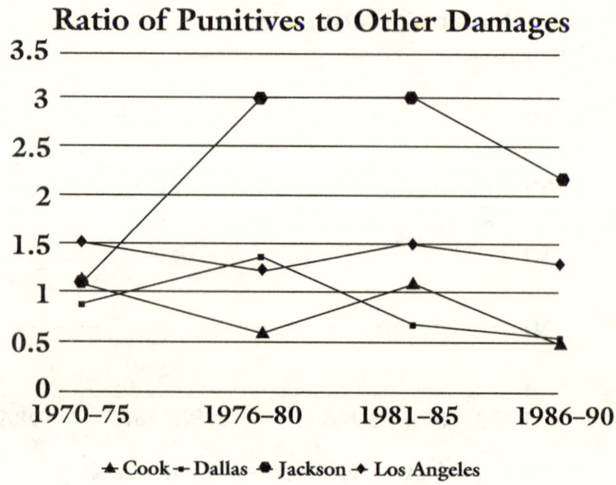

FIGURE 6.7 Mean Ratio of Punitives to Other Damages

53.0%, and in Los Angeles from 56.0% to 62.0%. Contrary to what one would expect in light of the rhetoric of reform, there is no trend evident in figure 6.6 of an increasing percentage of total awards being made up by punitive damages. In Dallas, the percentage actually decreased after 1970–75.

Another method of examining the proportionality issue is to examine the ratio of punitive damages to all other damages ($P/T - P$, where P = punitive award and T = total award). Again, the reformers' claims suggest that the ratio will be high and the size of the ratio will increase over time. Figure 6.7 shows the ratio of punitive damages to all other damages for Cook, Dallas, Jackson, and Los Angeles. We see here four different patterns, none of which are quite what we might expect based on the reform literature. Jackson exhibited the highest ratios, moving from 1.1 to 3.0 in 1976–80 then dropping to 2.2 in 1986–90. In Dallas, which had much lower ratios, there was an initial increase from 0.9 in 1970–75 to 1.4 in 1976–80 followed by a drop to below 0.8 in the last 2 five-year periods. Los Angeles exhibited a third pattern—one of relative stability over the years. The ratio of punitive to other damages moved from 1.5 in 1970–75 to 1.2 in 1976–80 to 1.5 in 1981–85 to 1.3 in 1986–90. Cook's ratios fluctuated over a somewhat broader range: 1.1 to 0.6 to 1.1 to 0.5.

Independent of the patterns in the ratios for the four counties in figure 6.7 is the question of whether these ratios are too high. If the reformers' claims are used as a standard, the four sets of ratios appear quite low because the reformers refer to ratios in the hundreds if not the thousands.[116] It is true that there have been some single cases where the punitive damage award exceeds the other damages by a considerable amount, but these instances were the exception. The issue of what ratio is too high is one that even the U.S. Supreme Court has declined to address head-on, leaving that issue to the state judicial systems to discern if appropriate. In searching for a comparative standard, however, one might turn to the various statutory provisions for multiple damages. Federal law allows treble damages in antitrust suits, and many states permit multiple damages in a variety of situations. For example, the Texas Deceptive Trade Practices Act allows multiple damages of up to three times compensatory damages.[117] Of more relevance, a series of tort reform measures enacted in Texas provided specific standards for punitive awards.[118]

The Texas Omnibus Tort Reform Act of 1987 limits the amount of punitive or exemplary damages recoverable in certain actions to the greater of $200,000 or four times actual damages.[119] Using the 4:1 standard for comparison, the median ratios for Dallas in figure 6.7 were quite low. Only 3.2% (17 of 529) of the punitive damage verdicts in Dallas between 1970 and 1990 exceeded the limits of the current Texas law. Only one of these was a malpractice case, and only one was a products liability case. Although the ratios for Jackson were higher than those for Dallas—and were the highest of all four counties in figure 6.7—most were still below the limits of the Texas law. Only 8.0% (21 of 264) of the punitive damage verdicts in Jackson exceeded the limits of the Texas law. Only 2.8% (5 of 176) of the verdicts in Cook County exceeded those limits. In Los Angeles, which experienced higher punitive awards generally, 16.2% (60 of 371) exceeded the limits of the Texas law (none of these 60 cases in Los Angeles involved products liability or medical malpractice). Thus, for these four sites, any problems that might exist with regard to the ratio of punitive damages to all other damages appear to be minor.

In summary, the results of our analysis do not provide support for the reformers' claims regarding patterns and changes in punitive damage awards over time. Juries did not routinely award punitive damages in Cook, Dallas, Jackson, and Los Angeles, and no consistent patterns of increasing frequency over time were evident among the sites. The punitive damage rates for physical harm cases, including the high-visibility areas of medical malpractice and products liability, were low throughout the 21 years examined. Furthermore, in three of the counties the typical punitive damage award remained modest; and in the fourth the increases in awards were the result of patterns in financial harm rather than physical harm cases. Upward trends in all four sites existed only in the highest 25% of the punitive damage award distribution, suggesting that there were effectively two punitive damage systems in these sites: one for the bulk of punitive damage cases, in which the size of awards did not increase greatly (except in Los Angeles), and another for a small proportion of the cases in which the size of awards did increase significantly (with only Los Angeles showing comparatively dramatic increases). Contrary to what might be expected, most cases in this higher award system tended to be financial harm rather than physical harm cases (except in Cook, which had a relatively low punitive award structure). Finally, the data do not show a general pattern of increase in the percentage of the total award represented by punitive damages over time or an increase in the ratios of punitive damages to other damages.

These four sites are only case studies and cannot be used to make a generalization about national trends. Alternatively, they do provide a context for interpreting the reformers' allegations about patterns and changes in the incidence and size of punitive damage awards. The diversity among these four sites belies the notion of a single national trend over time and suggests that a skeptical approach should be taken with regard to the empirical claims used by the reformers in justification for fundamental changes.

Conclusion and General Summary

As was the case in our discussions of medical malpractice and products liability verdicts, our examination of punitive damages verdicts shows a picture of reality quite different than the one portrayed in the reform rhetoric. We would like to use the conclusion of this chapter to present a summary of not just the verdict data in punitive damages, but of the jury verdict data presented in the previous three chapters as well. In examining the 1988–90 data in general, we saw that juries were not especially proplaintiff nor was there evidence of trends over time reflecting an increasing proplaintiff pattern in outcomes. What we did find was variability both among sites and among types of cases in the mix of cases, in who wins, and how much is awarded when plaintiffs do win. Variability, however, does not mean chaos. There were orderly patterns within these variations.

We found that the majority of the 82 sites covered had plaintiff win rates between 50% and 65%. Plaintiffs were more likely to win in cases involving a financial harm than in cases involving a physical harm. Median awards tended to be modest, although the overall median awards for some sites in California and Michigan exceeded $100,000—as did all but one New York site. At the other extreme, overall median awards did not reach as high as $40,000 in the Illinois, Missouri, and Oregon sites. A part of the reason for these differences can be found in the varying dollar amounts used in defining the respective courts' jurisdictions. Higher median awards are expected where the jurisdictional floor is set at a relatively high dollar amount. In California, for instance, the floor for the superior courts was $25,000, and as a consequence the median awards tended to be high. In contrast, four of seven Missouri sites, four of five Oregon sites, and three of seven Illinois sites had *median* awards of $25,000 or less—the general jurisdiction courts in these states have low jurisdictional floors. And, like win rates, median awards tended to be higher for financial harm cases than physical harm cases.

The variations among sites is one of the most striking of our findings from the 1988–90 data. Plaintiff win rates varied from 31.3% (Suffolk, N.Y.) to 75.7% (Portage, Oh.). Median awards ranged from $9,135 (Montgomery, Oh.) to $417,200 (Bronx, N.Y.). Attributing the variations to differences in jury bias or capriciousness, the so-called "Bronx effect,"[120] is much too facile. A full explanation, unfortunately, is not possible because simply too little is known. In part, the variations in overall patterns in win rates and awards are likely to have been the result of the selection processes that ultimately bring only a limited number of matters to trial in combination with local legal culture and differences in procedure and law. Additionally, different types of sites will have very different mixes of business because of their size and socioeconomic characteristics. Major urban areas, for instance, should experience a different mix of cases than less densely populated or less industrialized areas.

Cases in the high-visibility areas of products liability and medical malpractice made up a small proportion of the jury trials, generally less than 10% for each in most jurisdictions. Punitive damages, which can cut across a wide range of cases, were also relatively rare. Larger urban sites may have somewhat higher percentages of malpractice and products cases, again in part because of their socioeconomic characteristics. Plaintiffs, as a general proposition, were not likely to win these types of cases—30.4% in malpractice and 39.0% for products liability in our 1988–90 data. When plaintiffs did win, however, awards could be high. No site with 10 or more malpractice verdicts had a median award under $100,000, and only one site with 10 or more products verdicts had a median under $100,000. Win rates and awards varied by the setting from which the case arose for both malpractice and products, but generally speaking, win rates and awards for both were higher the more severe the injury involved.

The majority of medical malpractice verdicts in the 1988–90 data emerged from injuries occurring in a surgical setting. The plaintiff win rate in these cases was 29.3% with a median award of $385,000. Within the surgery setting, two surgical areas were responsible for almost half of the verdicts—obstetric/gynecology and orthopedic surgery. The plaintiff win rates in these two areas were 34.6% and 28.7% respectively. The median awards were $738,544 and $247,500. The higher median for ob/gyn is tied to the greater percentage of major injuries compared to orthopedic surgery. Ob/gyn did not simply generate more major injuries, it produced more of the most severe major injuries. The median award for the most severe major injuries in ob/gyn was over $4 million. The highest awards in ob/gyn were found in the most severe injury cases where problems in medical management had caused the injury—$4.7 million. These awards were so high because the injured patient was generally very young, meaning that costs (medical, etc.) must be calculated for a number of years in the future. These were primarily the "bad baby" cases.

The bulk of the products liability verdicts emerged from one of three settings—work, vehicle, or home. The work setting (people injured in the course of employment) generated more products verdicts than any other setting, and the injuries involved tended to be either serious temporary injuries or major injuries. Most of these verdicts involved products classified as industrial machinery. Overall, plaintiffs won 49.0% of the work cases, and the median award was $379,434. The win rate was higher for major injury work cases (55.4%) than for those involving minor injuries (40.0%), and the win rate for death cases was nearly the same as that for major injuries (54.1%). The highest win rate for work setting cases, however, was in death cases involving asbestos. Plaintiffs were successful in all but one of the 16 asbestos cases involving death. The highest products liability awards were not found in the work setting but in the vehicle setting which had the most severe injuries. The median award for vehicle major injury cases was $2.6 million, while for work major injury the median award was $367,500.

Turning to punitive damages, we saw that in the 1988–90 data punitive damages were awarded in 4.5% of all verdicts and in 8.3% of winning verdicts. There was, however, variation among the sites, with some (12) having no reported punitive damage cases and some (three) having punitive damage rates of over 20% of winning verdicts. Punitive awards were more likely to be given in cases involving a financial harm than a physical harm. Even the high-visibility areas of medical malpractice and products liability had low rates of punitive damages: 2.5% of successful malpractice verdicts and 8.6% of successful products verdicts. While individual punitive damage awards could be very high, the typical award was not. Half of the 22 sites with 10 or more punitive awards had a median below $50,000, and five had medians under $30,000. Alternatively, five of those 22 sites had median punitive awards in excess of $100,000.

The verdict data for 1988–90 present a very different picture than that found in the rhetoric of reform. Though limited, the verdict data for the years 1970–90 also provide reason for skepticism regarding the rhetoric's characterizations regarding change—allegations important for the rhetorical story of decline. It is difficult and dangerous to talk in general terms about temporal patterns for jury verdicts overall. Aggregate figures mask too many specific patterns for particular types of cases, and it is those specific patterns that are important. For medical malpractice our limited exploration of verdicts over the 21 years showed no large-scale consistent temporal patterns, even for sites in the same state. For instance, while win rates in San Francisco fluctuated over time, those in Los Angeles stayed stable. Perhaps most importantly, the patterns evident in our data suggest not a system that has devolved into chaos or some other degenerate state, but an orderly system that did not change in any major way over the 21-year period. Still, we found evidence of important but subtle shifts within this system that underlay temporal patterns in malpractice verdicts, especially those at the high end of the award structure. These shifts involved evidence of increases in cases with major injuries (especially the most severe levels of injury), medical management–caused injuries, and younger people. Such shifts cannot be simply explained as the result of increasingly generous or biased juries, or of even increasingly greedy lawyers. They reflect the dynamics of activities farther down the disputing pyramid—activities about which little is known.

Our exploration of products liability verdict data over the 21 years showed no consistent patterns over time either, even for sites within the same state. In Cook County there appears to have been a products liability system that did not change dramatically with regard to the settings from which cases emerged, with work setting cases predominating.

In contrast, Los Angeles showed a clear pattern over time. The proportion of verdicts emerging from the work setting increased, while the percentage from the vehicle setting decreased. Even though more cases emerged from the work setting, win rates for these cases changed little. The vehicle setting was different—the win rate increased up until the last time period and then decreased. While the median award for both settings increased, the increase for the vehicle setting was more dramatic. Underlying this pattern in the vehicle setting was a shift toward more severe injuries, and over time the most severe injuries made up an increasing proportion of verdicts. Like Los Angeles, San Francisco also experienced an increase in the proportion of verdicts from the work setting and a decrease from the vehicle setting. Those changes were much more dramatic in San Francisco, the primary reason being an influx of asbestos cases. There was no comparable influx in Los Angeles. As with malpractice, the temporal patterns in products liability verdicts suggest not a system in chaos, but one that is orderly yet dauntingly complex.

As we saw in this chapter, there was no single, consistent pattern over time for punitive damages either. Still, juries did not routinely award punitive damages nor was there any general pattern of an increasing rate of punitive damage awards. Punitive damage rates for physical harm cases including medical malpractice and products liability were low throughout the 21 years. Clear upward trends for awards were evident only in the highest 25% of the award distribution. Contrary to what might be expected from the reform rhetoric, most cases in this part of the award structure tended to be financial harm cases rather than physical harm cases.

As with medical malpractice and products liability, we explored temporal patterns in punitive damages in just a handful of sites. Consequently, generalizations about national trends cannot be drawn from these sites. What the discussions of temporal patterns in punitive damages as well as in malpractice and products can do is provide a set of detailed contexts for interpreting the reformers' allegations about change. What we found are temporal patterns quite different from the reformers' claims, patterns that reflect orderly but complex systems about which little is systematically known.

The jury verdict data we have presented along with the findings of other studies provide a context for interpreting the reform rhetoric's characterization of juries and the civil justice system. An important aspect of this context is that it highlights how little is systematically known about the bulk of the disputing pyramid—matters that are relevant to the policy debate. For instance, why do individuals choose to pursue claims in the legal arena? How do plaintiffs' lawyers select which claims they will pursue? How do insurance companies, self-insured entities, and defense lawyers evaluate claims and make decisions as to which matters to settle and which to actively defend? What is the relationship between the operation of medical disciplinary systems and malpractice claims or between risk management programs and malpractice claims? What is the relationship between the adequacy of workers' compensation system and products liability claims or between the operation of workplace safety regulation and such claims? These questions do not exhaust the issues warranting systematic, empirical research, but they illustrate the type of phenomena that we need to know more about.

The context provided by the jury verdict data we have presented and by the findings of other studies ultimately raises a question for the policy debate concerning what the "problem" actually is. That context points us in very different directions than those suggested in the reform rhetoric. Targeting reforms at those matters going to the courts begs the question of where and how injuries or other other harms occur. Focusing on formal processes that come into play only as a result of injuries is akin to shooting the messenger. Claims and lawsuits, in effect, report on potential problems elsewhere. They are not *the* problem.

CHAPTER SEVEN

Juries and Civil Justice Reform: Politics, Policy, and Knowledge

> If, sometime during the present decade, a consensus emerges in favor of serious judicial reform, it will be because millions of minds have been changed.[1]

Politics

As we noted at the very beginning of this book, juries lie at the heart of the ongoing public policy debate over reform in the American civil justice system. They are at the symbolic center of the debate and of the vigorously marketed image of a civil justice system not simply in trouble, but in crisis and requiring immediate reform. Reformers, Clermont and Eisenberg noted, "catalog problems with juries."[2] Juries are used to symbolize everything that is allegedly wrong or dysfunctional in the civil justice system.

Underlying this image is a normative standard that asks us to evaluate juries and the larger civil justice system on the basis of their allegedly substantial social and economic costs. There are apparently few, if any, benefits to balance against these costs in the reformers' estimation. Much of the reform rhetoric fostering this image consists of claims about the behavior and operation of the civil justice system that are causally linked to various problems in contemporary America—from the elimination of high school football programs to the plight of poor, pregnant women to the health of our national economy. These links are made in order to suggest that the sole reason such problems exist is the legal system. Implicit in this argument, of course, is the idea that the social and economic ills described will be remedied by the reformers' policy solutions.

There has been and continues to be political opposition to the crisis image and the reformers' proffered solutions. There has also been a persistent criticism by some scholars who study the civil justice system and juries arguing that there is a substantial gap between the reformers' characterization of the civil justice system and what is empirically known. Equally important, these academic critics note that despite the reformers' broad-ranging claims, there is still a great deal concerning the operation of the civil justice system about which we know very little. Some of these academic critics have questioned the soundness of key pieces of research utilized by the reformers,[3] and a few go farther still, questioning the motives and integrity of those doing such research.[4] Rustad and Koenig have, with intentional irony, described the worst of this research as "junk social science"[5]—a play on Peter Huber's complaints about what he calls "junk science" in the legal system. However, it is important to note that the academic critics of the reform rhetoric are *not* arguing that the civil justice system is operating flawlessly. They are concerned with the effects of enacted policies that have little connection to reality and with the troubling problems that systematic research uncovers.[6] Ultimately, these critics are skeptics who believe that common sense suggests "as in the case of Chicken Little, that it is best to check calmly to see if, figuratively speaking, the sky really is falling."[7]

The arguments and findings of these critics suggest that we must look beyond, but not ignore, the substantive claims of the reform rhetoric to the larger context in which these claims are made. In the context of a fierce political battle to change the civil justice system, the rhetoric of reform is an effort to present an image of the world carefully constructed to shape the policy agenda in ways favorable to the reformers' interests. This is, after all, what politics is all about—who gets what, when, and how.[8] Ultimately, the rhetoric is a contest over the public mind and is often a construct grounded more on passions and perceptions than on reliable empirical information. It is a part of the larger contemporary political phenomenon that David Ricci and others such as James Smith[9] describe as the politics of ideas, and should be treated accordingly.

Throughout this book we have been concerned with the rhetoric of reform and its claims. We have pursued this course because of the rhetoric's role in a political campaign which has as its goal fundamental change in the civil justice system, especially with regard to juries. At the extreme, some reform advocates even want to abolish civil juries. The politics of ideas, however, is not one-sided—though it is decidedly lopsided. The opponents of civil justice reform have not been idle. There is an antireform rhetoric that is equally as problematic because of its use of horror stories, appeals to passion over reason, misuse of quantitative data, and so on.

This antireform rhetoric strives to create its own images in the battle over the public mind. It is not as extensive nor as sophisticated as the reform rhetoric. We do not find the kind of public relations activity that characterizes the reform effort. There is nothing, for example, that compares to the *Punitive Damages Update* campaign discussed in chapter 6 or to the various insurance industry campaigns described in chapter 2. Nor do we find the direct mail strategy used by the various state-level, proreform lobbying organizations with symbolically charged names—like the Illinois Civil Justice League or the Texas Civil Justice League or the Pennsylvania Truth and Fairness in Litigation Committee.[10] This does not mean that the antireform movement is above such tactics and on the side of the angels. Perhaps it is merely an effect of a much smaller pool of resources. On the antireform side, there are no sophisticated, ideologically oriented organizations like the Manhattan Institute whose mission is to lobby the public mind and help shape the national mood. Additionally, we do not find an investment in support for academics and academic research at the levels exhibited by advocacy-oriented corporate foundations like the John M. Olin Foundation[11] or the Monsanto Foundation.[12]

Most of the antireform rhetoric is found in the political activity of trial lawyers' organizations and consumers' groups—both of whose political influence can be formidable.[13] This opposing rhetoric is primarily defensive in character and is largely defined by the reformers' claims. It is a rhetoric of response often in the posture of having to prove a variety of negatives in situations for which the relevant currency is emotion, passion, fear, and the co-optation of unassailable symbols. This positioning of the parties in the debate over reform is rather concisely described in the 1991 mission statement of the Manhattan Institute's Judicial Studies Program: "An essential element of successful policy advocacy is taking the initiative; the side proposing change most often ends up setting the agenda, while the side opposing change finds itself in the unenviable position of defending the status quo."[14]

Still, there are examples from the antireform side of efforts to take the initiative and offer competing images. An excellent example—on a par with some of the "best" offerings of the reform rhetoric—is Harvey Wachsman's 1993 book *Lethal Medicine: The Epidemic of Medical Malpractice in America*. Like Walter Olson's *The Litigation Explosion:*

What Happened When America Unleashed the Lawsuit, the message of this book is clear from its title. Most immediate and evocative is the contradictory idea of "lethal medicine," implying that the faith and trust we give to medicine is misplaced. Rather than a healing science or art, medicine is in reality deadly; it is not simply dangerous, it is lethal. Why is this so? It is so because of malpractice. Medicine becomes lethal because of negligence, and this implies fault and blame. Bad doctors are the real problem, but no one does anything about them even though their misdeeds are well known. How widespread is this deadly threat? Its scope has reached epidemic proportions.

Like the reform rhetoric's use of "explosion," the use of "epidemic" as a metaphor implies a rapid, destructive change. This imagery appeals to fear; and as with any epidemic, no one is safe. Says Wachsman, "We are all at risk. This epidemic cuts across all ages, races, sexes, and economic groups."[15] Where the reform rhetoric tells us that "we all pay the price" for the costs of the crisis in civil justice, Wachsman tells us that we are all potential victims of medical negligence. The cause of this scourge is incompetent and negligent physicians and a medical profession that refuses to discipline them.[16]

Like Olson's book and Peter Huber's *Liability*,[17] the argument of Wachsman's book is built around the use of anecdotes and horror stories as the primary means of describing the nature of the malpractice problem.[18] But the use of horror stories by Olson and Huber does not compare to Wachsman's effort. His book is unabashedly devoted to horror stories. They are not short, very general summaries to illustrate a point, but lengthy, detailed—sometimes graphically and gruesomely so—stories of serious injuries or death suffered at the hands of negligent and incompetent physicians. These physicians are known by their peers, but they are left undisciplined by the medical profession. In effect, Wachsman asks the reader to be a witness to medical malpractice and the suffering it causes as well as the medical profession's refusal or inability to deal with the problem.

For example, Wachsman devotes 13 pages to the activities of one physician—a non–board-certified general surgeon practicing as an ob/gyn—and three of his patients. These patients are merely examples of the doctor's surgical practices "that mutilated thousands of women."[19] This surgeon "dreamt up a new type of surgical procedure that he apparently believed would enhance women's enjoyment of sexual intercourse."[20] The procedure was often done without the consent or knowledge of the patients "while they were under sedation during deliveries or undergoing other surgical procedures that they had consented to."[21] The story tells the reader of the trust the three women placed in the doctor and the devastating consequences of his "bizarre" procedures on their lives, including their sex lives.

The purposes of this story were threefold. First, it illustrated vividly the existence of incompetent and negligent physicians—in this instance, one characterized as a "recidivist."[22] Second, it showed the unwillingness of the surgeon's peers, the hospital where he performed surgery, and the local medical society to discipline him despite the fact that his bizarre surgical procedure and its consequences had been known for years. Indeed, the hospital even appointed him to serve on its quality assurance committee.[23] Third, it "shows that the best way—perhaps the only way under present circumstances—of forcing incompetent doctors out into the open is through the courts. The only way of subjecting these practitioners to public scrutiny, and deterring malpractice is through the public attention attendant to lawsuits and trials. The courts have become the sole policing body for the medical profession, and malpractice lawyers have taken on the role of public prosecutors."[24]

Wachsman's book presents an image of "bad apples," cover-ups, and a conspiracy of silence. It is the patients who are the hapless victims and trial lawyers who are the heroes. And if one is concerned with the size and propriety of jury awards, especially for the various awards lumped under the term "pain and suffering," all she need do is consider the plight of those women maimed by the incompetent ob/gyn. Wachsman offers this alternative image as an authority and not merely as a critic or commentator. He is a well-known and very successful plaintiffs' attorney specializing in malpractice. His lengthy and detailed horror stories are actually cases he has handled. But more importantly, Wachsman speaks as an authority because he is also a physician—a neurosurgeon. He can speak of medicine as an insider, and indeed some of the book's first horror stories were drawn from his time as a surgeon-in-training.[25] Certainly there are other examples of the antireform rhetoric, but this particular one demonstrates that the politics of ideas encompasses both sides in this battle.

Policy

Analyzing the rhetoric of reform requires an examination of the symbolic devices used in the battle for the public mind *and* a comparison of those portrayals to systematic, empirical evidence. The appropriateness and efficacy of proposed and enacted policy solutions will depend, to a large degree, on their connection to reality.[26] Given that policy mistakes can be costly, it is troubling that so much of the reform rhetoric is accepted as being accurate. The argument presented in this book is that the characterization of juries and the civil justice system animating the tort reform movement is at odds with the findings of systematic empirical research or is based on claims about things for which there is little or no systematic research. This is especially true in terms of systematic evidence for the causal connections linking the legal system to a host of social and economic ills. Consequently, we are skeptical of the efficacy of enacted reforms and concerned about the possible unintended consequences of those measures. Beyond the self-interest of those groups lobbying for reform, we can see little reason for continuing or endorsing this reform movement.

Although there is much that we still need to learn, the research available presents a very different picture than that offered by the reform rhetoric. For instance, there is evidence that injuries occur frequently, but that most people who theoretically could pursue a claim for redress or file a lawsuit do nothing at all. For example, the RAND study discussed in chapters 3 and 5 found that only about one in 10 victims of accidental injuries in their surveys turned to the liability system for compensation. Few even considered making a claim for compensation, and attorneys were rarely consulted. The study found that people did not pursue claims because of their own judgments about responsibility for the injury, their judgments about norms of propriety and fairness in affixing blame, and because of the severity of the injury.

The disparity between injuries suffered and claims or lawsuits filed was also one of the key findings of the Harvard Medical Malpractice Study. It was described as the "first dramatic finding" of the study,[27] and led to the conclusion that "our analysis of malpractice litigation data demonstrates that the problem is not a litigation surplus, but a litigation deficit. The gap between torts occurring in American hospitals and tort suits being filed in American courts is far greater than has ever been supposed."[28] As we noted in chapter 5, Richard Abel made a similar argument regarding product-caused accidents,[29] and the findings of the RAND study of accident victims support his argument.[30]

While many people who could file a claim or lawsuit do not, there is still a concern about filings by those who supposedly have no grounds for doing so. The concern is usually tied to the issue of cost—the cost associated with sorting frivolous suits from those that are meritorious. This was, for instance, one of the major concerns raised by the authors of the Harvard Malpractice Study.[31] As a general statement, little systematic research has been done on how well claims and lawsuits are sorted on their merits. Some study has been made of the malpractice area, using malpractice insurance closed claims, and while far from conclusive, the findings suggest that the process is in fact quite effective in sorting out those situations involving negligence from those that do not.[32] Such findings counsel against blithely accepting the allegation that the process of resolving claims is "more a lottery than a rational system."[33] Given that there must be some kind of decision process for determining if an injury has occurred, whether compensation should be paid, and how much is to be paid, the question of the cost of sorting will not go away. But there appear to be no standards for determining what level of cost is too high. And "frivolousness" is likely to be in the eye of the beholder.

Contrary to what might be expected, when verdict data are viewed in the aggregate they suggest that civil juries are not especially sympathetic to plaintiffs. Within this aggregate, there are variations among sites and types of cases that reflect complex, yet orderly patterns in verdicts. Variations among sites, however, are inevitable and quite acceptable in a highly decentralized legal system with 50 state variants (plus the District of Columbia and others), each being organized, in turn, around smaller, local units. Some of the variation is likely to be the result of differences among the states in law and procedure, but some is also likely to be linked to socioeconomic differences among states and even within states. Underlying this decentralized system and institutions like the jury are, of course, fundamental political principles tied to the federal structure of the American polity and the idea of self-government.[34]

Variations in jury verdicts among different types of cases should also be expected—not all types of cases are the same, nor should they be handled the same. The question is whether orderly patterns exist within particular types of cases or the major settings within those case types. In terms of the data we presented on jury verdicts in medical malpractice, products liability, and punitive damages cases, the answer appears to be yes. These patterns, however, are complex, and they highlight how meager our collective knowledge really is concerning the processes that make up the respective disputing pyramids for these areas (and, by implication, others). One useful way of increasing our collective knowledge that can inform policy discussions as well as contribute to more theoretical pursuits is to take the epidemiological perspective that informed some of the studies from the medical literature discussed in chapter 4.

The reform rhetoric tells us that supposed patterns in claims, lawsuits, and verdicts are problems in themselves with a priori causes. No further inquiry or analysis is therefore needed, and policies should be enacted to eradicate these problems. An epidemiological approach suggests that we look at these issues in a different manner. Phenomena such as claiming or verdict patterns are not themselves the problem, but rather they are the endpoint of a process set in motion by some underlying phenomenon that requires a remedy. The analytical task in this approach is to start at the endpoint and trace the process backwards in order to identify the root problem. Solutions may then be crafted to deal with that matter or with those parts of the process close to it. For instance, there is a description in chapter 4 of an epidemiological study of closed malpractice insurance claims that used claims as a quality improvement tool.[35] Claims and lawsuits were not cast as the problem demanding attention in this study; the problem was injuries caused by substandard and/or negligent medical care. Proposed solutions focused on improving the quality of care.

This approach requires the disaggregation of data, looking for frequency, distribution, and patterns—and ultimately for the relationships driving or influencing those patterns. Using the disputing pyramid idea, this means asking first about the types of cases that go to a jury trial and their relative frequencies. Then we must look within different types of cases and ask about their major characteristics. For instance, for malpractice and products liability cases this would involve an examination of the different settings from which cases emerge. Within particular settings, more specific characteristics must be investigated—such as the severity of injury, the cause of injury or the product and industry involved. This approach also entails looking at the processes that bring different types of matters all the way to a jury trial and the key factors affecting those processes. Taken generally, then, we must work backwards down the disputing pyramids for different types of cases to their respective bases—all the way to the injuries or other harms suffered and the factors that affect their occurrence.

Consideration of this approach quickly points out the limits of current knowledge. In this sense, it outlines a series of research agendas surrounding different types of cases. At the same time, it points to connections with empirical literatures that might otherwise be overlooked. For instance, it directs us to the medical literature for studies on the occurrence of injuries and their causes as well as to the sociological literature of qualitative studies of medical work and error. For products liability, we must address the empirical literature on the regulation of safety and the literature on alternative compensation systems like workers' compensation. In other words, those research agendas will be interdisciplinary.

Such an epidemiological approach is likely to also point to a different set of potential policy problems than those offered by the reform rhetoric. For instance, there is the idea that there are many injury victims who go uncompensated—who "lump it." Still, the core issue is always injuries (or other harms), their causes, and the factors affecting them. The rhetoric of reform ignores this—or more importantly tries to obscure it from our view. The rhetoric concentrates on processes that are set in motion long after an injury or harm occurs. Consequently, the proposed and enacted reforms offer nothing to address this base problem—one that will not go away on its own. A more epidemiological approach would also have us look at existing processes and institutions for compensation and safety regulation that may require policy changes.

Knowledge

We conclude, then, like so many other social scientists by arguing that more research is needed. The reason is not simply the idea that there is still much about which little is known, although this is an important part of the reason. There is also the question of how much is reliably known in light of the intense politics surrounding the issue of civil justice reform. A related concern focuses on the character of future research given the larger political environment. Much of the current academic literature (including our own research) has been driven, in one way or another, by the politics of ideas and the political debate over reform. It is safe to say that if not for this debate, most of the research and commentary in the literature would not have been undertaken. That debate is likely to continue to shape research agendas in the future.

There is nothing inherently bad about the idea that research agendas may often be shaped by the policy agenda, the political debates surrounding that agenda, and the political efforts to gain a place on the policy agenda. While we might like to think that scholarly research is proactive, it is often reactive—sometimes uncritically so. This is especially true when funding is a concern, and as we all know, research agendas are sometimes altered to fit the interests of funders. The more serious problem arises when partisan political interests actively seek to shape research agendas in the social sciences and to influence the literature in ways that further their cause. This, we believe, is what has been happening with issues surrounding the reform debate. We say this not to suggest that there is a conspiracy of some kind underway; it is just partisan politics working its way into the research literature.

Efforts at shaping research agendas and the literature on civil justice follow a pattern that has been documented by those who have studied the politics of "think tanks," especially institutions that have staked out a position someplace to the right on the political spectrum.[36] James E. Smith, in his book *The Idea Brokers: Think Tanks and the Rise of the New Policy Elite* describes the efforts at developing a conservative counter-elite to combat what conservatives in the 1970s saw as an entrenched liberal elite or establishment "comprised of the nation's major foundations, Ivy League universities, New York publishing houses, research institutions, newspapers, and the broadcast media, which maintains the supremacy of liberal ideas and policies."[37] Starting in the 1970s, intellectuals like Irving Kristol set out to do battle with the so-called liberal elite and its ideas by creating institutions and outlets for conservative ideas. Universities, think tanks, and foundations were especially important in this battle because they were seen as "idea-generating" and "idea-legitimizing" institutions.[38] According to Smith:

> Defenders of the capitalist ethos would have to wage war both by creating their own counterparts and by taking the battle inside the university and, in time, political bureaucracy. Kristol asked whether it was in the long-term interest of corporations to continue to support institutions that had proved so hostile. He appealed for a more discriminating corporate philanthropy that would identify and support those academics and intellectuals who believed in a strong private sector. . . . In the early 1970s, executives in a handful of traditionally conservative foundations redefined their programs with the aim of reshaping the policy agenda and constructing a network of conservative institutions and scholars. The John M. Olin Foundation, for example, had directed its money to anti-labor organizations and to educational programs on free enterprise in undistinguished colleges. But in the 1970s, its patterns of giving became more sophisticated and more closely attuned to the potential of grantees for influencing debates on national policies.[39]

In short, philanthropy was to be a weapon in the political battle over ideas between right and left. In addition to more targeted funding for universities and individual scholars, this also involved funding for think tanks. This meant funding for already existing institutions like the American Enterprise Institute as well as for the creation of new institutions like the Heritage Foundation and the Manhattan Institute.

With regard to the battle over ideas as it relates to civil justice reform, we find this kind of targeted philanthropy in the funding of individual scholars through endowed chairs, funding for institutes and centers either at universities or free-standing, funding for conferences and lectures, and funding for research. Such financial support is an attempt to shape research agendas and influence the academic literature in ways consistent with the reformers' interests and which fit into a larger conservative political agenda. The more insidious aspect of this effort is not the direct attempt to determine the substance of a particular project, but rather the influence on the assumptions about the civil justice system with which researchers begin and the questions that they set out to answer. This has more to do with setting the theoretical tone of the literature, and here the reform movement has had success.

One of the most visible ways this has been done is by sponsoring and/or funding academic or quasi-academic conferences and lecture series. Conferences may be designed to bring together researchers and representatives of organizations seeking reform—lobbying not simply the literature but those who create and maintain it. Alternatively, these conferences may just bring researchers together for a meeting that explicitly or implicitly accepts the reformers' perspective on the civil justice system. Lecture series provide an accepted formal outlet for the reformer's view, usually in a context that gives those views at least a certain degree of legitimacy. Often the lectures or a series papers coming out of a conference will later be published either in a book or an academic journal.

Perhaps one of the most interesting examples of such targeted philanthropy in a lecture series is the annual Monsanto Lectures on Tort Law Reform and Jurisprudence at Valparaiso University Law School which started in 1987. Each lecture is a distillation of a monograph published in the *Valparaiso University Law Review*. The lecture series, according to the law review, "is endowed by a generous gift from the Monsanto Fund, the eleemosynary arm of the Monsanto Company."[40]

The stated purpose of this lecture series reads like a short summary of the reform movement's prime targets:

> to critically re-examine the deep theory of tort as it has evolved in this country and to explore avenues for its reform. This may include comment upon the contingent fee practice, punitive damages, strict liability concepts, the use and misuse of expert witnesses, the problem of causation in science and law, the role of insurance, the manner of bearing "process costs," and even the jury system itself.[41]

This series, then, is about reexamination in the interest of making changes in the civil justice system. It is not, apparently, a multisided symposium; instead, the reformers' perspective is accepted at the outset. The inaugural lecture was delivered by George Priest, John M. Olin Professor of Law and Economics at Yale Law School and a well-known reform advocate. Peter Huber gave the fourth lecture in 1990,[42] and Richard Epstein gave the fifth lecture in 1991.[43] The lectures in the series are, in effect, part of a brief for the reformers' policy agenda. Such a series should not be surprising in light of the Monsanto Company's public stand on civil justice reform as illustrated by the discussion in chapter 6 of the company's CEO, Richard Mahoney.

The Monsanto Lecture Series may be among the more blatant efforts at lobbying the academic literature by a corporation with a political agenda. But there are other corporations and their foundations that are also unabashedly partisan (on the right of the political spectrum) in their support in the civil justice arena. Among them are the John M. Olin Foundation, the Smith-Richardson Foundation, the Lynde and Harry Bradley Foundation, the Sarah Scaife Foundation, and the Aetna Foundation.[44] Corporations and conservative foundations have been providing support for research institutions such as the RAND Corporation's Institute for Civil Justice and the Manhattan Institute for a number of years.[45] The majority of the funding for George Priest's Program in Civil Liability at Yale Law School has come from manufacturing and insurance companies or their foundations.[46] In response to a question in a deposition for a trial in which he was called as an expert witness in 1989,[47] Priest listed his primary financial supporters as Aetna Life and Casualty Foundation, Bethlehem Steel, Chubb and Son, Signa, Exxon Education Foundation, General Electric Foundation, Mobil Corporation, Monsanto, Prudential Insurance, R. J. Reynolds Tobacco, Roman Haas Company, and 3-M.[48]

Support from these corporate funders has gone to conferences highlighting the reformers' perspective on the civil justice system. For instance, the Manhattan Institute along with the Academy of Political Science sponsored an academic conference in November 1987, entitled "New Directions in Liability Law." Papers from the conference were published in a special issue of the *Proceedings of the Academy of Political Science* edited by Walter Olson.[49] According to a conference brochure, funds for the conference were provided by the Charles A. Dana Foundation, Starr Foundation, Aetna Alliance of American Insurers, American Hoist and Derrick, AT&T, Dow Chemical, General Dynamics, Prudential, RJR Nabisco, Sea-Land Corporation, and Weyerhauser. The published proceedings also noted support from the Broyhill Foundation, Lounsbery Foundation, Monsanto Fund, Moses

Foundation, Schultz Foundation, Smith-Richardson Foundation, and Sunmark Foundation.[50] A similar conference was held in June 1987 at the Brookings Institution in Washington, DC. It was funded by the Starr Foundation, Dow Chemical, Bell Atlantic, Alex C. Walker Foundation, and Aetna Foundation.[51] Papers from the conference were published by Brookings in a book entitled *Liability: Perspectives and Policy*.[52] Among the contributors were Peter Huber and George Priest.

Brookings held another conference in 1990 which was devoted specifically to products liability. Papers were published in a Brookings book edited by Peter Huber and Robert Litan and entitled *The Liability Maze: The Impact of Liability on Safety and Innovation* (1991). As noted in chapter 6, this work figured prominently in the 1991 report of the Senate Committee on Commerce, Science, and Transportation recommending passage of S.640, the Product Liability Fairness Act. Funding for that conference was provided by the Starr Foundation, the Sloan Foundation, and Brookings' Center for Economic Progress and Employment. Brookings' Center, in turn, was funded by Donald S. Perkins, American Express, AT&T, Chase Manhattan Bank, Cummins Engine, Ford Motor Company, Hewlett-Packard, Morgan Stanley, Motorola, Springs Industries, Union Carbide, Warner-Lampert, Xerox Corporation, Aetna Foundation, Ford Foundation, General Electric Foundation, Prudential Foundation, Sloan Foundation, Smith-Richardson Foundation, Institute for International Economics, and Alex C. Walker Foundation.[53]

A 1993 conference held by the National Center for State Courts—the Williamsburg Conference on Civil Justice: A Focus on Torts—also received substantial corporate support. The conference brought together researchers, judges, and many of the major interests in the reform debate. It received support from Aetna, American International Group, Inc., Phillips Petroleum Company, and Monsanto. Funding also came from the Association of Trial Lawyers of America (ATLA), illustrating that groups on the antireform side have also become active in trying to lobby the literature. The Roscoe Pound Foundation, closely tied to ATLA, has funded a variety of conferences and research related to the reform debate. It funds the Chief Justice Earl Warren Conferences on Advocacy. Among conference topics during the 1980s were Product Safety in America (1984), Dispute Resolution Devices in a Democratic Society (1985), The American Civil Jury (1986), and Medical Quality and the Law (1989). The Roscoe Pound Foundation funded John Guinther's book *The Jury in America* (1989) and the surveys of jurors upon which it reported. Needless to say, the book is projury in tone.

The Roscoe Pound Foundation also helped fund Professor Michael Rustad's empirical research on punitive damages in products liability cases.[54] The findings of this research have found their way into the academic literature[55] and the policy debate. The Roscoe Pound Foundation monograph presenting Rustad's initial findings included as an appendix the prepared testimony of Rustad and his collaborator Professor Thomas Koenig before the U.S. Senate Committee on Commerce, Science, and Transportation from September 19, 1991 on S.640, The Product Liability Fairness Act.[56] Rustad also prepared an amicus curiae brief for the U.S. Supreme Court case *Honda Motor Co. v. Oberg* which raised constitutional questions about punitive damages. The brief was done for the Trial Lawyers for Public Justice, "a national public interest law firm devoted to representing victims of corporate and government abuse."[57]

The Roscoe Pound Foundation's support of Rustad's research has not escaped the attention of the reform interests. Because of this support his research has been dismissed as a piece of advocacy. For instance, a 1992 *ABA Journal* article quoted a proreform lawyer who had argued against the constitutionality of punitive damages before the Supreme Court as saying: "It (Rustad's research) is a selected, narrow, biased study that represents an advocacy position. . . . It's an assertion by a proponent in a controversy."[58] Both sides, then, have invested in influencing the literature, and as the statement above illustrates, this includes assaults characterizing one another's efforts as purely political.

The efforts at shaping research agendas and the academic literature for partisan political purposes raise some troubling issues for researchers and those concerned with the integrity of the academic literature. Most importantly, such efforts raise a question about just what the literature tells us about juries and the civil justice system—both with regard to the policy debate and to more theoretical concerns. We cannot assume that the findings and analyses in the literature can be taken at face value. A healthy skepticism is needed when deciding what in the literature is reliable knowledge rather than simply part of a political argument. To paraphrase David Ricci's remarks on think tanks, when research, conferences, or lectures take place in situations that are highly sensitive to political considerations or receive support (especially ongoing support) from funders with a partisan interest in the products of their support "we are entitled to assume that the setting will sway their observations."[59] Partisan funders are unlikely to be indifferent to the policy implications of the projects they subsidize, whether it is the John M. Olin Foundation on the right or the Roscoe Pound

Foundation on the left. Even for projects not directly supported by the partisans for either side, a healthy skepticism is still warranted because the partisans have largely set the terms of debate and research.

We argue for more research, then, not only because so little is systematically known about the civil justice system, but also because of the influence of partisan politics on the academic literature. We are not so naive as to think that partisan efforts to shape research agendas and the literature will cease; instead, they are likely to increase. More research in the marketplace of ideas—research that is critical of assumptions and methodologically sound as well as cognizant of the political interests at work—is the only way to respond to partisan efforts to lobby the academic literature. This presumes a vigorous idea of peer review in its most general sense. In his critique of studies supporting the "deep pockets" hypothesis in medical malpractice cases discussed in chapter 4, Neil Vidmar noted that many of them were published in venues not using a peer review process. That process, he said, is used by journals to assess the methodological and conceptual quality of a potential publication. He argued that a number of the studies he critiqued "would likely have failed peer review."[60] But this process also works on a more general level, as Vidmar's critique itself so well illustrates. And it is this more general review process that is needed in the marketplace of ideas along with more research. This is what science, even social science, is about—knowledge found to be reliable because it holds up under critical empirical testing and evaluation. The politics of ideas may result in problematic policies of questionable effectiveness, but left unchallenged it will thoroughly undermine the scientific enterprise.

Notes

CHAPTER 1

1. Clermont and Eisenberg, "Trial by Jury or Judge: Transcending Empiricism," 77 *Cornell L. Rev.* 1125 (1992).

2. J. Frank, *Law and the Modern Mind* 178 (1931).

3. *Id.* at 177–78.

4. Sales and Cole, "Punitive Damages: A Relic That Has Outlived Its Origins," 37 *Vand. L. Rev.* 1154 (1984).

5. P. Huber, *Galileo's Revenge: Junk Science in the Courtroom* (1991).

6. Clermont and Eisenberg, *supra* note 1.

7. D. Stone, *Policy Paradox and Political Reason* 7 (1988).

8. *Id.* at 309.

9. *Id.* at 121–22.

10. D. Ricci, *The Transformation of American Politics: The New Washington and the Rise of Think Tanks* 182–207 (1993).

11. *Id.* at 23.

12. *Id.* at 25.

13. Ideas have found their way into politics and the policy process, says Ricci, in a variety of ways: "ideas were what campaign advertising conveyed in the form of images; ideas and information were what public interest groups purveyed in research reports and press conferences; ideas helped to assemble facts into news 'stories' disseminated by the mass media; and ideas animated independent voters who decided they would no longer automatically toe a party line." *Id.* at 192.

14. *See* Vidmar, "On Libel and the Civil Jury" (unpublished manuscript delivered at the Annual Meeting of the Law and Society Association, June 11–14, 1987); MacCoun, "Inside the Black Box: What Empirical Research Tells Us about Decisionmaking by Civil Juries," in *Verdict: Assessing the Civil Jury System* (R. Litan ed., 1993).

15. McCormick, "The American Tort System: A Time to Rebalance the Scales of Justice," 52 *Vital Speeches of the Day* 267 (1986).

16. *Id.*

17. Malott, "America's Liability Explosion: Can We Afford the Cost?" 52 *Vital Speeches of the Day* 180 (1986).

18. *Id.* at 181.

19. *A Report from the President's Council on Competitiveness: Agenda for Civil Justice Reform in America* 5 (1991).

20. "Striking a Blow at 'Junk Science,'" *Chicago Tribune*, July 12, 1993, § 1, at 12 (editorial).

21. *See generally* Huber, *supra* note 5, at 4.

22. W. Olson, *The Litigation Explosion* 152–53 (1991).

23. Andresky, "A World without Insurance?" *Forbes* July 15, 1985, at 40.

24. For instance, a 1986 article in *U.S. News & World Rep.* entitled "Sky-high Damage Awards" reported that there were 401 $1 million-plus jury verdicts nationwide in 1984 (Gest and Work, "Sky-high Damage Awards," *U.S. News & World Rep.*, January 27, 1986, at 35). A 1986 *Wall St. J.* article, "Generous Juries", reported 400 such awards in 1984 (Langely, "Generous Juries," *Wall St. J.*, May 29, 1986, A1).

25. Tort Policy Working Group, United States Department of Justice, *Report of the Tort Policy Working Group on the Causes, Extent and Policy Implications of the Current Crisis in Insurance Availability and Affordability* [hereinafter *Report*], charts I and H (1986).

26. Mahoney and Littlejohn, "Innovation on Trial: Punitive Damages versus New Products," 246 *Science* 1396 (1989).

27. American Tort Reform Association, "Punitive Damages Update," April 12, 1989; *see* Daniels and Martin, "Myth and Reality in Punitive Damages," 75 *Minn. L. Rev.* 1 (1990) at 15–23 for a detailed explanation of the press kit.

28. *Pacific Mutual Life Insurance Co. v. Haslip*, 499 U.S. 1 (1991).

29. Brief for Petitioner, Appendix A, *Pacific Mutual Life Ins. Co. v. Haslip*, 499 U.S. 1 (1991); Brief of the American Institute of Architects, the American Tort Reform Association, the Council of Community Blood Centers, General Electric Co., the Minnesota Civil Justice Coalition, the National School Boards Association, and the Texas Civil Justice League as Amici Curiae in Support of Petitioner at 4, *Haslip*.

30. Nutter, "The Fight for Civil Justice Reform," *Ins. Rev.* November–December 1984, at 5.

31. *Id.*

32. Church, "Sorry, Your Policy Is Canceled," *Time*, March 24, 1986, at 16.

33. King, "Stopping the Bloodbath in Medical Malpractice," *Bus. Wk.*, April 22, 1985, at 93.

34. *Report*, *supra* note 25, at 35–42.

35. *Id.* at 35.

36. *Id.* at 35–36.

37. *Id.* at 36, 39.

38. *Id.* at 39, 42.

39. Council on Competitiveness, *supra* note 19, at 5–6.

40. P. Huber, *Liability: The Legal Revolution and Its Consequences* 10 (1988).

41. *Id.*

42. *Id.*

43. 125 L. Ed. 2d 366 (1993).

44. *TXO Production*, dissenting opinion of Justice O'Connor at 406.

45. Priest, "The Invention of Enterprise Liability: A Critical History of the Intellectual Foundations of Modern Tort Law," 14 *J. Legal Stud.* 461 (1985).

46. Priest, "The Current Insurance Crisis and Modern Tort Law," 96 *Yale L.J.* 1521 (1987).

47. Olson, *supra* note 22.

48. McCormick, *supra* note 15, at 267.

49. J. O'Connell and B. Kelley, *The Blame Game: Injury, Insurance and Injustice* 42 (1987).

50. Huber, *supra* note 5, at 3.

51. *Id.* at 5.

52. *Id.* at 4.

53. *Id.*

54. Council on Competitiveness, *supra* note 19, at 5.

55. McCormick, *supra* note 15, at 268.

56. Bowen, "Congressional Testimony on Senate Bill S.1804," 257 *JAMA* 816 (1987).

57. Huber, *supra* note 40, at 50–51.

58. *Id.* at 229.

59. J. O'Connell, *The Lawsuit Lottery* 4 (1979).

60. Ellis, "Punitive Damages, Due Process, and the Jury," 40 *Ala. L. Rev.* 975 (1989) at 996–97.

61. Mahoney, "Consumers, Competitiveness Suffer from Excesses in Punitive Damages," *Financier*, January 1989, at 12.

62. Bovbjerg, Sloan, Dor, and Hsieh, "Juries and Justice: Are Malpractice and Other Personal Injuries Created Equal?" 54 *Law & Contemp. Probs.* 37 (1991).

63. *Id.* at 37–38.

64. *Id.* at 38.

65. Malott, *supra* note 17, at 182.

66. *Id.*

67. McCormick, *supra* note 15, at 268.

68. "We All Pay the Price: An Industry Effort to Reform Civil Justice," *Ins. Rev.*, April 1986, at 58.

69. *Id.* at 59.

70. *Id.* at 58–59.

71. Church, *supra* note 32, at 16.

72. Gest and Work, *supra* note 24.

73. Farrell, "The Insurance Crisis: Now Everyone Is in a Risky Business," *Bus. Wk.*, March 10, 1986, at 88.

74. Wright, "Our Liability Mess Is No Asset," *Dallas Morning News*, February 9, 1986, at 38a.

75. Huber, *supra* note 40, at 3–4.

76. *Id.* at 4; Huber reached this figure in the following way: "The extent of these indirect costs can only be guessed at. One study concluded that doctors spend $3.50 in efforts to avoid additional charges for each $1 of direct tax they pay. If similar multipliers operate in other areas . . ." at 4.

77. Huber, *supra* note 5, at 165; P. Huber and R. Litan, eds., *The Liability Maze: The Impact of Liability Law on Safety and Innovation* (1991) at 2.

78. Huber, *supra* note 5, at 165.

79. Council on Competitiveness, *supra* note 15, at 1.

80. Huber, *supra* note 40, at 3.

81. Malott, *supra* note 17, at 182.

82. McCormick, *supra* note 15, at 269.

83. *Id.*

84. Mahoney and Littlejohn, *supra* note 26, at 1397.

85. *Id.* at 1395.

86. Mahoney, *supra* note 61, at 21–22.

87. Council on Competitiveness, *supra* note 19.

88. Prepared Remarks by the Vice President at 2, Annual Meeting of the American Bar Association, Atlanta, Georgia, August 13, 1991; *see also* Curriden and Baxter, "Quayle Riles Lawyers with Legal Reform Speech," *Atlanta Constitution*, August 14, 1991, at D3.

89. Prepared Statement of Robert A. Mosbacher, Secretary, Department of Commerce, Hearings before the Subcommittee on Commerce, Science and Transportation, United States Senate on the Product Liability Fairness Act, S.640, September 12, 1991 (S. Hrg. 102–727 at 16).

90. *Id.* at 17.

91. The Trial Lawyers for Public Justice is a plaintiff-oriented, "national public interest law firm devoted to representing victims of corporate and government abuse." Brief of Trial Lawyers for Public Justice as Amicus Curiae in Support of Respondents at 1, Pacific Mutual Life Insurance Co. v. Haslip, 499 U.S. 1 (1991).

92. *Id.* at 9.

93. *Id.* at 22.

94. *See* Chesebro, "Galileo's Retort: Peter Huber's Junk Scholarship," 42 *Am. U. L. Rev.* 1637, 1641–50 (1993); Bell, "Analyzing Tort Law: The Flawed Promise of NeoContract," 74 *Minn. L. Rev.* 1177 (1990). Regarding Huber's status, Bell wrote: "Huber has traveled far and wide since the publication (of his book *Liability*), engaging in debates and explaining his thesis. Memoranda from the Manhattan Institute discuss his extensive speaking tours, provide glowing reviews of his writing and even offer for sale audio tapes of Huber's performances on radio talk shows. At recent scholarly meetings, law professors from Yale, Stanford and the University of Houston have spoken of the sensation created by recent Huber visits. An entire panel at the annual meeting of the American Political Science Association in Atlanta in September 1989, was devoted to Huber's book, with the author there to confront his 'critics.' Huber has been featured in front-page *New York Times* discussions of risk and public policy. He regularly writes a column in *Forbes* magazine. In short, to a much greater degree than any other writer about tort-related issues, Huber is a visible public figure." (*Id.* at 1178–79, n. 7.)

95. Saks, "Do We Really Know Anything about the Behavior of the Tort Litigation System—And Why Not?" 140 *U. Pa. L. Rev.* 1147 (1992).

96. Sanders and Joyce, "Off to the Race: The 1980s Tort Crisis and the Law Reform Process," 27 *Hous. L. Rev.* 207 (1990).

97. Saks, *supra* note 95, at 1156.

98. *Id.* at 1149.

99. *Id.* at 1287.

100. *Id.*

101. Saks, "Malpractice Misconceptions and Other Lessons about the Litigation System," 16 *Just. Sys. J.* 7, 19 (1993).

102. *See* Abel, "The Real Tort Crisis—Too Few Claims," 48 *Ohio St. L.J.* 443 (1986).

103. Sanders and Joyce, *supra* note 96.

104. *Id.* at 257.

105. *Id.* at 226–34.

106. *Id.* at 234–55.

107. *Id.* at 258.

108. Saks, *supra* note 95, at 1152.

109. *Id.* at 115–56.

110. Sanders and Joyce, *supra* note 96, at 276.

111. *Id.* at 277–78.

112. *E.g.*, New York Advisory Commission on Liability Insurance (1986); Governor's (Massachusetts) Task Force on Liability Issues (1986); Governor's (Alabama) Commission on the Insurance Crisis and Tort Reform (1986); Florida Academic Task Force for Review of the Insurance and Tort Systems (1986); Governor's (Tennessee) Task Force on Tort and Liability Insurance Reform (1987).

113. Sanders and Joyce, *supra* note 96, at 278.

114. *Id.*

115. *Id.* at 216–17.

116. *Report*, *supra* note 25.

117. Sanders and Joyce, *supra* note 96, at 214–55.

118. *Id.* at 278.

119. *Id.*

120. *Id.* at 279.

121. Saks, *supra* note 101, at 18.

122. M. Feeley, *Court Reform on Trial: Why Simple Solutions Fail* at xii (1983).

123. Chesebro, *supra* note 94.

124. *E.g.*, Huber, "Injury Litigation and Liability Insurance Dynamics," *Science* 31, October 2, 1987; "No-Fault Punishment," 40 *Ala. L. Rev.* 1037 (1989); "Are We Afraid of the Future," *Reader's Digest*, December 1988, at 191.

125. *See* Bell, *supra* note 94.

126. *See* Chesebro, *supra* note 94.

127. J. Kingdon, *Agenda, Alternatives, and Public Policies* 129 (1984).

128. *Id.* at 214.

129. *Id.*

130. Jost, "Tampering with Evidence: The Liability and Competitiveness Myth," 78 *A.B.A. J.* 44 (1992).

131. *Id.* at 44.

132. Huber and Litan, *supra* note 77.

133. Jost, *supra* note 130, at 48.

134. *Id.* at 49.

135. *Id.*

136. *Id.* at 47.

137. *Id.*

138. *Id.*

139. Chesebro, *supra* note 94.

140. The "*Fyre* Rule" is a common law rule dating to the 1920s, dealing with admissibility of scientific testimony and evidence in criminal trials. It limits admissible information to those matters generally accepted by scientists in a given field. *See* Chesebro, *supra* note 94, at 1687–95.

141. *Id.* at 1642–43.

142. *Id.* at 1688.

143. *Id.* at 1643.

144. *Id.* at 1687.

145. *Id.* at 1691

146. *Id.* at 1705–15.

147. *Id.* at 1710–11.

148. *Id.* at 1709, n. 325.

149. Huber, *supra* note 40.

150. Page, "Deforming Tort Reform: Liability, the Legal Revolution and Its Consequences," 78 *Geo. L.J.* 649 (1990).

151. *Id.* at 659–60.

152. Hayden, "Neocontract Polemics and Unconscionable Scholarship," 24 *Law & Soc'y Rev.* 863 (1990) at 863–64.

153. Hager, "Civil Compensation and Its Discontents: A Response to Huber," 42 *Stan. L. Rev.* 540 (1990).

154. *Id.* at 540.

155. *Id.* at 579.

156. *Id.* at 580.

157. Geyelin, "Tort Bar's Scourge: Star of Legal Reform Kindles Controversy but Collects Critics," *Wall St. J.*, October 16, 1992, § A, at 1.

158. *Id.* at § A, at 4.

159. Jost, *supra* note 130, at 46.

160. *See* Stone, *supra* note 7, at 309.

161. Manhattan Institute Judicial Studies Program, "Mission Statement and Overview," November 12, 1991, at 1.

162. *Id.* at 1–2.

163. Ricci, *supra* note 10, at 193.

CHAPTER 2

1. J. Kingdon, *Agenda, Alternatives, and Public Policies* (1984).

2. *Id.*

3. D. Stone, *Policy Paradox and Political Reason* (1988).

4. Kingdon, *supra* note 1, at 95–121.

5. *Id.* at 4.

6. *Id.*

7. *See generally* R. Cobb and C. Elder, *Participation in American Politics: The Dynamics of Agenda Building* (1983).

8. *Id.* at 85.

9. *Id.* at 86.

10. *Id.* at 87.

11. Manhattan Institute Judicial Studies Program, "Mission Statement and Overview," November 12, 1992, at 1.

12. Kingdon, *supra* note 1, at 95.

13. Cobb and Elder, *supra* note 7, at 172–73.

14. Stone, *supra* note 3, at 106.

15. *E.g.*, Saks, "Do We Really Know Anything about the Behavior of the Tort Litigation System—And Why Not?" 140 *U. Pa. L. Rev.* 1993 (1992); Sanders and Joyce, "Off to the Race: The 1980s Tort Crisis and the Law Reform Process," 27 *Hous. L. Rev.* 207 (1990).

16. Kingdon, *supra* note 1, at 91.

17. *Id.* at 204.

18. *Id.* at 207.

19. *Id.* at 208.

20. Manhattan Institute Judicial Studies Program, *supra* note 11, at 1–2.

21. Kingdon, *supra* note 1, at 137.

22. Casey, "Tort Reform Coalitions Flourish in Midwest," *Nat'l Underwriter*, July 18, 1986, at 14.

23. *See* Nutter, "The Fight for Civil Justice Reform," *Ins. Rev.*, November–December 1984, at 3 (Nutter was president of the Alliance of American Insurers); *see also* Casey, *supra* note 22. The Alliance of American Insurers is located in Schaumburg, Illinois (a Chicago suburb), and has been vigorously involved in the efforts to gain access to the public agenda for the insurance industry's characterization of the crisis, its causes, and remedies.

24. Casey, *supra* note 22.

25. With regard to Project Justice's efforts to defeat a prejudgment interest bill in the Illinois General Assembly in 1986, the *National Underwriter* reported (approvingly): "Hundreds of publicity pieces were mailed to the media throughout the state which resulted in supportive news coverage." *Id.*

26. *Id.* at 54–55; "Civil Justice Coalitions: A National Awakening," 62 *J. Am. Ins.* 4–5 (1986). We find the establishment of the following: Indiana Project Justice, Kansas Project Justice, the Pennsylvania Truth and Fairness in Litigation Committee, the Washington Liability Reform

Coalition, Florida Project Civil Justice, the Wisconsin Coalition for Justice, the Minnesota Tort Reform Coalition, the Ohio Basic Fairness in Litigation Coalition, the Michigan Committee for Civil Justice Equity, Iowa Project Civil Justice Reform, Nebraska Project Justice, and the Texas Tort Reform Coalition, which changed its name to the Texas Civil Justice League.

27. "We All Pay the Price: An Industry Effort to Reform Civil Justice," *Ins. Rev.*, April 1986, at 58 [hereinafter "We All Pay the Price"].

28. *Id.*

29. *Id.* at 59.

30. *Id.* at 58–59.

31. *Id.* at 59.

32. "The Lawsuit Crisis Is Bad For Babies," *Newsweek*, June 30, 1986, at 27; "No One Is Immune from the Lawsuit Crisis," *Time*, June 9, 1986, at 32; "No One Is Immune from the Lawsuit Crisis," *Newsweek*, June 9, 1986, at 87; "The Lawsuite Crisis Is Penalizing School Sports," *Newsweek*, April 28, 1986, at 37; "The Lawsuit Crisis Is Penalizing School Sports," *Time*, April 28, 1986, at 25; "Even the Clergy Can't Escape the Lawsuit Crisis," *Time*, March 31, 1986, at 69; "The Lawsuit Crisis Is Bad for Babies," *Time*, March 31, 1986, at 67 (all advertisements sponsored by the Insurance Information Institute).

33. *We All Pay the Price*, *supra* note 27, at 58–59.

34. *Wall St. J.*, November 19, 1985, at 3 and February 14, 1986, at 3.

35. Kingdon, *supra* note 1, at 115.

36. Stone, *supra* note 3, at 6.

37. *See* M. Edelman, *Political Language: Words That Succeed and Policies That Fail* (1977) and *Constructing the Political Spectacle* (1988).

38. Manhattan Institute Judicial Studies Program, *supra* note 11, at 1.

39. *See* Geertz, "Common Sense as a Cultural System," in *Local Knowledge: Further Essays in Interpretive Anthropology* 75 (1983).

40. F. Bailey, *The Tactical Uses of Passion* 26 (1983).

41. *Id.* at 23, 26.

42. Stone, *supra* note 3, at 108.

43. *Id.*

44. As Peter Huber wrote: "Once lawyers take charge of an area of life, the person of low cunning acquires mastery over the person of high simplicity. With lawyers in charge, the mean person gets the better of the generous one. How long such conquests last is another matter; that they are regularly achieved in the courts is an everyday experience." *Liability: The Legal Revolution and Its Consequences* 223 (1988).

45. Stone, *supra* note 3, at 109, 113.

46. *Id.* at 115.

47. *Id.* at 109.

48. Priest, "The Invention of Enterprise Liability: A Critical History of the Intellectual Foundations of Modern Tort Law," 14 *J. Legal Stud.* 461 (1985).

49. Priest, "The Current Insurance Crisis and Modern Tort Law," 96 *Yale L.J.* 1521 (1987).

50. Huber, *supra* note 44, at 4.

51. *Id.* at 7.

52. *Id.*

53. *Id.* at 221–22.

54. *Id.* at 222.

55. *Id.* at 231.

56. Stone, *supra* note 3, at 113.

57. Huber, *supra* note 44, at 224.

58. W. Olson, *The Litigation Explosion: What Happened When America Unleashed the Lawsuit* 348 (1991).

59. Quoted in Daniels, "The Question of Jury Competence and the Politics of Civil Justice Reform: Symbols, Rhetoric, and Agenda-Building," 52 *Law & Contemp. Probs.* 269, 288 (1989).

60. *Id.*

61. Stone, *supra* note 3, at 116.

62. *Id.*

63. *Id.* at 117.

64. Malott, "America's Liability Explosion: Can We Afford the Cost?," 52 *Vital Speeches of the Day* 180 (1986).

65. Olson, *supra* note 58, at 152.

66. "The Pinto and the Horse"—As told in *Forbes* (Greene, The Hanging Judges of Business," *Forbes*, April 7, 1986, at 63), the story goes: "Ford Motors . . . lost a $1.5 million jury decision to the estate of a woman who was killed when her car hit a horse, causing it to jump through the roof of her 1980 Ford Pinto." In reality, the horse did not jump through the roof, but rather slid across it. The car's roof collapsed under the weight of the horse. Federal safety standards required that a car roof withstand 5,000 pounds of pressure in order to protect the occupants in a rollover. Here the roof collapsed under much less weight (*see* Brill and Lyons, "The Not-So-Simple Crisis," *Am. Law.*, May 1, 1986 at 1; *see also* "Litigation Myths," *Charleston (W. Va.) Gazette-Mail*, June 1, 1986 at 1).

"The Ladder in the Manure"—Here a workman who was shingling a barn set up his ladder in a pile of manure. The man fell and was injured when the ladder slipped in the manure. He was awarded $300,000 from the manufacturer of the ladder because the manufacturer did not warn buyers of the danger of setting the ladder up in something as slippery as manure. This story got its widest exposure as part of a *60 Minutes* broadcast in early 1986. In reality, the manure had nothing to do with the verdict. The jury found that the ladder broke with less than a 450-pound load on it. The ladder's safety rating indicated that it could support 1,000 pounds (*see* Brill and Lyons, "The Not-So-Simple Crisis;" "Litigation Myths").

"The Drunk and the Phone Booth"—This story was originally circulated as a part of the political campaign to deny reelection to Rose Bird, then Chief Justice of California. As told in the *Wall Street Journal*: "A man is injured when a drunk driver crashed into a telephone booth and California Chief Justice Rose Bird rules that the company that designed the booth is liable." According to the *Charleston (W. Va.) Gazette-Mail*, however, the booth had been the site of a prior accident, the driver that hit it was not drunk, the plaintiff—who had one leg crushed and the other severed—said he had time to get out of the booth, but the door wouldn't open. The California Supreme Court's ruling merely said the issues he had raised were proper for a jury to consider (*see* "Capping the Courts," *Wall St. J.*, December 3, 1985, at 30, "Litigation Myths").

"The Fat Man and the Lawnmower"—As told in *Forbes* (Andresky, "A World without Insurance?" *Forbes*, July 15, 1985, at 40) the story goes: An overweight man with a history of coronary disease suffered a heart attack while trying to start a Sears lawnmower. He sued Sears, charging that too much force was required to yank the mower's pull rope. A jury in Pennsylvania awarded him $1.2 million, plus damages of $550,000 for delays in settling the claim. In fact, the case involved a 32-year-old medical doctor with no history of heart disease and a product that was defectively manufactured (*see* Church, "Sorry, Your Policy Is Canceled," *Time*, March 24, 1986, at 16).

These stories and others have appeared frequently since the middle 1980s. For a critical discussion, *see* Daniels, *supra* note 59, at 292–97.

67. Hayden, "The Cultural Logic of a Political Crisis: Common Sense, Hegemony and the Great American Liability Famine of 1986," Disputes Processing Research Program Working Paper, Series 9, March 1989, Institute for Legal Studies, University of Wisconsin–Madison at 10.

68. *Id.* at 32–37.

69. American Tort Reform Association letter of October 10, 1986, soliciting membership and monetary contribution and addressed to John P. Heinz, then Executive Director of the American Bar Foundation, Chicago, IL, at 1–2.

70. Bailey, *supra* note 40, at 123–43.

71. *Id.* at 125.

72. *Id.* at 133.

73. *Id.* at 132.

74. *Id.* at 139.

75. McCormick, "The American Tort System: A Time to Rebalance the Scales of Justice," 52 *Vital Speeches of the Day* 269 (1986). Bailey noted that another characteristic of assertive rhetoric is the invocation of danger (*supra* note 40, at 138). The horror stories serve as a notice of crisis and a warning of further calamity if corrective action is not immediately taken.

76. Bailey, *supra* note 40, at 139.

77. Jost, "Tampering with Evidence: The Liability and Competitiveness Myth," 78 *A.B.A. J.* 50 (1992).

78. M. Edelman, *Political Language: Words That Succeed and Policies That Fail* 43–55 (1977).

79. Cox, "Tort Tales Lash Back," *Nat'l Law J.* vol. 14, no. 48, August 3, 1992, at 1, 37.

80. Stone, *supra* note 3, at 118.

81. *See* Galanter, "Reading the Landscape of Disputes: What We Know and Don't Know (and Think We Know) about Our Allegedly Contentious and Litigious Society," 31 *UCLA L. Rev.* 4, 6, n. 4 (1983).

82. *USA Today*, June 6, 1986, at 12A, col. 1.

83. *See* Wermiel, "Courting Disaster: The Cost of Lawsuits Growing Every Larger Disrupts the Economy," *Wall St. J.*, May 16, 1986, at A1, col. 6.

84. Richey, "Administration Proposes New Limits on Product Liability Awards," *Christian Sci. Monitor*, May 2, 1986, at 5, col. 1.

85. Tort Policy Working Group, United States Department of Justice, *Report of the Tort Policy Working Group on the Causes, Extent and Policy Implications of the Current Crisis in Insurance Availability and Affordability* 2 (1986) [hereinafter *Report*].

86. *Id.* at 35–42.

87. Appleman, "Jury Verdicts and Insurance Rates," *Ins. L.J.*, November 1962, at 714.

88. "How Can We Save Doctors from Themselves?" *Parade Magazine*, December 29, 1985, at 16.

89. "New Product Liability Law Advanced by Senate Panel," *Chicago Sun-Times*, June 13, 1986, at 60.

90. Wermeil, *supra* note 83.

91. Gest and Work, "Skyhigh Damage Suits," *U.S. News & World Report*, January 27, 1986, at 35.

92. 492 U.S. 257, 282 (1989).

93. 499 U.S. 1 (1991).

94. 125 L. Ed.2d 366 (1993).

95. Olson, *supra* note 58, at 1.

96. McCormick, *supra* note 75, at 267–68.

97. Church, "Sorry, Your Policy Is Canceled," *Time*, March 24, 1986, at 16.

98. *Id.*

99. Flemma, "Medical Malpractice: A Dilemma in the Search for Justice," 68 *Marquette L. Rev.* 237, 241–42 (1985).

100. *Report of the Senate Committee on Commerce, Science, and Transportation: Product Liability Fairness Act*, Senate Report 102–215 (1991), at 12.

101. Cook et al., "The Liability Crisis in the United States: Impact on the Accounting Profession," *J. Acct.*, November 1992, at 19.

102. *Id.*

103. *Id.*

104. Stone, *supra* note 3, at 127.

105. Kingdon, *supra* note 1, at 98–99.

106. *Id.* at 98.

107. *Id.* at 96.

108. *Id.* at 97.

109. Stone, *supra* note 3, at 133–34.

110. Kingdon, *supra* note 1, at 96.

111. Stone, *supra* note 3, at 130.

112. One exception is Alabama where the state supreme court has begun charting jury verdicts in cases involving punitive damages.

113. Bovbjerg, Sloan, Dor, and Hsieh, "Juries and Justice: Are Malpractice and Other Personal Injuries Created Equal?," 54 *Law & Contemp. Probs.* 37 (1991).

114. *Report*, *supra* note 85, at 35–42.

115. *Id.* at 35.

116. *Id.* at 36.

117. *A Report from the President's Council on Competitiveness: Agenda for Civil Justice Reform in America* 5–6 (1991).

118. Kingdon, *supra* note 1, at 98.

119. *Id.* at 99.

120. *Update*, Tort Policy Working Group, United States Department of Justice, *An Update on the Liability Crisis* (1987) [hereinafter *Update*].

121. *Id.* at 39–40.

122. H. Blalock, *Social Statistics* 69–70 (rev. 2d ed. 1979).

123. *Id.*

124. *Update*, *supra* note 120, at 39.

125. King, "Stopping the Bloodbath in Medical Malpractice," *Bus. Wk.*, April 22, 1985, at 93.

126. Stone, *supra* note 3, at 148.

127. *Id.* at 147.

128. *Id.* at 154.

129. *Id.* at 159.

CHAPTER 3

1. Clermont and Eisenberg, "Trial by Jury or Judge: Transcending Empiricism," 77 *Cornell L. Rev.* 1125 (1992).

2. *See* Saks, "Malpractice Misconceptions and Other Lessons about the Litigation System," 16 *Just. Sys. J.* 7, 19 (1993).

3. *See* Daniels and Martin, "Don't Kill the Messenger 'till You Read the Message: Products Liability Verdicts in Six California Counties, 1970–1990," 16 *Just. Sys. J.* 69 (1993).

4. Greene, "On Juries and Damage Awards: The Process of Decision-making," *Law & Contemp. Probs.*, Autumn 1989, at 225.

5. *See* Vidmar, "Making Inferences about Jury Behavior from Jury Verdict Statistics: Cautions about the Lorelei's Lied," unpublished paper, Duke University School of Law (1993); *see also* Vidmar, "Empirical Evidence on the 'Deep Pockets' Hypothesis: Jury Awards for Pain and Suffering in Medical Malpractice Cases," 43 *Duke L.J.* 217 (1993).

6. Metzloff, "Researching Litigation: The Medical Malpractice Example," 51 *Law & Contemp. Probs.* 199, 235 (1988).

7. McCormick, "The American Tort System: A Time to Rebalance the Scales of Justice," 52 *Vital Speeches of the Day* 268 (1986).

8. Galanter, "The Radiating Effects of Courts," in *Empirical Theories about Courts* 117 (K. Boyum and L. Mather eds., 1983).

9. Galanter, "Reading the Landscape of Disputes: What We Know and Don't Know (and Think We Know) about Our Allegedly Contentious and Litigious Society," 31 *UCLA L. Rev.* 4, (1983) and M. Galanter, "Jury Shadows: Reflections on the Civil Jury and the Litigation Explosion," paper presented at the 1986 Warren Conference On Advocacy in the United States 19 (June 12–15, 1986).

10. M. Galanter, "Jury Shadows: Reflections on the Civil Jury and the Litigation Explosion," paper presented at the 1986 Warren Conference On Advocacy in the United States 19 (June 12–15, 1986).

11. Galanter, *supra* note 8, at 121.

12. *E.g.*, Galanter, *supra* note 9; Miller and Sarat, "Grievances, Claims and Disputes: Addressing the Adversary Culture," 15 *Law & Soc'y Rev.* 823 (1980–81).

13. J. Ladinsky and C. Susmilch, "The Processing of Consumer Disputes in a Metropolitan Setting," paper delivered at the Annual Meeting of the Midwest Political Science Association, Chicago, Ill., April 1980.

14. *See generally* Miller and Sarat, *supra* note 12.

15. P. Danzon, *Medical Malpractice: Theory, Evidence and Public Policy* 20 (1985).

16. P. Weiler, *Medical Malpractice on Trial* 12 (1991).

17. See chapter 4 for a more detailed discussion of these data.

18. Miller and Sarat, *supra* note 12, figure 1B, at 544.

19. *Id.*

20. D. Hensler et al., *Compensation for Accidental Injuries in the United States*, RAND Corporation, Santa Monica (R-39990HHS/ICJ, 1991). For a review of earlier research see Galanter, *supra* note 9, at 11–32.

21. *Id.* at 3.

22. *Id.*

23. *Id.* at 173.

24. *Id.* at 110.

25. *Id.*

26. *Id.* at 122, figure 5.2.

27. *Id.* at 172.

28. *Id.* at 110, 129.

29. *See* Galanter, *supra* note 9 at 28, n. 131.

30. Ostrom, Rottman, and Hanson, "What Are Tort Awards Really Like? The Untold Story from the State Courts," 14 *Law & Pol'y* 77, 81 (1992).

31. Clermont and Eisenberg, *supra* note 1, at 1137.

32. Galanter, *supra* note 8, at 136.

33. *Id.* at 136.

34. *Id.*

35. Galanter, *supra* note 8 at 121–24; Galanter, *supra* note 10; Mnookin and Kornhauser, "Bargaining in the Shadow of the Law: The Case of Divorce," 88 *Yale L. Rev.* 950 (1979).

36. M. Feeley, *The Process Is the Punishment* 154–98 (1979).

37. *E.g.*, J. Eisenstein and H. Jacob, *Felony Justice: An Organizational Analysis of Criminal Courts* (1977); M. Heumann, *Plea Bargaining: The Experiences of Prosecutors, Judges, and Defense Attorneys* (1979); M. Lipetz, *Routine Justice: Processing Cases in Women's Court* (1984); D. Neubauer, *Judicial Process: Law, Courts & Politics in the United States* 221–32 (1991).

38. Feeley, *supra* note 36, at 159.

39. District 6 includes the 19 counties in the Texas Sixth District Court of Appeals which sits in Texarkana. Located in the northeast corner of the state, those counties are Bowie, Camp, Cass, Delta, Fannin, Franklin, Gregg, Harrison, Hopkins, Hunt, Lamar, Marion, Morris, Panola, Red River, Rusk, Titus, Upshur, and Wood. District 9 includes the 11 counties in the Texas Ninth District Court of Appeals which sits in Beaumont. Located on the eastern edge of the state, those counties are Angelina,

Hardin, Jasper, Jefferson, Liberty, Montgomery, Newton, Orange, Polk, San Jacinto, and Tyler.

40. See Galanter, *supra* note 8.

CHAPTER 4

1. Vidmar, "Empirical Evidence on the Deep Pockets Hypothesis: Jury Awards for Pain and Suffering in Medical Malpractice Cases," 43 *Duke L.J.* 217, 218 (1993).

2. Thomas, "The Medical Malpractice 'Crisis': A Critical Examination of a Public Debate," 65 *Temple Law Rev.* 459 (1992).

3. The proposed AMA plan is a "fault-based" process that replaces the jury system with an administrative process.

4. Phillips and Kalk, "Replacing the Tort System for Medical Malpractice," *Stan. L. & Pol'y Rev.* 210–15 (Fall 1991).

5. Bowen, "Congressional Testimony on Senate Bill S.1804," 257 *JAMA* 816 (1987).

6. Johnson, "Beyond Tort Reform," 257 *JAMA* 827 (1987).

7. *Id.*

8. Johnson, "A Radical Proposal," 78 *A.B.A. J.* 48 (1988).

9. *Id.*

10. *E.g.*, Bovbjerg et al., "Juries and Justice: Are Malpractice and Other Personal Injuries Created Equal?" 54 *Law & Contemp. Probs.* 4 (1991).

11. Vidmar, *supra* note 1, at 219, n. 5.

12. *Id.* at 219, n. 6.

13. J. Frank, *Law and the Modern Mind* 178 (1931).

14. Vander Kolk, "Is That All There Is?" 152 *Am. J. Obstetrics & Gynecology* 139 (1985).

15. *Id.* at 142.

16. *Id.* at 140.

17. *Id.* at 142.

18. Tort Policy Working Group, United States Department of Justice, *Report of the Tort Policy Working Group on the Causes, Extent and Policy Implications of the Current Crisis in Insurance Availability and Affordability* [hereinafter *Report*] (1986), chart D.

19. *Id.* at 36.

20. *Id.* at 46–47.

21. Bowen, "Keynote Address," in 1 *Medical Professional Liability and the Delivery of Obstetrical Care* 1 (V. Rostow and R. Bulger eds., 1989).

22. *See* S. Law and S. Polan, *Pain and Profit: The Politics of Malpractice* 161–94 (1978).

23. *Id.* at 1–27.

24. Church, "Sorry, Your Policy Is Canceled," *Time*, March 24, 1986, at 16.

25. *E.g.*, "Liability: Injustice for All," Manhattan Institute (1992): video; Domenici, "Health Care Reform," *A.B.A. J.*, August 1992, at 42.

26. *Ins. Rev.*, April 1986, at 58; *see* chapter 2, at 32–36.

27. *Ins. Rev.*, *id.* at 58.

28. P. Huber, *Liability: The Legal Revolution and Its Consequences* 3 (1988).

29. W. Olson, *The Litigation Explosion: What Happened When America Unleashed the Lawsuit* 165 (1991).

30. "Maternity Care in the United States," in Rostow and Bulger eds., *supra* note 21, at 14–34.

31. *See* Rostow and Bulger eds., *supra* note 21, vols. 1 and 2.

32. D. Ricci, *The Transformation of American Politics: The New Washington and the Rise of Think Tanks* 9–17, 182–207 (1993).

33. Bulger, "Chairman's Preface," in Rostow and Bulger eds., *supra* note 21, at vii.

34. *Id.* at viii.

35. "Summary of Conclusions and Recommendations," in Rostow and Bulger eds., *supra* note 21, at 2.

36. *Id.*

37. *Id.*

38. *See* Rostow and Bulger eds., *supra* note 21, at 212–15, appendix D: State and National Liability Surveys Summarized.

39. *Id.*

40. *Supra* note 35, at 1.

41. *Id.* at 2.

42. *See Report*, *supra* note 18.

43. F. Bailey, *The Tactical Uses of Passion* 132 (1983).

44. *Supra* note 35, at 3.

45. *Supra* note 30.

46. Lewis-Idema, "Medical Professional Liability and Access to Obstetrical Care: Is There a Crisis?" in Rostow and Bulger eds., *supra* note 21, vol. 2, at 86: figure 1, Changes in number of rural physicians practicing obstetrics.

47. The data used to generate this graph were drawn from member surveys conducted by physician organizations; *id.* at 85.

48. Three such alternatives were viewed favorably by the committee: a no-fault administrative process, a fault-based administrative process (the AMA's plan), and Professor Richard Epstein's private contract

scheme; "The Legal System: The Committee's Findings and Proposals for Changes," in Rostow and Bulger eds., *supra* note 21, vol. 2, at 132–41.

49. *E.g.*, Budetti, "Malpractice and Access to Care," 36 *St. Louis U. L.J.* 879 (1992); Saks, "Do We Really Know Anything about the Behavior of the Tort Litigation System—And Why Not?" 140 *U. Pa. L. Rev.* 1993 (1992); "Malpractice Misconceptions and Other Lessons about the Litigation System," 16 *Just. Sys. J.* 7 (1993); Vidmar, *supra* note 1.

50. P. Weiler et al., *A Measure of Malpractice: Medical Injury, Malpractice Litigation, and Patient Compensation* 140–41 (1993).

51. *Id.* at 13.

52. *Id.*

53. Thomas, *supra* note 2, at 465.

54. *Id.*

55. *See* Vidmar, *supra* note 1.

56. K. DeVille, *Medical Malpractice in Nineteenth Century America* 25 (1990).

57. Law and Polan, *supra* note 22, at 97.

58. Bovbjerg, "Legislation on Medical Malpractice: Further Developments and a Preliminary Report Card," 22 *U.C. Davis L. Rev.* 449, 504 (1989).

59. *Id.* at 506.

60. *Id.* at 506–7.

61. *Id.* at 507.

62. *Id.* at 507.

63. *Id.* at 514–19.

64. *Id.* at 519–21.

65. *Id.* at 522.

66. *Id.*

67. *Id.* at 523, n. 103.

68. *Id.* at 523–24.

69. *Id.* at 525.

70. *Id.*

71. *Id.*

72. *Id.*

73. *Id.* at 525–27.

74. *Id.* at 531.

75. *See* "Legal System," *supra* note 48, at 128–29, table 7.1.

76. A 1985 study by Frank Sloan is an exception in that it focused on physicians' malpractice insurance premiums rather than claims. His analysis found no indication that civil justice–related reforms affected premiums

for any of the three types of physicians he looked at: general practitioners, ophthalmologists, and orthopedic surgeons. Sloan, "State Response to the Malpractice Insurance 'Crisis' of the 1970s: An Empirical Assessment," 9 *J. Health Politics, Policy, and Law* 629 (1985).

77. P. Danzon, *The Resolution of Medical Malpractice Claims* (1982); *Medical Malpractice: Theory, Evidence, and Public Policy* (1985) [hereinafter cited as Danzon, *Medical Malpractice*]; "The Frequency and Severity of Medical Malpractice Claims: New Evidence," 49 *Law & Contemp. Probs.* 57 (1986) [hereinafter cited as Danzon, *New Evidence*].

78. P. Danzon, *Medical Malpractice*, *supra* note 77.

79. *Id.* at 52.

80. Danzon, *New Evidence*, *supra* note 77.

81. *Id.* at 71–72.

82. *Id.* at 76–77.

83. *Id.* at 78.

84. P. Danzon, *Medical Malpractice*, *supra* note 77, at 68–79; *New Evidence*, *supra* note 7, at 69, 70, 78–79.

85. Sloan et al., "Effects of Tort Reforms on the Value of Closed Medical Malpractice Claims: A Microanalysis," 14 *J. Health Pol., Pol'y and L.* 663, 668 (1989).

86. *Id.*

87. *Id.* at 675–76, table 2.

88. *Id.*

89. *Id.* Seven reforms evidenced a significant relationship to the number of months from injury to filing. Three of the reforms were related to shorter time spans between injury and claim filing: mandatory pretrial screening, caps on noneconomic damages, and collateral source offsets. Changes in the statute of limitations, restrictions on the *ad damnum* clause in pleadings, tighter requirements for expert witnesses, and the existence of joint underwriting pools were significantly related to a longer time between injury and filing.

Finally, 15 reforms produced significant relationships to the number of years between a claim's filing and its closing. Twelve were related to fewer years between filing and closing: mandatory screening, admissibility at trial of screening results, arbitration provisions, limits on the use of the *res ipsa loquitur* doctrine, restrictions on the *ad damnum* clause, limits on contingency fees, cost shifting, caps on noneconomic damages, caps on total damages, provisions making the periodic payment of awards mandatory, provisions allowing for the discretionary use of periodic payments, and the existence of joint underwriting pools. Three reforms were significantly related to longer times between filing and closing: the existence of a patients' compensation fund to pay for the largest awards, mandatory collateral source offsets, and discretionary collateral sources offsets.

90. *Id.* at 684–87, appendix 1. Longer times from injury to filing were found in those claims involving younger claimants, especially those under one year of age. Claims arising from events occurring in a nursing home were related to shorter times from injury to filing while those occurring in a doctor's office were aligned with longer times. Misdiagnosis claims, surgery claims, and monitoring claims were tied to longer times to filing, while anesthesia claims were related to shorter filing times. More serious injury were also associated with longer filing times. Misdiagnosis, ob/gyn, surgery, anesthesia, drug, and blood-related claims all were significantly related to longer times from filing to closing and to higher payments plus costs. More serious injuries were significantly related to longer closing times, while less serious injuries were associated with shorter times.

91. *See*, "Legal System," *supra* note 48, at 126–31; P. Weiler, *Medical Malpractice on Trial* 32–38 (1991).

92. *See* Vidmar, *supra* note 1.

93. As Neil Vidmar has remarked in this regard: "Propagandists have no interest in methodological confounds when the statistics appear consistent with their goals." Vidmar, *supra* note 1, at 266.

94. Kapp, "Solving the Medical Malpractice Problem: Difficulties in Defining What 'Works,'" 17 *Law, Medicine and Health Care* 156 (1989).

95. *Id.*

96. Sloan, *supra* note 76.

97. *See* Abel, "The Real Tort Crisis—Too *Few* Claims," 48 *Ohio St. L.J.* 443 (1987); "The Crisis Is Injuries, Not Liability," in "New Directions in Liability Law," 37 *Proceedings of the Academy of Political Science* (W. Olson ed., 1988).

98. *See* P. Weiler et al., *supra* note 50, at 141–42.

99. Sloan et al., *supra* note 85, at 674.

100. P. Danzon, *New Evidence*, *supra* note 77, at 77.

101. P. Danzon, *Medical Malpractice*, *supra* note 77, at 75.

102. Sloan et al., *supra* note 85, at 678.

103. *Id.* at 684–89, appendix 1.

104. Julian et al., "Investigation of Obstetric Malpractice Closed Claims: Profile of Event," 2 *Am. J. Perinatology* 320 (1985).

105. *Id.* at 323.

106. Kinney et al., "Indiana's Medical Malpractice Act: Results of a Three-Year Study," 24 *Ind. L. Rev.* 1275, 1278 (1991).

107. *Id.* at 1279.

108. *Id.* at 1297.

109. Gronfein and Kinney, "Controlling Large Malpractice Claims: The Unexpected Impact of Damage Caps," 16 *J. Health Pol., Pol'y and L.* 441, 444 (1991).

110. *Id.* at 458.

111. *Id.* at 446.

112. *Id.* at 458.

113. *Id.* at 448.

114. *Id.* at 450.

115. Kinney et al., *supra* note 106, at 1302–3.

116. *Id.*

117. *Id.* at 1296.

118. *Id.* at 1305.

119. *See* chapter 1 at 21; M. Feeley, *Court Reform on Trial: Why Simple Solutions Fail* at xii (1983).

120. *E.g.*, C. Inlander et al., *Medicine on Trial: The Appalling Story of Medical Ineptitude and the Arrogance That Overlooks It* (1988).

121. *E.g.*, H. Wachsman, *Lethal Medicine: The Epidemic of Medical Malpractice in America* (1993).

122. For instance, the forward of the People's Medical Society book, *Medicine on Trial* (*supra* note 120, at 11) begins with the following: "I warn you. What you will read is not very reassuring. This book presents a grave indictment of American medicine. It is a catalog of ineptitude, malfeasance, gross neglect, indifference, and incredible arrogance. . . . We have culled from this research [medical and public health research] the bits and pieces of an ugly story to present for the first time a complete picture of this American tragedy. . . . Critical comments by experts in medicine, epidemiology, and public health have been added to help communicate how serious the situation is. 'Serious' is too tame a word. We could with justification call this a conspiracy against the public. One has to wonder why the facts presented in this book have not heretofore been put on public view."

123. P. Danzon, *Medical Malpractice*, *supra* note 77, at 20.

132124. The estimate is probably low, Danzon said, because of the California study's design. It did not include injuries occurring outside of hospitals. In addition, some injuries may not have been recorded in the hospital charts, the study's data source. Finally, certain injuries were specifically excluded from the study, "such as non-indicated treatments that did not result in adverse outcomes; unauthorized treatments; and injuries resulting in emotional damage only or disability that did not prolong hospitalization and probably would not cause continuing disability following discharge." (*Id.* at 20.)

125. Weiler et al., *supra* note 50, at 43.

126. *Id.* at 43–44.

127. *Id.* at 44.

128. *Id.* at 44.

129. *Id.* at 55.

130. *See* M. Paget, *The Unity of Mistakes* 20–27 (1988); *see also* Fox, "The Evolution of Medical Uncertainty," 58 *Milbank Memorial Fund Q.* 1 (1980).

131. *See* A. Strauss et al., *Social Organization of Medical Work* (1985); C. Bosk, *Forgive and Remember: Managing Medical Failure* (1979).

132. Daniels, "The Pragmatic Management of Error and the Antecedents of Disputes over the Quality of Medical Care," in *Quality and Regulation in Health Care* 138 (R. Dingwall and P. Fenn eds., 1992).

133. *See* Bosk, *supra* note 131.

134. *See* Daniels, *supra* note 132.

135. *See* R. Schulz and A. Johnson, *Management of Hospitals* (2d ed. 1983).

136. Strauss et al., *supra* note 131, at 19–20.

137. *Id.*

138. P. Danzon, *Medical Malpractice*, *supra* note 77, at 24.

139. Weiler et al., *supra* note 50, at 70.

140. *Id.* at 69–73.

141. *Id.* at 73.

142. *Id.* at 140–41.

143. Abel, *supra* note 97.

144. *See* May and DeMarco, "Patients and Doctors Disputing: Patients' Complaints and What They Do about Them," Dispute Processing Research Program Working Paper, Institute for Legal Studies, University of Wisconsin–Madison (1986).

145. Meyers, " 'Lumping It:' The Hidden Denominator of the Medical Malpractice Crisis," 77 *Am. J. Pub. Health* 1544 (1987).

146. *See* Felstiner et al., "The Emergence and Transformation of Disputes: Naming, Blaming and Claiming," 15 *Law & Soc'y Rev.* 631 (1980–81).

147. Meyers, *supra* note 145, at 1546.

148. *Id.*

149. *Id.* at 1547.

150. *Id.*

151. Hickson et al., "Factors That Prompted Families to File Medical Malpractice Claims following Perinatal Injuries," 267 *JAMA* 1359 (1992).

152. *Id.* at 1362.

153. *Id.*

154. *Id.* at 1361.

155. *Id.*

156. Grossman et al., "An Empirical Analysis of Closed Medical Malpractice Insurance Claims: The Wisconsin Health Care Liability Insurance Plan, 1976–1988," American Bar Foundation Working Paper Series 9209, at 29–30.

157. Taragin et al., "The Influence of Standard of Care and Severity of Injury on the Resolution of Medical Malpractice Claims," 117 *Annals Internal Med.* 780, 781 (1992).

158. Hatch, "Medical Malpractice Study: Minnesota," 20(2) *Trial Law. Q.* 10 (1989). At the time the study was done, Hatch was Minnesota's Commissioner of the Commerce Department.

159. *Medical Malpractice Statistical Report*, Texas State Board of Medical Examiners, Austin, Tex., 1982 through 1988.

160. Hatch, *supra* note 158, at 12.

161. *Medical Malpractice in Missouri, 1986–1988*, at 91, Missouri Division of Insurance, Statistical Section, Jefferson City, Mo. (1989).

162. Taragin et al., *supra* note 157, at 780.

163. M. P. Souka ed., *Malpractice Claims: Final Compilation*, National Association of Insurance Commissioners, Brookfield, Wisconsin [hereinafter NAIC] (1980).

164. Kinney et al., *supra* note 106, at 1287.

165. *Id.*

166. *Medical Malpractice: Case Study on Indiana 7*, United States General Accounting Office, GAO/HRD–87–215–4 (1986).

167. Grossman et al., *supra* note 156.

168. 38% of market; Grossman et al., *supra* note 156, at 7.

169. *Id.* at 9–10.

170. *See* the above discussion of Taragin et al., *supra* note 157.

171. Taragin et al., *supra* note 157.

172. *Id.* at 782.

173. *Id.* at 780–81.

174. *Id.* at 781.

175. *Id.* at 782.

176. *Id.*

177. *Id.*

178. *Id.*

179. Weiler et al., *supra* note 50, at 75. Weiler et al. argued that even though many claims may not involve negligence, "the legal system appears to do a surprisingly, accurate job of sifting out the valid from the invalid claims."

180. Grossman et al., *supra* note 156, at table 2a and table 7, adjusted to 1990 from 1988 dollars.

181. *Id.* at table 2a, adjusted to 1990 dollars.

182. Kinney et al., *supra* note 106, at 1287.

183. *E.g.*, *Medical Malpractice: Six State Case Studies Show Claims and Insurance Costs Still Rise despite Reforms*, United States General Accounting Office, GAO/HRD-87-21 (1986); Kinney et al., *supra* note 106; Grossman et al., *supra* note 156; Nye et al., "The Causes of the Medical Malpractice Crisis: An Analysis of Claims Data and Insurance Company Finances," 76 *Geo. L.J.* 1495 (1988); Daniels and Andrews, "The Shadow of the Law: Jury Decisions in Obstetrics and Gynecology Cases," in Rostow and Bulger eds., *supra* note 21 (1989).

184. Grossman et al., *supra* note 156, at Table 4.

185. *Medical Malpractice in Missouri*, *supra* note 161, at 83–91.

186. *Id.*

187. Kinney et al., *supra* note 106, at 1293.

188. The injury categories used in the table are a collapsed version of widely used nine-point scale for injury severity developed by the insurance (*see* NAIC, *supra* note 163, at 10). The full nine-point scale can be found in appendix 4.1 of this chapter.

189. Grossman et al. reported payments in 1988 dollars, and we report them unchanged for this table.

190. Grossman et al., *supra* note 156, at 23.

191. *Id.*

192. Grossman et al., *supra* note 156, at 23–25.

193. Galanter, "Jury Shadows: Reflections on the Civil Jury and the Litigation Explosion," at 19, paper presented at the Warren Conference, Boston, Mass. (1986).

194. Galanter, "Justice in Many Rooms," 19 *J. Legal Pluralism* 1, 6 (1981).

195. *See* Daniels, "Tracing the Shadow of the Law: Jury Verdicts in Medical Malpractice Cases," 14 *Just. Sys. J.* 4, 13 (1990).

196. *Id.* at 17.

197. NAIC, *supra* note 163, at 306.

198. Grossman et al., *supra* note 156, at 17.

199. NAIC, *supra* note 163, at 306.

200. *Id.*

201. *See* Kravitz et al., "Malpractice Claims Data as a Quality Improvement Tool: Epidemiology of Error in Four Specialties," 266 *JAMA* 2087 (1991).

202. *See* MacCoun, "Inside the Black Box: What Empirical Research Tells Us about Decisionmaking by Civil Juries," at 150 in *Verdict: Assessing the Civil Jury System* (R. Litan ed., 1993).

203. *E.g.*, Grossman et al., *supra* note 156; Kinney et al., *supra* note 106; Kravitz et al., *supra* note 201.

204. The hospital or other institutional setting covers situations in which the injury was the result of hospital or custodial care and no indication of a specific ailment or type of treatment was given.

205. *E.g.*, P. Danzon, *Medical Malpractice*, *supra* note 77, at 26–28. Medical management refers to the overall planning and handling of patient care, including cases involving the use and management of medications, failure in nursing management, and failure in physician planning and management. Specific procedure includes diagnostic as well as therapeutic procedures. The diagnostic categories are self-explanatory.

206. *E.g.*, Grossman et al., *supra* note 156, at 18–19; Kinney et al., *supra* note 106, at 1292; Nye et al., *supra* note 183, at 1543.

207. Win rates also varied across the different sites for individual settings. For instance, taking the five highest volume malpractice sites win rates for ob/gyn cases were 58.8% in New York County, 47.6% in Cook, 30.4% in Wayne, 26.9% in Los Angeles, and 16.7% in Harris. Two other New York City sites had win rates over 60%: Bronx, 66.7%, and Queens, 64.3%. One should not assume, however, that similar win rates would be found for other settings in these sites. In Cook, for example, while plaintiffs won 30.4% of ob/gyn cases, they won 71.4% (five of seven) for neurological surgery but none (zero of five) of the plastic surgery cases. Even in New York County there was a variation among settings with plaintiffs winning at a rate of 25.0% in surgery-general and 21.4% in orthopedic. At the same time, Harris showed relative consistency in win rates across surgical settings with no setting except ophthalmology (two of five cases) having a win rate over 25%. The reasons for such variations across sites are likely to be complex and remain unknown at our present state of knowledge; but we assume those reasons are knowable.

208. Looking at internal medicine, win rates in the five largest sites were: Los Angeles, 40.0%; Cook, 32.1%; Harris, 31.8%; New York, 29.6%; and Wayne, 13.6%.

209. Similar evidence of orderly patterns in the malpractice system can be found in epidemiology studies of closed malpractice claims. *See* Julian et al., *supra* note 104; Kravitz et al., *supra* note 201.

210. Kravitz et al., *supra* note 201.

211. In their closed claims study, Kravitz et al., found that the most frequent cause of patient injury was a management problem, and that these claims tended to have more serious injuries and higher payments. *Id.* at 2091.

212. *Id.* at 2087–88.

213. *Id.* at 2091.

214. Los Angeles, 1,290; Cook, 681; San Francisco, 235; San Diego, 231; Alameda, 208; Dallas, 199; Sacramento, 144; and Jackson, 132.

215. Los Angeles, 418 (win rate of 32.4%); Cook, 253 (37.2%); San Francisco, 76 (32.3%); San Diego, 65 (28.1%); Alameda, 59 (28.4%); Dallas, 38 (19.1%); Sacramento, 46 (31.9%); and Jackson, 39 (29.5%).

216. *See* Kelley and Smith, "Torts," 11 *S.Ill. U. L.J.* 1001, 1045–58; Turk and Elward, "Developments in Tort Law," 13 *S. Ill. U. L.J.* 723, 754–64 (1989).

217. *Id.*

218. *See* O'Brien, "Medical Malpractice—$250,000 Cap on Pain and Suffering—California Civil Cook Section 3333.2—Does the Statute Meet Its Constitutional Burden and Legislative Goals?" 8 *Whittier Law Rev.* 601 (1986).

219. Dallas, with its small numbers of winning cases, had a more dramatic pattern, being as low as $18,043 in 1976–80 and as high as $313,719 in 1986–90.

220. *See* Turk and Elward, *supra* note 216.

221. In Cook, the percentage of surgery verdicts from ob/gyn went from 26.3% to 18.0% to 22.0% to 24.8%. In both counties, over one-half of the surgery verdicts in each time period came from three specific settings: ob/gyn, orthopedic surgery, and general surgery. In neither county did orthopedic surgery or general surgery show any directional trend or fluctuate within a range greater than 11 percentage points.

222. There was no consistently upward trend over time in the median award for orthopedic surgery, the second largest surgery setting in Los Angeles. It went from $112,385 to $243,270 to $113,400 to $289,800. In Cook, the number of winning ob/gyn cases was below five in the first three time periods. In 1986–90 there were 30 winning ob/gyn cases with a median award of $229,125.

223. Those seven awards were $892,500, $2,651,250, $9,146,609, $9,183,158, $10,045,129, $11,203,471, $15,475,897.

224. Those nine awards were 1970–75: $9,039, $64,600, $202,800, $290,700, $516,800; 1976–80: $150,000, $222,600, $1,780,000; 1981–85: $55,962, $484,000, $648,000, $1,475,060, $3,780,000; 1986–90: $11,900, $275,000, $460,000, $2,651,250, $9,146,609, $9,183,158, $10,045,129, $11,203,471, $15,475,897.

225. *See* chapter 2 at 31; D. Stone, *Policy Paradox and Political Reason* 107 (1988).

226. Weiler et al., *supra* note 50, at 144–52.

227. *See* Kravitz et al., *supra* note 201.

228. *See* Kinney et al., *supra* note 106; Gronfein and Kinney, *supra* note 109.

229. Vidmar, *supra* note 1, at 243.

230. *Id.* at 255.

231. *Id.* at 248–49.

232. Vidmar and Rice, "Assessments of Noneconomic Damage Awards in Medical Negligence: A Comparison of Jurors with Legal Professionals," 78 *Iowa L. Rev.* 883 (1993).

233. *Id.* at 890.

234. *Id.* at 896.

235. *Id.* at 897.

236. *Id.* at 900.

CHAPTER 5

1. *See* Birnbaum, "Legislative Reform or Retreat? A Response to the Product Liability Crisis," 14 *The Forum* 251, 259–63 (1978).

2. *See* Schwartz, "Federal Action on Product Liability: What Has Occurred and What May Occur," 14 *The Forum* 287 (1978); Report of the Senate Committee on Commerce, Science, and Transportation: Product Liability Fairness Act, S.640 U.S. Senate Report 102–215:12–15 (1991).

3. S.640, 1991.

4. U.S. Senate Report 102–215:12 (1991).

5. Schwartz, *supra* note 2.

6. Tort Policy Working Group, United States Department of Justice, *Report of the Tort Policy Working Group on the Causes, Extent and Policy Implications of the Current Crisis in Insurance Availability and Affordability* [hereinafter *Report*], 45 (1986).

7. *Id.* at 35–36.

8. P. Huber, *Liability: The Legal Revolution and Its Consequences* 221 (1988).

9. *E.g.*, *Report*, *supra* note 6 at 35–36; Malott, "Let's Restore Balance to Product Liability Law," *Harv. Bus. Rev.*, May/June 1983, at 72; Malott, "America's Liability Explosion," 52 *Vital Speeches of the Day* 182 (1986). *See also* discussion of metaphors in chapter 2.

10. Huber, *supra* note 8 at 222; *see also* chapter 2's discussion of stories of decline.

11. Malott, 1986, *supra* note 9, at 182; *see also* chapter 2's discussion of stories of decline and chapter 1's discussion of consequences.

12. Washington Legal Foundation, "The Negative Impact of Product Liability on U.S. Competitiveness: Liability Law Reform Reinforced by New Studies," Critical Legal Issues Working Paper Series No. 43 (1990).

13. Malott, 1986, *supra* note 9 at 180; *see also* chapter 2's discussion of stories of decline.

14. *Report*, *supra* note 6, at 36.

15. Huber, *supra* note 8, at 3–5; *see also* chapter 1's discussion of consequences.

16. *See* J. Rawls, *A Theory of Justice* (1971) and "Justice as Fairness," 57 *Philosophical Rev.* 164 (1958).

17. McCormick, "The American Tort System: A Time to Rebalance the Scales of Justice," 52 *Vital Speeches of the Day* 268 (1986).

18. Malott, 1983, *supra* note 9.

19. McCormick, *supra* note 17.

20. See Daniels, "The Question of Jury Competence and the Politics of Civil Justice Reform: Symbols, Rhetoric, and Agenda-Building," 52 *Law & Contemp. Probs.* 269, 287–92 (1989).

21. *Supra* note 2.

22. Malott, 1983, *supra* note 9, at 67.

23. *Id.* at 67–68.

24. *Id.* at 67.

25. *Id.* at 72.

26. Malott, 1986, *supra* note 9, at 180.

27. *See* Washington Legal Foundation, *supra* note 12, at 18.

28. P. Huber and R. Litan eds., *The Liability Maze: The Impact of Liability Law on Safety and Innovation* 15 (1991).

29. *Id.* at 16.

30. *Id.* at 2–13.

31. *Id.*

32. Hearings before the Subcommittee on the Consumer of the Committee on Commerce, Science, and Transportation, U.S. Senate, S. Hrg. 102–727 (1991) at 164–67. Similar arguments about the consequences of the products liability system can also be found in testimony in 1990 on Senate bill 1400—the Product Liability Reform Act—by Assistant U.S. Attorney General Stuart Gerson before the Senate Committee on the Judiciary. Gerson testified that "the current system serves more to deter innovation, commercial development, domestic production and employment opportunities than it does to promote the manufacture of safer products. . . . To these concerns should be added lost jobs from decreased competitiveness of American products on international markets and stifled innovation" (U.S. Dept. of Justice, Statement of Stuart M. Gerson, July 31, 1990: 3).

33. *See* chapter 1's discussion of consequences and chapter 2's discussions of stories of decline and metaphors.

34. The Vice President's Office, Office of the Press Secretary, press release of August 13, 1991, "Fact Sheet," at 2.

35. Malott, 1986, *supra* note 9, at 182. On the value of high school football as a part of the tactical use of passion, *see* H. G. Bissinger, *Friday Night Lights* [1990] on high school football in Texas. High school football also played a part in the 1986 Insurance Information Institute's major public relations campaign: "We All Pay the Price: An Industry Effort to Reform Civil Justice," *Ins. Rev.* 58 (April 1986) (*see also* Daniels, *supra* note 20, at 283–85).

36. Malott, 1986, *supra* note 9, at 182.

37. McCormick, *supra* note 17, at 269.

38. Mahoney and Littlejohn, "Innovation on Trial: Punitive Damages versus New Products," 246 *Science* 1397 (1989).

39. *Id.*

40. *Id.* at 1395; punitive damages will be the subject of the next chapter.

41. 15 *Eng. Rep.* 402 (1892); R. Epstein, C. Gregory, and H. Kalven, Jr., *Cases and Materials on Torts* 413–17 (4th ed. 1984). Our discussion in this section draws primarily from Epstein et al., 413–35; 637–78.

42. Quoted in Epstein et al., *supra* note 41, at 414.

43. 217 N.Y. 382, 11 N.E. 1050 (N.Y. 1916).

44. 217 N.Y. 382 (N.Y. 1916) at 389.

45. *Id.* at 391.

46. Epstein et al., *supra* note 41, at 425.

47. 32 N.J. 358, 161 A.2d 69 (N.J. 1960).

48. Epstein et al., *supra* note 41, at 650.

49. *Id.*; *see also* Henningsen, *supra* note 47, at 371–73.

50. 24 Cal. 2d 453, 150 P.2d. 436 (Cal. 1944).

51. 24 Cal. 2d 453 (Cal. 1944) at 461, Traynor concurring.

52. *Id.* at 462, Traynor concurring.

53. *Id.*

54. 59 Cal. 2d 57, 27 Cal. Rptr. 697, 377 P.2d 897 (Cal. 1963).

55. 59 Cal. 2d 57 (Cal. 1963) at 63.

56. *Id.*

57. American Law Institute (1965), Restatement (Second) of Torts, Topic 5, Strict Liability, Comment c.

58. Epstein et al., *supra* note 41, at 638.

59. K. Viscusi, *Reforming Products Liability* (1991).

60. Consumer Product Safety Commission Annual Report, 1981, at 1.

61. Consumer Product Safety Commission Annual Report, 1990, at iii.

62. U.S. Department of Labor, *Occupational Injuries and Illnesses in the United States by Industry*, 1990, at 1.

63. *Id.* at table 3.

64. Priest, "Products Liability Law and the Accident Rate," in *Liability: Perspectives and Policy* (R. Litan and C. Winston eds., 1988) at 198–203; Viscusi, *supra* note 59, at 16–20.

65. Viscusi, *supra* note 59, at 19.

66. *Id.* at 19–20.

67. Priest, *supra* note 64, at 203.

68. Abel, "The Real Tort Crisis—Too *Few* Claims," 48 *Ohio St. L.J.* 443 (1987) [hereinafter cited as "The Real Tort Crisis"]; "The Crisis Is Injuries, Not Liability," *New Directions in Liability Law* (W. Olson ed., 1988) [hereinafter cited as "The Crisis Is Injuries"].

69. Abel, "The Crisis Is Injuries," *id.* at 40.

70. Abel, "The Real Tort Crisis," *supra* note 68, at 443–44.

71. Abel, "The Crisis Is Injuries," *supra* note 68, at 37. It is worth noting that Abel raises another issue relevant to the arguments of Priest and Viscusi. It has to do with the integrity of the kinds of governmental data they uncritically rely upon. He said, "Although the National Safety Council estimated that there were 11,600 workplace deaths in 1985, employers reported only 3,750 to the U.S. Bureau of Labor Statistics. Chrysler recently paid over $300,000 in fines to settle charges that it willfully failed to report worker injuries, and the U.S. Department of Labor has filed similar charges against other major corporations including Union Carbide, Monsanto, Shell Oil, Fina, and USX Corporation. The California Supreme Court has allowed employees to sue the Johns-Manville Corporation in tort (rather than claiming workers' compensation, usually the exclusive remedy), because for decades the company concealed health records showing that those workers were suffering from asbestos exposure" (*Id.* at 32).

72. May and DeMarco, "Patients and Doctors Disputing: Patients' Complaints and What They Do about Them," Dispute Processing Research Program Working Paper Series, Institute for Legal Studies, Madison: University of Wisconsin Law School (1986).

73. Meyers, " 'Lumping It': The Hidden Denominator of the Medical Malpractice Crisis," 77 *Am. J. Pub. Health* 1544 (1987).

74. D. Hensler et al. *Compensation for Accidental Injuries in the United States* (1991).

75. *Id.* at 3.

76. *Id.*

77. *Id.* at 23.

78. *Id.* at 110.

79. *Id.*

80. *Id.* at 124, table 5.4.

81. *Id.* at 111.

82. *Id.*

83. *Id.*

84. *Id.* at 142–72.

85. *Id.* at 156

86. *Id.* at 156–57, table 6.5.

87. *Id.*

88. *Id.* at 163, table 6.11.

89. *Id.* at 169–72.

90. Viscusi, *supra* note 59, at 43.

91. Missouri Department of Insurance, Statistical Section, *Missouri Product Liability Insurance Report, 1990* (1991); *Products Liability Insurance-Missouri, 1981–84* (1985).

92. Texas Liability Insurance Closed Claim Annual Report, prepared by the Texas State Board of Insurance, 1988, 1989, 1990.

93. Missouri Department of Insurance, 1990 Report, *supra* note 91, at 2.

94. Viscusi, *supra* note 59, at 48.

95. *Id.* at 58.

96. Missouri Department of Insurance, 1981–84 Report, *supra* note 91 at 3–9.

97. Missouri Department of Insurance, 1988–90.

98. *E.g.*, *Report*, *supra* note 6; Washington Legal Foundation, *supra* note 12; Malott, 1983, *supra* note 9, at 67.

99. *Report*, *supra* note 6.

100. *Product Liability: Extent of "Litigation Explosion" in Federal Courts Questioned*, GAO/HRD 88-36BR (1988) [hereinafter GAO]; T. Dunworth, *Product Liability and the Business Sector: Litigation Trends in Federal Courts*, RAND Institute for Civil Justice (1988).

101. GAO, *id.* at 2; Dunworth, *id.* at vii.

102. GAO, *id.* at 2.

103. Dunworth, *supra* note 100, at vii.

104. *Id.*

105. *Id.*

106. *Id.*

107. *E.g.*, C. Inlander, L. Levin, and E. Weiner, *Medicine on Trial: The Appalling Story of Medical Ineptitude and the Arrogance That Overlooks It* 172–88 (1988).

108. *See* Daniels and Martin, "Don't Kill the Messenger 'till You Read the Message: Products Liability Verdicts in Six California Counties, 1970–1990," 16 *Just. Sys. J.* 69 (1993), Although the logic of our argument regarding settings is similar to Galanter's concept of "case congregations," Galanter, "Case Congregations and Their Careers," 24 *Law & Soc. Rev.* 371 (1990), it is not identical. Our setting-defined subsystems are far smaller than Galanter's "case populations," which he defines as "such immensely large and enduring and ordinary categories of litigation as automobile injury cases" (*Id.* at 372). In fact, our settings exist within what can be considered a case population—products liability. On the other hand, these settings are more persistent and orderly than Galanter's other,

smaller groupings of cases—case congregations—which he sees as fleeting and highly contingent (*Id.*). What Galanter would see as congregations in products liability, those that form around particular products, we think will emerge from and be parts of particular settings that are not fleeting but persistent. They make sense as parts of particular settings because of the other characteristics shared beyond the particular product itself.

109. *See* Viscusi, *supra* note 59.

110. *E.g.,* within SIC 34, Fabricated Structural Metal Products, SIC 344.

111. *E.g.,* within SIC 344, Metal Door/Sash/Trim, SIC 3442.

112. *E.g., American Law Institute Reporter's Study,* 1991:114–20.

113. *E.g.,* Walters, "Workers' Compensation: A New Approach to an Old System," 3 *Cal. Law.* 40 (1983); Erlich, "Workers' Comp. Blues," 12 *Cal. Law.* 38 (1992).

114. Erlich, *id.* at 38–40.

115. *See* Erlich, *id. generally.*

116. *E.g.*, K. Meier, *Regulation: Politics, Bureaucracy, and Economics* 202–31 (1985); Viscusi, *supra* note 59.

117. For instance, Saks notes that the cost of acute care for the first two years for a head injury patient is $435,000 (from a 1990 source) and that lifetime care for a child with a head injury could cost over $4 million (Saks, "Do We Really Know Anything about the Behavior of the Tort Litigation System—And Why Not?" 140 *U. Pa. L. Rev.* 1147, 1266 (n. 449) (1992).

118. Meier, *supra* note 116, at 45–100.

119. Hensler et al., *supra* note 74, at 171, table 6.16; 52% of those claiming stated that a very important factor in their decision was the lack of any other way to pay the expenses.

120. *E.g.,* Meier, *supra* note 116, at 100–106.

121. Hans and Lofquist, "Jurors' Judgments of Business Liability in Tort Cases: Implications for the Litigation Explosion Debate," 26 *Law & Soc. Rev.* 85 (1992).

122. *Id.* at 93.

123. *Id.* at 106.

124. Vidmar, "Empirical Evidence on the Deep Pockets Hypothesis: Jury Awards for Pain and Suffering in Medical Malpractice Cses," 43 *Duke L.J.* 217, 252–55 (1993).

125. Hans and Lofquist, *supra* note 121, at 102–3.

126. Hans, "Robin Hood Myth Challenged," *Nat'l L.J.*, June 6, 1994, § C, at C1, C8.

127. Galanter, *supra* note 108, at 373.

128. *See* figure 4.2a.

129. Major injuries as a percentage of all vehicle setting cases including those alleging only property damage: 39.2%, 44.4%, 40.7%, and 65.0%; major injuries as a percentage of just personal injury vehicle cases: 40.8%, 45.7%, 45.8%, and 68.4%.

130. *E.g.*, Bovbjerg et al., "Juries and Justice: Are Malpractice and Other Personal Injuries Created Equal?" 54 *Law & Contemp. Probs.* 5, 37–39 (1991).

131. Gross and Syverud, "Getting to No: A Study of Settlement Negotiations and the Selection of Cases for Trial," 90 *Mich. L. Rev.* 319, 348–52 (1991); Daniels et al., "Why Kill All the Lawyers? Repeat Players in Medical Malpractice Claims," American Bar Foundation Working Paper 9210, 27–41 (1992).

132. The pattern of increasing asbestos cases can also be found in Alameda County adjacent to San Francisco. In the first two time periods, there were no reported asbestos verdicts in Alameda. In 1981–85 there were five (29.4% of work setting verdicts, 14.8% of all products verdicts), and in 1986–90 there were 21 (78.0% of work cases and 58.3% of all verdicts).

133. Galanter, *supra* note 108, at 373.

134. K. Viscusi, *Risk by Choice: Regulating Health and Safety in the Workplace* 3 (1983).

135. OSHA Act, § 26.

136. Viscusi, *supra* note 134, at 11.

137. *Id.* at 23.

138. *Id.*

139. Viscusi, *Fatal Tradeoffs* 181 (1992).

140. *Id.* at 188–89.

141. Viscusi, "Occupational Accidents and Illnesses," in *Liability: Perspectives and Policy*, in R. Litan and C. Winston eds., *supra* note 64, at 163.

142. *Id.* at 163–64.

143. Presidential Task Force, *OSHA Safety Regulation* 13–14 (1977).

144. D. Lofgren, *Dangerous Premises: An Insider's View of OSHA Enforcement* 213 (1989).

145. G. Eads and M. Fix, *Relief or Reform: Reagan's Regulatory Dilemma* 197 (1984).

146. *Id.* at 196.

147. *See generally* J. Rees, *Reforming the Workplace: A Study of Self Regulation in Occupational Safety* (1988).

148. L. Darling-Hammond and T. Kniesner, *The Law and Economics of Workers' Compensation* 4 (1980).

149. Viscusi, *supra* note 59, at 179.

150. Victor, "Major Challengers Facing Workers' Compensation Systems in the 1990s," in *Challenges for the 1990s* (R. Victor ed., 1990).

151. ALI-Weiler, *Enterprise Responsibility for Personal Injury: Reporter's Study*, 106–7 (1991).

152. *Id.* at 110–11.

153. *Id.* at 113.

154. *Id.* at 111.

155. Viscusi, *supra* note 59, at 182–83.

156. *Id.* at 183.

157. *Id.*

158. ALI-Weiler, *supra* note 151, at 115.

159. *See* Walters, Erlich, *supra* note 113.

160. ALI-Weiler, *supra* note 151, at 116.

161. *Id.* at 116–17.

162. *Id.* at 117.

163. Viscusi, *supra* note 59, at 186.

164. *E.g.*, vehicle setting: J. Mashaw and D. Harfst, *Regulating the Automobile* (1986); Graham, "Product Liability and Motor Vehicle Safety," in *The Liability Maze: The Impact of Liability Law on Safety and Innovation* (P. Huber and R. Litan eds., 1991), relating to the National Highway Traffic Safety Administration; home setting: Viscusi, "Consumer Behavior and the Safety Effects of Product Safety Regulation," 28 *J. L. & Econ.* 527 (1985); K. Meier, *supra* note 116, at 100–106, relating to the Consumer Product Safety Commission.

CHAPTER 6

1. Much of discussion in this chapter drawn from Daniels and Martin, "Myth and Reality in Punitive Damages," 75 *Minn. L. Rev.* 1 (1990)

2. *Fay v. Parker*, 53 N.H. 342, 382 (1873).

3. This debate includes an often cited article that argued that punitive damages are an unjust absurdity and that "[t]he doctrine is an anachronism and should be abolished." Duffy, "Punitive Damages: A Doctrine Which Should Be Abolished," in Defense Research Institute, Inc., *The Case against Punitive Damages* 8 (1969). *But see* Harris, "Rereading Punitive Damages: Beyond the Public/Private Distinction," 40 *Ala. L. Rev.* 1079, 1082–83 (1989) (arguing that traditional criticisms of punitive damages are no longer valid).

4. *E.g.*, Mahoney and Littlejohn, "Innovation on Trial: Punitive Damages versus New Products," 246 *Science* 1395-96 (1989); P. Huber, *Liability: The Legal Revolution and Its Consequences* 3–10 (1988).

5. *See* Johnston, "Punitive Liability: A New Paradigm of Efficiency in Tort Law," 87 *Colum. L. Rev.* 1385, 1388 (1987). Johnston notes that "Virtually no aspect of current tort doctrine has been immune to

criticism and legislative reform. However, attention has been focused on spectacular punitive damages cases. Despite empirical evidence suggesting that any increase in the size or frequency of punitive damages has been limited to a few geographical areas, large punitive damages awards have come to symbolize the problems perceived in the current system. Many recently enacted tort reform measures severely limit punitive damages." *Id.* at 1387–88 (footnotes omitted). According to Robert Prentice, "The attack on punitive damages is part of a wide-ranging, well-organized attack on the current tort law system. Claims of a 'litigation explosion' and an 'insurance crisis' have supported a nationwide tort reform movement. No doubt there is some substance to these claims, though the reports of a litigation explosion, like Mark Twain's death, have been greatly exaggerated and the insurance crisis is, at least in part, an invention of the insurance industry. There is also substantial evidence that the claims of runaway punitive damages are greatly exaggerated." Prentice, "Reforming Punitive Damages: The Judicial Bargaining Concept," 7 *Rev. Litig.* 113, 123 (1988). *See also* Hayden, "The Cultural Logic of a Political Crisis: Common Sense, Hegemony and the Great American Liability Insurance Famine of 1986," at 2–3 (Institute for Legal Studies Working Paper Series No. 9, 1989) (arguing that the tort reform movement was an attempt to divert political attention from the crisis caused by insurance companies) [hereinafter Hayden, "Cultural Logic"]; Daniels, "The Question of Jury Competence and the Politics of Civil Justice Reform: Symbols, Rhetoric and Agenda-Building," 52 *Law & Contemp. Probs.* 269, 269–73 (1989) (arguing that the criticism of juries is part of a comprehensive attack on the civil justice system as a whole); Hayden, "Neocontract Polemics and Unconscionable Scholarship," 23 *Law & Soc'y Rev.* 863, 863–64 [1989] [reviewing P. Huber, *Liability: The Legal Revolution and Its Consequences* [1988] [arguing that the book fails to support the position that there is in fact a liability crisis]).

6. For instance, the amicus brief prepared by a number of major tort reform groups in *Pacific Mut. Life Ins. Co. v. Haslip*, 499 U.S. 1 (1991), claims that: "Punitive damages are today awarded with a frequency and in amounts that are startling. . . . And these awards may be enormous: punitive verdicts exceeding $1 million, while certainly not the norm, have become almost commonplace. . . . This system of punitive damages—where punitive awards are routine and fantastic verdicts receive little attention—is entirely a product of the last 20 years." Brief of the American Institute of Architects, the American Tort Reform Association, the Council of Community Blood Centers, General Electric Company, the Minnesota Civil Justice Coalition, the National School Boards Association and the Texas Civil Justice League as Amici Curiae in Support of Petitioner at 4, *Pacific Mut. Life Inc. Co. v. Haslip* [hereinafter Brief of the American Institute of Architects]. For an extended discussion of the politics of tort reform, see Daniels, *supra* note 5.

7. The American Tort Reform Association recently noted that 27 states had passed some form of legislation affecting punitive damages in the 1986–89 period. American Tort Reform Association, "Legislative

Reform in the Punitive Damages Area (1986–1989)," *Punitive Damages Update*, at 1–3 (Nov. 9, 1989) [hereinafter "Legislative Reform"] (Punitive Damages Update, 2201 Wisconsin Ave., NW, Suite 240, Washington, D.C. 20007).

8. *Browning-Ferris Industries v. Kelco Disposal*, 492 U.S. 257 (1989); *Pacific Mutual Life Insurance Co. v. Haslip*, 499 U.S. 1 (1991); *TXO Production Corporation v. Alliance Resources Corporation*, 125 L. Ed. 2d 366 (1993); *Honda Motor Co. v. Oberg*, 129 L. Ed. 2d 336 (1994).

9. 98 *Eng. Rep.* 489 (K.B. 1763).

10. 95 *Eng. Rep.* 768 (K.B. 1763).

11. *See Wilkes*, 98 *Eng. Rep.* at 498–99; *Huckle*, 95 *Eng. Rep.* at 769.

12. 1 N.J.L. 90 (Sup. Ct. 1791).

13. *Id.* at 91 (emphasis in original).

14. *Id.*

15. Ellis, "Fairness and Efficiency in the Law of Punitive Damages," 56 *S. Cal. L. Rev.* 1, 3 (1982).

16. *E.g.*, Ellis, "Punitive Damages, Due Process, and the Jury," 40 *Ala. L. Rev.* 975, 991–99 (1989). *See also* Peters, "Punitive Damages in Oregon," 18 *Willamette L. Rev.* 369, 406–11 (1982) (arguing for the abolition of punitive damages except as specifically provided by statute to "promote clarity of the law and fairness in its administration"); Brief of Association for California Tort Reform as Amici Curiae in support of Petitioner at 2–3, *Pacific Mut. Life Ins. Co. v. Haslip* (arguing that unlimited punitive damages are per se a violation of due process).

17. Ellis, *supra* note 16, at 991–99; Peters, *supra* note 16, at 407.

18. Ellis, *supra* note 16, at 996–99.

19. Peters, *supra* note 16, at 420–23.

20. Sales and Coles, "Punitive Damages: A Relic That Has Outlined Its Origins," 37 *Vand. L. Rev.* 1117, 1158–64 (1984).

21. *Id.* at 1165.

22. *Id.* at 1159–64.

23. *Id.* at 1168–69.

24. *Id.* at 1154–58.

25. Mallor and Roberts, "Punitive Damages: Toward a Principled Approach," 31 *Hastings L.J.* 639, 644–47 (1980).

26. According to the American Tort Reform Association, 18 states had adopted the "clear and convincing" standard between 1986 and 1988. "Legislative Reform," *supra* note 7, at 2.

27. Johnston, *supra* note 5, at 1403–4.

28. *Id.* at 1406.

29. Galanter and Luban, "Poetic Justice: Punitive Damages and Legal Pluralism," 42 *Am. U. L. Rev.* 1393 (1993).

30. *Id.* at 1428.

31. *Id.* at 1440.

32. *Id.* at 1440–41.

33. *Id.* at 1442.

34. Hampton, "The Retributive Idea," in *Forgiveness and Mercy* (J. Hampton and J. Murphy eds., 1988).

35. Galanter and Luban, *supra* note 29, at 1432.

36. *Id.* at 1432.

37. *Id.* at 1433.

38. The Pellerin Group Public Relations, Inc., 2201 Wisconsin Avenue, NW, Suite 240, Washington, D.C. 20007.

39. American Tort Reform Association, *Punitive Damages Update*, Cover Letter at 1 (April 12, 1989) [hereinafter Cover Letter]. Other mailings have included a November 6, 1989, missive presenting an American Tort Reform Association (ATRA) report on legislative changes in the punitive damages area along with a reprint of Goldberg, "Punitives in Peril," *A.B.A. J.*, October 1989, at 46. *See* "Legislative Reform," *supra* note 7, at 4. The article was touted as featuring comments from ATRA's president and other tort reform experts. Another mailing announced that the United States Supreme Court had granted a stay of a state court judgment in an Alabama punitive damages case pending a timely filing of a writ of certiorari. American Tort Reform Association, Punitive Damages Update, Supreme Court Grants Stay in Alabama Punitive Case (Nov. 7, 1989). The case involves fraud, and the Employment Retirement Income Security Act, an award of $2,412 in compensatory damages, and an award of $1,797,588 in punitive damages. *HealthAmerica v. Menton*, 551 So. 2d 235 (Ala.), *cert. denied*, 110 S. Ct. 1166 (1989). Other mailings by ATRA include *Punitive Damages Update*, "Ten Punitive Damages Petitions for Certiorari before United States Supreme Court" (Oct. 12, 1989) (summary of the issues involving punitive damages awaiting the Supreme Court as it began the 1989 term); *Punitive Damages Update*, "Five Punitive Damages Petitions for Certiorari Pending before United States Supreme Court" (Jan. 29, 1990); *Punitive Damages Update*, "Pennsylvania Bar Association Recommends Reform of State Punitive Damages Law" (Aug. 16, 1990) (explaining that a package of 22 recommendations for reforming the Pennsylvania tort system was adopted by the Commonwealth's bar association); *Punitive Damages Update*, "California Punitive Damages Awards Increase 266 Percent Since 1987" (Dec. 28, 1989) [hereinafter "California Punitive Damages" (reporting on a study by the Association for California Tort Reform on the increase in the size of punitive damage awards); *Punitive Damages Update*, "Legal Uncertainty Forces Beneficial Products off the Market" (Dec. 15, 1989) [hereinafter "Legal Uncertainty"] (touting Mahoney and Littlejohn, *supra* note 4); *Punitive Damages Update*, "Legal Expert Calls for Curbing Abuses of Punitive Damages Awards" (July 31, 1989) (presenting the highlights of Peter Huber's speech before the National Governor's Association annual meeting in Chicago).

40. Cover Letter, *id.* The first three paragraphs of the cover letter read:

Dear Editor/Correspondent:

On April 18 the U.S. Supreme Court will hear oral arguments on *Browning-Ferris Industries, Inc. v. Kelco Disposal, Inc.* The Court will review a Vermont jury's award of $51,000 in compensatory damages and $6 million in punitive damages.

For the first time the Court will directly examine the question of whether disproportionately large punitive damage awards are in violation of the Excessive Fines clause of the 8th Amendment to the Constitution.

Because you might be considering coverage of the oral arguments and/or the decision expected later this year, we have put together a number of background materials for your unrestricted use. These materials include:

- An overview of the case;
- An overview of punitive damages in general;
- A list of qualified experts who have agreed tointerviews on the case;
- A press release on the case from the Lawyers for Civil Justice;
- Relevant studies on punitive damages;
- Quotations from Supreme Court Justices on the issue;
- An article on a recent ruling by a New Jersey judge on mass tort cases;
- A list of states enacting punitive damage legislation since 1986;
- A press release on testimony in Minnesota on punitive damages;
- A press release on punitive damages legislation that passed in Utah; and
- Relevant news clippings.

Id.

41. 492 U.S. 257 (1989).

42. Cover Letter, *supra* note 39, at 6.

43. *Id.* at 4.

44. *Id. See also* Mahoney, "Consumers, Competitiveness Suffer from Excess in Punitive Damages," *Financier*, January 1989, at 23 (arguing that U.S. advantage in aircraft production is eroding) [hereinafter Mahoney, "Consumers, Competitiveness"]; Mahoney, "Punitive Damages: The Courts Are Curbing Creativity," *N.Y. Times*, December 11, 1988, § 3, at 3 [hereinafter Mahoney, "Punitive Damages"] (arguing punitive damages affect United States' international competitiveness).

45. Mahoney, "Consumers, Competitiveness," *id.*; Mahoney, "Punitive Damages," *id.*

46. Mahoney and Littlejohn, *supra* note 4, at 1395.

47. "Legal Uncertainty," *supra* note 39, at 1.

48. Mahoney, "Punitive Damages," *supra* note 44 (general readership); Mahoney, "Consumers, Competitiveness," *supra* note 44 (business and financial audience); Mahoney and Littlejohn, *supra* note 4 (intellectual and scientific audience).

49. Mahoney and Littlejohn, *supra* note 4, at 1397; Mahoney, "Consumers, Competitiveness," *supra* note 44, at 22; Mahoney, "Punitive Damages," *supra* note 44, at 3.

50. Mahoney and Littlejohn, *supra* note 4, at 1395.

51. *Id.*

52. Mahoney, "Punitive Damages," *supra* note 44, at 3. Nearly the same words occur in Mahoney and Littlejohn, *supra* note 4, at 1396, and in Mahoney, "Consumers, Competitiveness," *supra* note 44, at 21.

53. Mahoney, "Consumers, Competitiveness," *supra* note 44, at 21. One finds Dorsey Ellis making the same claim in a recent symposium article on punitive damages. Ellis, *supra* note 16, at 988–1003. In a burst of excess and invective, Ellis says: "Jury bias in favor of an injured plaintiff and against the defendant is a major concern for the defendant against whom punitive damages are sought. This is especially true for institutional defendants. Profit-making entities, such as insurance companies, banking institutions, and manufacturing corporations, do not rank high in the public's esteem, even when a cross-section of the community is systematically surveyed. And, regardless of our aspirations, juries do not reflect a cross-section of the community. Noticeably absent from most panels are those who are most likely to understand the functions of profits in an enterprise economy—managers and professionals. Hence, the antagonism toward large, profit-making institutions is likely to be greater in a cross-section of jurors than in a cross-section of the community. There is good reason to believe, moreover, that this bias will manifest itself in the jury's decision on the defendant's liability for punitive damages. . . ." *Id.* at 996–97. Such sloppy reasoning and shallow analysis could be simply dismissed out of hand if it were not written by a major legal scholar in this area.

54. Mahoney and Littlejohn, *supra* note 4, at 1396; Mahoney, "Consumers, Competitiveness," *supra* note 44, at 20.

55. Mahoney, *Punitive Damages*, *supra* note 44, at 3. The same stories appeared in Mahoney, "Consumers, Competitiveness," *supra* note 44, at 20. There is, however, reason to be quite skeptical of Mahoney's protestations of innocence—at least in terms of the Minnesota Copper-7 judgment he rails against. It was a trial in which numerous internal Searle documents were introduced into evidence. These materials showed that the company had been aware of problems with the Copper–7 for many years (problems with a higher incidence of pelvic infections that can lead to sterility in a clearly identifiable group of women) and that management ultimately decided not to make changes in the product for the American market. *See* Mintz, "The Selling of an IUD: Behind the Scenes at G. D. Searle during the Rise and Fall of the Copper-7," *Washington Post*, August 9,

1988, Health Section, at 12, col. 1. In fact, the company's public posture was to deny any link between the Copper-7 and pelvic infections despite evidence to the contrary. *Id.* These Searle documents also raised questions about the quality of the company's own research involving the testing of the device with regard to pelvic infections. *See* "Judge Denies Searle Bid for New IUD Liability Trial," *Chicago Tribune*, February 17, 1989, § C, at 3; "Claimant in Searle IUD Liability Case Seeks $15 Million in Punitive Damages," *Wall St. J.*, August 26, 1988, at 9, col. 1; Mintz, *supra*, at 12, col. 1; "Contraceptive Trial Opens with Charges Monsanto Knew of Copper-7 Defects," *Wall St. J.*, May 18, 1988, at 6, col. 2; "Records Raise Question: Did Monsanto Know of IUD Problem in Buying Searle?" *Wall St. J.*, March 15, 1988, at 9, col. 2; *see also Kociemba v. G. D. Searle & Co.*, 707 F. Supp. 1517, 1526 (D. Minn. 1989) (denying G. D. Searle's motion for a new trial because the jury could have concluded reasonably that Searle intentionally misrepresented the safety of the Copper-7).

56. Mahoney and Littlejohn, *supra* note 4, at 1397.

57. *Id.* A "study" conducted by the Association for California Tort Reform "informs" us that the average punitive damage award in California rose from $1.69 million in 1987 to $3.01 million in 1989. "California Punitive Damages," *supra* note 39, at 1.

58. Mahoney and Littlejohn, *supra* note 4, at 1397.

59. *Id.*; Mahoney, "Consumers, Competitiveness," *supra* note 44, at 22.

60. Mahoney, "Consumers, Competitiveness," *supra* note 44, at 22; Mahoney and Littlejohn, *supra* note 4, at 1397.

61. Mahoney and Littlejohn, *supra* note 4, at 1397.

62. The parade of horrors continues with an antinausea morning sickness drug being withdrawn from the market even though it was "widely used by health care professionals and approved by FDA." *Id.* Medical equipment is also at risk. Union Carbide halted development of a suitcase-sized kidney dialysis machine because of the threat of punitive damages. *Id.* This company also stopped offering intravenous equipment. *Id.* Moreover, the only U.S. manufacturer of gas anesthesia machines withdrew from the market, leaving the market to two foreign companies. *Id.* The alleged explosion in punitive damage awards has also affected foreign suppliers. For instance, "the Japanese maker of a vaccine for Japanese encephalitis withdrew the product from the U.S. market . . . because of liability concerns, leaving American travelers to Asia unprotected." *Id.*

63. Mahoney, "Consumers, Competitiveness," *supra* note 44, at 20–21.

64. *Id.* at 23.

65. Mahoney and Littlejohn, *supra* note 4, at 1397.

66. Mahoney, "Consumers, Competitiveness," *supra* note 44, at 24; Mahoney, "Punitive Damages," *supra* note 44, at 3.

67. Mahoney, "Consumers, Competitiveness," *supra* note 44, at 24; Mahoney, "Punitive Damages," *supra* note 44, at 3.

68. Mahoney and Littlejohn, *supra* note 4, at 1398.

69. *See* Hayden, "Cultural Logic," *supra* note 5, at 13–14; Daniels, *supra* note 5, at 280.

70. *See supra* note 55 and accompanying text. *See also* P. Brodeur, *Outrageous Misconduct: The Asbestos Industry on Trial* (1985) (approving of punitive damage awards for known dangers in asbestos-related litigation). Edelman provides an apt illustration of the general point about masking alternative explanations for events: "Many crises are precipitated by an event that rather suddenly makes clear the serious consequences of activities that have been going on for a long time without occasioning much concern. Limitations on refining capacity and long-standing tax and price arrangements among American oil companies and Middle East oil-producing countries set the stage for an energy crisis long before the sudden declaration in 1973 that oil was in short supply." M. Edelman, *Political Language: Words That Succeed and Policies That Fail* 46–47 (1977).

71. *See* Edelman, *id.* at 29–32.

72. *See* Daniels, *supra* note 5, at 309–10; R. Hayden, *Cultural Logic*, *supra* note 5, at 21–23. In fact, a major amicus brief in *Pacific Mutual* is premised on this logic: "[I]t is only in recent years that punitive damage awards subject to challenge as unconstitutionally excessive and arbitrary have been imposed upon defendants. From 1789 to 1970, the limited availability and small magnitude of punitive damage awards gave no serious basis for anyone to claim protection under the Due Process Clause. In recent years, however, the need for constitutional scrutiny of punitive damage awards has become increasingly clear." Brief of the American Institute for Architects, *supra* note 11, at 28. The brief's argument is dominated by the presentation of quantitative data to show the alleged change. *Id.* at 23–28.

73. Mahoney and Littlejohn, *supra* note 4, at 1396.

74. American Tort Reform Association, *Punitive Damages Update, Relevant Studies on Tort Reform/Punitive Damages* (April 12, 1989) [hereinafter *Relevant Studies*].

75. *Id.*

76. *Id.*

77. *See also* Brief of the American Institute of Architects, *supra* note 6, at 23 ("This impressive body of anecdotal evidence of growth in the size and frequency of punitive awards is supported by the available empirical data. By far, the most comprehensive empirical study was one conducted by the RAND Institute for Civil Justice.").

78. *See also* Daniels, *supra* note 5, at 299 (noting that "[e]ven more widely used are data from Jury Verdicts Research, Inc. ('JVR') on awards in malpractice and products liability cases").

79. M. Shanley and M. Peterson, *Comparative Justice: Civil Jury Verdicts in San Francisco and Cook Counties, 1959–1980*, appendix A at 79–88 (1983).

80. For instance, the data were used to demonstrate the seriousness of the problem in *Tort Policy Working Group, United States Department of Justice, Report of the Tort Policy Working Group on the Causes, Extent, and Policy Implications of the Current Crisis in Insurance Availability and Affordability* (1986) [hereinafter *Report*] (charts G–I), and later in *Tort Policy Working Group, United States Department of Justice, An Update on the Liability Crisis* 33–38 (1987) [hereinafter *Update*] (charts C–H, K, L). The data were used to demonstrate the lack of any serious problem in *Special Committee on Punitive Damages, Section of Litigation, American Bar Association, Punitive Damages: A Constructive Examination* 17–26 (1986) [hereinafter *Constructive Examination*].

81. *Report*, *id.* at 39–45 (charts G–I).

82. *Update*, *supra* note 80, at 33–38 (charts C–H, K, L).

83. *E.g.*, "What the U.S. Government Thinks about Tort Reform: Look Who's on Our Side, Uncle Sam," *J. Am. Ins.*, 2d Q., 1986, at 23–24.

84. *Report*, *supra* note 80, at 68–69; *Update*, *supra* note 80, at 47–48.

85. *Report*, *id.* at 39–42 (footnotes and chart references omitted).

86. *Id.* at 43 (chart H).

87. *Id.* at 42, n. 39.

88. *Relevant Studies, supra* note 74.

89. *Report*, *supra* note 80, at 39.

90. *Relevant Studies, supra* note 74.

91. *Report*, *supra* note 80, at 42.

92. Mahoney and Littlejohn, *supra* note 4, at 1396.

93. *Relevant Studies, supra* note 74.

94. *Report*, *supra* note 80, at 42.

95. *Relevant Studies, supra* note 74.

96. *Report*, *supra* note 80, at 39.

97. *Update*, *supra* note 80, at 49.

98. *Id.* at 49, n.62.

99. *Report*, *supra* note 80, at 42.

100. *See Update*, *supra* note 80, at 47, n.54 (referring to M. Peterson, S. Sarma, and M. Shanley, *Punitive Damages: Empirical Findings* 4 (1987).

101. The problematic nature of the "hard data" is further illustrated by the fact that the reformers' opponents use the same study to argue an entirely different categorization of the punitive damages system. In

1986, the same year of the *Report*'s publication, the Special Committee on Punitive Damages of the ABA's Section of Litigation published a report. *See Constructive Examination*, *supra* note 80. This report is based upon a study of punitive damages commissioned by the Special Committee and conducted by the ICJ. *Id.* at 1. This is the ICJ study of punitive damages in Cook County and San Francisco. According to the Special Committee's report: "The major findings of the RAND study . . . suggest that contrary to the common perception, punitive damage awards are neither routine nor routinely large, especially in personal injury cases including [product] liability and malpractice litigation. While punitive damages awards have grown in frequency and size over the past 25 years, the bulk of this growth has been in cases of intentional torts, unfair business practices or contractual bad faith. The punitive damages picture in personal injury cases has changed very little in 25 years. Moreover, while the size of punitive damages awards has increased, most awards are moderate in amount and the ratio of punitive to compensatory damages is generally not excessive. The multimillion-dollar punitive award 10 to 20 times the plaintiff's actual damages is, in empirical terms, not a pattern but an aberration. In short, the findings of this study suggest that the notion of a punitive damages "crisis" is exaggerated overall and focused on the wrong types of cases." *Id.* at 17–18. The use of the same study for opposite conclusions in the punitive damage debate should make clear the problematic nature of the "hard data" used in the debate. Again, the purpose is not a reasonably accurate picture of the punitive damage system, but gaining support for a political agenda.

102. R. Yin, *Case Study Research: Design and Methods* 21 (1984).

103. Even some academics and researchers working in this area have slipped into this habit. *E.g.*, D. Hensler, M. Vaiana, and M. Peterson, *Trends in Tort Litigation: The Study behind the Statistics* 14 (1987); Litan, Swire, and Winston, "The U.S. Liability System: Background and Trends," in *Liability: Perspectives and Policy* 8–10 (R. Litan and C. Winston eds., 1988); Danzon, "Medical Malpratice Liability," *id.* at 106–7.

104. 499 U.S. 1 (1991).

105. Amicus Curiae Brief of the Chamber of Commerce of the United States, the National Association of Manufacturers, the Chemical Manufacturers Association, and the American Corporate Counsel Association, In Support of Petitioner at 9, *Pacific Mut. Life Ins. Co. v. Haslip.*

106. 125 L. Ed. 2d 366 (1993).

107. *Id.* at 389.

108. *Id.*

109. *Id.* at 406.

110. This database did not include Alaska; Adams and El Paso Counties in Colorado; Idaho; Michigan; Montana; Ohio; Oregon; Jefferson, St. Charles, St. Louis (City), St. Louis (County); and Travis, District 6, and District 9 Counties in Texas.

111. *See* Daniels and Martin, *supra* note 1, at 32 for comparable figures on the 1981–85 period.

112. *See* Mahoney and Littlejohn, *supra* note 4, at 1396; *Report, supra* note 71, at 35–42.

113. Daniels and Martin, *supra* note 1, at 38 (table V).

114. Sales and Coles, *supra* note 20, at 1154–58; Brief of the American Institute of Architects, *supra* note 6, at 21–28.

115. Mo. Rev. Stat. § 290.140 (Vernon Supp. 1990); *see also* "Comment, Missouri's Service Letter Statute: Its Reach, Effect and Constitutionality," 52 *UMKC L. Rev.* 641 (1984) (describing the scope and effect of recent amendment to this statute).

116. *See* Mahoney and Littlejohn, *supra* note 4, at 1397.

117. Tex. Bus. & Com. Code Ann. § 17.50(b)(1) (Vernon 1987).

118. *See* Montford and Barber, "1987 Texas Tort Reform: The Quest for a Fairer and More Predictable Texas Civil Justice System (parts 1 and 2)," 25 *Hous. L. Rev.* 59, 66, 245, 314–41 (1988).

119. Tex. Civ. Prac. & Rem. Code Ann. § 41.007 (Vernon Supp. 1990).

120. *See* T. Eisenberg and M. Wells, "Trial Outcomes and Demographics," paper presented at the Annual Meeting of the Law and Society Association, Phoenix, Ariz., June 1994.

CHAPTER 7

1. Manhattan Institute Judicial Studies Program, "Mission Statement and Overview," November 12, 1991, at 1.

2. Clermont and Eisenberg, "Trial by Jury or Judge: Transcending Empiricism," 77 *Cornell L. Rev.* 1125 (1992).

3. *E.g.*, Vidmar, "Empirical Evidence on the Deep Pockets Hypothesis: Jury Awards for Pain and Suffering in Medical Malpractice Cases," 43 *Duke L.J.* 217 (1993); Daniels and Martin, "Myth and Reality in Punitive Damages," 75 *Minn. L. Rev.* 1 (1990).

4. *E.g.*, Rustad and Koenig, "The Supreme Court and Junk Social Science: Selective Distortion in Amicus Briefs," 72 *N.C. L. Rev.* 91 (1993).

5. *Id.*

6. The authors of the Harvard Malpractice Study, for instance, expressed concern not only over the amount of injury caused by negligent medical care, but also that many injured patients receive no compensation. In their view, the present tort system is not serving many injured patients well, and this leads the authors to arguing for a no-fault system of compensation for medical injuries. *See* P. Weiler et al., *A Measure of Malpractice: Medical Injury, Malpractice Litigation, and Patient Compensation* (1993).

7. D. Ricci, *The Transformation of American Politics: The New Washington and the Rise of Think Tanks* 228 (1993).

8. *See* H. Laswell, *Politics: Who Gets What, When, How* (1958).

9. J. Smith, *The Idea Brokers: Think Tanks and the Rise of the New Policy Elite* 214–39 (1991).

10. *See* "Civil Justice Coalitions: A National Awakening," 62 *J. Am. Ins.* 4–5 (1986).

11. *See* McMillen, "Olin Foundation Gives Millions to Conservative Activities in Higher Education: Critics See Political Agenda," *Chronicle of Higher Education*, January 22, 1992, at A31–A32; Smith, *supra* note 9, at 180–89; Chesebro, "Galileo's Retort: Peter Huber's Junk Scholarship," 42 *Am. U. L. Rev.* 1705–22 (1993).

12. *See* "The Monsanto Lectures on Tort Reform and Jurisprudence," 22 *Val. U. L. Rev.* (1987).

13. An interesting recent example of the political clout of trial lawyers is recounted in Walters, "Let a Million Tort Actions Blossom," *Cal. Law.*, February 1994, at 39–41. Walters describes the tactics used by the California Trial Lawyers Association to stop a move for a ballot measure to reduce contingency fees. He opened the article with the following: "Mao Tse-tung would be proud of the California Trial Lawyers Association. Mao preached that large armies can be defeated by much smaller forces that strike at their enemies' weakest points and avoid direct confrontations. In late 1993, the CTLA, which has only a few thousand members, humbled a seemingly powerful coalition of manufacturers, medical care providers and insurance companies that was gathering behind a proposed ballot measure to reduce contingency fees greatly for personal injury cases." *Id.* at 39.

14. Manhattan Institute Judicial Studies Program, *supra* note 1, at 1.

15. Wachsman, *supra* note 15, at 13.

16. *Id.* at 1–23, 76–103.

17. P. Huber, *Liability: The Legal Revolution and Its Consequences* (1988).

18. *See* chapter 2, at 43–46.

19. Wachsman, *supra* note 15, at 106.

20. *Id.* at 107.

21. *Id.* at 110.

22. *Id.* at 104.

23. *Id.* at 110–13.

24. *Id.* at 128.

25. *Id.* at xii–xiii.

26. *See* Ricci, *supra* note 7, at 208–38.

27. Weiler et al., *supra* note 6, at 137.

28. *Id.* at 140–41.

29. Abel, "The Real Tort Crisis—Too *Few* Claims," 48 *Ohio St. L.J.* 443 (1987).

30. D. Hensler et al., *Compensation for Accidental Injuries in the United States* 111 (1991).

31. Weiler et al., *supra* note 6, at 139–41.

32. Taragin et al., "The Influence of Standard of Care and Severity of Injury on the Resolution of Medical Malpractice Claims," 117 *Annals Internal Med.* 780 (1992).

33. Bowen, "Keynote Address," in *Medical Professional Liability and the Delivery of Obstetrical Care*, vol. 1 (V. Rostow and R. Bulger eds., 1989).

34. *See* Madison, Federalist Papers 10 and 51.

35. Kravitz et al., "Malpractice Claims Data as a Quality Improvement Tool: Epidemiology of Error in Four Specialties," 266 *JAMA* 2087 (1991).

36. *See* Ricci, *supra* note 7; Smith, *supra* note 9; Chesebro, *supra* note 11.

37. Smith, *supra* note 9, at 169.

38. *Id.* at 181, summarizing Irving Kristol's argument.

39. *Id.* at 181–82.

40. "The Monsanto Lectures on Tort Law Reform and Jurisprudence," 22 *Val. U. L. Rev.* (1987). The connection between the law school and Monsanto is found in the following: "Valparaiso University wishes to give special acknowledgment to two men whose vision and hard work have nurtured this project—alumnus Richard W. Dusenberg, Senior Vice President, General Counsel and Secretary of the Monsanto Company, and John L. Mason, President of the Monsanto Fund." *Id.*

41. *Id.*

42. Huber, "On Law and Sciosophy," 24 *Val. U. L. Rev.* 319 (1990).

43. Epstein, "A Clash of Two Cultures: Will the Tort System Survive Automobile Insurance Reform?" 25 *Val. U. L. Rev.* 173 (1991).

44. *See* McMillen, *supra* note 11; Chesebro, *supra* note 11; Smith, *supra* note 9.

45. *See* RAND Corporation, *Institute for Civil Justice: An Overview of the First Six Program Years* 75–78 (1986); RAND Corporation, *The Institute for Civil Justice: Annual Report*, April 1, 1989–March 31, 1990, 108–11 (1989); Manhattan Institute for Policy Research, *Manhattan Forums: The First Five Years*, 28 (1986).

46. Deposition of George Priest in the case of *Thomas Wayne Trawick and Judy R. Trawick v. Michaels of Oregon* (Case No. 88-C–413-N), in the U.S. District Court for the Middle District of Alabama, Northern Division at 6; deposition taken on October 18, 1989, in New York.

47. *Trawick v. Michaels of Oregon*, 88-C-413-N, U.S. District Court for the Middle District of Alabama, Northern Division.

48. Deposition of George Priest, *supra* note 48, at 39.

49. "New Directions in Liability Law," 37 *Proceedings of the Academy of Political Science* (W. Olson ed., 1988).

50. *Id.* at iv.

51. MacLaury, "Forward" in *Liability: Perspectives and Policy* at viii (R. Litan and C. Winston eds., 1988).

52. *Id.*

53. *Id.* at viii.

54. Rustad, "Demystifying Punitive Damages in Products Liability Cases: A Survey of a Quarter Century of Trial Verdicts," Papers of the Roscoe Pound Foundation (1991).

55. Rustad, "In Defense of Punitive Damages in Products Liability: Testing Tort Anecdotes with Empirical Data," 78 *Iowa L. Rev.* 1 (1992).

56. Rustad, *supra* note 60, at 41–49

57. Brief of Amicus Curiae Trial Lawyers for Public Justice in support of Respondent, *Honda Motor Co. v. Oberg*, in the Supreme Court Court of the United States (No. 93–644) at 1.

58. DeBenedictis, "Punitives under Control. But Tort Reform Boosters See Bias in Study Findings," 78 *A.B.A. J.*, May 1992 at 38; quoting Theodore Olson.

59. Ricci, *supra* note 7, at 213.

60. Vidmar, *supra* note 3, at 217, 265.

Index

Abel, Richard, 117, 163, 165, 249
Accidental injuries
  claims frequency, 149, 164–65, 167, 249
  data sources, 162, 163, 181, 249
  work versus nonwork settings, 162, 164–65, 170–72, 174–81
Accounting industry statement on liability crisis, 50–51
Aetna Foundation, 255, 256
Aetna Insurance
  public relations campaign, 35, 42, 155
  underwriting of Manhattan Institute, 25
Aetna Life and Casualty Foundation, 255
Agenda-setting. *See also* Research agendas
  causal assertions in, 56–58
  decision agendas, 30, 35
  governmental agendas, 30
  policy agendas, 30–31
  public agendas, 30–31
  quantification tactics, 51–57
  role of elections, 33, 35–36
  softening up process, 33–34
  symbolic devices in, 37–51
  tactics, 29–32, 37–51, 51–57
  timing factors, 32–34
  windows of opportunity, 32–33, 35–36
Alabama Governor's Commission on the Insurance Crisis and Tort Reform, 264n. 112
Alabama State Supreme Court, 271n. 112
Alaska
  award sizes, 70, 75, 84
  number of punitive awards, 215
  plaintiff success rates, 70–72, 75, 79, 215
Alliance of American Insurers, 255, 266n. 23
American Bar Association Section of Litigation Special Committee on Punitive Damages report, 300n. 101
American Bar Foundation study of surgical intensive care unit error, 116
American Enterprise Institute, 26, 253
American Institute of Architects, 260n. 29, 293n. 6, 299n. 72
American Journal of Perinatology, 111
American Law Institute 1965 Restatement (Second) of Torts, 160
American Medical Association
  on biomedical research deterioration, 207
  on negative impact of product liability system, 157
  on reform effectiveness, 105
  reform package, 92, 274n. 3, 275n. 48
American Tort Reform Association, 260n. 29, 269n. 69

amicus brief for *Pacific Mutual Life Ins. Co. v. Haslip*, 7, 212, 293n. 6
press kit on punitive damage awards, 6, 205–6, 209–10
use of horror stories, 5, 44
Antireform movement
constituents, 246
data misuse, 246
emotional appeal, 246, 247
metaphors, 247
use of horror stories, 246, 247–48
Arbitration panels, 104, 106, 107, 277n. 89
Arizona
award sizes, 70, 75, 84, 86, 222
number of punitive awards, 215, 218, 219–20
personal injury award rates, 220
plaintiff success rates, 70–72, 75, 79, 215, 220
products liability cases by setting, 171
Asbestos cases, 167, 173, 175, 176, 191, 240
Assertive rhetoric, 45, 46, 97, 99
Association of Trial Lawyers of America, 256

"Bad baby" cases, 96, 119, 128, 134, 141, 240
Bailey, F. G., 45, 46, 97, 99
Bailey, William O., 35, 42
Balance metaphor in products liability rhetoric, 154–56
Bendectin, 14, 167
Binding arbitration, effect on malpractice claims filed, 106, 107, 277n. 89
Blalock, Hubert, 54
The Blame Game: Injury, Insurance and Injustice (O'Connell and Kelley), 10
Bovbjerg, Randall
on jury bias, 12
on medical malpractice insurance crisis, 103–5
Bowen, Otis
on civil justice system image, 92–93
on medical malpractice awards, 11, 98
on medical malpractice insurance premiums, 95, 98
on public health problems and medical malpractice, 98–99
Lynde and Harry Bradley Foundation, 25, 255
Brain Damage from a Drug Overdose story, 156
Bronx effect, 239
Browning-Ferris Industries, Inc. v. Kelco Disposal, Inc., 6, 48, 205–6
Burger, Warren, 41
Burglar through the Skylight story, 5
Bush administration position on tort reform, 5, 8, 10, 14, 15, 23, 35, 41, 101, 157
Business Week insurance crisis story, 7, 13, 55–56, 57

California
award sizes, 70, 72–73, 75, 77, 84, 86, 90, 139–42, 142–43, 146, 184–85, 209–12, 221–22, 238
number of jury verdicts over time, 87–89, 126, 138–41, 142–43, 168, 170–71, 183–92, 214, 215, 218
personal injury award rates, 220
plaintiff success rates, 70–72, 75, 79, 82–83, 138–39, 144, 145, 184–85, 215, 220, 222–38
punitive damage awards over time, 222–38
workers' compensation system, 178–79, 190, 1978
California Medical Association/California Hospital Association study on medical malpractice, 106, 117
California Trial Lawyers Association, 303n. 13
Cardozo, Benjamin, 159
Case congregations concept, 183, 289n. 108
CAT scan story, 5, 10, 43–44
Chase Manhattan Bank, 25, 256
Chesebro, Kenneth, 24–25
Chicago Tribune use of CAT scan story, 5
Chief Justice Earl Warren Conferences on Advocacy, 256–59
Christian Science Monitor, 47
Civil Justice Campaign, 34
Civil justice system. *See also* Tort reform movement
effect on competitiveness, 15, 23, 208
empirical research regarding, 16, 19–20

negative characterization, 21, 22, 23, 243, 249
public image, 2–3, 26–27, 36, 58, 92–93, 94
Civil Litigation Research Project study of claim filing, 64, 65
Claimant characteristics and malpractice claim success, 107–8, 110, 278n. 90
Clermont, Kevin M., 2, 241
Cobb, Richard, 30
Collateral source offsets, effect on malpractice claims filed, 106, 277n. 89
Colorado
award sizes, 70, 75, 83, 84, 222
number of punitive awards, 215, 218, 220
personal injury award rates, 220
plaintiff success rates, 70–72, 75, 79, 215, 220
products liability cases by setting, 171
Common Sense Legal Reform Act, 35
Compensation for Accidental Injuries in the United States (RAND), 164–65, 182, 249
Consumer Product Safety Commission, 194
report on product-related injuries, 162
Contingency fee system
effect on products liability vehicle injury cases, 191
enacted reforms effectiveness, 106, 107
relationship to litigation explosion, 4–5, 103
restrictions, 104, 106, 107, 112, 277n. 89
as tort incentive, 2, 103
wounding corporate offenders, 202–5
Contract with America, 35
Copper 7 intrauterine device, 207
Coryell v. Colbaugh, 200
Costs
fueled by litigation explosion, 4, 12–13, 24, 103
indirectly incurred from jury decisions, 34, 154, 156
reforms aimed at, 105, 107
statistics regarding, 52
Cost shifting, 107, 277n. 89
Council on Competitiveness, 15, 35
use of CAT scan story, 5, 10
use of Huber tort tax figures, 14
use of Institute for Civil Justice awards figures, 8, 53

Dalkon Shield cases, 167
Danzon, Patricia, 64, 112, 115
on effects of malpractice reforms, 105–6, 107, 109, 110, 114
on negligent injury claims filing, 117
DeMarco, Laura, 117, 163
DeVille, Kenneth Allen, 102
Direct mail strategy, 246
Disputing pyramid concept, 251
in medical malpractice
differences by medical setting, 123–25
frequency of events within, 115, 117, 119
patient injuries as base, 114–17
structure, 126
overall structure, 62–63, 65, 66
in products liability
claims frequency, 163–67
data availability, 161–67
frequency of injury, 161–63
structure, 161, 165
Dow Chemical, 254, 256
DPT vaccine, 14, 157
The Drunk and the Phone Booth story, 44, 269n. 66
The Drunk Driver story, 44
Dunworth, Terry, 167

Economic competitiveness
threatened by products liability system, 15, 22–23
threatened by punitive damages awards, 208
Eisenberg, Theodore, 2, 243
Elder, Charles, 30
Elections, role in agenda-setting process, 33, 35–36
Ellis, Dorsey, 11, 298n. 53
Epstein, Richard, 159, 161, 255
medical malpractice reform proposal, 275n. 48
Escola v. Coca-Cola Bottling Co., 159
Expert testimony
admissibility, 265n. 140
jury confusion regarding, 2, 9–10
witness requirements, 105

Family practice medicine malpractice verdicts, 134
The Fat man and the Lawnmower story, 5, 156, 181, 269n. 66
Federal Trade Commission, 194
Feeley, Malcolm, 21, 67, 112
 on tort reform movement veracity, 21
Florida Academic Task Force for Review of the Insurance and Tort Systems, 264n. 112
Florida Project Civil Justice, 266n. 26
Food and Drug Administration, 194
Forbes, 6
Frank, Jerome, 1, 4, 11, 93
Fyre Rule, 24, 265n. 140

Galanter, Marc, 47, 126, 183, 193
 defense of punitive damages, 202–4
Galileo's Revenge: Junk Science in the Courtroom (Huber), 24
General Accounting Office
 study of federal products liability filings, 166–67
 study of Indiana malpractice, 123
General surgery malpractice verdicts, 131–33, 137, 142
Georgia
 award sizes, 70, 75, 84, 222
 number of punitive awards, 215, 218, 219–20
 personal injury award rates, 220
 plaintiff success rates, 70–72, 75, 79, 215, 220
Gerson, Stuart M., 286n. 32
Greenman v. Yuba Power Products, Inc., 160
Gronfein, William P., 112–13
Grossman, Mary, 120, 121, 123, 124–25
Guinther, John, 256

Hager, Mark, 25–26
Hampton, Jean, 203
Hans, Valerie, 182–83
Harvard Malpractice Study, 101, 115, 117, 123, 147, 249
Hayden, Robert, 25, 44
Henningsen v. Bloomfield Motors, 159
Hensler, Deborah, 65
Heritage Foundation, 26, 253
Hewlett-Packard, 256
Hickson, Gerald, 119
Home setting injuries in products liability
 award sizes, 169, 172, 180, 181
 claims frequency, 171, 187, 191, 192
 frequency by industry, 180–81
 horror stories, 182
 severity data, 169, 180–81, 189
 win rates, 169, 172, 181, 189
Honda Motor Co. v. Oberg, 257
Hoover Institute, 26
Hot Air Balloon and the Dryer story, 156
Huber, Peter
 agenda-setting tactics, 30
 on contract law, 40
 on costs of liability system, 34, 154, 156–57
 Galileo's Revenge: Junk Science in the Courtroom, 24
 on junk science, 10, 24
 on jury awards sizes, 8, 11, 53
 lawyer-bashing, 267n. 44
 Liability: The Legal Revolution and Its Consequences, 8, 11, 25, 39, 41, 44, 48, 96, 153, 247
 The Liability Maze, 23, 156–57, 256
 renown, 263n. 94
 tort tax concept, 14, 23–24, 39
 use of horror stories, 5, 10, 44, 96, 153, 154
 as the voice of reform, 17, 21–26, 152–53, 255, 256
 writings on civil liability rules, 9, 39, 48, 57, 154
Huckle v. Money, 200

Idaho
 award sizes, 70, 75, 84
 number of punitive awards, 215
 plaintiff success rates, 70–72, 75, 79, 215
The Idea Brokers: Think Tanks and the Rise of the New Policy Elite (Smith), 253
Illinois
 award sizes, 6, 7, 8, 70, 72–73, 75, 77, 83, 84, 90, 139–41, 184–86, 207, 209–11, 238
 number of jury verdicts over time, 87–89, 126–27, 139–42, 142–43, 168, 170, 183–92, 215, 218
 personal injury award rates, 219

plaintiff success rates, 70–72, 75, 79, 83, 138–39, 144, 146, 184–86, 214, 215, 219, 222–38
punitive damage awards over time, 223–39
Illinois Civil Justice League, 246
Image-making. *See also* Strategic representation
influence on public policy, 3–4, 26–27, 245–46
as strategic representation, 37, 58
Implied warranty concept, 159
Indiana
malpractice insurance market, 121–22
malpractice reforms, 104, 112–13, 148
medical malpractice awards cap, 104, 112
Indiana Project Justice, 266n. 26
Infant mortality rates, relationship to medical malpractice crisis, 96, 97, 98–99
Informed consent doctrine, 105
Institute of Medicine Committee to Study Medical Professional Liability and the Delivery of Obstetrical Care
authority of, 97
on reform effectiveness, 105
report, 98–101
Insurance crisis
award reports during, 6, 7, 53
concept, 50
consequences, 12–13
legal changes underpinning, 9
relationship to punitive damages, 199
responses to, 19–20
Insurance industry
claims handling patterns, 121–23
public relations campaigns, 34–35, 42–43, 96–97, 155
strategic representation by, 266n. 23
underwriting of Manhattan Institute, 25
Insurance Information Institute, 267n. 32
on litigation explosion, 13
public relations campaign, 34–35, 96–97, 286n. 35
Insurance Services Office Products Liability Closed Claim Survey, 166
Insurance underwriting pools, 103, 107, 277n. 89
Internal medicine malpractice verdicts, 135, 137, 138, 142, 146
Iowa Project Civil Justice Reform, 267n. 26

Johnson and Higgins (brokerage firm), 35
Jost, Kenneth, 37, 46
analysis of Huber's work, 22–24, 25, 26
Joyce, Craig, 147, 182, 193
analysis of tort reform movement, 17, 19–21, 23, 26, 32, 36, 37, 59
Julian, Thomas M., 111, 112
Junk science, 10, 24
Junk social science, 245
Juries
claims made about, 1–2, 4, 9–12, 243
competence questioned, 1–2, 9–12, 103, 104, 148, 207
empirical research regarding, 16, 148
negative characterization, 21, 27, 92–93, 148, 249
plaintiff bias claims, 4, 11–12, 93, 103, 104, 149, 150, 201–2, 207
plaintiff bias data, 88, 182–83, 190, 238, 250
Jury awards
appelate litigation regarding, 6
restrictions, 104–5, 106, 107, 112, 202, 204, 237, 277n. 89
size assumptions, 7, 53, 154–57
size data, 69–73, 75–78, 83–86, 89–90, 127, 130–31, 168, 238–39
statistics regarding, 52–57
structured versus lump-sum, 105, 277n. 89
summary figures frequently quoted, 5–8, 52–57, 156
The Jury in America (Guinther), 256
Jury verdicts. *See also* Medical malpractice; Products liability; Punitive damages
activity across time, 87–90, 137–41, 183–93, 213–42
automobile cases, 78–87. *See also* Vehicle-related injuries
award size, 69–73, 75–78, 83–87, 89–90, 127, 130–31, 147, 168–72, 178–81, 184–85, 221–42
bodily harm cases, 74–78, 169, 173, 178–81, 217–21, 225, 233, 238

effect of statutory differences, 73, 89–90, 201, 236, 250
financial harm cases, 74–78, 78–87, 217–21, 224, 225, 233, 238
overall patterns, 250–51
plaintiff win rates, 69–83, 87–89, 127, 130–31, 147, 168–70, 171, 177, 181, 184–85, 214–27, 238–39
reporters, 66–68, 91–92
statistics, 271n. 112
symbolic value, 62, 66
trend-setting aspects, 62, 66, 126, 136, 137
unpredictability, 60
urban patterns, 69, 239

Kalk, Paul, 92
Kansas
award sizes, 70, 72, 75, 84, 90
number of jury verdicts over time, 87–89, 215
plaintiff success rates, 70–72, 75, 79, 82, 215
Kansas Project Justice, 266n. 26
Kapp, Marshall, 108–9
Kelly, Brian, 10
Kingdon, John
on agenda setting, 29–32, 36
model of agenda-setting process, 32–33, 36, 51, 54
on policy entrepreneurs, 22
Kinney, Eleanor, analysis of Indiana malpractice reform, 112–14, 120–21, 123
Koenig, Thomas, 245, 257
Kravitz, Richard J., 137
Kristol, Irving, 253

The Ladder in the Manure story, 44, 268n. 66
Ladinsky, Jack, 63
Law, Medicine and Health Care (Kapp), 108–9
Law, Sylvia, 103
The Lawsuit Lottery (O'Connell), 11
Lawyers for Civil Justice, 296n. 10
Legal standards, changes incurred through jury verdict trends, 9, 39–40, 103, 155, 157–58
Lethal Medicine: The Epidemic of Medical Malpractice in America (Wachsman), 246–48
Liability: The Legal Revolution and Its Consequences (Huber), 8, 11, 25, 39, 41, 44, 48, 96, 247
Liability litigation. *See also* Medical malpractice; Products liability; Punitive damages
changes in law regarding, 9, 39–40, 103, 155, 157–58
deficit in, 101, 117, 118, 147, 163, 249
explosion concept, 4, 12–15, 47, 87–90, 103
jury trials versus bench trials, 66
popular perception, 13
success rates. *See* Jury verdicts
undercompensation in, 18
The Liability Maze (Huber and Litan), 23, 156–57, 256
Liability tax concept, 23–24
Litan, Robert, 23, 156–57, 256
The Litigation Explosion (Olson), 9, 41, 42, 44, 46, 47, 48–49, 57, 96, 246–47
Litigation lottery, 41
Littlejohn, Stephen
on product liability awards, 157
on punitive damage awards, 6, 157, 206–9
use of hard data, 209
Little League baseball player story, 5
Lobbying groups, name choices, 34, 38, 246
Luban, David, 202–4

McCormick, William
on consequences of the litigation explosion, 13–14, 41, 45, 57, 155, 157
on insurance crisis, 5, 10–11
on legal systems changes, 9, 10–11, 49, 155
use of balance metaphor, 155
MacPherson v. Buick Motor Co., 158–59, 161
Mahoney, Richard, 254
on jury bias, 11, 207
on product liability awards, 157
on punitive damage awards, 6, 14–15, 157, 206–9
use of hard data, 209
Malott, Robert
on consequences of the litigation explosion, 12–14, 41, 57

on liability awards, 5, 154, 155, 156, 157
use of balance metaphor, 155
Manhattan Institute
agenda-setting tactics, 30, 41
financial backing, 25, 253, 255
mission statement, 30, 33, 37
political objectives, 24–25, 26, 27, 246
Manhattan Institute Judicial Studies Program mission statement, 27, 246
Massachusetts Governor's Task Force on Liability Issues, 264n. 112
Mass communications media
metaphors purveyed by, 47–49
and politics of ideas, 3
May, Marlyn, 117, 163
Mediation, 105
Medical care
consumer's groups concern, 114
effect of punitive damage awards, 208
error frequency, 115–17, 130, 137, 144
impact of malpractice crisis, 95
standards, 111
Medical malpractice. *See also* Negligent injury situations
antireform rhetoric, 247–48
claims
closed with payment, 120–23, 147
defensibility, 122
differences by medical setting, 123–25, 129–37, 141–46, 239–40
frequency, 64, 95, 104, 110, 111, 117–19
claims frequency reduction, 106
formal adjudication rates, 119–20, 147, 239
horror stories, 247–48
insurance market differences by state, 121–22
insurance premiums, 93, 95, 96, 276n. 76
jury verdicts, 79–87, 93, 126–48, 239, 241
litigation deficit, 101, 117, 118, 147, 249
litigation delays, 278n. 90
pervasiveness, 247–48
Medical malpractice awards
age discrimination, 108, 146, 278n. 90
caps, 104–5, 106, 107, 112, 277n. 89
causal assertions veracity, 18, 21, 56
compared with product liability awards, 168
negligent injury situations, 111, 127–29, 130–37, 141–46
punitive, 221, 226–27, 237, 239, 240
size
claims, 6–7, 53, 93, 95, 104
data, 84–87, 127, 130–31, 239
influences on, 107–8, 110, 111
Medical malpractice crisis
adversarial dialogue, 101–2
anecdotal evidence, 101–2
causal assertions, 95
consequences, 50, 95
empirical research, 101
historical roots, 102
indicators, 93
legislative response, 103
ob/gyn focus, 95–101
relationship of infant mortality rates, 96, 97, 98–99
strategic representation, 94–101, 137
Medical Malpractice in Nineteenth Century America (DeVille), 102
Medical malpractice reform
aimed at cost reduction, 105
arbitration panels, 104, 106, 107, 277n. 89
changes in legal standards, 103
contingency fee restrictions, 104, 112, 277n. 89
cost shifting, 107, 277n. 89
effectiveness, 106
fault-based proposals, 274n. 3, 275n. 48
focused on medical quality, 103–4
focused on success likelihood, 105
insurance underwriting pools, 103, 107, 277n. 89
irrelevancy, 111
no-fault administrative process proposals, 275n. 48
patient compensation funds, 103, 112–13
as politics of ideas, 108, 113–14
pretrial screening panels, 104, 105, 106, 107, 113, 277n. 89
private contract scheme proposals, 275n. 48
unintended consequences, 112–13

Medical malpractice reform evaluation studies
 choice of indicators, 108–9
 on claim payment rate, 106–7, 110, 111
 on frequency of claims, 106, 111
 interpretation problems, 109–11
 nonlegal factors significance, 107–8, 110–11
 on payment size, 106
 scientific character, 108, 114
Medical Protective Insurance Company of Fort Wayne, Indiana (MedPro), 121
Metaphors
 antireform rhetoric, 247
 rhetoric of reform, 42–43, 46–51, 94, 154–56
 in strategic representation, 46–51, 94, 154–56
Meyers, Allan, 118, 163
Michigan
 award sizes, 70, 75, 77, 81, 86, 127, 221–22, 238
 number of jury verdicts over time, 127, 171, 214, 215, 218
 personal injury award rates, 220
 plaintiff success rates, 70–72, 75, 79, 82, 214, 215, 220
Michigan Committee for Civil Justice Equity, 38, 267n. 26
Miller, Richard, 64
Minnesota Civil Justice Coalition, 260n. 29, 293n. 6
Minnesota Commerce Department study on malpractice claims, 121
Minnesota Tort Reform Coalition, 267n. 26
Missouri
 award sizes, 71, 76, 77, 85, 86, 90, 222, 238
 number of jury verdicts over time, 87–89, 171, 214, 216, 218
 personal injury award rates, 220
 plaintiff success rates, 71–72, 76, 80, 82–83, 216, 220
 punitive damage awards over time, 220, 222–38
Missouri Division of Insurance
 malpractice claims, 120
 reports on products liability insurance claims, 166
Monsanto Company, 246, 255, 256
 fear of liability litigation, 14–15, 157, 206–9
Monsanto Fund, 255
Monsanto Lectures on Tort Law Reform and Jurisprudence, 254–55
Montana
 award sizes, 71, 76, 85
 number of punitive awards, 216
 plaintiff success rates, 71–72, 76, 80, 216
Mortality rates in negligent injury situations, 115
Mosbacher, Robert, 15
Multiple damages, statutory provisions, 236

National Academy of Sciences, 97, 100
 on vaccine research, 208
National Association of Insurance Commissioners study of malpractice claims, 120, 129
National Center for State Courts, 256
National Highway Traffic Safety Administration, 194
Nebraska Project Justice, 267n. 26
Negligent injury situations in medical malpractice
 awards, 111, 127–29, 130–37, 141–46
 claims filing, 117–18, 119
 differences by medical setting, 123–25, 129–37, 141–46
 frequency of occurrence, 115, 117, 146, 147
 mortality rates, 115
 patient inaction regarding, 117–18, 147, 249
 rating scale, 127
Neurology malpractice verdicts, 133, 134–35
New York Advisory Commission on Liability Insurance, 264n. 112
New York (state)
 award sizes, 71–73, 76, 77, 83, 85, 86, 127, 222, 238
 number of jury verdicts over time, 126, 171, 214, 216, 218, 219
 personal injury award rates, 220
 plaintiff success rates, 71–72, 76, 80, 82, 220, 239
North Carolina Hospital Association study of medical malpractice crisis, 92

Notice of intent to sue requirements, 105, 277n. 89

Obstetrics/gynecology field
as focus for malpractice crisis strategic representation, 95–101, 137
malpractice verdicts, 131–34, 137, 142, 239–40
risk management, 111
stories of decline, 94–96, 137
Occupational Safety and Health Administration (OSHA), 179, 194–96
O'Connell, Jeffrey, 10, 11
O'Connor, Sandra Day, 8, 48, 212–13
Ohio
award sizes, 71–72, 76, 83, 85, 127, 222
number of jury verdicts over time, 214, 216, 218, 220
personal injury award rates, 220
plaintiff success rates, 71–72, 76, 80, 83, 216, 220, 239
products liability cases by setting, 171
Ohio Basic Fairness in Litigation Coalition, 38, 267n. 26
John M. Olin Foundation, 25, 157, 246, 253, 255
Olson, Walter, 255
The Litigation Explosion, 9, 41, 42, 44, 46, 47, 48–49, 57, 96, 246–47
use of horror stories, 5, 44, 46
Ophthalmic surgery malpractice verdicts, 133
Oregon
award sizes, 71–72, 76, 77, 85, 238
number of jury verdicts over time, 214, 216
plaintiff success rates, 71–72, 76, 80, 216
products liability cases by setting, 171
Orthopedic surgery malpractice verdicts, 131–34, 137, 142, 240

Pacific Mutual Life Ins. Co. v. Haslip, 6–7, 16, 48, 212
Page, Joseph, 25
Patient compensation funds, 103, 112–13
Pediatrics malpractice verdicts, 134, 146
Pennsylvania Truth and Fairness in Litigation Committee, 246, 266n. 26
Personal injury awards
punitive, 217–21
size claims, 6, 8, 11, 53–55, 207, 209–12, 231–34
size data, 75–77
Personal injury litigation
filing frequency, 63–66, 172, 178–81, 219–20
success rates, 74–78, 225, 233, 238
Pharmaceutical industry, underwriting of Manhattan Institute, 25
Phillips, Carter, 92
The Pinto and the Horse story, 44, 268n. 66
Plastic surgery malpractice verdicts, 133
Polan, Steven, 103
Politics of ideas. *See also* Agenda-setting
influence of rhetoric of reform, 3, 21–26, 27–28, 245–46
marketing, 29
pervasiveness, 259n. 13
regarding malpractice reform, 108, 113–14
use of expert proof, 97, 100
Prentice, Robert, 293n. 5
Pretrial screening panels, 104, 105, 106, 107, 112, 277n. 89
Priest, George, 152, 255, 256
concern with the past, 41
on products liability litigation, 162–63
writings on civil liability rules, 9, 39, 53
Privity of contract doctrine
background, 158
in products cases, 158–59
Products liability
changes in law regarding, 152–53, 155, 157–58
claims
closed with payment, 166
differences by setting, 162, 164–65, 171–72, 175–81, 240
frequency, 152, 164–65, 167, 170, 178
crisis representation, 152, 153–57
data availability, 161–67
effect of workers' compensation, 178
federalization, 152
formal adjudication rates, 165–66, 239
insurance availability, 152
litigation deficit, 163, 249

regulatory programs, 178, 194–99
rhetoric of reform regarding, 153
strict liability doctrine, 152, 155
Products liability awards
compared with medical malpractice awards, 168
consequences, 14
economic competitiveness threatened by, 15, 22–23
size claims, 6, 7–8, 153, 154–57
size data, 84–87, 168, 169, 171–72, 178, 179, 180, 181, 184–85, 238, 239
Products liability cases
defendants, 167
frequency by industry, 173–74, 175–77, 178–79, 180–81
injury severity, 169, 172, 178, 179, 180–81
jury verdicts, 79–87, 152–53, 167–68, 169–72, 177, 179, 180–81, 183–93, 240–41
lack of empirical knowledge regarding, 26
negotiation process, 191
punitive damage awards, 168, 221, 226–27, 237, 239, 240
statistics regarding, 167
win rates, 169, 171, 179, 181, 184–85
Products Liability Fairness Act, 1991, 50, 152, 155, 157, 256, 257
Professional standard of care idea, 105
Project Justice (Illinois), 34, 38, 266n. 25
Psychiatry malpractice verdicts, 134
Psychic and the CAT scan story, 5, 10, 43–44
Public policy
changes needed, 252
influence of rhetoric of reform, 3, 22–26, 27, 36, 245–46
special interests' influence, 25–26
Public policy problems
agenda status, 31
preexisting solutions, 32, 101
socially constructed, 31
strategic representation, 31–32, 97, 99
Public relations campaigns by insurance companies, 34–35, 42–43, 96–97, 155
Punitive damage awards
arguments against, 201–2
arguments for, 201, 202–4
caps, 105, 202, 204, 237
consequences of, 12–15, 157, 206–8
constitutional challenges, 6, 7, 8, 200, 205–6
data sources, 6, 8, 209–12
effect on medical care, 208
frequency and size reports, 5–8, 52–57, 156, 168, 207, 209–12, 213–17, 221–42
by harm category, 217–21, 226–27, 231–34, 240
historical background, 199, 200–201
jury bias, 201, 202, 207
medical malpractice cases, 221, 226–27, 239, 240
moral justification, 203–4
objectives, 201
patterns, 242
personal injury cases, 217–21
products liability cases, 168, 221, 226–27, 239, 240
punishment rationale, 201–2
purpose, 200
relationship to insurance crisis, 199
research and development curtailed by, 159, 206–8
standards of proof, 202
state statutory provisions, 201
statistical generalizations, 212
strategic representation, 199, 205–13
wounding corporate offenders, 202–5
Punitive damages reform
horror stories, 206–8
politicization, 206
scientific characterization, 206–8
Punitive Damages Update press kit, 6, 205–6, 209–12

Quayle, Dan, 5, 8, 10, 14, 35, 41, 156
on self-inflicted competitive disadvantage, 15, 23

Radiology malpractice verdicts, 134, 135
RAND Corporation Institute for Civil Justice
Compensation for Accidental Injuries in the United States, 163–65, 181, 248
funding, 255
study of Cook County, Illinois, awards, 6, 7, 8, 53–54, 209–12

study of San Francisco awards, 209–12
study of tort liability system, 65
Reactionary intelligentsia, 26, 253
Reagan administration
OSHA during, 195–96
position on medical malpractice, 99, 101
Report of the Tort Policy Working Group on the Causes, Extent and Policy Implications of the Current Crisis in Insurance Availability and Affordability, 35, 47
data sources, 6, 8, 210–11
on medical malpractice award size, 6, 7–8, 53, 54, 95
on personal injury award sizes, 6, 8, 53, 54, 210–11
on products liability suits, 6, 7–8, 53, 54, 152, 154, 166
Update
data sources, 6, 210, 211
punitive damage award figures, 6, 54–55, 210, 211
veracity, 20, 36, 54–55
Research agendas
corporate funders, 254–57
influences, 252–54
interdisciplinary, 251–52
targeted philanthropy for, 253–54
Research and development, effect of punitive damage awards, 157, 206–8
Rhetoric of assertion, 45, 46, 97, 99
Rhetoric of reform
causal assertions, 18, 19, 21, 23, 56–58, 95, 97, 99, 245
emotional appeal, 38, 43, 44, 46, 49, 157, 206, 208–9
gap from empirical knowledge, 2, 23, 26, 32, 38, 58, 147, 240–41, 245, 249
importance, 2–3
influence on politics of ideas, 3, 21–28, 245–46. *See also* Strategic representation
influence on public policy, 3, 22–26, 27, 245–46
metaphors, 42–43, 46–51, 94, 154–56
stories of decline, 38–42, 48–49, 53, 57, 94–95, 96–97, 137, 153–57
stories of helplessness and control, 41–43
symbolic devices, 29, 37–51, 248
synecdoches, 43, 98
use of visual displays, 55–57, 95, 100
Ricci, David
on the politics of ideas, 3, 27–28, 97, 245
on think tanks, 257
Rice, Jeffrey J., 149–50
Roscoe Pound Foundation, 256–58
Rustad, Michael, 245, 257

Saks, Michael, 147, 182, 193
analysis of tort reform movement, 17–19, 21, 23, 26, 32, 36, 59
Sanders, Joseph, 147, 182, 193
analysis of tort reform movement, 17, 19–21, 23, 26, 32, 36, 59
Sarat, Austin, 64
Sarah Scaife Foundation, 25, 255
Schwartz, Victor, 152
Science, 157, 206, 207, 208
Screening panels, effect on malpractice claims, 106, 107
G. D. Searle, 207
Senate Committee on Commerce, Science, and Transportation report on products liability, 50, 152, 156–57, 256, 257
Sloan, Frank, 105, 106–7, 109, 110, 111–12, 114, 276n. 76
Smith, James E., 245, 253
Smith-Richardson Foundation, 25, 255, 256
Springs Industries, 256
Standard Industrial Classification Manual (SIC), 173
Starr Foundation, 25, 255, 256
State Farm Insurance, 25
Statutes of limitation reforms, effect on malpractice claims, 106, 107, 277n. 89
Stone, Deborah
on public policymaking power struggles, 3, 27
on strategic representation of policy problems, 31, 37, 39, 41, 43, 46–47, 51, 57, 58
on symbolic devices, 30, 43
Stories and anecdotes
award sizes quoted, 53–57, 154–56
Brain Damage from a Drug Overdose story, 156
The Burglar through the Skylight, 5

as crisis-oriented folklore, 44, 269n. 75
of decline, 38–41, 48–49, 53, 57, 94–95, 96–97, 153–57
The Drunk and the Phone Booth, 44, 269n. 66
The Drunk Driver story, 44
The Fat man and the Lawnmower, 5, 44, 156, 181, 269n. 66
of helplessness and control, 41–43
of hope through restoration, 41, 42
Hot Air Balloon and the Dryer story, 156
innocent victims in, 39, 45
The Ladder in the Manure story, 44, 268n. 66
The Little League baseball player story, 5
major themes, 43, 45, 94, 96
The Pinto and the Horse story, 44, 268n. 66
The Psychic and the CAT scan story, 5, 10, 43–44
as rhetorical devices, 45, 46
scapegoats in, 46, 58
tactical uses, 43, 58, 154–57, 247
veracity, 46, 58, 156
villains in, 38–39, 45–46
Strategic representation, 31–32, 37
causal assertions in, 56–58, 95, 97, 99
quantification tactics, 51–57
symbolic devices in, 37–51
use of metaphor, 46–51, 94, 154–56
use of visual displays, 55–57, 95, 100
Strauss, Anselm, 116–17
Strict liability doctrine, 152, 155
evolution, 160–61
origins, 160
Symbolic politics
emotional appeal, 38, 43, 44, 46, 49, 247
rhetoric, 37–58, 248
stories of decline, 38–41, 48–49, 53, 57
stories of helplessness and control, 41–43

Tactical use of passion, 38, 44, 157, 286n. 35
Taragin, Michael, 119–20, 121–23
Targeted philanthropy
forms and forums, 254–57
for research agendas, 253–54
Tennessee Governor's Task Force on Tort and Liability Insurance Reform, 264n. 112
Texas
award sizes, 71, 76, 77, 85, 86, 90, 139, 221–22
number of jury verdicts over time, 88, 126–26, 138–39, 168, 170, 171, 184, 214, 216, 218
personal injury award rates, 219–20
plaintiff success rates, 71–72, 76, 80, 138, 184, 214, 216, 219–20, 222–38
punitive damage awards over time, 222–38
Texas Civil Justice League, 246, 260n. 29, 267n. 26, 293n. 6
Texas Deceptive Trade Practices Act, 237
Texas House/Senate Joint Committee on Liability and Tort Reform, 20
Texas Omnibus Tort Reform Act of 1987, 20, 237
Texas reform proposals, 19–20, 237
Texas State Board of Insurance reports on products liability claims, 166
Texas State Board of Medical Examiners report on malpractice claims, 120
Texas Tort Reform Coalition, 267n. 26
Thomas, W. John
on anecdotal nature of malpractice debate, 101–2
on medical malpractice torts, 92
Time magazine insurance crisis story, 7, 13, 49–50, 55, 96
Tort reform movement
agenda-setting tactics, 29–59
Bush administration position, 5, 8, 10, 14, 15, 23, 35, 41, 101, 157
causal assertions veracity, 18, 19, 21, 23, 56, 245
coalitions, 34, 38
damages done by, 19
federal legislation, 35
opposition to, 245–48
Reagan administration position, 6, 7–8, 35, 47, 53, 54, 95, 152, 154, 166, 210–11
rhetoric. *See* Rhetoric of reform
state commissions, 6, 19–20, 58, 236–37, 264n. 112
theoretical justification, 9, 243
veracity, 16, 23

Tort tax concept, 14, 23–24, 39
Traynor, Roger, 159–60
Trial Lawyers for Public Justice, 38, 257
  amicus brief supporting *Pacific Mutual Life Ins. Co. v. Haslip*, 16
  nature of, 263n. 91
Truth and Fairness in Litigation Committee (Pennsylvania), 38
TXO Production Corporation v. Alliance Resources Corporation, 8, 48, 212–13

Urbanization as factor in malpractice claims, 110, 239
Urology malpractice verdicts, 134
U.S. Department of Labor report on accidental injuries, 162, 163
U.S. News & World Report, 13, 48
USA Today, 47

Valparaiso University Law School, 254–55
Vander Kolk, Kenneth, 94, 95, 97
Vehicle-related injuries in products liability
  award sizes, 172, 179, 187, 190, 192, 240
  claims frequency, 171, 178, 187, 191, 192
  frequency by industry, 174, 178–79
  selective handling, 190–91
  severity data, 173, 178, 179, 189
  win rates, 172, 179, 189
Vidmar, Neil
  on medical malpractice juries, 92, 93, 148–50, 182, 258
  on noneconomic damages awards, 148–50
  on politics of ideas, 278n. 93
Viscusi, W. Kip
  on OSHA ineffectiveness, 195–97
  on products liability litigation, 162–63, 165–66, 197–98
Visual displays in strategic representation, 55–57, 95, 100

Wachsman, Harvey, 246–48
Wall Street Journal
  on civil justice system reform, 47–48
  on the Manhattan Institute political objectives, 26
Washington Legal Foundation, 154
Washington Liability Reform Coalition, 266n. 26
Washington (state)
  award sizes, 72, 77, 85
  plaintiff success rates, 72, 77, 81, 82
  products liability verdicts, 168, 171
Weiler, Paul, 197–99
Wilkes v. Wood, 200
Williamsburg Conference on Civil Justice: A Focus on Torts, 256
Windows of opportunity in agenda-setting process, 32–33, 35, 36
Winterbottom v. Wright, 158
Wisconsin Coalition for Justice, 266n. 26
Workers' compensation, 164
  effect on products liability system, 178, 196–98
  handling of occupational diseases, 196
  insufficient coverage, 196–97
Work-related injuries in products liability
  award sizes, 7, 175–77, 189–90, 191, 197, 240
  cases brought by employers, 197
  claims frequency, 162, 164–65, 167, 170–72, 173–74, 175–77, 178, 187, 192
  employers liability, 196
  frequency by industry, 173–74, 175–77, 178
  OSHA ineffectiveness, 195
  severity data, 169, 172, 175–76, 189, 197
  win rates, 175–77, 178, 190, 191, 240

Yale Law School Program in Civil Liability, 255